BULLETS TO BALLOTS

BULLETS TO BALLOTS

Collective De-radicalisation of Armed Movements

Edited by Omar Ashour

EDINBURGH
University Press

Edinburgh University Press is one of the leading university presses in the UK. We publish academic books and journals in our selected subject areas across the humanities and social sciences, combining cutting-edge scholarship with high editorial and production values to produce academic works of lasting importance. For more information visit our website: edinburghuniversitypress.com

Edinburgh University Press Ltd
The Tun – Holyrood Road
12 (2f) Jackson's Entry
Edinburgh EH8 8PJ

First published in hardback by Edinburgh University Press 2021

Typeset in 11/15 Adobe Garamond by
Servis Filmsetting Ltd, Stockport, Cheshire,
printed and bound by CPI Group (UK) Ltd, Croydon, CR0 4YY

A CIP record for this book is available from the British Library

ISBN 978 1 4744 6711 7 (hardback)
ISBN 978 1 4744 6712 4 (paperback)
ISBN 978 1 4744 6714 8 (webready PDF)
ISBN 978 1 4744 6713 1 (epub)

CONTENTS

List of Illustrations   vii

Acknowledgements   viii

Abbreviations   x

Notes on Contributors   xvii

1. Revisiting Collective De-radicalisation: A Comparative Perspective   1
   Omar Ashour

2. Lessons from South Africa: A First-hand Testimony   23
   Ronnie Kasrils

3. The Collective De-radicalisation of the Islamic Group in Egypt:
   A First-hand Testimony   45
   Osama Rushdi

4. From Arms to Talks: Transformations of Three Syrian Armed
   Islamist Movements   68
   Hamzah Almustafa

5. The Mahdi Army and the Sadrist Movement in Iraq: The
   Struggle for Transformation   95
   Haider Saeed

6. A Draw or a Defeat? How the IRA Transitioned from Bullets to Ballots 116
   Gordon Clubb

7. Transformations and Defeats: ETA and the End of the Armed Campaign 134
   Nick Hutcheon

8. The Afghan Taliban and the Peace Negotiations: Are the Taliban 'De-radicalising'? 153
   Thomas H. Johnson

9. Transformations after 'Defeats': The Cases of the Tupamaros and the Armed Left in Latin America 186
   Aldo Marchesi

10. Leaving the Weapons without Losing the War: Understanding the Transformation of the FMLN 213
    Alberto Martín Álvarez

11. Negotiated Revolution in South Africa, 1990–1994 238
    Thula Simpson

12. Transformations in Ethiopia: From Armed Struggle to the Politics of Coalition 265
    Mehari Taddele Maru

13. Transformations of Armed Nonstate Actors: Enduring Challenges and Strategic Implications 282
    Omar Ashour

Bibliography 304
Index 323

ILLUSTRATIONS

Figures

8.1	War crimes claimed by the Taliban in 2018	166
8.2	Military/govt employee defections claimed by the Taliban in 2018	168
8.3	Attacks/defensive engagements claimed by the Taliban forces in 2019	170
8.4	War crimes claimed by the Taliban in 2019	170
8.5	Military/govt employee defections claimed by the Taliban in 2019	171
8.6	Attacks/defensive engagements claimed by Taliban forces in 2020	173
8.7	War crimes claimed by the Taliban in 2020	174
8.8	Military/govt employee defections claimed by the Taliban in 2020	175

Table

12.1	List of influential armed groups in Ethiopia	267

ACKNOWLEDGEMENTS

The story of this edited book began in the summer of 2017. In November 2018, the Strategic Studies Unit of the Arab Centre for Research and Policy Studies (ACRPS) organised the first international conference of its kind in the Arab world. Titled 'Bullets to Ballots: Transformations from Armed to Unarmed Political Activism', scholars and practitioners qualitatively examined a crucial issue-area that occupies public opinion and public policy in many countries. The conference provided the solid foundations for this book. In the following chapters, twelve scholars, practitioners and activists re-examine collective transformations towards non-violence and rethink collective de-radicalisation processes. The authors utilised systematic, integrated, multi-dimensional and multi-disciplinary approaches as well as first-hand testimonies to explain cases of collective transformations and de-radicalisation processes from Latin America to South Asia, including cases in the Arab world. Hence, they contributed to the bodies of literature impacting democratic transition; ending civil wars; demobilisation, disarmament and reintegration of ex-combatants; peacebuilding; countering violent extremism; counterinsurgency and counterterrorism.

Overall, so many mentors, friends and colleagues contributed to this edited book, and in many direct and indirect ways. Let me start by thanking the Arab Centre for Research and Policy Studies (ACRPS) for the support of this research project. I owe thanks to Dr Azmi Bishara, the General Director of ACRPS, Ronnie Kasrils, Osama Rushdi, Hamzah Almustafa, Dr Haider Saeed, Dr Gordon Clubb, Dr Nick Hutcheon, Professor Thomas H. Johnson, Dr Aldo Marchesi, Dr Alberto Martín Álvarez, Dr Thula Simpson, Mehari Taddele Maru, Frank Pearl, Maria Jimena Duzan, Alejandro Eder, Professor Rex Brynen, Richard Barrett, Professor Larry Goodson, Professor Gareth Stansfield, Dr Shadi Hamid, Dr Mohammad Almasri, Jamal Barout, Abdou Moussa, Nagham al-Akkad and last but not least, Dr Hae Youn Chung.

I am grateful to my research team at the Arab Centre's Strategic Studies Unit: my assistants Sofia Hnezla and Majd Abuamer for their bibliographic assistance and multiple research tasks; and Christopher Huw Hitchcock, Abby Lewis and Michael Scott for their editorial assistance.

Finally, I am thankful to my copy-editor, George MacBeth, and to Kirsty Woods, Bekah Dey, Eddie Clark, Helena Heald, Louise Hutton and Caitlin Murphy of Edinburgh University Press and all their colleagues for their support throughout the writing and the editing processes. I would also like to thank two anonymous peer-reviewers for their insightful comments and critical feedback.

Omar Ashour
Doha, 1 November 2020

ABBREVIATIONS

ADB	African Development Bank
AIS	Islamic Salvation Army, Algeria
AKP	Turkish Adalet ve Kalkınma Partisi (Justice and Development Party)
Al-Shabaab	Harakat Shabaab al-Mujahidin (Party of the jihadist Youth)
ANA	Afghanistan's National Army
ANC	African National Congress, South Africa
ANC-MK	African National Congress-Spear of Nation, South Africa
ANDM	Amhara Nationalist Democratic Movement
ANDSF	Afghanistan's National Defence and Security Forces
ANP	Afghanistan's National Police
AoC	Army of Conquest, Syria
AoI	Army of Islam, Syria
AQ	al Qaida
ARENA	Alianza Republicana Nacionalista (Nationalist Republican Alliance)
ASU	Arab Socialist Union, Egypt
AU	African Union
AUC	African Union Commission

AWB	Afrikaner Weerstandsbeweging (Afrikaner Resistance Movement)
BAC	Basque Autonomous Community
BDP	Building and Development Party, Egypt
BDS	Boycott Divestment and Sanctions
BPR	Bloque Popular Revolucionario (People's Revolutionary Bloc), El-Salvador
CAS	Cárcel de Alta Seguridad (Maximum Security Prison)
CD	Democratic Convergence
CODEPU	Corporación de Promoción y Defensa de los Derechos del Pueblo (Corporation for the Promotion and Defense of the People's Rights), Chile
CODESA	Convention for a Democratic South Africa
COMESA	Common Market for Eastern and Southern Africa
Concertación	Concertación de Partidos por la Democracia (Coalition of Parties for Democracy), Chile
COSAG	Concerned South Africans Group
CP	Conservative Party
CPC	Civilian Protection Committee, Syria
CPM	Political-Military Coordination
CRM	Revolutionary Coordinating Committee of the Masses
DP	Democratic Party
DRU	Unified Revolutionary Direction
EAC	East African Community
EASP	Egyptian Arab Socialist Organisation
EDP	Ethiopian Democratic Party
EE	Euzkadiko Ezkerra (the Left of the Basque Country)
EFFORT	Endowment Fund for the Rehabilitation of Tigray
EIU	Economist Intelligence Unit
EJO	Egyptian Jihad Organization
ELN	Ejército de Liberación Nacional (National Liberation Army), Bolivia
EPRDF	Ethiopian People's Revolutionary Democratic Front
ERP	Ejército Revolucionario del Pueblo (People's Revolutionary Army), Argentina

ETA	Euskadi Ta Askatasuna (Basque Homeland and Liberty), Spain
ETA-m	ETA Military
ETA-pm	ETA Political-Military
EU	European Union
FA	Frente Amplio (Broad Front), Uruguay
FAL	Fuerzas Armadas de Liberación (Armed Forces of Liberation)
FANSPS	Foreign Affairs and National Security Policy and Strategy
FAPU	Frente de Acción Popular Unificada (Unified Popular Action Front), El-Salvador
FARC	Fuerzas Armadas Revolucionarias de Colombia (Revolutionary Armed Forces of Colombia)
FARN	Fuerzas Armadas de la Resistencia Nacional (National Resistance Armed Forces), El-Salvador
FDR	Revolutionary Democratic Front
FMLN	Frente Farabundo Martí para la Liberación Nacional (Farabundo Front for National Liberation), El-Salvador
FPL	Fuerzas Populares de Liberación (Farabundo Martí Liberation People's Forces)
FPMR	Frente Patriótico Manuel Rodríguez (Manuel Rodríguez Patriotic Front), Chile
FRAP	Fuerzas Revolucionarias Armadas del Pueblo (People's Revolutionary Armed Forces), Mexico
FRELIMO	Front for the Liberation of Mozambique
FSA	Free Syrian Army
FTA	Free Trade Agreement
FTO	Foreign Terrorist Organization
FUSADES	Fundación Salvadoreña para el Desarrollo Económico y Social (Salvadoran Foundation for Social and Economic Development)
GAP	Government of Broad Participation
GIA	Armed Islamic Group, Algeria

Ginbot 7	Ginbot 7 (May 7th) for Democracy and Justice
GoIRA	Government of the Islamic Republic of Afghanistan
GTP	Growth and Transformation Plan
HB	Herri Batasuna/Popular Unity
HIG	Gulbuddin Hekmatyar's Hezb-e-Islami (Party of Islam) Party
HIK	Yunas Khalis' Hezb-e-Islami (Party of Islam) Party
HNC	High Negotiations Committee, Syria
HTS	Hay'at Tahrir al-Sham (Levant Liberation Organisation), Syria
IA	Izquierda Abertzal (Basque Nationalist Left)
ICRC	International Committee of the Red Cross
IDPs	Internally Displaced Persons
IEA	Islamic Emirate of Afghanistan
IF	Islamic Front, Syria
IFP	Inkhata Freedom Party, South Africa
IG	Islamic Group, Egypt
IGAD	Inter-Governmental Authority on Development
IMF	International Monetary Fund
IRA	Provisional Irish Republican Army, Northern Ireland
IS	Islamic State
ISI	Pakistan's Army Inter-Service Intelligence unit
ISIL	Islamic State of Iraq and the Levant
ISIS	Islamic State of Iraq and Syria
JCR	Junta de Coordinación Revolucionaria (Revolutionary Coordination Board)
JN	Jabhat al-Nusra, Syria
LIFG	Libyan Islamic Fighting Group
LP-28	Ligas Populares 28 de Febrero (Popular League of February 28)
MAS	Movimiento al Socialismo (Movement toward Socialism), Bolivia
MB	Muslim Brothers, Egypt
MDGs	Millennium Development Goals
Medrek (Forum)	Forum for Democratic Dialogue in Ethiopia

MIDROC   Mohammed International Development Research and
              Organization Companies
MIR   Movimiento de Izquierda Revolucionaria (Left
              Revolutionary Movement), Chile
MK   Umkhonto we Sizwe (Spear of the Nation), South
              Africa
MLNT   Movimiento de Liberación Nacional Tupamaros
              (Tupamaros's National Liberation Movement),
              Uruguay
MNR   Social-democratic National Revolutionary Movement
MOC   Military Operations Centre, Jordan
MoFED   Ministry of Finance and Economic Development
MPLA   People's Movement for the Liberation of Angola
MPP   Movimiento de Participación Popular (Popular
              Participation Movement), Uruguay
MPSC   Social Christian Popular Movement
MRTA   Tupac Amaru's Revolutionatry Movement, Peru
MTP   Movimiento Todos por la Patria (Everyone for the
              Homeland Movement), Argentina
NAG   National Action Group, Syria
NATO   North Atlantic Treaty Organization
NCSR   National Coalition for the Syrian Revolution
NDP   National Democratic Party, Egypt
NEBE   Electoral Board of Ethiopia
NEC   National Executive Committee
NEPAD   New Partnership for Africa's Development
NP   National Party
NPSA   National Peace and Security Architecture
NWC   National Working Committee
OAU   Organisation of African Unity
OEF   Operation Enduring Freedom (U.S. original
              Afghanistan mission name)
OLF   Oromo Liberation Front
ONLF   Ogaden Nationalist Liberation Front
OPDO   Oromo People Democratic Organization

OPM	Organización Político Militar (Political Military Organisation)
PAC	Pan Africanist Congress
PCS	Partido Comunista de El Salvador (Communist Party of El Salvador)
PDC	Partido Demócrata Cristiano (Christian Democratic Party), Chile
PEGA	Political, Economic and Governance Analytical approach
PESTLE	Political, Economic, Social, Technological and Legal Environment
PLO	Palestinian Liberation Organisation
PNV	Partido Nacionalista Vasco (Basque Nationalist Party)
PP	Partido Popular/Popular Party
PRTC	Partido Revolucionario de los Trabajadores Centroamericanos (Revolutionary Party of Central American Workers)
PRT-ERP	Partido Revolucionario de los Trabajadores-Ejército Revolucionario del Pueblo (Workers Revolutionary Party-People Revolutionary Army), Argentina
PSOE	Partido Socialista de Obrero Español (Spanish Socialist Worker's Party)
PT	the Partido dos Trabalhadores (Worker's Party), Brazil
REC	Regional Economic Community
SACC	South African Council of Churches
SACP	South African Communist Party
SADF	South African Defence Force
SANDF	South African National Defence Force
Sandanistas/SNLF	Sandinista National Liberation Front of Nicaragua
SEPDM	Southern Ethiopian People Democratic Movement
SILF	Syrian Islamic Liberation Front
SNA	Syrian National Army
SNC	Syrian National Coalition
SOPs	Standard Operating Procedures
SSI	State Security Investigations

SWAPO	South West African Peoples Organisation of Namibia
Syrian MB	The Muslim Brotherhood in Syria
TPDM	Tigrai People Democratic Movement
TPLF	Tigrai People Liberation Front
UCA	Jesuit Central American University
UDF	United Democratic Front
UES	University of El Salvador
UNAMA	United Nations Assistance Mission in Afghanistan
UNDP	United Nations Development Programme
UP	Unidad Popular (Popular Unity), Chile
USAID	United States Agency for International Development
UWHP	University of the Witwatersrand
WTC	World Trade Centre
ZANU	Zimbabwe African National Union
ZAPU	Zimbabwe African People's Union

NOTES ON CONTRIBUTORS

Hamzeh Almustafa

Doctoral candidate in Middle Eastern Politics at University of Exeter (UK) and a researcher at the Arab Center for Research and Policy Studies (ACRPS). He is the General Director of Syria TV and the author of *The Virtual Public Sphere in the Syrian Revolution: Features, Orientations, and Mechanisms to Create Public Opinion* [in Arabic] (2012).

Alberto Martín Álvarez

Research Fellow at the Research Institute Dr José María Luis Mora (Mexico City). He holds a PhD in Latin American Studies from the Universidad Complutense, Madrid. He has extensively researched the Salvadoran revolutionary left. His interests are framed in the study of collective action, social movements and political violence in Latin America and Europe.

Omar Ashour

Founding director of the Critical Security Studies Programme in the Doha Institute for Graduate Studies and the Strategic Studies Unit in the Arab Centre for Research and Policy Studies. He is the author of *The De-Radicalization of Jihadists: Transforming Armed Islamist Movements* (2009) and *How ISIS Fights: Military Tactics in Iraq, Syria, Libya and Egypt* (Edinburgh University Press, 2021). He served at the University of Exeter

(UK) as a tenured faculty member for ten years (2008–18). He also served as a senior consultant for the United Nations on security sector reform, counterterrorism and de-radicalisation issues (2009–13; 2015) and co-authored the United Nations' Economic and Social Commission for West Asia's (UN-ESCWA) document on security sector reform during the transitional periods of the 'Arab Spring'. He was a research fellow at the Brookings Institution (2010–15) and an associate fellow at the Royal Institute of International Affairs (Chatham House) in London (2015–17). He holds a PhD from McGill University, Canada.

Gordon Clubb

Lecturer in International Security at the University of Leeds. His research focuses on de-radicalisation, conceptualising it as a social process, and on the role of former combatants in preventing and countering violent extremism. His most recent book is *Social Movement De-Radicalization and the Decline of Terrorism: The Morphogenesis of the Irish Republican Movement* (2017). He is a research fellow at the German Institute on Radicalization and De-radicalization Studies.

Nick Hutcheon

A researcher focused on the qualitative study of first- and second-generation intra-state immigrants in Basque nationalist movements. His research included twelve-month fieldwork period in the Basque Country, conducting in-depth interviews with activists and supporters of ETA and the larger Basque nationalist movements in the provinces of Araba, Bizkaia, Gipuzkoa and Nafarroa. He holds a PhD from the University of Leeds.

Thomas H. Johnson

Research professor in the National Security Affairs Department at the Naval Postgraduate School (Monterey, California) as well the director of the Program for Culture and Conflict Studies. For over three decades, Professor Johnson has conducted research and published widely on Afghanistan and South Asia. At the Naval Postgraduate School, Professor Johnson teaches courses on Afghanistan, Central and South Asian crises, and historical insurgencies and counterinsurgencies. He has taught at the University of Southern

California and the Foreign Service Institute, and frequently lectures at Service Academies. Before joining the faculty of the Naval Postgraduate School, he served on the faculty of George Mason University. He is the author of the recent book, *Taliban Narratives: The Uses and Power of Stories in the Afghanistan Conflict* (2018). His most recent book is *The Historical Dictionary of Afghanistan* with the late Professor Ludwig Adamic (2021).

Ronnie Kasrils

The Sharpeville Massacre prompted Kasrils to join the African National Congress (ANC) in 1960, serving as the secretary of the ANC-aligned Congress of Democrats (CoD) in Natal until it was banned in 1962. He was a co-founder of Umkhonto we Sizwe (MK), the ANC's military wing, from its inception in 1961, and the head of its intelligence at a later stage. In 1994 until June 1999, Kasrils was appointed deputy minister of defence. During this period, he assisted Joe Modise in the amalgamation of the previous adversarial military forces into a new South African National Defense Force. He was the minster of intelligence services between 2004 and 2008, and he led a few reforms in both the military and the intelligence establishments.

Aldo Marchesi

Director of the Uruguayan Interdisciplinary Studies Center (CEIU), a specialised centre on Uruguayan Recent History, and a history lecturer at the Universidad de la República (Montevideo, Uruguay). He holds a PhD from New York University (2012). He has published widely on the recent history and collective memory of Uruguay and the Southern Cone. His most recent book is *Latin America's Radical Left: Rebellion and Cold War in the Global 1960s* (2018).

Mehari Taddele Maru

Programme head of the Institute for Security Studies and a lecturer at Addis Ababa University. He is a specialist in human rights and humanitarian law, and lectures at the UN Institute for Economic Development and Planning (Senegal), the African Center for Strategic Studies (USA) and NATO Defense College (NDC). He was a Member of the African Union High

Advisory Group and a Consultant for the Intergovernmental Authority on Development (IGAD).

Osama Rushdi

Former spokesperson of the Islamic Group of Egypt and former Political Advisor to its Building and Development Party. He is an Egyptian politician and a former member of the Egyptian National Council for Human Rights. He is also a member of the British and International Federation of Journalists and the director of the *Najda* Human Rights Foundation (United Kingdom).

Haider Saeed

Head of the Research Department and editor-in-chief of *Siyasat Arabiya* journal at the Arab Centre for Research and Policy Studies. Saeed earned his PhD in Linguistics from Baghdad's Al-Mustansiriya University. Saeed's writing focuses on intellectual history, critical theory and the politics of Iraq. He has contributed to the 'National Report on Human Development in Iraq' for the 2009 and 2014 editions. He is the author of *The Politics of the Symbol and the End of National Culture in Iraq* (2009) [in Arabic] and with others *The Status of Social Sciences in Iraqi Universities* (2008) [in Arabic]. He is also the editor of *The Arab Shiites: Identity and Citizenship* (2019) [in Arabic].

Thula Simpson

Associate professor at the University of Pretoria, department of historical and heritage studies. He holds a BA from King's College, University of London and a PhD from Birkbeck, University of London. His most recent publication is *The ANC and the Liberation Struggle in South Africa: Essential Writings* (2017). Professor Simpson's research interests include the liberation struggle in Southern Africa; South African historiography and historians; the rise and fall of segregation and apartheid; and African revolutionaries.

1

REVISITING COLLECTIVE
DE-RADICALISATION:
A COMPARATIVE PERSPECTIVE

Omar Ashour

Introduction

In March 2010, an official conference was held in the Libyan capital of Tripoli with academics, western journalists and officials. It marked the release of the leaders of the Libyan Islamic Fighting Group (LIFG) in a 'reconciliation' process led by Saif al-Islam Gaddafi, the then heir-apparent of Libya's late dictator, Muammar Gaddafi. 'De-radicalisation' was a major component of the process. The LIFG did not just abandon armed activism against the Gaddafi regime, but also produced 416 pages of thorough theological, ideological, instrumental and socio-psychological argumentation de-legitimating various forms of nonstate political violence, including national and international terrorism. Back then, the document served, and was celebrated, as a counter-narrative to the rhetoric and ideas of violent extremist groups, particularly al-Qaida.[1]

In August 2011, in the middle of an armed revolution, Abdul Hakim Belhaj, the former Emir of the LIFG spearheaded an attack on Bab al-Aziziya compound, Colonel Gaddafi's headquarters.[2] This was more of a counteroffensive to the regime's onslaught, however, than 'reneging on the deal' or abandoning the transformation. Between February and August 2011, the political environment had no room for de-radicalisation or reconciliation. From March 2010[3] to February 2011,[4] institutionalised mechanisms of non-violent conflict-resolution had not been introduced in Libya. Security sector reform processes, revisions of standard operating procedures (SOPs) in times of political crises, and a credible transitional justice process were unheard of. In other words, a sustained transformation from violent to non-violent activism had little-to-no chance of surviving, despite significant investments in creating and initiating it.

This has not been just a Libyan story. Officers, soldiers and employees of Task Force 134 – the unit commanding all detention operations in Iraq, including Camp Bucca (the former home of Abu Baker al-Baghdadi, the deceased leader of the so-called 'Islamic State Organisation') – understand this well.[5] A 'rehabilitation' programme with a de-radicalisation component was introduced by the United States and the Iraqi government in Iraqi prisons in 2007. It had some initial effects[6] and by 2008 about 10,000 prisoners were freed while the country was in a process of an initial de-escalation. By late 2010, almost all of the effects dissipated. Rather than a transformation towards unarmed, less-sectarian, constitutional and institutionalised politics, the Islamic State of Iraq and Sham (ISIS) was established in April 2013 on the ashes of both this programme and the whole de-escalation process.

This is not to conclude that transformation processes and de-radicalisation programmes in the Arab World are destined to fail. The failures are just a reminder of how critical macro-level reforms are to sustaining transformations, as exemplified by some of the European, Latin American and African cases reviewed below and discussed in the following chapters. After all, processes of transformation to unarmed activism are critical to national reconciliation, social cohesion, the functioning of state institutions, human security and human rights.[7] They are worth investing in and fighting for.

Collective transformations from armed to unarmed political activism remain a global phenomenon that merits revisiting and further investigation despite setbacks, the global rise of nationalist populism and the persistence of violent extremism. In this book, we qualitatively examine a sample of seventeen cases of armed organisations that transformed into political parties or nonviolent social movements in fifteen countries. These countries are Afghanistan, Algeria, Argentina, Chile, Colombia, Egypt, El Salvador, Ethiopia, Iraq, Libya, South Africa, Spain, Syria, the United Kingdom and

Uruguay. The seventeen organisations examined were inspired by ideologies ranging from religious to leftist to ethno-nationalist and nationalist. In order of analysis in this book, these organisations are:

- The African National Congress-Spear of Nation (ANC-MK) of South Africa
- The Islamic Group of Egypt
- The Levant Corps (*Faylaq al-Sham*), Army of Islam (*Jaysh al-Islam*) and Freemen of the Levant (*Ahrar al-Sham*) of Syria
- The Mahdi Army (*Jaysh al-Mahdi*) of Iraq
- The Provisional Irish Republican Army (IRA)
- The Basque Homeland and Liberty (ETA)
- The Taliban of Afghanistan
- The People's Revolutionary Army (ERP) and the Montoneros of Argentina
- The Left Revolutionary Movement (MIR) and Manuel Rodríguez Patriotic Front (FPMR) of Chile
- The Tupamaros National Liberation Movement (MLNT) of Uruguay
- The Farabundo Martí National Liberation Front (FMLN) of El Salvador
- The Ethiopian People's Revolutionary Democratic Front (EPRDF)

In addition to the aforementioned seventeen organisations, four others are comparatively revisited and briefly discussed:

- The Islamic Salvation Army (AIS) of Algeria
- The Libyan Islamic Fighting Group (LIFG)
- The Revolutionary Armed Forces of Colombia (FARC)
- The Sandinista National Liberation Front of Nicaragua (The Sandinistas or FSLN)

Organisations operating in other countries are referred to when relevant as well. The abovementioned cases hail from the four continents, covering the Middle East, South Asia, Western and Southern Europe, Sub-Saharan Africa, and Latin America.[8] In this book, scholars, a former state official and a non-state activist either reflect on their direct involvement in leading collective de-radicalisation processes or analyse them as academic experts.

The organisations discussed across the six abovementioned regions represent a qualitative sample of a larger global phenomenon. One quantitative study demonstrated that among 268 identified armed groups that operated between 1968 and 2006, only 20 (7 per cent) were defeated militarily.[9] In contrast, 114 (43 per cent) joined the political mainstream, either as political parties or socio-political movements. Policing, intelligence and public responses were responsible for dismantling 107 (40 per cent) organisations, the majority of them small ones.[10] For larger groups (especially those with over 1,000 members), by far the most common trajectory was the conversion to unarmed political or social activism.[11] Smaller datasets have produced similar results. Of 133 armed groups fighting against regimes of different types between 1990 and 2009, 54.8 per cent transformed into political parties in about fifty countries across the globe.[12]

How do such transformations happen? Why do they happen? What are the conditions for initiating such transformations? And what are the conditions for sustaining them? What are the different trajectories of moving away from violent activism? Do these transformations happen after a military victory, a military defeat, or a draw in an armed conflict between an insurgent group(s) and an incumbent authority(ies)? These are the main research questions that this book engages with to explain collective transformations from armed to unarmed political activism.

This chapter provides an analytical overview of the phenomenon, its defining terms, causal variables and dynamic trajectories, and presents a number of empirical cases. The transformations and the de-radicalisation of the selected movements are intertwined with processes of democratisation, national reconciliation, peacebuilding, civil–military relations and security sector reform, countering and preventing violent extremism and countering terrorism and insurgency.[13] This chapter is composed of five interrelated sections. After this first section, the following (second) section lays out a theoretical framework for collective transformations. It also discusses the relevant terminology used during approaching and analysing this issue-area. The third section empirically overviews some of the most salient cases of collective de-radicalisation and transformations from armed to unarmed political activism discussed in this book. The fourth section proffers scholarly observations on the phenomenon, based on the empirical overview. The last section outlines the book's structure.

Collective De-radicalisation: A Conceptual Framework

Collective transformation from armed to unarmed activism is a process of relative change, in which an armed group can reverse its ideology, narratives, rhetoric, behaviour and/or organisational structure away from armed action, and towards unarmed political or social activism. In security and terrorism studies literature, this phenomenon is sometimes referred to as 'collective de-radicalisation' or a process whereby an armed organisation abandons and/ or de-legitimises the use of armed tactics to achieve political goals, while also moving toward an acceptance of gradual social, political and economic change and reforms within an existing status-quo. But scholars have never agreed on one precise term for it and the security studies community has debated both the definition and the dimensions of 'de-radicalisation'.[14]

Revisiting Terminology

In earlier works,[15] I argued that the concept of 'de-radicalisation' should be centred on changing attitudes toward *political violence* and the *pace* of socio-political change, rather than towards *constitutional liberalism*.[16] This means that deradicalised groups will reject violence and accept slow and gradual institutional reform within a relatively reformed status quo, but may still maintain intolerant, xenophobic and other illiberal views. Other scholars have argued that deradicalised groups and individuals must uphold constitutional liberalism. If they abandon violence, but still uphold a radical ideology (or elements of it), then the term used to describe them is 'disengaged' (from terrorism) as opposed to 'deradicalised'.[17] The distinction between behaviour and ideology (as well as organisational structures) is a critical contribution to both scholarship and practice, regardless of the terms used to make the distinction.

In this volume, as in previous works, I have found it useful to distinguish between 'de-radicalisation' and 'moderation',[18] as well as to use three qualifiers with the term 'de-radicalisation': behavioural, ideological and organisational. This is based on an understanding of radicalisation as a process of relative change in which a group undergoes ideological and/or behavioural transformations that lead to the rejection of the socio-political status quo (if the status quo is democratic, then the rejection will include peaceful alternation of power and the legitimacy of ideological and political pluralism, among other democratic principles) and possibly to the utilisation of violence, or to an increase in the levels of violence to achieve socio-political goals and to bring about change. A *radical* collective entity in that sense exhibits three features:

1. It demands and/or acts to bring about sweeping, revolutionary changes to undermine an existing status quo.
2. It has low-to-no tolerance for alternative views or forms of activism (both alternative radical and all reformist ones) and hence dismisses, marginalises, or attacks them.
3. It *may* utilise and legitimise social and political violence. A radical collective entity can initiate violence against the forces, supporters and/or acceptors of the status quo. A radical collective entity *may* also retaliate to a crackdown by the forces of the status quo.

In this sense, the term 'radical' alone – without a qualifier – should have no negative connotations. Abolitionists, democracy, racial and gender equality, anti-apartheid and anti-colonial activists were all radicals challenging a dominant socio-political status quo at one point in time, but so are groups like al-Qaida and the 'Islamic State'. Hence, qualifiers are merited with terms associated with 'radicalisation' and 'de-radicalisation'.

The qualifier 'behavioural de-radicalisation' reflects an empirical reality outlined in the following chapters by both scholars and practitioners: the behavioural abandonment of violence is almost always intertwined with the acceptance of slow, gradualist reforms within an existing status quo. The acceptance of a reformist, gradualist approach is by definition *not* radical. It is a constituent component of de-radicalisation processes. Most groups discussed in the following chapters did develop a gradualist, constitutional electoral political platform. All accepted to work within the existing status quo, usually a reformed one based on a compromise. Many of these groups – including Islamist, leftist and ethno-leftist ones – did not fully embrace constitutional liberalism and still uphold *some* radical ideas/rhetoric or modifications of them. Still, the argument here is that they 'behaviourally de-radicalised'; a step further than mere disengagement from terrorism and political violence and a term coined to better capture the complex realities of these groups.

Costs and Co-optations in Practice and Scholarship

Clearly, there are political costs and policy implications for upholding either of the two aforementioned approaches to de-radicalisation. The first approach (transforming to unarmed politics behaviourally but upholding illiberal views ideologically and rhetorically) risks undermining social cohesion, especially in multicultural, multi-ethnic and multi-religions societies. The second definition can be abused to dismiss mere transitions from armed to unarmed activism as 'failed de-radicalisations' and therefore politically and legally exclude particular groups on the basis that they did not become liberal democratic entities, even if the contexts in which they operated were ruled by brutal, illiberal dictatorships. Indeed, setting the standard of 'de-radicalisation' and even mere transformations to unarmed politics as full embrace of constitutional liberalism may mean that many political parties, social movements and particularly armed groups will fail below that standard. Based on previous works analysing experiences within parts of the Middle East and Central Asia,[19] I have found it useful here to distinguish between *de-radicalisation* and *moderation*. The latter is also a process of relative change that is mainly concerned with attitudes toward liberal democracy. Still, as Jillian Schwedler concluded,[20] there is also no scholarly consensus on the definition of *moderation*.[21]

Within authoritarian regimes, de-radicalisation and transformation to unarmed activism are sometimes conflated with political co-optation and buy offs. Only groups and individuals that toe the regime's line and show loyalty to the leader – whether an authoritarian president or a regressive king – are considered 'de-radicalised' or 'moderates'. As demonstrated in the following chapters, if a group transforms its means for change – from violent to non-violent – but remains in opposition, it is still 'radical,' 'extreme' or 'terrorist'. Regime-type in these processes is as crucial to understand as the rebel-type.

Causes of Collective De-radicalisation: Initiation versus Sustenance

As mentioned above, transformations from armed to unarmed activism can occur across three dimensions: ideological, behavioural and organisational.

Based on these dimensions several types of collective de-radicalisation were identified. *Comprehensive de-radicalisation* refers to a successful collective transformation process on all the three dimensions (ideological, behavioural and organisational). *Substantive (or factional) de-radicalisation* entails a successful process of transformation on both the ideological and behavioural dimensions, but not on the organisational one. Usually, a failure on that level is followed by splits, factionalisation and internal organisational conflict, and/or the marginalisation of the de-radicalised leadership. A third type of collective de-radicalisation is *pragmatic de-radicalisation*. which refers to a successful behavioural and organisational transformation process, but without an ideological de-legitimisation of political violence.

Previous findings indicated that a combination of meso-level (organisational level) variables interact to successfully *initiate*, and in the short term *sustain*, a collective de-radicalisation process.[22] Charismatic leadership within the organisation, state repression, interactions with the non-like-minded 'other' as well as between the layers of the organisation, and selective inducements from the state within a de-escalatory environment are common causal variables initiating transformations.

The argument is qualified in this book as an explanatory framework. Within the meso-level (organisational and institutional levels), a charismatic leader/centralised leadership may include leaders of relevant state institution(s) (such as the presidency or the dominant armed institution within the state) who support collective de-radicalisation rather than being limited to the leader/leadership of the insurgent organisation. The 'combat pressure' on *both* sides replaces the 'state repression' variable. As the empirical cases in the following testimonies and chapters indicate, the pressures of combat and armed confrontations affected the calculations of *both* incumbent and insurgent leaderships, regardless of the insurgency outcome (defeat, destructive draw or victory). Internal and external interactions remain critical and unchanged. Selective inducements, however, can be proffered by both local incumbents/ruling regimes and also other regional and international actors.

There is a pattern of interaction between these meso-level variables.[23] The combat pressures of armed confrontations and interactions with non-like-minded actors often affect the ideas and the behaviour of the leadership of an

armed organisation and are likely to lead those leaders to initiate three endog-
enous processes: strategic calculations based on cost-benefit analysis; political
learning based on interaction with the non-like-minded; and modification of
the group's worldview as a result of severe crises, frustration, bloodshed and
violent changes in the environment. Following these processes, the leadership
of an armed organisation sets off a transformation process that is bolstered by
selective inducements from the incumbent authorities as well as by internal
interactions within the group(s). Also, transformed group(s) often interact
with armed groups and sometimes influence them in a controlled, pressured
environment (such as prisons, areas of exile, or rugged strongholds). A mir-
roring process usually occurs within the armed institutions of the state and
the incumbent authorities. Finally, it is important to differentiate between
initiating and sustaining a collective de-radicalisation process. Two macro-
level (state and interstate) variables are arguably critical in sustaining (as
opposed to initiating) the transformations. The proposed two variables are
democratisation and regional/international support. Democratisation is used
here as a proxy entailing security sector reform processes, balanced/reformed
civil-military relations and a credible transitional justice process. All of the
aforementioned findings, hypothesised arguments and variables will be re-
examined in the following empirical chapters.

Cases of Collective De-radicalisation: An Overview

After the Arab Uprisings of 2010 and 2011, very basic political freedoms
were briefly gained within fragile democratisation processes. This showed
how macro-level changes can affect collective de-radicalisation processes.
Formerly armed large groups have upheld their transformation from armed
to unarmed activism, and the Egyptian Islamic Group (IG), factions and
individuals from the Egyptian al-Jihad organisation, and the LIFG have not
only turned into political parties, but also participated in elections, constitutional crafting and mainstream political compromises. In 2011, for example,
the IG held internal elections, asked its members to fill in party registration
forms, held rallies against sectarian violence and issued joint statements with
the Coptic Church of Asyut promoting peaceful coexistence. However, their
stance on constitutional liberalism did not change much. For example, the
IG still did not support the right of specific minorities and women to run for

presidency. And in general, ultraconservative regressive ideologies, such as Saudi Wahhabism, partly shape the worldview of the organisation. In Algeria, organisations such as the Islamic Salvation Army (AIS) and smaller groups have laid down arms since the late 1990s. Despite the selective (and relatively successful) socioeconomic reintegration of some of their leading commanders and members, these organisations were not allowed to participate in electoral politics.[24] Additionally, any research or investigation of the security sectors' procedures, behaviours and policies during the 'national tragedy'[25] and/or into a post-war transitional justice process are punishable by Algerian law.[26] In Syria, Iraq and Afghanistan, an under-researched dimension is highlighted in this book. Ideological, rhetorical and behavioural transformations – below but relevant to de-radicalisation – have been exhibited by groups such as the Levant Corps (*Faylaq al-Sham*), Army of Islam (*Jaysh al-Islam*), Freemen of the Levant (*Ahrar al-Sham*) of Syria, the Mahdi Army of Iraq and the Taliban of Afghanistan. Moreover, the Syrian and the Afghan cases in particular have shown transformations *during* combative phases and insurgency. This can be contrasted with other cases of collective de-radicalisation examined in this book and elsewhere, in which the transformations are demonstrated after the battle/conflict/war outcomes (defeat, draw or victory).

In comparison, European cases of (or attempted) collective transformation and de-radicalisation from armed to unarmed activism show some differences in terms of the initiation and sustainability of the processes, institutional maturity, strength and flexibility, resilience and tolerance at both societal and official levels, elite and leadership awareness and reintegration capacities. The two cases of the Provisional Irish Republican Army (IRA) in the United Kingdom and the Basque Homeland and Liberty (ETA) in Spain are discussed in the following chapters. In the United Kingdom, macro- and meso-level factors initiated the peace process and sustained the Good Friday agreement. They included charismatic leaderships, the British government's innovative counterterrorism strategy, the European Union peace funding (inducements, and the role of ex-combatants, particularly at the community level (interactions).[27] In Spain, the continuous factional transformation of ETA – from the 1970s to 2017 – has shown the critical importance of meso-level factors (especially charismatic leadership), even when macro-level changes occur (such as the democratic transition in Spain and the EU's consistent support for de-radicalisation and transformations to unarmed politics). Macro-level factors can certainly reduce the risk of a strong insurgent organisation, with significant local support.[28] However, these elements do not guarantee a comprehensive transformation of an armed organisation to non-violent activism, without the meso-level (organisational-level) variables. In Turkey, the PKK has failed to transform to unarmed politics, despite the presence of charismatic leaderships on both of the warring sides, and despite available opportunity structures, and possibilities to participate in electoral and constitutional politics.[29] In a way, the PKK represents an outlier case, where some of the incentives were lined up against de-radicalisation and the combat pressure and the costs of the armed path were deemed tolerable by the PKK guerrilla commanders. Hence, the perceived strategic benefits of using bullets outweighed any estimated gains from transforming to compete at the ballot box.

Whereas levels of both democratic maturity and professional competence of the security establishments are quite high in Western Europe, Latin American democratic consolidation and security sector reforms are relatively recent. Hence, the lessons learned from Latin America's successful (and failed) cases of transformations are highly relevant and comparable to the Arab cases. Latin America and the Caribbean region offered cases of transformation via different trajectories. Transformations after military defeats include the cases of the Tupamaros in Uruguay and, more generally, the armed left-wing organisations in Chile, Argentina and Brazil. This is well-contrasted with the case of the Revolutionary Armed Forces of Colombia (FARC),[30] where the transformation followed a destructive stalemate, and the case of the Sandinistas in Nicaragua, where the transformation into a ruling political party happened after a decisive military victory.[31] As detailed in the following chapters, the case studies and experiences in Latin America show how a combination of the aforementioned meso- and macro-level variables (i.e. organisational and state/interstate levels) can both initiate and sustain collective transformations to unarmed activism, despite relatively limited wealth and resources in comparison to the Arab World.

Finally, Africa provides cases of successful transformations also with limited resources. Recent developments in Ethiopia have shown a trajectory of transformation of former guerrilla organisations to coalition partners; a process that is still ongoing with other armed groups. A more successful transformation and a transition to democracy took place in South Africa during the 1990s. It is a transformation via a destructive draw and a hurting stalemate.[32] In this case, the charismatic leadership of Nelson Mandela was able to push the transformation and initiate peaceful negotiations, despite the capacity to use arms, internal resistance and even defections within the armed wing of the ANC (Spear of the Nation or MK), and the 'war within the war' fought by the ANC and the Zulu Nationalist Inkatha movement.[33] Unlike the Arab cases (such as the IG in Egypt and LIFG in Libya), and some of the Latin American cases (such as the M-19 and the FARC in Colombia), the ANC in South Africa was quite successful in electoral politics and managed to win via ballots, not bullets.

Scholarly Observations

The primary focus of this book is *collective* transformation and de-radicalisation processes. However, de-radicalisation programmes that target *individuals* have been examined in the scholarly literature and used by practitioners as an integral part of counterterrorism and security strategies in several parts of the world, including the Middle East. For example, Saudi Arabia,[34] Iraq[35] and pre-2011 Yemen[36] employed structured prison programmes under the control of the state/authorities in which interactions between prisoners and religious/spiritual leaders and civil society members were introduced. Selective inducements were also employed under state-control to support the individual de-radicalisation and the abandonment of political violence by selected individuals. These programmes employed varying types and levels of socioeconomic incentives, psychological counselling, theological and religious guidance, and sports and arts therapy. But the results in the Arab World specifically were meagre.

In the Iraqi context, the programme failed to reduce the recruitment, rise and risk potentials of ISIS. In the Saudi context, tens of the graduates of the Saudi '*Munasaha*' programme joined al-Qaida in the Arabian Peninsula (AQAP) in Yemen and became leading commanders.[37] The problem was not always with the programmes per se.[38] It was the unreformed and sustained repressive, corrupt and sectarian socio-political environment in which these programmes and the individuals benefiting from them were embedded in. As a result, the rates of success (and failure) were highly contested, mainly due to macro-level structural challenges and inhospitable environments. So far, there is no consensus on how to measure the success of these programmes,[39] although it is more feasible to measure collective transformations (organisations and factions), than individual ones.

Additionally, the sustainability of these programmes as well as collective transformation processes – without a thorough process of political and security reform and some form of transitional justice – is questionable. Regardless of the approach taken to explain transformations towards unarmed politics, a consensus among scholars and practitioners has almost developed: these processes are extremely context sensitive. In other words, in a political context where authoritarian repression, military coups and other forms of political violence and social instability are the common features, attempted processes and programmes of transformations and de-radicalisation are more likely to fail or collapse in the short to mid-term.

A few observations can be deduced from the above overview. Firstly, it is clear that revisiting collective transformations to unarmed political activism is worthwhile, indeed critical – especially in the Arab World. Twelve out of twenty-two Arab regimes are either at war with components of their own societies, or at war with their neighbours. The Arab region has the highest armed conflict ratio per capita in the world,[40] as well as the highest number of victims of all forms of political violence in the world.[41] Hence, transformations to forms of non-violent activism and contestation – from bullets to ballots and from IEDs to irenic activism– is of particular importance to the region.

A second observation is related to the literature on collective transformations from armed to unarmed activism. The trans-regional, qualitative-comparative dimension has hitherto received relatively limited attention. There has been a considerable amount of work on the related but distinct topic reframed in some of the security studies literature as 'how terrorism ends'. This body of literature examines a litany of possible reasons that an organisation employing terror tactics may forgo political violence.[42] Nevertheless, exploring what happens when an organisation goes beyond armed activism and participates in peaceful activities merits more work to answer several of the above-mentioned research questions. The state-centric (or status-quo-centric) assumptions in some of the security studies literature impede deeper research into the phenomenon of collective transformation. The near-exclusive reliance on secondary sources has a similar effect.

A third observation concerns the relatively limited interdisciplinary collaboration and approaches in this area of research. This is despite valuable contributions from disciplines and subfields as diverse as security studies, criminology, psychology, sociology, politics, history, theology and religious studies, peace studies, conflict studies, strategic studies, military studies, and media and communications.

A fourth observation involves the relatively limited collaboration between scholars, practitioners and nonstate leaders of these transformations. When pursued, this type of collaboration proved to be invaluable to academics, governmental officials and nonstate leaders of the transformations and has had an overall positive impact on the research agenda. This book pursues this type of collaboration.

A final observation involves a few hypotheses-engendering research questions that still merit revisiting and further research investigation. Many scholarly works in this field have concentrated on how such transformations happen and why they happen, with a focus on either a single case-study or on a comparative approach in one particular region. However, a differentiation between initiating and sustaining the collective transformations, as well as the conditions for their endurance merit more investigation. The different trajectories taken after moving away from armed action have also been relatively underexplored.[43] Both of these issue-areas are revisited in the following chapters.

Book Structure

The book is composed of thirteen chapters, taking into consideration the abovementioned observations. Following this chapter, there are two chapters representing first-hand testimonies by leaders involved in collective deradicalisation and transformation processes of armed organisations. Both chapters reflect the experiences and the opinions of their authors on critical periods of transformations. They are activists' testimonies as opposed to scholars' analysis.

Chapter Two is authored by Ronnie Kasrils, the former South African minister of intelligence services. Kasrils was also a co-founder and a former leader of Umkhonto we Sizwe (MK), the ANC's military wing since its inception in 1961. As one of the co-founders of the MK and as a former deputy minister of defence of South Africa, Kasrils reflects on his personal experiences as a statesman and as a guerrilla commander and the challenges faced by the ANC and the MK during the transition to non-violent political activism.

Chapter Three is another testimony given by a leader from the other end of both the political spectrum and the African continent. Osama Rushdi is the former spokesperson of the Islamic Group (IG) of Egypt and the former political advisor to its Building and Development Party (BDP). His chapter includes personal reflections on the various developments within the group's ideology and structure, from a student to an armed movement and finally on the transformations towards a political party and the de-legitimation of political violence and terrorism.

The following two chapters are authored by scholars focused on collective transformations of armed nonstate actors in the Middle East. In Chapter Four, Hamzah Almustafa explores the ideological, rhetorical, behavioural and organisational transformations undergone by three armed Islamist movements in Syria over the past nine years. The chapter addresses an under-researched topic in the literature by analysing relevant transformations below the level of de-radicalisation, developing during combat and without abandoning arms. The chapter also assesses the strategic implications and potential impact on the future of the Syrian Civil War. In Chapter Five, Haider Saeed analyses the transformations of the Mahdi Army in Iraq. He argues that the militia is an outlier to the common mode of relationship between Iraqi ideological parties and their armed wings. The chapter focuses on the reasons behind the transformations of the Mahdi Army since the formation of the militia in 2003 and up to 2020.

The following three chapters are focused on comparative collective transformations and the attempted de-radicalisation of armed nonstate actors in Western Europe and South Asia. In Chapter Six, Gordon Clubb analyses the de-radicalisation process undertaken by the Provisional IRA. He argues that the UK government's counter-terrorism strategy facilitated intra-movement dynamics which enabled (and constrained) agency to transition to nonviolent activism. To account for the transformations, the chapter analyses the interplay between structure and agency over two periods, the first leading up to the Good Friday Agreement and the second following the agreement. In Chapter Seven, Nick Hutcheon examines the factional transformations of ETA away from violent ethnonationalist secessionism. This chapter argues that the dissolution of ETA was partly driven by the political leadership of the Basque nationalist left and necessarily validated via their external interactions with prestigious political figures. It elaborates on the six variables outlined above (leadership, combat pressures, interactions, inducements, democratisation and regional/international support). The chapter describes the process leading to ETA's dissolution and explains how and why the organisation dissolved. In Chapter Eight, Tom Johnson proffers a critical analysis of the Afghan Taliban's transformations and asks a timely question: is the Taliban de-radicalising? The chapter focuses on the impact of leadership, external interactions, regional support and democratisation on the transformations of the Taliban. The chapter also addresses the implications for the Taliban after their participating in and signing the Doha peace agreement with the United States based on Qatar's mediation.

After that, the focus of the book shifts to Latin America. In Chapter Nine, Aldo Marchesi analyses the transformations from armed organisations to political parties and social movements in the context of the democratisation of the 1980s and 1990s in the Southern Cone of Latin America. The chapter focuses on three variables that are integral to understanding the ways in which armed organisations were successful in their adaptation to new democratic regimes: leadership, state repression, interactions and inducements within democratisation including amnesties and transitional justice processes. In Chapter Ten, Alberto Martin Álvarez explores the transformations of the FMLN in El Salvador from a coalition of armed insurgent organisations to a political party. The chapter analyses the main transformations experienced during combat as a function of leadership (of the armed Left), internal interactions (within the armed Left), and changes within the US policy on the armed conflict (regional support and inducements).

Then, the focus of the book shifts back to Africa. In Chapter Eleven, Thula Simpson analyses the decisive phase of the liberation struggle in South Africa beginning in September 1984 with the commencement of the great township uprising against the apartheid regime. The chapter explores in detail the question of why the transition towards negotiations happened, despite the capacity to use arms. The chapter also analyses issues such as defections within the MK and the clashes between the ANC and the Zulu Nationalist Inkatha movement. In Chapter Twelve, Mehari Maru explores the transformations of Ethiopian armed organisations to a ruling political coalition. The chapter overviews the military victory against the former regime, the transformations of the coalition partners from armed guerrillas to statesmen and the challenges of transition towards unarmed politics and, generally, to democratisation in Ethiopia.

Finally, in Chapter Thirteen, I conclude with final reflections and implications. These are represented as a framework for explaining and sustaining collective de-radicalisation and transformations towards unarmed activism based on the cases analysed. As such, the book aims to contribute to revisiting understandings of collective de-radicalisation and to offer further insights into how and why armed groups *may* or *will* transform to unarmed activism and how to sustain such transformations in the future.

Notes

1. Omar Ashour, 'Post-Jihadism: Libya and the Global Transformations of Armed Islamist Movements', *Terrorism and Political Violence*, vol. 23, no. 3 (2011), pp. 377–97. See also: Mary Fitzgerald and Emad Badi, 'The Limits of Reconciliation: Assessing the Revisions of the Libyan Islamic Fighting Group (LIFG)', *Institute for Integrated Transitions* (2020), pp. 36–42.
2. Omar Ashour, 'Fears Over Islamists within Libyan Rebel Ranks', *BBC News*, 31/8/2011, accessed on 11/12/2018, at: https://bbc.in/34rLutt. See also: Abdul Hakim Belhaj, 'From the 'Fighting Group' to the 'Homeland Party': Observations on the Transformations in Libya', paper presented at the first annual conference of the Strategic Studies Unit entitled 'From Bullets to Ballots: Transformations from Armed to Unarmed Political Activism', Arab Centre for Research and Policy Studies, Doha, 3–4/11/2018.
3. The month in which the 'reconciliation' was officially declared.
4. The month in which the Libyan Revolution started.
5. Major-General Douglas Stone, Commander of Task Force 134, Interview by the author, Singapore, 24/2/2008.
6. Babak Dehghanpisheh, 'Iraqi Prison Tries to Un-Brainwash Radical Youth', *Newsweek*, 8/8/2007, accessed on 11/12/2018, at: https://bit.ly/2rj0eX6

7. Azmi Bishara, 'Opening Remarks', paper presented at the first annual conference of the Strategic Studies Unit entitled 'From Bullets to Ballots: Transformations from Armed to Unarmed Political Activism', Arab Centre for Research and Policy Studies, Doha, 3–4/11/2018.

8. Despite its trans-regional nature, this sample is incomprehensive. It neither includes North American nor Australian cases of transformations, such as the factional cases from the Black Panthers Organisation in the United States (especially the Illinois Chapter of the organisation) and *Le Front de Libération du Québec* (FLQ) in Canada.

9. That is by exclusive military means. See for example: Seth G. Jones and Martin C. Libicki, *How Terrorist Groups End: Lessons for Countering al Qa' ida* (Santa Monica: RAND Publications, 2008), p. 19.

10. Ibid., pp. 141–85. Most of these small organisations have fewer than 200 members.

11. Omar Ashour, *The De-Radicalization of Jihadists: Transforming Armed Islamist Movements* (London and New York: Routledge, 2009), pp. 12–18.

12. Carrie Manning and Ian Smith, 'Political Party Formation by Former Armed Opposition Groups after Civil War', *Democratization*, vol. 23, no. 6 (2016), p. 973.

13. See: United Nations, 'Plan of Action for Preventing Violent Extremism', *Report of the Secretary-General*, 24/12/2015, accessed on 11/12/2018, at: https://bit.ly/1n0F1wu

14. For a detailed review see: Jillian Schwedler, 'Can Islamists Become Moderates? Rethinking the Inclusion-Moderation Hypothesis', *World Politics*, vol. 63, no. 2 (2011), pp. 347–76; Alex Schmid, 'Radicalization, De-Radicalization, and Counter-Radicalization: A Conceptual Discussion and Literature Review', *ICCT Research Papers* (2013), pp. 20–31. For some of the foundational literature on the concept within armed Islamist, jihadist, ethnonationalist and leftist groups see: Robert Tucker, 'Deradicalization of Marxist Movements', *American Political Science Review*, vol. 61, no. 2 (1967), pp. 343–58; Omar Ashour, 'Lions Tamed? An Inquiry into the Causes of De-Radicalization of Armed Islamist Movements', *Middle East Journal*, vol. 61, no. 3 (2007), pp. 598–600; Toro Bjørgo and John Horgan (eds), *Leaving Terrorism Behind: Individual and Collective Disengagement* (Abington: Routledge, 2009); John Horgan, *Walking Away from Terrorism: Accounts of Disengagements from Radical and Extremist Movements* (London and New York: Routledge, 2009); Ashour, *The De-Radicalization of Jihadists*; Angel Rabasa et al., *Deradicalizing Islamist Extremists* (Santa Monica: RAND, 2010); Veronique Dudouet (ed.), *Civil Resistance and Conflict Transformation:*

Transitions from Armed to Nonviolent Struggle (London: Routledge, 2015); Daniel Koehler, *Understanding De-Radicalization: Methods, Tools and Programs for Countering Violent Extremism* (London, New York: Routledge, 2016).

15. See for example: Ashour, 'Lions Tamed', p. 598; Ashour, *The De-Radicalization of Jihadists*, pp. 4–7.

16. Ibid, pp. 6–7. For a summarised review, see: Thomas Hegghammer, 'The De-Radicalization of Jihadists: Transforming Armed Islamist Movements', *Perspective in Politics*, vol. 9, no. 2 (2011), pp. 472–4.

17. See for example: John Horgan, 'De-radicalization or Disengagement?', *Perspectives on Terrorism*, vol. 2, no. 4 (2010), pp. 3–8. For a comprehensive review of the concepts see: Rabasa et al.

18. The term is also contested in the literature. In this book, we mean by 'moderation' a process of relative change that is mainly concerned with the attitudes towards liberal democracy. On the ideological level, the key transformation is the acceptance of democratic principles, the legitimacy of diversity and pluralism and peaceful alternation of power. A higher level of moderation would be the endorsement of constitutional liberal democracy as opposed to the electoral elements of democracy.

19. Ashour, *The De-Radicalization of Jihadists*, pp. 4–5.

20. Jillian Schwedler, 'Why Academics Can't Get Beyond Moderates and Radicals', *Washington Post*, 12/2/2015, accessed on 25/10/2020, at: https://wapo.st/3knWgX4

21. Ibid. See also: Schwedler, 'Can Islamists Become Moderates?'; see also Jillian Schwedler, *Faith in Moderation: Islamist Parties in Jordan and Yemen* (Cambridge: Cambridge University Press, 2006).

22. See for example: Ashour, *The De-Radicalization of Jihadists*, pp. 136–46; Rabasa et al., pp. 157–77.

23. By micro-level, we mean individual-level variables. By meso-level, we mean organisational and institutional level variables. By macro-level, we mean state- and interstate-level variables.

24. Omar Ashour, 'Islamist De-Radicalization in Algeria: Successes and Failures', *Middle East Institute*, 1/11/2008, accessed on 11/12/2018, at: https://bit.ly/2rlZVLd

25. A politically charged term that Algerian officials use to refer to the civil war of the 1990s.

26. Rachid Tlemçani, 'Algeria Under Bouteflika: Civil Strife and National Reconciliation', *Carnegie Papers*, no. 7 (2008); 'Algeria: New Amnesty Law

Will Ensure Atrocities Go Unpunished: Muzzles Discussion of Civil Conflict', *Human Rights Watch*, 28/2/2006, accessed on 5/12/2018, at: https://bit.ly/2KXglTc

27. See the chapter 7 by Gordon Clubb entitled 'A Draw or a Defeat? How the IRA Transitioned from Arms to Peace?'; see also: Jonathan Powell, *Talking to Terrorists: How to End Armed Conflicts* (London: The Bodley Head, 2014).

28. Barbara Walter, 'Why Bad Governance Leads to Repeated Civil War', *Journal of Conflict Resolution*, vol. 59, no. 7 (2015), pp. 1–31; Anna Gemtansky, 'You Can't Win If You Don't Fight', *Journal of Conflict Resolution*, vol. 57, no. 4 (2012), p. 710; Philip Keefer, 'Insurgency and Credible commitment in Autocracies and Democracies', *The World Bank Economic Review,* vol. 22, no. 1 (2008), pp. 33–61.

29. Murat Yesiltas, 'When Politics is not Enough: Explaining the Failure of the Peace Process and the PKK's Urban Insurgency in Turkey (2015–2016)', paper presented at the first annual conference of the Strategic Studies Unit entitled 'From Bullets to Ballots: Transformations from Armed to Unarmed Political Activism', Arab Centre for Research and Policy Studies, Doha, 3–4/11/2018.

30. Frank Pearl, 'Talking to Guerrillas: Reflections on the FARC and the Colombian Peace Accords', paper presented at the first annual conference of the Strategic Studies Unit entitled 'From Bullets to Ballots: Transformations from Armed to Unarmed Political Activism', Arab Centre for Research and Policy Studies, Doha, 3–4/11/2018.

31. Roberto Cajina, 'The Changing Ethos of the Nicaraguan Military: Three Stages and Three Different Identities', paper presented at the first annual conference of the Strategic Studies Unit entitled 'From Bullets to Ballots: Transformations from Armed to Unarmed Political Activism', Arab Centre for Research and Policy Studies, Doha, 3–4/11/2018.

32. See for example the original 'ripeness' argument after 'hurting stalemates' in Africa, in: William Zartman, *Ripe for Resolution: Conflict and Intervention in Africa* (Oxford: Oxford University Press, 1989).

33. See Chapter 2 by Ronnie Kasrils and Chapter 12 by Thula Simpson.

34. Christopher Boucek, 'Saudi Arabia's 'Soft' Counterterrorism Strategy: Prevention, Rehabilitation and Aftercare', *Carnegie Papers,* no. 97 (September 2008).

35. Jeffrey Azarva, 'Is U.S. Detention Policy in Iraq Working?', *Middle East Quarterly,* vol. 16, no. 1 (Winter 2009); Amit R. Paley, 'In Iraq, "A Prison Full of Innocent Men",' *Washington Post,* 6/12/2008.

36. Christopher Boucek et al., 'Opening Up the Jihadi Debate: Yemen's Committee for Dialogue', in: Tore Bjørgo and John Horgan (eds), *Leaving Terrorism Behind* (New York: Routledge, 2009).

37. Marisa L. Porges, 'The Saudi Deradicalization Experiment, Expert Brief', *Council on Foreign Relations*, 22/1/2010.

38. The Saudi Programme specifically was highly problematic from the beginning, in comparison to European, and Latin American Programmes that target individuals. This is partly due to the strong emphasis on sectarian (*Wahabbi*) interpretations of Islamic texts to stress the religious authority of the king, the inferiority of the 'others' (including non-Sunnis and non-Muslims), and the other elements.

39. See for example: John Horgan and Kurt Braddock, 'Rehabilitating the Terrorists? Challenges in Assessing the Effectiveness of De-radicalization Programs', *Terrorism and Political Violence*, vol. 22 no. 2 (2010), pp. 267–91.

40. Since 1945 or their independence, 90 per cent of all states in the Middle East and the Maghreb have participated in at least one violent conflict. The comparable violence ratio worldwide is 64 per cent. See for example: Frank Pfetsch and Christoph Rohloff, *National and International Conflicts, 1945–1995: New Empirical and Theoretical Approaches* (London: Routledge, 2000), p. 77.

41. Scott Gates et al., 'Trends in Armed Conflict, 1946–2014', Peace Research Institute Oslo (PRIO), *Conflict Trends* (2016), p. 4; Kendra Dupuy and Siri Aas Rustand, 'Trends in Armed Conflict, 1946–2017', Peace Research Institute Oslo (PRIO), *Conflict Trends* (2016), p. 4.

42. See for example: Audrey Kurth Cronin, 'How Al-Qaida Ends: The Decline and Demise of Terrorist Groups', *International Security*, vol. 31, no. 1 (2006); Audrey Kurth Cronin, 'Historical Patterns in Ending Terrorism', in: *Ending Terrorism: Lessons for Defeating al-Qaeda*, The Adelphi Papers, vol. 47, no. 394 (2007), pp. 23–50; Jon B. Alterman et al., 'How Terrorism Ends', United States Institute of Peace, *Policy Brief* (1999); Martha Crenshaw, 'Why Violence Is Rejected or Renounced: A Case Study of Oppositional Terrorism' in: Thomas Gregor (ed.), *A Natural History of Peace* (Nashville: Vanderbilt University Press, 1996); Jones and Libicki; Jeffrey Ian Ross and Ted Robert Gurr, 'Why Terrorism Subsides: A Comparative Study of Canada and the United States', *Comparative Politics*, vol. 21, no. 4 (1989), pp. 405–26.

43. Some of the civil war literature engaged with these two-issue areas. For a background, see: Cara Jones and Katrin Witting, 'The 2015 Legislative and Presidential Elections in Burundi: An Unfinished Post-Conflict Transition',

Electoral Studies, vol. 43 (September 2016); Gervais Rufyikiri, 'The Post-Wartime Trajectory of CNDD-FDD Party in Burundi: A Facade Transformation of Rebel Movement to Political Party', *Civil Wars*, vol. 19 no. 2, (2017), pp. 220–48; Matthew Shugart, 'Guerrillas and Elections: An Institutionalist Perspective on the Costs of Conflict and Competition', *International Studies Quarterly*, vol. 36, no. 2 (June 1992), pp. 121–51; Dominik Klapador, 'From Rebels to Politicians: The Case of Nepal', *London School of Economics Paper Series*, (February 2009), pp. 4–54.

2

LESSONS FROM SOUTH AFRICA:
A FIRST-HAND TESTIMONY*

Ronnie Kasrils

Introduction

South Africa is a country where there was a successful negotiated settlement from a virtual civil war catastrophe – characterised by armed contestation and mass uprisings – to a peaceful outcome. The result saw the replacement of the universally detested apartheid system by a democratic dispensation. This has become something of a model for the resolution of conflicts elsewhere but of course no two situations are identical. The African National Congress (ANC), which led this struggle, proved itself capable of operating within the environment of both armed and unarmed political activism.[1]

This chapter seeks to draw some lessons from the South African experience. In doing so I will try to answer such questions as how the transformation to 'unarmed politics' happened; and why and what were the conditions for its initiation. There are other pertinent points, both objective and subjective – macro and micro – which bear consideration. Incidentally I believe a better term than 'unarmed politics' is 'non-violent struggle'. There is an important element that I believe should not be overlooked: why groups decide to move from non-violent struggle to armed struggle in the first place. I hope to show how that informs the development of armed struggle and becomes integral to its outcome.

The South African struggle overthrew apartheid by a combination of violent and non-violent means which ultimately led to a negotiated settlement. To understand the nature of this transition one needs to look at the particular South African and international context and the era in which the conflict and transformation occurred.

The Resort to Armed Force

Where the right of a people to vote for a government of its choice does not exist or where their suffering has become unbearable, what often happens is a resort to armed contestation. In 1962 a world leader of note stated 'those who make peaceful change impossible make violent change inevitable'. That was not Che Guevara or Chairman Mao speaking but none other than John Fitzgerald Kennedy, the president of the USA.[2]

Those who have risen in rebellion – in a just war against repression – invariably have a political goal. If that goal is democracy, it is possible that the outcome will be the ballot box. However, where objectives are loosely defined the outcome may very well be confusion, nihilism and anarchy. That latter case all too often spells disaster; and more particularly when the space opens up for the intervention of foreign forces with their own agenda. The outcomes of the guerrilla struggles in the latter part of the twentieth century, where the main issue was independence from colonial rule, were decidedly different from the upheavals of the twenty-first century – in the Middle East most dramatically.

In the case of the ANC, deep, sober deliberation by its leadership was taken to move from non-violent activism to armed struggle and very clear political objectives were established from the start. One of the ANC's foremost leaders, Walter Sisulu, commented of the deliberations in which he was intimately involved: 'They had a sober approach. You could reason everything, and they did not have a mechanical party approach: they relied on people.'[3] There was robust debate, however the decisive factor was the charismatic leadership of Nelson Mandela arguing for a change in policy. He would not have succeeded in convincing fellow comrades, however, if the conditions had not been ripe. The end result was a success story, although the peaceful negotiated settlement after 30 years of dogged struggle came as a surprise. The primacy of the political leadership and the movement's aims created the opportunity for negotiated conflict resolution irrespective of the severity and length of that struggle. This is in marked contrast with situations in which armed struggle has been subjective in its response to injustice with ill-defined strategy and aims.

The ANC was not unique in its victory. Its move from non-violent to violent struggle in 1961, following the Sharpeville massacre,[4] was reflected in the similar decisions and paths taken by other liberation movements in the Southern African region at that time – in Angola, Namibia, Mozambique and Zimbabwe – but which undoubtedly started with the inspirational victory of the Algerian people over the French in 1962.[5]

These national liberation movements had all resorted to utilising guerrilla methods of warfare – irregular contestation by a weaker protagonist against a more powerful conventional adversary – linked to the mobilisation of their people in what is called both a Just War and a People's War. These movements had the correct policies in perspective to gain the support of Africa's independent states through the Organisation of African Unity (OAU) providing political, moral and material backing – although the socialist countries played a major role in providing weapons and training. The independent African states never relented under the pressure of the Western powers nor the military aggression carried out by racist South Africa against Angola, Mozambique, Zimbabwe and other front-line states.[6] And when they in turn became independent in 1975 and 1980, they were steadfast in the solidarity they provided the ANC and SWAPO of Namibia until the latter two became independent.

I hope to demonstrate that there are lessons to be learnt by those who wish to see an outcome of freedom and independence in countries experiencing unimagined violence in today's world. South Africa's struggle provides lessons in the effectiveness of both armed and unarmed forms of struggle: in the art of negotiations, the role of leaders, reconciliation, transformation of the military, the crafting of an inclusive constitution, mass political activity and interacting with foreign states whilst not allowing them to direct national affairs.

In expressing the hope that South Africa's experience may be of assistance elsewhere, I refer to the tragic convulsions in the Middle East which is being torn asunder at the expense of the suffering of millions of people who have lost their lives, homes and countries. We cannot overlook the plight of the Palestinians, who were part of the guerrilla struggles that commenced in the 1960s. The Palestinian Liberation Organisation emerged and became allied with liberation forces in Africa and elsewhere. The ANC and the PLO enjoyed particularly strong relations. Nelson Mandela stated after South Africa's liberation: 'we know too well that our freedom is incomplete without the freedom of the Palestinians.'[7]

As far as foreign intervention is concerned, it is necessary to point out – in my opinion – that the involvement of the Cubans and Russians in Angola at decisive moments was at the express invitation of the government of that country. This followed various invasions by South Africa's armed forces. South Africa and the USA supported rival groups in Angola and Mozambique. It is also necessary to point out that it was the former Soviet Union, Cuba, China and other socialist countries, that provided the liberation movements with the necessary weapons and training they so sorely needed against an enemy which enjoyed overwhelming resources. And it was the major Western powers that provided support for South Africa, through trade and investments, including the sale of weapons, that prolonged apartheid rule. Israel was a covert partner of South Africa's, going as far as assisting the apartheid regime to manufacture nuclear weapons.[8]

The Universal Context of Guerrilla Warfare

Any consideration of how to promote negotiations, must embrace the reasons why force was utilised in the first place. Here, we are not contemplating conventional warfare between nation states which is another matter entirely, although irregular guerrilla warfare is used in support of war between conventional forces of nation states. Our focus is rather on a situation whereby a populace's yearning for freedom, independence and human dignity has been obstructed and denied. This takes place in a universal historical context.

People all over the world from ancient times have risen in response to cruel forms of persecution, conditions of slavery and serfdom, colonial conquest and dispossession of their land, foreign invasion, dictatorship and tyranny of various forms. The post-World War Two era witnessed the collapse of the shameful colonial system and the rise of modern guerrilla movements fighting for independence. Apart from the struggles already mentioned in this context were those ranging across continents from Cuba to Vietnam, Malaya and Burma, Palestine to Oman and Aden, Cyprus and Kenya, Nicaragua and Salvador, Ireland and the Basque Country of Spain and many more. All went through an initial phase of protest against colonial or neo-colonial repression and were generally rooted in much earlier anti-colonial uprisings. Non-violent activism, however, was generally met by batons and bullets. Whereas nonviolent protest, as in India, Ghana, Tanzania, Zambia and others, resulted in a decision by the colonial powers to hand over independence peacefully, armed contestation was unnecessary.

Where independence was not conceded, guerrilla warfare became the norm – the utilisation of irregular methods against the superior forces of a conventional army. Such warfare is the weapon of the weak against the strong and aims not simply to defeat an enemy but to win popular support and political influence to the enemy's cost. In the classical Maoist dictum, 'the guerrilla moves among the people like fish in in the sea.' When synergy is reached guerrilla warfare turns into the all-embracing 'People's War' seen in the inspirational revolutionary struggles of the twentieth century in Cuba and Vietnam, Algeria and Southern Africa and preceding them the heroic partisan (guerrilla) movements of the Second World War against the Nazis or in the Far East against Japanese imperialism – and earlier still in the Middle East against the Ottoman Empire, and the various brands of European colonialism.

A pertinent observation was made by the master revolutionary strategist V. I. Lenin that unless guerrilla forces were imbued with revolutionary politics, they would have the tendency to descend into banditry. And both he and Mao Tse Tung, in their definitive writings on guerrilla warfare, pointed out the vast difference between those fighting for a just cause and those involved in insurgency on behalf of imperialist aggressors or in the 'unorganised and undisciplined activities that are anarchism'.[9] That was a prescient reflection, as can be seen in the regression to criminality and drug smuggling from Afghanistan to Colombia. And we have seen the appalling development among irregular forces and paramilitary groups descending into the nihilistic barbarism of Al Qaeda, Daesh/Isis, Al Shabab and Boko Haram, amongst other groups. These have no clear politics, debase religion to their own ends, and bask in the use of terrorism and the cult of bloodletting, rape and beheadings.

Terrorism

This serves as a cue to make clear that terrorism is not a tactic that has been embraced by genuine guerrilla movements. Terrorism is a method which is used against a civilian population, in order to sow mass panic and destabilise a country and its government. The African National Congress (ANC), and the fraternal movements of Southern Africa rejected outright the use of terrorist tactics, although Mandela made reference to the possibility of using such tactics in discussions leading to the establishment of the ANC's armed wing, the Spear of the Nation (MK). He wrote:

> In planning the direction and form that MK would take, we considered 4 types of violent activities: sabotage, guerrilla warfare, terrorism and open revolution. For a small and fledgling army, open revolution was inconceivable. Terrorism inevitably reflected poorly on those who used it, undermining any public support it might otherwise garner. Guerrilla warfare was a possibility, but since the ANC had been reluctant to embrace violence at all, it made sense to start with a form of violence that inflicted the least harm against individuals: sabotage.[10]

When a tendency towards acts of terrorism appeared, the leadership immediately moved to halt them. These actions began to make their appearance in the mid-1980s when some units, out of touch with headquarters, began placing bombs in the 'Wimpy-Bar' hamburger chain. I was called upon to engage with some recalcitrant commanders and chastised them by reminding them we were engaged in a People's War and not a 'Wimpy-Bar War.' It was this factor that consistently gave the ANC the moral high ground and the credit of waging a just war.

The attempt by the apartheid regime and its Western backers, leaders such as Margaret Thatcher and Ronald Reagan, to smear Mandela and the ANC with the 'terrorist' brush was widely rejected. In fact, it was seen precisely in the counter-insurgency methods of the colonial powers and is glaringly evident in Israel's utilisation of state terrorism. Because MK did not descend to the level of waging a dirty war, the ANC held the moral high ground. Guerrilla armies fight in accordance with the rules of warfare and respect the rights of civilians. In accordance with its principles and values the ANC signed the Geneva Convention on the rules of warfare in 1980.[11]

Where there were divergences in this regard, such as abuses in the detention of suspected and proven apartheid spies that had infiltrated its ranks, the ANC established four commissions of inquiry and publicly expressed regret for the lapses.[12]

South Africa's Historical Background

That struggle for South Africa's freedom in modern times is well known: a struggle for national liberation during the twentieth century against a white minority colonial regime which had developed a system of extreme discriminatory rule known as apartheid. Colonial conquest and the dispossession of land had taken place from the seventeenth century, first under Dutch and then British rule. In 1910 the British handed independence to the settler white community which had grown to just under 10 per cent of the population. In 1948, the most fanatically nationalistic section of the white community – the Dutch-descended Afrikaners, who formed 60 per cent of the white minority – voted in the National Party, which immediately set about establishing its apartheid version of white colonial settler domination.

The Apartheid System 1948

Apartheid was a system of racial discrimination and segregation even more severe than what had already evolved over three centuries – which was gruesome enough. It was a brutal system of political and economic dominance by the white minority which increased the restrictions on the indigenous black majority and made their exploitation even more severe.

Under this system the races were kept strictly apart, with even social interaction forbidden. The indigenous people were deprived of virtually all rights. The 13 per cent of South Africa's land in the hands of black people in backward and remote rural areas was divided into fragmented Bantustans. Stripped of their rights in the rest of South Africa, where they laboured in mines and factories and on farms, the apartheid regime cynically stated that 'the black man could enjoy self- government' in his own Bantustan homeland. The aim of the system was ultra-exploitation of the majority black people whose labour made the upper echelons of the white settler population extremely wealthy.[13]

South Africa 1960

In 1960, following the Sharpeville massacre, the ANC and other liberation movements were outlawed, leaders banned, imprisoned, executed. A state of emergency was declared allowing people to be detained without charge. After much deliberation, the leaders of the ANC and their ally the South African Communist Party (SACP) agreed to embark on the path of armed struggle and established its military wing Umkhonto We Sizwe (MK) – The Spear of the Nation. The manifesto of MK declared:

> The time comes in the life of any nation when there remain only two choices: submit or fight. That time has now come to South Africa. We shall not submit, and we have no choice but to hit back by all means with enough power in defence of our people, our future and our freedom . . . [14]

The declaration gave the reasons why the liberation movement was embarking on this new method of struggle, and placed responsibility for violence at the door of the regime. MK combatants vowed to spare no effort in the struggle to free the oppressed people but made it clear that the aim was establishing an inclusive democratic state of all the people – black and white. The following words of the manifesto were to prove prescient in the long run:

> We hope, even at this late hour, that our first actions will awaken everyone to a realisation of the disastrous situation to which the Nationalist [government] policy is leading. We hope that we will bring the government and its supporters to their senses before it is too late, so that both the government and its policies can be changed before matters reach the desperate stage of civil war . . .[15]

Three Decades of War 1960–90

The hope expressed in the manifesto for peace landed on deaf ears at the time, and for decades to come. It is history that it took 30 years of bloodshed and suffering, with increased repression being met by increased resistance, before the apartheid regime came to accept that the way to end the conflict was to do precisely what the MK manifesto had demanded in 1961 and opt for change.

Let us now turn to consider why the regime which had been seemingly so immovable and obdurate in its policies experienced a sea change and what the conditions were that brought about the coming transformation.

By 1990, apartheid's political and business elite, and their Western supporters, had conceded that the political and military costs had become too heavy a burden to sustain. Mass political struggle led by the ANC, directed by its internal underground network, reinforced by the military blows of MK and the international solidarity movement's BDS campaign (Boycott Divestment and Sanctions) – drove the apartheid regime to the negotiating table. The last straw was when international banks refused to roll over the apartheid debt, denying a beleaguered South Africa the loans on which it had become dependent.

It was quite clearly the political policy and strategy of the ANC which won worldwide support, as well as inspiring South Africa's masses, in the words of its President Oliver Tambo, in a January 1985 address 'to make apartheid unworkable and the country ungovernable'.[16] The ANCs political work, side-by-side with the prosecution of the armed struggle, had been building alliances and isolating the apartheid regime. At this stage white business and sections of the white population including a part of its political elite, its academics and intellectuals, sections of white youth who were refusing to be conscripted into the apartheid armed forces,[17] were making it impossible to stave off change.

Reasons for Change

At this point apartheid's traditional partners, particularly Britain and the United States, and other Western powers, were pressing the apartheid regime to make reforms and avoid the prospects of revolution. No doubt the fact that the Soviet Union was on the point of unravelling, contributed to the Western view that the time was opportune. The international communist bogeyman had clearly lost its potency, and the fear that South Africa would fall prey to communism had abated. There are those who claim that was the key factor. In fact, there was a coalescence of the following factors:

• the ANC's politics gave it a distinctive advantage over its adversary's ideology

- the armed struggle was growing in strength
- working class activism, reflected in the powerful trade union movement (Cosatu), was growing; as was the militancy among women and young people; religious and cultural organisations and civil society in general united in a mass democratic movement under the umbrella of the United Democratic Front (UDF)
- the BDS campaign was highly effective in isolating the Pretoria regime, weakening the economy and psychologically draining the will of the white minority whilst inspiring the oppressed
- growing divisions, war weariness and confusion within the ruling class were manifest
- in contrast, far from flagging, the mass insurrectionary mood in South Africa was reaching unprecedented heights
- the ruling power could no longer rule in the old way and the people were not prepared to live under the old conditions
- the apartheid regime's armed forces suffered an immense setback following their defeat at the Battle of Cuito Cuanavale in Angola (October 1987 to March 1988)[18] by the combined Cuban and National Army, paving the way for the independence of neighbouring Namibia
- the balance of power between the status quo and the revolutionary forces had tilted in favour of revolutionary change.

The Move to Negotiations

Notwithstanding the above factors, the liberation movement still did not have the strength to overthrow the regime; and the regime was unable to defeat the people. The realisation dawned on both that if they wished to avoid a devastating civil war, they shared a common responsibility to save the country from such a fate. Some of the forward-looking thinkers in the regime, especially in its intelligence services, had begun to secretly sound out the imprisoned Mandela as to whether the organisation would be conducive to entertaining talks about talks as a first step towards negotiations. Similar secret overtures were taking place externally in contact with Oliver Tambo's inner circle. Tambo was the highly respected president of the ANC in exile, but was in fact linked at a crucial period directly to Mandela by the underground's secret means of communication.[19] They were able to keep one another briefed on what could in fact be a dangerous new phase. The question was whether the ANC could really trust the advances being made by representatives of the regime?

Both Mandela and Tambo, lifelong friends and one-time partners in their Johannesburg firm of attorneys, were men of tremendous integrity and stature, inspirational figures enjoying the devotion of their followers and commanding international respect. Mandela, having faced the prospect of a death sentence in an apartheid court, which translated into 27 years of incarceration, became the charismatic leader of the revolution. Although he often stressed that it was the masses who make history, his role as an individual, in an impressive collective of fellow revolutionaries, was incalculable. It was his study of the enemy that enabled him to grasp from behind prison bars that the time had been ripening for the exploration of the possibilities of a negotiated settlement – and he had the courage to break new ground even whilst his fellow comrades in prison had serious doubts almost to the point of mistrusting him.[20] In his interaction as a prisoner with the regime, the non-like-minded 'other', who had the advantage of controlling him 'in the pressurised environment of prison',[21] it proved to be the canny Mandela who outplayed his adversary. The game was conducted, with Mandela being relocated from incarceration on Robben Island to more comfortable prison conditions on the mainland and separated from his comrades, the regime offering him various inducements including his freedom if he renounced armed struggle; Mandela countering with the inducement that peaceful negotiations were possible if the regime released all prisoners, allowed exiles to return home and permitted free political activity.[22]

February 1990 – ANC Unbanned, Mandela Freed

The actual turning point occurred on 2 February 1990 when South Africa's president, F. W. de Klerk, announced to the all-white parliament that the government was lifting the ban on the ANC and all outlawed organisations, and Mandela's release would take place the following week.

He stated: 'The season of violence was over. The time for reconstruction and reconciliation has arrived.'[23] Mandela was released on 11 February to mass adulation; his closest colleagues having already been released over previous months. The prerequisite for talks between the former adversaries had arrived. President de Klerk had played what he considered was his masterstroke – aiming to seize the strategic initiative. This was an inducement from the state within a de-escalating environment to win over Mandela and the ANC and gain credit in the country and abroad for initiating transformation. The regime thought they had stolen a march on the ANC and could outmanoeuvre them in the political arena. They also hoped to split the unity of the ANC and had hopes of uniting with its moderates against its radical left alliance and the communists.

What helped keep the unity of the ANC intact, preparing it for just such a turnaround, was its preparation for negotiations even when the likelihood seemed distant. The ANC in exile had been discussing the possibility and had been in consultation both with forces inside the country and key African states. Tambo had mobilised the Organisation of African Unity (OAU) in support of the ANC's strategic document, the Harare Declaration of 1989.[24] This agreement articulated the necessary conditions for negotiations and its goals. The OAU's endorsement, followed by the approval of the United Nations, was a diplomatic and strategic masterstroke by the ANC. The principles of the Harare Declaration became the basis for the negotiations with the apartheid regime. Unfortunately, the heavy work took its toll on Tambo's health, and he suffered a stroke from which he never recovered.

Negotiations Begin

Formal negotiations kicked off with a historic meeting between the ANC and the South African government on 4 May 1990 in Cape Town.[25] This resulted in a commitment between the two parties towards the resolution of the existing climate of violence and intimidation as well as the removal of practical obstacles to negotiation including immunity from prosecution for returning exiles and the further release of political prisoners.

Within three months this agreement was extended to include commitment by the ANC to suspend the armed struggle.[26] This was a test for MK. Although some quarters within the regime expected division to break out within MK, and were hoping for just that, such expectation did not materialise. There was heated debate amongst MK combatants, particularly among those in external bases, some of whom suspected a sell-out, but the political consciousness and discipline which had been installed into the military by the ANC prevailed. MK remained a disciplined and united force taking instructions from the political leadership. It was not just Mandela's leadership that was influential in this regard, but moreover that the ANC enjoyed a remarkable collective leadership that had been steeled in battle over the years, in exile, in prison, in the underground and in the mass political movement.

A multi-party forum was convened so as to create inclusivity and bring everybody on board.[27] It had its ups and downs and even broke down, although it was reconvened after some months. Violence and tensions in the country created a very bumpy ride indeed. In order to salvage the situation, the two chief protagonists – the ANC and de Klerk's National Party, who by now were partners in the project – returned to bilateral talks and brokered a Record of Understanding between themselves. They agreed to reach bilateral consensus on issues before taking them to the other parties in the forum. This put considerable pressure on those lesser players to agree with the consensus or be left behind. A Transitional Executive Council was agreed upon, which drafted an interim constitution and oversaw the run up to the first democratic national elections at the end of April 1994.

During the negotiation process, de Klerk's government had attempted to delay elections; sought a two-phase transition with an appointed transitional government and a rotating presidency; argued for a period of power-sharing; and sought privileges for minorities. The ANC rejected these proposals and insisted on a transition in a single stage to majority rule. Other sticking points included decisions on a unitary or federal state, property rights and indemnity from prosecution for politically motivated crimes. A major concern for the regime was the security of jobs and pensions for those in the service of the state. The ANC displayed great flexibility and proposed a breakthrough 'sunset clause' guaranteeing state pensions and jobs and accepting a coalition government for the five years following a democratic election.

Once the two adversaries had come to agreement on the principles and modalities of moving forward, a multi-party conference was convened, and an interim constitution was agreed. This was not without difficulties for the regime and certain parties still sought a federal rather than a unitary state. The ANC insisted on the latter and pressed for early elections. It won most of its key points but was prepared to make concessions regarding property and land rights. It argued within its ranks that the immediate requirement was to move towards achieving political power.

National Elections April 1994

The elections held on 27 April 1994, went extremely smoothly with no violence being reported. The ANC won 62 per cent of the vote, reflecting the support it enjoyed amongst the masses and its ability to run a superb election campaign without prior experience. Nelson Mandela became president, with F. W. de Klerk as one of his two deputy presidents. The National Party, with 20 per cent of the vote, joined the ANC in a Government of National Unity in which the once ruling party was given a few cabinet posts. The country's new constitution was agreed in 1995 and a Truth and Reconciliation Commission established dealing with politically motivated crimes committed during the apartheid era.

With the benefit of hindsight, the transition from apartheid to democracy appears smooth. However, the new democracy was bitterly negotiated, with many compromises on both sides. Many lives were lost during the process, and from the start of negotiations in mid-1990 to the elections in April 1994, 14,000 people died and 22,000 were injured. These were mainly black victims who were killed in clashes between ANC supporters and those of Buthelezi's Inkatha Freedom Party (IFP) with its largely Zulu ethnic rural constituency. Hand-picked IFP members had been trained and armed by apartheid agents from the police and the military. When the carnage wreaked by such murderous gangs was exposed, F. W. de Klerk denied any connection. It is clear that a so-called 'third force' from the security services was operating to attack ANC aligned communities in an attempt to both weaken the ANC and disrupt the process.

Under pressure from the right wing of his party, de Klerk withdrew from the Government of National Unity within a few years, and his National Party began to wither away. Most whites however continued to support opposition parties. For a time, Mandela's attempts at reconciliation settled nerves among the white population.

The ANC's Political Activism

The ANC was able to take the move from armed to unarmed political activism in its stride. The years of non-violent struggle and the mobilisation of the masses prior to its proscription in 1960 had given it considerable experience, confidence and organisational skill within the political arena, as did the incalculable experience gained over three decades working in the international arena, interacting with the UN, the OAU, a range of governments, diplomats and NGOs.

The stature that it had achieved over decades of hard work and its influence on mass political activity, which increased during the 1980s, had seen the rise of the ANC-aligned United Democratic Front (UDF), composed of 600 grassroots organisations, and the emergence of Cosatu, the pro-ANC trade union federation, in 1983 and 1984 respectively. This meant that by 1990, with such allies on the ground, the ANC was well placed to operate openly and publicly. The fact that politics had always been primary, and the military secondary, that whether in prison or in exile ANC leaders were always at ease in a political role, was extremely advantageous. This was no movement fresh out of the bush that had to learn the political game. It was widely accepted that the ANC was leagues ahead of the apartheid National Party leadership and in fact totally outclassed them. And the ANC adroitly mobilised the masses behind its negotiating positions. As the time for the country's first democratic elections approached, the ANC's campaign showed its organisational flair – which was proven by its electoral success. In that first election, and in all the succeeding ones to 2004, its majority increased from 62 per cent in 1994 to 69 per cent. That was a remarkable achievement for a national liberation movement that was still to constitute itself as a party.

Having to meet people's expectations is never easy, and the ANC's popularity has begun to wane. Although its share of the national vote has not dropped below 62 per cent, in the 2016 local elections alarm bells began to ring, when its vote dropped just below 54 per cent. With unemployment and the wealth gap between rich and poor widening obscenely, giving rise to widespread protests over delivery failures, it is more than evident that the economic, property and land concessions that the ANC made in the early 1990s to aid the smooth transition have come back to haunt it.

The Military in the Negotiations

The military of both sides were involved in the negotiations within a commission of their own which was not independent but under political control. The MK command staff formally engaged with the apartheid generals and arrived at a programme of integration of former adversarial armies – small and large – into a unified, national defence force. This new transformed South African National Defence Force (SANDF) swore to uphold the democratic constitution, follow the orders and policy of the government of the day and keep out of politics. It accepted its primary role of protecting the sovereignty of South Africa and the well-being of its people. It has proved its mettle, remained stable, and seen remarkable transformation, with black officers in the majority of top posts. Its training and curricula have been developed in keeping with the constitution and civil-military relations. It has come to play a significant role in peacekeeping operations in Africa.

What proved advantageous to military cooperation was that both sides had imbibed the professional ethic of accepting loyalty to, and leadership of, their political principals. On the regime side this was almost 'apolitical' in the sense of career soldiers under apartheid and before that being obedient to the 'government of the day'. For MK cadres, the liberation ideology and subordination of the military wing to the political leadership was sacrosanct. The objective circumstance of negotiations over a democratic dispensation already arrived at provided this positive convergence, stiffened by the fact that the democratic dispensation upheld property laws. If Mandela's economic changes had been more radical at that time, I have no doubt there would have been no such buy-in by the previous system and of course by the apartheid military. In fact, for this reason the Western powers and neighbouring states were fully behind the transition and used all their influence to keep change on track. Whilst there was mistrust among MK cadres of the ANC being lured into a trap by the regime, the trust in the charismatic leadership proved decisive. Briefings and consultations with the cadres in the camps by leaders they had come to trust over many years calmed fears, in an intensive process of internal interactions between the grassroots, the middle ranks and the commanders of the MK and the ANC leadership. There was no mutinous reaction, no breaking away or formation of extremist rejectionist groupings by 'spoilers', which would have played into the hands of reactionary forces. This was a testimony to the deep level of political education and training which had been sustained over the years and provided to new recruits. This outlook was also reflected in the fact that a group of senior leaders of MK, including myself, found ourselves on the run or arrested within the country, when in the midst of the negotiation process in August 1990 'spoilers' within the security forces convinced de Klerk that we were planning to ferment an armed uprising against even Mandela's wishes. They had evidence of the work we had been carrying out since before de Klerk lifted the ban on the ANC. We had instructions to remain in place until the ANC could be assured the negotiation process was genuine. The secret police used this to portray our activity as a plot against the negotiations. Mandela rejected the 'evidence', but it took over six months for the episode to be settled. If it hadn't been for the firm ideological fusion of the ANC's military and political leadership, the secret police spoilers might well have initiated the split that de Klerk and his cohorts had been hoping for. There were a few senior ANC members advocating that I should secretly leave the country so as to defuse the situation, but Mandela would have none of that.

The politicians on both sides had agreed on mutual integration of the former adversarial forces, with recognition of rank – and, crucially, with the ANC guaranteeing the pensions and retirement conditions the SADF serving officers expected. This was a major card on the MK side, for it neutralised the influence of the most conservative officers in the apartheid forces against the meaningful change we envisaged. A major sticking point of theirs was a rear-guard attempt to minimise the number of MK generals to three. We insisted on 18, including the first woman general in South Africa's history, and won the day. This encouraged former MK combatants at lower rank level, who, fearing that they would be discriminated against owing to their lack of educational qualifications and the need to upgrade to conventional military training, were demanding to be recognised as mid-level officers – majors and up. It was quite surprising how naïve some former SADF officers could be, especially after a few drinks. During a break in proceedings one such claimed to me that we could create the best defence force in the world, 'with white officers and black troops'. I told him we weren't intent on emulating the days of the British Raj in India. The 18 generals were a tenth of the top brass in our new armed forces, but with political power on our side, and intense upgrading courses, the disparity has been completely overcome. The former SADF officers who genuinely shifted loyalties to serve the democratic government have proven themselves over the years. Those who stuck it out to obtain their pensions on retirement, or had hoped to control or even sabotage the transformation process, have more or less departed.

One cannot claim that the ranking process was a happy experience for all ranks, and in fact it was a matter of some ongoing dissatisfaction. So too was the deal struck for those former guerrillas who opted for demobilisation. Attempts at training for civil society occupations, and inadequate pensions given the low base they started conventional service from, have left many with grievances to this day.

As the ranking system and retraining programme was being instituted in 1995, such dissatisfaction proved to be more challenging to resolve than the previous decision concerning the ceasefire and integration process. Once in the middle of the night I joined President Mandela, straight from an interrupted sleep, to address a protest of former MK rank-and-file, who had marched from their assembly camp outside Pretoria to the seat of govern-ment. We listened patiently to their grievances and on Mandela's assurance that these grievances would be attended to, the former guerrillas returned to camp. Ironically, one aspect of the protest was not about former SADF officers, but about an allegation that a general, formerly of the MK, had not been taking their disquiet seriously. The selective inducements and amounts provided for collective demobilisation pay-outs, and pension levels, which had appeared satisfactory in 1994, have been offset by inflation and poorly prepared settlement into civil society. Those with higher levels of education, who went into political office, into the professions and particularly business, have fared far better.

Conclusion

It is a matter of historical record that the determined struggle of South Africa's people forced the apartheid regime to talk to their representatives by 1990. This opened the way for a negotiated settlement and peaceful transition to a democratic dispensation. The ballot and not the bullet, the pen and not the sword, were the final arbiters of change.

In summation, and to make clear the historic forces that brought about the remarkable change, the following ten points are worthy of note:

1. the move to violent confrontation could be characterised as a just war because the regime's repression gave the ANC no other choice than to bring about change by force of arms
2. the armed forces of the ANC were under charismatic political leadership
3. the armed struggle was part of a range of methods of struggle such as strikes, protests and demonstrations
4. the use of terrorist tactics against the white population was discouraged
5. military operations were aimed at the security forces, state structures, communication and economic targets, and not at unarmed civilians
6. the 'just war' character of the struggle gave the ANC forces the moral high ground, and the basis to mobilise international support and win over sections of the white population in support of change
7. the political objective of the struggle was constantly stressed, and it was made clear that the struggle was against a system, the apartheid system, and not the colour of a person's skin
8. over time the movement developed a strategy based on what were called the four pillars of struggle, namely: mass political struggle; armed struggle; clandestine underground activity; and international solidarity, which was vital in isolating the apartheid regime through boycott, disinvestment and sanctions (BDS)
9. even during the times of the fiercest confrontation and repression, the ANC never lost sight of the possibility of seeking a negotiated settlement. This was a leadership choice. It was bolstered by a process of internal (within the ANC and the MK) and external interactions (with the regime)
10. the negotiation process was strictly between the protagonists within South Africa with both sides endeavouring to minimise the effect of foreign interference.

The concessions Mandela's ANC was prepared to make to finalise negotiations – particularly in the economic sphere, where a huge disparity in wealth between the rich and the poor continues to exist – has become a source of frustration and protest especially for the younger generation.[28] In a sense the ANC was faced with the dilemma of partial success. The debate within was whether to secure what it deemed possible or risk a reversal of fortune by insisting on achieving all of its objectives at one go. Its prudent choice was to follow the dictum of Ghana's Kwame Nkrumah of first securing the political kingdom, after which all things would follow – a controversial expectation.[29] Whatever transpires in the future a remarkable revolutionary change occurred peacefully in South Africa – from bullets to ballots – with considerable advantages for its people, for the African continent and the international community.

Notes

* This chapter is based on a testimony presented at the First Annual Conference of the Strategic Studies Unit at the Arab Centre for Research and Policy Studies (ACRPS), titled 'From Bullets to Ballots: Transformations from Armed to Unarmed Political Activism', held in Doha from 3 to 4 November 2018. The author is grateful to Dr Omar Ashour, the director of Strategic Studies Unit at ACRPS.

1. ANC, the oldest national liberation movement in Africa, founded 1912 committed to non-violent struggle; banned 1960: resorted to armed struggle 1961; unbanned February 1990, entered into negotiations July 1990; won first democratic elections April 1994 and formed South Africa's first democratic government.

2. John Fitzgerald Kennedy in a speech to Latin American diplomats at the White House 1962 (13 March 1962). He was referring to Fidel Castro's overthrow of the dictator Batista who in his view had made peaceful change impossible. The quotation is sometimes stated as 'those who make peaceful revolution impossible make violent revolution inevitable'.

3. Anthony Sampson, *Nelson Mandela: The Authorised Biography* (Johannesburg: Harper Collins and Jonathan Ball publishers, 1999), p. 151. Sisulu was one of the foremost leaders of the ANC, stood alongside Nelson Mandela at the Rivonia trial when they were sentenced to life imprisonment.

4. 21 March 1961, following a peaceful protest at a police station, in which 69 people were shot dead and over 200 wounded

5. The People's Movement for the Liberation of Angola (MPLA), Front for the Liberation of Mozambique (FRELIMO), South West African Peoples

Organisation of Namibia (SWAPO), and the Zimbabwe African People's Union (ZAPU) and Zimbabwe African National Union (ZANU). All led successful armed struggles which reached their apex in negotiated settlements either with the colonial powers or internal settler communities. The Portuguese colonies, including Guinea-Bissau, won their independence in 1975; Zimbabwe was freed from white settler rule in 1980 and Namibia won its independence from South Africa in 1990.

6. Botswana, Lesotho and Swaziland.

7. Nelson Mandela, address at the International Day of Solidarity with the Palestinian people, Pretoria, 4 December 1997.

8. Sasha Polakow-Suransky, *The Unspoken Alliance: Israel's Secret Relationship with Apartheid South Africa* (Johannesburg: Jacana Media, 2010), Ch. 3, Ch. 8.

9. 'Mao Zedong', *Marxists*, accessed on 8/9/2020, at: https://bit.ly/2Gy0mga

10. Sampson, p. 270.

11. Luli Callinicos, *Oliver Tambo: Beyond the Engeli Mountains* (Cape Town: David Philip Publishers, 2004), pp. 471–2. Signed by ANC President Oliver Tambo, 28 November 1980.

12. Stuart 1984, Sachs 1989, Skweyiya released 1992 and Motsuenyane Commission 1993. See: South African History Online, at: https://bit.ly/2GwtZ1p

13. The white minority never constituted more than 10 per cent of the population, which was a large number in colonial terms. By the end of the twentieth century they numbered approximately 5 million, outnumbered by a black population of approximately 50 million.

14. Sampson, pp. 274–5.

15. Ibid. p. 274.

16. Callinicos, p. 548.

17. The 'End Conscription Campaign' was run by white youth who refused to serve in the apartheid armed forces and by the late 1980s was growing in support despite persecution and presentment by its adherents.

18. Fidel Castro stated of the seismic consequences: 'The history of Africa will have to be written as before and after Cuito Cuanavale'. See: Piero Gleijeses, *Visions of Freedom* (Cuito Cuanavale: Wits University Press, 2013), Ch. 15.

19. Padraig O'Mailey, *Shades of Difference: Mac Maharaj and the Struggle for South Africa* (New York: Viking Press, 2007), Ch. 14.

20. Ibid.

21. Omar Ashour, 'From Bullets to Ballots: Transformations from Armed to Unarmed Political Activism', *Strategic Papers*, The Arab Centre for Research

and Policy Studies, 13/8/2020, accessed on 8/9/2020, at: https://bit.ly/2Zz6hsj; See also: Omar Ashour, *The De-Radicalization of Jihadists: Transforming Armed Islamist Movements* (London, New York: Routledge, 2009), pp. 14–28.

22. Sampson, pp. 352, 363–72. And see: Niel Barnard, *Secret Revolution: Memoirs of a Spy Boss* (Cape Town: Tafelberg, 2015). Barnard was head of apartheid's National Intelligence Service, and played a key role on behalf of the government in the secret discussions with Mandela from May 1988 until Mandela's release in February 1990.

23. Ibid., p. 266.

24. Callinicos, pp. 108–9.

25. Known as the Groote Schuur talks, May 1990.

26. Set out in a document entitled the Pretoria Minute dated 6 August 1990.

27. Referred to as the Codesa talks, constituting 19 different parties.

28. Ronnie Kasrils, *A Simple Man: Kasrils and the Zuma Enigma* (Johannesburg: Jacana Media, 2017).

29. Dr Kwame Nkrumah's motive was clear in his landmark statement. 'Seek ye first the political kingdom and all else shall be added unto you'. The motive behind this statement as opined by Ama Biney in her book *The Political and Social Thought of Kwame Nkrumah* was a promise of an economic paradise and riches for newly independent Ghana. Ama Biney, *The Political and Social Thought of Kwame Nkrumah*, 1st edn. (New York: Palgrave Macmillan, 2011).

3

THE COLLECTIVE DE-RADICALISATION OF THE ISLAMIC GROUP IN EGYPT: A FIRST-HAND TESTIMONY*

Osama Rushdi

Introduction

My interest in political activism started at an early age with the outbreak of the 1973 October War. At the time I was only fifteen years old, and just finishing my middle school education. On entering high school, I joined the youth wing of the only political organisation that existed at the time: the Arab Socialist Union. I soon became secretary of the ASU's Maghaha Secondary School Branch. Maghagha, in central Upper Egypt's Minya Governorate, is the city where I was born. The first great shock of my life came with the January 1977 uprising – called the 'Thieves' Uprising' by then President Anwar Sadat (1970–81) – during which one of my relatives was killed. He was a distinguished student at the Faculty of Science in Cairo University.

When schools reopened after the obligatory shutdown, I gave a speech at the morning assembly – I was responsible for the school loudspeaker system. I said that the uprising of 17–18 January was neither a 'thieves' uprising' nor a 'communist revolution' and said that there was a need for more political freedoms. I was immediately summoned by the headmaster, who was a long-time army reservist. He reprimanded the teacher overseeing the students responsible for the loudspeaker system, and I was officially banned from using it; the military officer responsible for military education, at that time a subject taught in schools, threatened me with expulsion and arrest.

This was the first political punishment I remember receiving for trans-
gressing the limited margin of freedom then available. It was enough of
a shock that I paid wary attention to the steps taken by President Sadat
in March 1976, when he established three 'platforms' [*manabir*] within
the ASU: the right-wing Liberal Socialists, the leftist National Unionist
Organisation and the centrist Egyptian Arab Socialist Organisation
(EASP). In November 1976, in a famous speech to the Egyptian parliament, he subsequently ordered that these 'platforms' to become fully-
fledged political parties; the unitary ASU came to an impromptu end and
its property and branch headquarters were inherited by the new ruling
party, the EASP.

The EASP's performance did not satisfy Sadat. On 31 July 1978, he
unexpectedly announced the establishment of the National Democratic Party
(NDP) under his chairmanship. Overnight, the EASP membership trans-
ferred their allegiance *en bloc* to the NDP, which also inherited all its proper-
ties without any official ruling dissolving the older party. After Sadat's death,
the NDP was headed by President Hosni Mubarak (1981–2011) until its
formal dissolution on 16 April 2011 by order of the Supreme Administrative
Court, in the wake of the 25 January Revolution.

We used to joke that even the new NDP signs put up on what had formerly been the EASP headquarters (and before that the ASU headquarters)
were no different from the signs that had been there before – that the different party names were just 'redecorations' of a single political organisation
whose philosophy of absolute totalitarian rule never changed.

In the academic year 1977–8, I enrolled in the pharmacy faculty of the
University of Asyut, a religiously conservative city. From the beginning I
paid close attention to the political debates taking place between the communists, the Nasserites and the Islamic Group (IG). The IG's membership
was expanding steadily at the time, and in 1979 its candidate won the chairmanship of the Union of University Students (which represented students at
universities across Upper Egypt in Sohag, Qena and Aswan). I joined the IG
that same year, and from 1984 to 1986 – after my release from a three-year
spell in prison between October 1981 and October 1984, when I was found
innocent by a court – I became its official representative at Asyut University.
Given my proximity to the group, and my involvement in many of the events

surrounding it, I think my testimony in this chapter regarding the IG's positive and negative features may be useful.

From Call to Collision: A Reading of Causes and Consequences

The atmosphere of freedom that marked the first period of Sadat's rule did not last long. The clash with the Islamist student movement came to a rapid head in the late 1970s, ending with the dissolution of the Egyptian Students Union and the arrest of its members. However, the conflict between Sadat and the Islamist movement now expanded, moving from the university to society at large and turning into a popular opposition movement which showed fierce opposition to the president's policies – especially after his famous visit to Jerusalem in 1977 and his signing of the Camp David Accords in September 1978. Restrictions on movement and on student work in universities steadily intensified up to the night of 3 September 1981, when in a shocking and unprecedented step amounting to political suicide, Sadat arrested some 1,536 people representing all intellectual, political and religious tendencies, causing widespread public anger.

Those IG leaders who had managed to avoid arrest could not help but recall the stories of torture and the other horrors of prison that the Muslim Brotherhood had faced during their 'Ordeal' (*Mihna*) under Nasser, which decided the matter in favour of armed confrontation. On 28 September 1981, it was decided that President Sadat would be assassinated in a military parade to be held on 6 October 1981. By chance, artillery officer First-Lieutenant Khaled Islambouli – whose older brother Mohammed had been detained the week before, meaning that he had a personal grudge against Sadat – had been chosen to march in the parade a few days earlier. The Islambouli group's assassination plot, which formed part of a multi-front plan to achieve regime change by popular revolution, was successful.

Mohamed Hosni Mubarak, assuming the presidency in the wake of President Sadat's assassination, realised immediately that massive popular anger and broad opposition to Sadat had made his assassins into popular heroes enjoying the sympathy of many Egyptians and Arabs. Leftist poets like Ahmed Fouad Negm (1929–2013) and Abd al-Rahman al-Abnoudi (1938–2015) gave voice to this broad wave of feeling, eulogising Islambouli after his execution.

At the beginning of his tenure Hosni Mubarak tried to put these events to rest. While five of those directly involved in Sadat's assassination were sentenced to execution and others given prison terms, thousands of detainees arrested in the aftermath of the assassination were set free. On several occasions Mubarak even declared that 'violence generates violence' – referring, in this case, to state violence. But by 1986 he was back to the old ways, making regular allusions to the Islamist threat to his regime and playing on the West's inability to contain the 1979 Islamic Revolution in Iran. By doing so, he hoped to secure urgently needed economic aid and a rescheduling of Egypt's foreign 'Paris Club' debts without application of stringent IMF diktats, which he feared could kindle social unrest akin to that of the January 1977 uprising.

Although the IG began its confrontation with the Egyptian state with the Sadat assassination, the 1980s was a period of marked detente between the two sides. IG opposition to state policy took place through non-violent public activity: organising conferences, calling for mass demonstrations and issuing communiques condemning government policies. For example, the IG:

1. Organised a campaign against Mubarak's 1987 re-nomination for the presidency. It was the only movement to run such a campaign, amid a wave of enthusiastic support for the nomination that incorporated all other Islamist groups as well as other political parties and currents.
2. Called in late 1988 for a mass demonstration proceeding from the Al-Azhar Mosque in solidarity with the first Palestinian uprising; the march was broken up by the security forces.
3. Organised conferences at the Egyptian Bar Association to expose the repressive practices of the Mubarak regime.

After the Central Security Forces mutinied in February 1986, however, the Minister of the Interior, Major-General Ahmed Rushdi (1984–6), was replaced by Major-General Zaki Badr (1986–90).[1] Badr's policies had a major role in driving the IG towards confrontation. He expanded arrests of Islamic Group activists in universities and approved the use of torture and very harsh conditions both in prisons and at the State Security Investigations

(SSI – *Mabahith Amn El Dawla*) headquarters. Through the use of administrative detention under newly promulgated emergency laws (which remained in effect for the thirty years of Mubarak's rule) and through a redoubled policy of frame-ups and faked police records, he rounded up and imprisoned as many people as possible. He used the constant threat of terrorism to justify his policies and convince Mubarak and the government to allow him free rein.[2] Indeed, he was to announce publicly that his policy was to 'shoot them right in the heart' – that is, extra-judicial execution.

I was no stranger to Major-General Badr's abuses. Between October 1986 and March 1989 – when I was able to leave Egypt – he ordered my arrest on several occasions, for four–six months each time. During these periods of detention, I was tortured at the SSI headquarters in Lazoughli in Cairo.

After returning to Egypt in June 2011 after the 25 January Revolution, I worked on a documentary film about torture during President Mubarak's rule. One of the people I met with during this period was Major-General Ibrahim Abdel Ghaffar, who had at one point served as a warden at the infamous Scorpion Prison and by that point was a Deputy-Director of the Prisons Authority. Abdel Ghaffar enjoyed a good reputation among ex-prisoners, who attested to the role he played in bringing an end to torture and ill-treatment of prisoners and in particular in improving food rations, regularly stolen before his intervention.

The first time that we met, Abdel Ghaffar told me that he knew who I was and that because of me he had been reprimanded and docked a week's salary during his service in Asyut in 1989, when he had learned of a plan to assassinate me on orders given by Badr to the then chief of security in the governorate, Major-General Ali al-Banna. After we had finished our interview on torture, I asked if he would be willing to record his account of the assassination plot and his role in foiling it. He agreed, and his testimony is publicly available on YouTube.[3]

The intensification of arrests, torture, framing of suspects and the renewal of extrajudicial murders (beginning in February 1989 with the assassination of IG activist Majid Al-Otaifi on 26 July Street in Cairo) all show a steady escalation that Badr was able to bring about in state policy towards the IG. Primarily as a result of these policies, the IG began to consider returning to

violence in response to state violence and filling out the ideological groundwork required to legitimize fighting regimes that 'refuse to implement the
laws of Islam', based on Ibn Taymiyya's *fatwas* (which served as an inspiration for all armed Islamist organisations that became active in the 1980s and
1990s). And this is, unfortunately, what happened.

The most significant violent operations included:

- An attempt to assassinate Badr by blowing up his motorcade on a bridge
  in Cairo in January 1990 (which failed for technical reasons).
- Several attempts to assassinate President Mubarak, the most famous of
  which was the 1993 attempt (foiled at the last moment) to booby-trap the
  Sidi Barrani airport bypass.
- An attempt to assassinate Mubarak while he was in Addis Ababa for the
  1996 African Summit (the attempt failed).
- Extensive clashes between IG armed units and the police resulting in more
  than 1,000 deaths from both sides in the period from 1993 to 1997.

More than 20,000 IG members and sympathisers were arrested and tried
in military courts, with seventy-five of them executed alongside widespread
torture and ill-treatment, years spent without family visits, and outbreaks of
disease among detainees.

The Initiative for Ceasing Violence: Causes of Collective De-radicalisation

Between 1992 and 1997 the cycle of violence and incitement to violence
(from both sides) reached devastating levels in many Egyptian regions, especially the governorates of Upper Egypt. The regime increasingly resorted
to mass arrests, torture and extrajudicial killings, declining to differentiate
between groups that engaged in violence and those who had no part in it.

After years of reciprocal violence, the question posed to IG leaders in
prison was: how do we break this vicious circle in which violence seems to be
more about revenge than regime change? The IG had previously accepted a
number of initiatives seeking an end to arrests and torture in exchange for an
end to violent reprisals; these efforts did not succeed because within the security services and the nationalist-left (which controlled the media) there were

many who resisted any attempt to bring an end to violence with ideological foes, from which they could garner some benefit.

The horrific experiences of young IG members in prison – as well as the suffering inflicted on their families, whose crops were often burned and whose houses were demolished by police who ignored the law entirely and no longer differentiated in any way between the IG's military wing, its broader membership and sympathisers – placed great pressure on the group's leaders, who began to seek a way out. On 5 July 1997, during his trial before the military court, Muhammad Amin made a statement on behalf of six IG leaders in prison, calling on IG members to unconditionally and unilaterally cease all domestic and foreign military operations as well as all communiqués encouraging violence against the state.

The July 1997 initiative was not a response to external pressures or to a direct request from the regime. It was a unilateral declaration intended to forestall those who stood to benefit from the continuing spiral of violence. Much of the Egyptian security apparatus were hesitant in their response to the initiative: after the loss of hundreds of officers and soldiers and numerous assassination attempts against the president as well as other senior officials (including Major-General Raouf Khairat, the deputy head of SSI) attributed to the IG, there was a lack of trust.

The initiative caused a great deal of discussion among IG supporters at home and abroad. At a time when prisoners were entirely isolated, nobody had any clear idea of why the declaration had been made or what its implications were, apart from a few scraps of information gleaned by lawyers while attending trial sessions; the announcement of the initiative raised more questions than it answered. Nearly one hundred days later, on 17 November 1997, a group of six youths opened fire on a tour group in the Deir el-Bahari temple in Luxor, in the complete absence of the security forces. In what was then an unprecedented act of terrorism, they killed fifty-eight foreign tourists and four Egyptian citizens. The peace initiative faced a baptism of fire.

The Initiative's Fate after the Luxor Massacre

I pause to consider this massacre not only because it took place just a few weeks after the IG initiative was announced, but also because of how repellent the act was and the shock that it caused even amongst IG's leaders. The incident dealt a serious blow to the credibility of their initiative, particularly given that the IG was immediately accused of responsibility. To make matters worse, one of the IG's leaders abroad, Rifai Taha (1954–2016), claimed that the IG was responsible for the attack. I myself confronted Taha, condemning the massacre in the following statement:

> Honesty and courage of conviction force me to proclaim my deep regret and sorrow at the incident in Luxor and the deaths of such a huge number of innocent victims. Whatever the possible motives, there can be no justification for such unprecedented and indiscriminate killing, which is totally at odds with the ideological and political literature of the Islamic Group.

Before making this statement, I had already confirmed that Taha – who had claimed responsibility from Afghanistan – had nothing to do with the massacre and had first heard about it on the radio. His aim had simply been to thwart the IG initiative, which he objected to. Analysis of his statement and the course of events confirm that his claim was based on initial and inaccurate media reports of the hijacking of a tourist bus, with kidnappers demanding that Dr Omar Abdel-Rahman (1938–2017), imprisoned until his death in the US, be released in exchange for the hostages. No such hijacking took place.

The Luxor Massacre sounded the alarm for an entire society on the verge of losing its moral compass amid paroxysms of violence escaping the control of all parties. This only served to increase the importance of the initiative to stop the violence.

Was the IG Initiative a Statement of Defeat or a Strategic Transformation?

The initiative for ceasing violence in July 1997 was not, in my view, a declaration of defeat, as some argued, so much as a reflection of a strategic political vision that had concluded that violence only perpetuates tyranny and social breakdown at all political and economic levels, eroding freedoms and human rights, and that violence cannot be an end in itself. While these ideas were taking shape within the Egyptian IG, the situation was reaching crisis point in other jihadist hotspots around the world (hotspots that had emerged because of the state's failure to incorporate citizens and young people who it had systematically excluded). The IG was acutely aware of these developments and staunchly resisted any attempt to mix it up in them.

In February 1998, Osama bin Laden (1957–2011) had appropriated the name 'Islamic Group in Egypt', claiming that it was part of his 'global front to fight the Jews and the Crusaders', founded 'to fight Americans and plunder their money everywhere' as part of his policy of fighting the 'far enemy' (i.e., the West). The IG protested, surprised to see its name used in this way, and asked al-Qaeda to correct the error. When this was not forthcoming, in the last week of July 1998 we published an interview with Rifai Taha on the IG's *al-Murabitun* website (of which I was editor-in-chief). In this interview, Taha – who had been listed among the signatories of Bin Laden's declaration – categorically denied the Islamic Group had joined this 'global front': 'The IG has not been presented with any project of this kind, and if this were to happen, it would be for the leadership to decide'.[4]

The IG leadership had the maturity and responsibility to see that al-Qaeda was trying to drag the Islamic Group into a confrontation and to distance itself from any such entanglement. Messages attributed to Ayman al-Zawahiri, found on his private computer and published by the USA after its invasion of Afghanistan, have since revealed al-Zawahiri's opposition to the initiative.

Ideological De-radicalisation and Revisions as a Break with the Past

Implementing the initiative, the Islamic Group halted all combat operations, dismantled its armed wing and revised its ideology, bringing about a structural change. After the Luxor Massacre no further violent acts were attributed to the IG either within or outside Egypt.

However, the Egyptian state's responses to the initiative remained inadequate until the 9/11 attacks against the USA and the launch of the broad-front 'War on Terror', when the Mubarak regime was identified as an 'exporter' of terrorism rooted in anger at his despotic policies. During his March 2012 visit to the United States, Mubarak faced criticism from the US media for failing to cooperate with America in the 'War on Terror', despite Egyptian intelligence coordination and support for the campaign in Afghanistan, and congressmen objecting to a deal offering modern missiles to Egypt. After a famously difficult visit to President George W. Bush's

(2001–9) farm in Crawford, Texas in 2004 – during which President Bush Jr. criticised many aspects of 'democratisation' in Egypt – Mubarak declined to return to the US for five years, breaking with a long tradition of annual visits. At around this time, the Mubarak regime began to remember the IG initiative and its success in checking the cycle of violence in Egypt. A new openness to the initiative enabled a shift in Ministry of Interior policy, with journalists allowed to visit IG leaders in prison to learn about the initiative and cultivate public support.

Major-General Mustafa Rifaat (also known as *El-Hagg*), SSI Deputy-Director and the official responsible for IG affairs, began an expanded dialogue with IG leaders in prison, who were allowed to visit other prisons throughout Egypt to conduct public seminars, explain the origins, implications and dimensions of the IG initiative, and respond to questions. Most members of the Islamic Group were receptive to government dialogue because of the close links between IG members and leaders.

These reviews brought about intellectual developments and a strategic, methodological and practical shift in orientation. A series of studies titled *Conceptual Corrections* (*Tashih al-Mafahim*) was penned by the 'Historical Leadership' (*al-qiyadat al-tarikhiyya*) of the group as represented by its Shura Council: Karam Zuhdi, Najih Ibrahim, Assem Abdul Majid, Osama Hafez, Essam Derbala and Ali al-Sharif. These studies did not only seek to provide a legal and methodological foundation for the initiative. They laid the groundwork for an entirely new ideological method, breathing new life into pragmatic approaches to Islamic jurisprudence (*fiqh al-waqi', fiqh al-ma'alat*) and revitalising the IG's efforts to be self-critical and to root its positions in the realities of its working environment. Moreover, they engaged in a bold reconsideration of all of the central issues of jihadi thought: the principles of jihad itself, the concept of 'enjoining good and forbidding evil' (*al-amr bi'l-ma'ruf wa'l-nahy 'an al-munkar*), the question of tourism and safe passage for foreigners, the targeting of urban infrastructure and civilians, *takfir* and the relationships of Muslim countries with their neighbours. The Islamic Group has remained committed to this methodology and strategic path ever since.

The Islamic Group presented its 'corrective vision' to society and its institutions and to al-Azhar (the largest religious university in Egypt), through a series of books, including:

- *The End to Violence Initiative: An Ideological Vision and a Realistic Consideration*
- *The Forbidden Status of Extremism in Religion and Excommunications of Muslims*
- *Errors Committed During the Jihad*
- *Advice and Clarification Correcting the Concepts of those Who Judge Others*
- *On Distinguishing Ends and Means*
- *The Strategy and Bombings of al-Qaeda: Errors and Dangers*
- *Memories: Jurisprudential Recantations by the Islamic Group*
- *The Inevitability of Confrontation and the Jurisprudence of Results*
- *Much-Needed Advice to the Leaders of Al-Qaeda*
- *Islam and the Rules of War*
- The book *No to Bombings* was published on the IG Portal on 13 August 2014. It dealt with the issue of terrorist bombings and their theological prohibition.
- A handbook explaining why targeting infrastructure is forbidden: *Destruction of Infrastructure: Legitimate Struggle or Forbidden Sabotage?* (later republished on the official IG website on 13 August 2014).[5]

My Position on the Ideological De-radicalisation

I resigned from the IG in January 1999 as part of an internal agreement stipulating that I, Rifai Taha and Muhammad Shawqi al-Islambouli would all resign membership of the Shura Council after sharp disagreement and internal polarisation between myself and Rifai Taha over the initiative that became public. This allowed the IG's Overseas Shura Council under its new president Mustafa Hamzah to release an official statement announcing its approval of the initiative, which was of great importance (despite these developments) in securing support for the initiative once all IG factions had indicated their agreement. Despite my resignation, IG affairs have continued to be of great interest to me as someone interested in Islamist political activism.

My insistence on upholding the IG de-radicalisation initiative stems from my belief that authoritarian regimes foment violence to justify impediments to democratisation, state violence and continuous violations of human rights. In Egypt, the threat of terrorism has also been used as a mean of securing concessions such as debt rescheduling or economic aid from a West concerned that Egypt might go the way of Iran. Violence only serves these regimes – regimes which do not respect human rights, whether these rights are those of soldiers and officers in the military or of other citizens. However, at the time I repeatedly expressed fear that the future of the initiative was being put at risk by a short-sighted security strategy that failed to recognise the strategic importance of the transformations taking place. Had they been presented properly to public opinion and to young people searching for answers to their concerns, these transformations could have become a significant achievement, with an international strategic impact beyond solely Egyptian issues and IG membership.

When the Mubarak regime began to actively respond to the initiative and the press began to enter prisons and publish interviews with leaders who had been imprisoned for more than twenty years, these dialogues no longer seemed to be about presenting the IG model to young people around the world vulnerable to violent extremism. This audience might benefit from the intellectual and ideological clarity of transformative vision and perhaps, in some cases, reconsider their haste to join the ranks of violent extremist transnational organisations. Instead, the narratives accompanying the transformations/de-radicalisation processes took on a self-flagellating character, undermining the initiative's long-term impact in favour of a short-sighted and narrow-minded Egyptian security focus, without regard to the impact this could have on the initiative's future and the future of peaceful political transformations in Egypt and beyond. Abandoning harmful means and methods should not mean abandoning principles.

In 2003, in response to these developments, I published a number of articles on my *Al-Mahrousa* website. In one article, subsequently reprinted in the Saudi-funded London newspaper *Asharq al-Awsat's* 20 July 2003 edition after an interview with IG leader Karam Zuhdi (15–16 July 2003), I said the following:

> Healing the wounds of the past and dispelling doubts and misgivings about the initiative is a matter of successfully and practically implementing it on the ground and of those responsible for it remaining steadfast in the face of trouble until all complaints have been dealt with. Press 'interviews' of this kind conducted in an atmosphere of great difficulty are no more

than opportunities for self-flagellation and defamation of those behind the initiative . . . Al-Sharq Al-Awsat's Karam Zuhdi Interview from Scorpion Prison in Egypt served only to disparage the course correction announced by the IG six years ago, based on a theological and a political vision that continues to enjoy wide support, stressing peaceful support for Islamist political and media activism to spare the country and its people the sort of tragedies that all have suffered during the bloody confrontations of the last ten years.

I went on to write:

If Karam Zuhdi really believes what he says, then why doesn't he follow up his acknowledgment of error by taking responsibility for these errors and announcing his withdrawal from a leadership role to make way for a new generation – a generation who do not have the same reputation as the Karam Zuhdi who filled thousands in Minya and Asyut with fighting spirit, and who were not involved in these errors? Or are we going to operate like those groups whose political history is one long list of contradictions, for whom it is better to reign in hell than serve in heaven![6]

The Domestic and Foreign Repercussions of Ideological De-radicalisation

It is no exaggeration to claim that the success of the initiative effectively robbed the spectre of terrorism that had been constantly invoked by the Mubarak regime to justify restrictions on democratisation and political and civil freedoms of its sting. The initiative thus paved the way for the gradual liberalisation and interaction that in turn set the stage for the January 2011 Revolution. For other jihadist movements inside and outside Egypt, the success of the Islamic Group's initiative as a basis for societal reconciliation paved the way for similar initiatives such as that associated with the founder of the Egyptian Jihad Organisation (EJO), Dr Sayyed Imam al-Sharif.

The Jihad Organisation and Ideological Revisions: A Critique

Dr Sayyed Imam, one-time Emir of the Egyptian Jihad Organisation before his split with the Zawahiri faction in 1993, published his *Righting the Course of Jihad in Egypt and the World* from prison, where he was serving a twenty-five-year sentence after being repatriated from Yemen following the September 11 attacks. This document was published simultaneously in the Kuwaiti news-paper, *al-Jarida*, and the Egyptian newspaper, *al-Masry al-Yawm*, in episodes beginning on 18 November 2007.[7]

Although the EJO differs from the IG in not having a centralised leader-ship, Imam is still an important intellectual and ideological authority for both EJO in particular and many other Arab jihadist groups. He had no qualms declaring the EJO (whose leader he had been until quite recently, a title that he continued to claim in spite of this) to be apostates, apparently after Zawahiri had published a book of his in edited form (under the title *Guide to the Righteous Path*) without *fatwa*s declaring the IG and Saudi Arabia's chief Mufti Abdulaziz bin Baz to be apostates – a move which angered Bin Laden and in turn Imam. His *Essential Guide for Preparation* was the first item for study for al-Qaeda's recruits in its Afghan training camps. Imam's ideas laid the foundation for the Armed Islamic Group (GIA) in Algeria, which com-mitted massacres of civilians in Algerian villages and could be considered a beta-version of what ISIS was to become in subsequent years. Abu Musab al-Zarqawi, the 'spiritual father' of the Islamic State Organisation (ISIS) also drew on Imam's ideology and book.

The *Compendium of the Pursuit of Divine Knowledge*, published in 1993, is Imam's most extreme work, tarring whole societies as infidels and apostates and justifying application of the Shari'a provisions on fighting apostates to anyone in possession of a voter registration card (even if unused!): poten-tial voters are apostates for acquiescing to democracy. His *Advice to Draw Close to God Almighty* (2006) continues his earlier excoriation of the Muslim Brotherhood as well as democracy and elections. Imam has also been credited with a book published under Ayman al-Zawahiri's name, *The Bitter Harvest* (also branding the Muslim Brotherhood apostates).

Imam's *Righting the Course* – supposedly a document of ideological de-radicalisation – does not include any repudiation of his previous work, despite the role that his *fatwas* (theological edicts) have played as the ideologi-cal basis of Salafi-Jihadi groups including al-Qaeda and ISIS and the colossal suffering they have caused Islamic societies and the world more broadly. After reading the first few sections, I realised that he was in fact sidestepping any responsibility for the acts of Ayman al-Zawahiri and Bin Laden and avoiding explicitly addressing the ideology that legitimised and instigated these acts.

I have written an article elsewhere[8] criticising Imam's previous writings and rejecting his claims to be simply quoting scholarly opinion or providing abstract rulings – claims which serve to obscure the fact that he mixes together quotation with opinion, personal judgement and interpretation, producing arbitrary and sometimes fatuous *fatwas*. As I noted there, the *fatwas* on declaring other Muslims to be apostates, which have caused so much damage to so many Muslims worldwide, are so lengthy (some 1,000 pages in large font) that they cannot be appropriately dealt with in only a few lines of print. In fact, it would be difficult in a single article or even several articles to cover even some of the violent extremist incitement presented in these books, which are still readily available online or in print to excitable and gullible young people with an interest in Islamic jurisprudence – young people who are at the current moment particularly susceptible to large doses of *takfir* and obscurantism. At the end of my article, I called on Imam to explicitly repudiate these books and indeed to suggest burning them, and to rewrite them if he so desired on new foundations. It subsequently became clear that *Righting the Course* was simply part of the long personal war between Imam and Ayman al-Zawahiri that began with their public falling out in 1993.

On 4 December 2008, after Imam published another booklet responding to attacks on him in Zawahiri's *Exoneration* (2008), I returned to the subject with another article in *al-Masry al-Youm* Egyptian newspaper entitled 'From Reviews to Polemics: When will Sayyed Imam respond to himself?'[9] I ended this article by reiterating what I have said repeatedly on various occasions: ideological de-radicalisation is a serious matter and playing games with it is tantamount to playing with fire. Wrong treatments may result in the emergence of ideas and groups that are even more closed, ossified and resistant to listening, thus hearing neither this voice nor that, young men will think that whatever ideological de-radicalisation literature is produced is merely a product of the security services or of pressure exercised in prison.

The revisions attributed to Imam did nothing but allow him to distance himself from the EJO and al-Qaeda against a background of dissent and disagreement, without signalling any reconsideration of an ideology of which he was one of the most important sources. This undermines the credibility of his condemnations of these groups or his denial of any link to them. This can be contrasted with the IG's reassessment of its ideology, which has not only produced two decades of broad reconciliation with all segments of society and condemnation of all forms of past violence lasting to the present day but has confronted and dismantled the entire ideological structure underpinning jihadist violence.

The IG's new positions show just how structurally, ideologically and strategically different it is from organisations like al-Qaeda and ISIS. There are fundamental differences in the structure and foundational premises of the movements; in their visions; in their interpretation and implementation of Islamic rulings; in how they understand reality; in goals and priorities, and in working out how to respond to different challenges.

The Outcome and Fate of Collective De-radicalisation

Even if over a long span of time, the ideological revisions of the IG achieved the goals envisioned by their participants: a gradual release of detainees has been underway since 2002; death sentences are no longer being carried out against those sentenced in military or supreme state emergency security courts; and violence has been effectively brought under control. The IG did not see any major defections, and although there was an element of dissatisfaction with some of the positions taken by the leaders at the time, it found expression in the results of the General Assembly and Consultative Council elections conducted among members in all governorates and resulting in the expulsion of several founders from the council. Dr Essam Derbala[10] was elected to head the council. This corrective process took place in an atmosphere that was far from contentious or divisive, possible only in the aftermath of the 25 January Revolution.

The 25 January Revolution: A Test for Collective De-radicalisation?

Egypt's 25 January Revolution, the biggest transformation in the country's history, was the great test of the IG initiative. The Revolution placed the IG at a crossroads between its new convictions as embodied in the initiative and its violent past, without impediment or barrier from a state security apparatus. The state security system had broken down entirely – a golden opportunity for acts of violence and retaliation without costs. There were ample incentives to retreat from the initiative's founding principles, and all the obstacles preventing the IG from returning to arms and giving free reign to a spirit of retribution had disappeared overnight. The IG proved at this moment that its belief in the initiative and collective de-radicalisation was irreversible, and that abandoning weapons and rejecting violence was a strategic choice that could not be undone. Moreover, IG leaders were able to direct IG members' energies positively and constructively: key IG members stood publicly to protect churches and property, helping to prevent a total collapse into chaos in Upper Egyptian towns. With their participation in popular committees and traditional councils, little by little the risks of this chaos happening disappeared.

Establishment of the Building and Development Party

The IG General Assembly put a great deal of effort into the creation of the Building and Development Party (BDP),[11] whose founding was announced on 20 June 2011. Although it was initially denied a licence by the Party Affairs Committee on 19 September 2011 because of its 'purely religious' programme, on 10 October 2011, the Supreme Administrative Court overturned the Committee's decision, stating that the party's programme was in accordance with the constitution.

This move represented another qualitative leap in the transition to peaceful political action via a legal and a constitutional political party, for an organisation whose members were once armed militants. The party was one product of the IG's initiative, ushering in perhaps the most important phase in the history of the Islamic Group. Ten years after the initiative began, the IG turned to open political action, winning fifteen out of 498 contested seats in the People's Assembly (lower house of the parliament) and two out of 180 contested seats in the Consultative (Shura) Council (upper house of the parliament), in the first free and fair parliament elections to ever take in Egypt's history. The party only fielded twenty-two candidates in the People's Assembly elections, of whom fifteen won, mostly in individual seats (the highest success rate compared to the percentage of candidates). The result reflected the relative local satisfaction with the Building and Development Party, itself a result of convictions established in the community with the de-radicalisation and transformation of the members of the Islamic Group from bullets to ballots, and from secret armed action to overt political activism.

The Building and Development Party sought to end the state of division between Islamist and civil political forces over the formation of the Constitutional Drafting Assembly, ceding its two seats to civil society by nominating two persons not associated organisationally with the party; it also issued a statement clarifying its vision and undertaking to uphold the good of the nation above all other considerations. The IG and the BDP also launched a national dialogue initiative on 10 January 2013.[12] When opposition figures felt that the president was monopolising power, the BDP submitted a proposal to solve the legislative crisis engendered by the abolition of the Military Council's supplemental constitutional declaration which had preserved the right to legislate, by creating a balance within the Shura Council – dissolved in June 2012 – so that the ninety seats appointed by the president would devolve to Copts, women, youth and other secular forces, and thus legislation would be passed by a rebalanced Shura Council until new parliamentary elections could be held. The BDP's quorum of those appointments was to be twelve seats (which it offered to waive) in accordance with the established rules that were the outcome of the National Dialogue.[13] The IG and the BDP also offered an integrated project to solve the Sinai crisis and end the state of violence there. The BDP offered former President Mohamed Morsi its acceptance of the referendum on early presidential elections, on 21 July 2013.[14]

On 5 July 2013 – after the military coup of 3 July – the BDP presented its first political initiative, aimed at resolving the crisis before it came to a head.[15] The essence of this initiative was that if transition away from the Morsi government had to happen, it should take place through ballot boxes to preserve the gains of the 25 January Revolution. The party thus presented a procedural initiative including the following steps to resolve the crisis:

- Popular referendum on the Military Council's 'road map'
- The return of the army to its barracks.
- Calming the political climate and working towards national reconciliation.[16]

The BDP suffered the brutality of the 3 July 2013 military coup led by Defence Minister Abdel Fattah El-Sisi (2014–) against the first elected civilian president after the revolution, President Mohamed Morsi. The BDP peacefully opposed the coup and the ensuing breakdown of human rights and of the justice system, with the massacres of political activists and violent dispersal of peaceful sit-ins organised to protest the coup in which hundreds of Egyptians were killed. The IG and BDP were subjected to severe pressure to compel them to support the existing regime and withdraw from the National Alliance to Support Legitimacy, a coalition of parties and movements formed prior to the coup. The IG refused, stressing the right to peaceful opposition. Although the IG and BDP were not involved in any of the violence and condemned all use of violence, this was not enough for a regime that eliminated any space for freedom in Egypt. Dr Essam Derbala, head of the Islamic Group's Shura Council, was still arrested on 13 May 2015, after leaving a mosque in the Qena governorate, southern Egypt. He was on a lecture tour intended to warn young people away from the ideas of ISIS.

On 9 August 2015, Dr Essam Derbala died in the Scorpion Prison, where he had been imprisoned after his arrest. He was denied access to his family and to medicine despite suffering from diabetes; this is now a common policy in Egypt, whereby patients are denied treatment until they die.[17] On the same day that he died, Derbala was brought before the State Security Court in a clearly dangerous condition, with a temperature of 41°.

This was not a sufficient cause for the prosecution to order him medical care. He died immediately following his return to his prison cell. Three years ago, Dr Safwat Abdel-Ghani, a member of the Consultative (Shura) Council (the upper-house of the Parliament) and the head of the party's Political Bureau, and Alaa Abu al-Nasr, the party's Secretary General, were also arrested. Although each of them has been ordered released by a court five times, on each occasion a security objection has been raised, and as of the writing of this chapter they remain in prison alongside other IG members.

The Parties Affairs Committee submitted a request to the Supreme Administrative Court to dissolve the BDP based on the party's opposition to military rule. The party was dissolved in April 2020. After the 2013 military coup, there is a *de facto* criminalisation of political activity. I had the honour of being a political advisor to the BDP until January 2019, when myself and others abroad submitted resignations due to attempts to pressure the party using threats of dissolution. This was done to free the party from the consequences of my political opposition abroad.

The International Position on the Islamic Group

US support of the Mubarak regime against its jihadist opponents began in 1993 and developed further in 1995. On 13 September 1995, Talaat Fouad Qassem (1957–95), one of the émigré leaders of the IG, was disappeared on his way from Denmark to Croatia and secretly extradited to Mubarak's Egypt. This was despite the fact that he had been granted political asylum in Denmark, held a Danish travel document granting him protection under the UN Refugee Convention (to which all the parties that participated in his abduction are signatories), and despite the fact that he was resident in Denmark, a country that respects the law and which could have prosecuted him for any suspected wrongdoing. Egypt has thus far refused his family in Denmark's requests for a death certificate.

Although the IG initiative was launched on 5 July 1997, the US government nonetheless included it on the list of foreign terrorist organisations on 10 August 1997, and despite the initiative's lasting success the designation has been renewed automatically ever since. The United Kingdom followed suit and included the IG on its list of foreign terrorist organisations in March 2001; the European Union reproduced the American list in December 2001 list. However, neither the IG nor any of its members were included on the United Nations sanctions listings, such as persons and entities associated with both al-Qaeda and ISIS.

On 15 February 2011, the British newspaper *The Daily Telegraph* published a WikiLeaks report of a letter dated 14 October 2008 from the American Embassy in Cairo's Intelligence Working Group to their bosses in Washington, giving their opinion on the proposed removal of the Egyptian IG from the Sponsors of Terrorism blacklist. After the Working Group meetings with the SSI deputy director in Cairo and with the Assistant Minister for Terrorism Affairs at the Egyptian Foreign Ministry, the Working Group in Cairo recommended leaving the IG on the list in order to keep the Egyptian regime happy.[18] This shows clearly that the ongoing blacklisting of the IG does not have the sort of objective reasons stipulated by Article 219 of the act regulating the FTO list.

In Europe, the IG's Dr Tariq Al-Zomor, a member of the Shura Council, filed a lawsuit in 2016 before the European Court of Justice against the

European Commission's decision to include the group on the European Union's list of foreign terrorist organisations, where the listing is renewed automatically. The court had already issued a ruling on 10 April 2019 for the removal of the IG name from the European Union's list, and the ruling became final with the passage of the appeal deadline. However, a new European Commission decision relisted the Islamic Group on the foreign terrorist organisations list. Such a step sent a negative political message: that the European Commission is evading the implementation of the court's final judgements and that law is respected in dealings with European citizens, but not with foreigners.

Conclusion

The de-radicalisation initiative of the Egyptian IG, transforming itself into a non-violent political and social actor, has succeeded. Based on lengthy conversations and interactions conducted with all the leaders of the IG who were active before or after the military coup of 3 July 2013, whether inside or outside Egypt, I have no doubt that the IG has definitively and irreversibly turned the page on violence. There is now a completely internalised under-standing of the adverse consequences of resorting to violence, and of the merit of peaceful political and media approaches – even if they require long and open-ended application.

But given the repression and the collapse of any structure for upholding human rights in Egypt, other groups will emerge to judge the experiences of those who preceded them as failures and may revive the cycle of violence and instability. This only reinforces the urgency of the need for political reform that welcomes diversity and opens the door to peaceful political action, to promoting societal peace and economic development. One only needs to recall that the Arab Spring was tantamount to an earthquake among violent groups, chief among them Al Qaida, whose leader, Osama bin Laden, real-ised immediately before his death that the Arab Spring could have had put an end to jihadism.

Notes

* This testimony was presented at the first annual conference of the Strategic Studies Unit in Arab Center for Research and Policy Studies, titled 'From

Bullets to Ballots: Transformations from Armed to Unarmed Political Activism',
Doha, 2–3 November 2018. The initial paper was written in Arabic and was
subsequently translated to English. I am grateful to the Arab Center for Research
and Policy Studies in Doha and to Prof Dr Omar Ashour for organising the
conference and for gathering much valuable experience from around the world
to achieve civil peace and security after periods of violence and confrontations.
I am reflecting here on the case of the Islamic Group as a first-hand witness.
Hopefully, these studies will help researchers and readers with lessons learned
to help enhance security, development and societal peace in all their countries.
I am also grateful to Prof Dr Azmi Bishara, the founder and general director of
the Arab Center, and for Prof Dr Abdel Fattah Madi of the Arab Center. The
statements, opinions and any mistakes made here are entirely mine.

1. Michael Ross, 'Egyptian Army Storms Mutineers' Camp', *Los Angeles Times*,
1/3/1986, accessed on 11/6/2019, at: https://lat.ms/2oRxW8B
2. Alaa Ibrahim, 'Generals and Terrorists: Zaki Badr', *Al-Bawaba*, 10/28/2016,
accessed on 11/6/2019, at: https://bit.ly/2NLmjbB
3. Osama Rushdi, 'Testimony Revealing the Brutality of the Mubarak Regime
and Its Interior Ministry', *YouTube*, accessed on 6/11/2019, at: https://bit.
ly/2NPB3pQ
4. Diaa Rashwan, *Transformations of Islamic Groups in Egypt*, Strategic Pamphlets,
no. 92 (Cairo: Al-Ahram Center for Political and Strategic Studies, 2000), p. 24.
5. The official portal of the *Islamic Group*, accessed on 26/10/2020, at: https://bit.
ly/33nLsj8
6. Abd al-Latif al-Manawi, 'Osama Rushdi Criticises the Leader of the *Islamic
Group* in the Middle East and Affirms His Support for the Initiative to Stop
Violence', *Asharq Al-Awsat*, 20/7/2003, accessed on 6/11/2019, at: https://bit.
ly/2NnHEZL
7. Sayyed Imam, 'The Document for the Right Guidance of Jihad Activity in
Egypt and the World (Episode One)', *Islamists Today*, 11/18/2008, accessed on
6/11/2019, at: https://bit.ly/2PRcdc0
8. The Egyptian newspaper, *Al-Masry Al-Yawm*, 23/11/2007.
9. Osama Rushdie, 'From Reviews to Polemics … When Will Syed Imam
Respond to Himself?' *Al-Masry Al-Youm*, 4/12/2008, accessed on 6/11/2019,
at: https://bit.ly/2pP6Krk
10. Yousri al-Badri, 'A Security Source Explains the Cause of the Death of Essam
Derbala', *Al-Masry Al-Youm*, 9/8/2015, accessed on 6/11/2019, at: https://bit.
ly/33nebEX

11. 'The Islamic Group in Egypt: From the Battlefields to the Fora of Politics (3–3)', *Arab 21*, 15/6/2019, accessed on 6/11/2019, at: https://bit.ly/2pzMslP

12. Tariq Al-Zomor, 'A Talk About the Experience of the Building and Development Party', Al-Asr Channel, *Masreya Files Program - The Egyptian Affair*, 10/13/2015, accessed on 6/11/2019, at: https://bit.ly/2pNj5MH

13. Ibid., minute 38.

14. Ibid., minute 24.

15. Published in: 'The Islamic Group Proposes an Initiative to Get Out of the Crisis', *al-Ahram*, 5/7/2013.

16. Ibid.

17. 'Al-Jama'a al-Islamiyya Accuses the Egyptian Authorities of Killing the Head of the Shura Council, Issam Derbala in Prison', *BBC Arabic*, 9/8/2015, accessed on 6/11/2019, at: https://bbc.in/2NIsehC

18. WikiLeaks, 'Al-Gama'at Al-Islamiya: Concerns Regarding Possible Revocation of Foreign Terrorist Organization Status', *The Daily Telegraph*, 15/2/2011, accessed on 6/11/2019, at: https://bit.ly/36AIjyy

4

FROM ARMS TO TALKS: TRANSFORMATIONS OF THREE SYRIAN ARMED ISLAMIST MOVEMENTS

Hamzah Almustafa

Introduction

'Killing Politics' – this was the title Lisa Wedeen gave the second chapter of her famous *Ambiguities of Domination* published in 1999, which deconstructs the physical and symbolic oppression used by the previous Syrian president Hafiz al-Assad to consolidate his thirty-year rule over society. According to Wedeen, the power of the Syrian regime lies not only in its ability to control material resources and to construct institutions of punishment, but also in its ability to manage the symbolic world,[1] by encouraging the cult of the ruler, destroying the image of the opposition in the popular conscience and using first force to punish them and then rhetoric to defame them. Syria thus experienced decades of exceptional political desertification, even in comparison to other authoritarian or authoritarian-competitive regimes in the Arab world. This can be traced to the constitutional clause (Article 8) added by the Arab Socialist Baath Party after they took power on 8 March 1963, by which it legitimised its 'leading' role in state and society in a way that robbed party pluralism of any real competitive element.[2]

This is not to say that there was no opposition. Secular political parties and forces such as the Balad and Kurdish parties have worked within a narrow elite space framed by cultural associations, forums and political salons without any effective influence on the street. The Syrian Muslim

Brotherhood (MB), on the other hand, no longer has any affiliates left in Syria since the 1982 uprising and its subsequent criminalisation under Law 49 of 1980, Article 1 of which states that 'all those affiliated with the Muslim Brotherhood shall be considered criminals and punished by execution'.[3] Although the beginning of the current president Bashar al-Assad's rule did witness a degree of political liberalisation or *infitah* (the Damascus Spring 2000, the Damascus Declaration 2005), promises of political reform and a gradual transition towards democracy soon dissipated, and repression by the security forces returned as the main and sole determinant of the regime's way of dealing with its opponents.[4]

After decades of exclusion and domestication, the Syrian revolution in both its peaceful and armed stages paved the way for opponents of the regime in general – and Islamists in particular – to break into the political sphere, creating a public space outside government control allowing political and social actors to put forth their own ideas and agendas.[5] Various Islamist groups have emerged within this framework, united in their general aims (establishing an Islamic state) but differing on how to achieve them depending on their school of thought (Salafi-jihadi, Salafi, Muslim Brotherhood, Sufi and so forth). Guided by the experience of Islamists in other Arab revolutions, these movements have sought to seize the opportunities presented by the revolution to expand their social base and to assume a central political position in the Syrian crisis. This has led to ideological, behavioural and organisational changes.

Since mid-2014, Islamist battalions have become the centre of gravity for armed activity against regime forces and their foreign sponsors while simultaneously becoming a major problem for regime change in Syria. This is due to the different evaluations made by various international and regional powers influential in the Syrian crisis on how best to deal with them, in the face of demands on the one hand to list them as terrorist organisations in preparation for their military elimination, and on the other to absorb them into opposition institutions and encourage them to engage in negotiations for a political settlement.

This chapter does not intend to present political prescriptions or value judgments and attempts to avoid these two issues. Instead, it adopts an alternative approach accounting for behavioural, organisational and ideological transformations within Islamist movements in Syria, focusing on the processes of transformation more than discussing their inevitable end or making normative judgments. Likewise, it investigates the mechanisms that help determine the outcome of these transformations. Ideological transformation involves the restructuring and redirecting of a radical group's ideology, delegitimising the use of violent means to achieve political ends. While this process also involves moving towards an acceptance of gradual socio-political change within a pluralist context, it does not require the adoption of liberal or democratic principles. Behavioural transformation, meanwhile, is a process leading to the abandonment of armed methods as a tactic of attaining revolutionary political goals, without a concurrent process involving the ideological delegitimization of violence. Finally, organisational de-radicalisation refers to the process leading to dismantlement of an armed group[6].

Hence, the central puzzle of this chapter is how to assess the impact of political-diplomatic engagements on Syrian Islamist battalions' discourse, behaviour and organisational structures. This will raise a series of secondary questions about the analytical models that can explain the transformations of these movements, as well as their response and the extent to which they differ from each other. In order to answer these questions, I have selected three cases to serve as the subjects of comparative analysis. These are *Ahrar al-Sham* (Freemen of the Levant), *Jaysh al-Islam* (the Army of Islam, AoI), and *Faylaq al-Sham* (the Sham Legion). The chapter uses two research methods: discourse analysis and semi-structured interviews. Most of these interviews were conducted with leaders of these movements, influential figures in the opposition, and activists and researchers with substantial knowledge of the research topic.

Ahrar al-Sham: Gradual Emancipation from Salafi Jihadism

Upon their release from prison in 2011, Syrian Salafis were surprised by the outbreak of the Syrian Revolution and its spread throughout almost all the governorates, adopting a peaceful approach and raising unfamiliar slogans about democracy, the civil state and so on. Despite their initial reservations, the revolution was their only gateway to make contact with local communities outside of their ideological circles. The reality of the revolution, their re-evaluations and previous experiences – especially in Sednaya Prison – and their experience with the regime all played a part in their discussions, which revolved around an 'imagined' project based on a dichotomy between the ideological and the local. This project was then given a tangible organisational structure by Hassan Abboud when he founded the *Ahrar al-Sham* (Freemen of the Levant) battalions on 11 November 2011. Abboud described the battalions as an armed wing intended to 'protect peaceful demonstrations',[7] and as the foundation-stone of a 'local' jihadist project similar to the Taliban[8] but unaffiliated with global jihad and its organisational frameworks such as al-Qaeda.

Beyond Salafi Jihadism

Ahrar al-Sham has always distinguished itself from both al-Qaeda and the Free Syrian Army (FSA). This has caused it intellectual confusion, because it has been forced to use the vocabulary of revolutionary discourse in order to differentiate itself from its jihadist counterpart and vice versa – although at the time of its establishment the Salafist element was more dominant than the revolutionary one.[9] Throughout the revolutionary years, the movement has been unable to define itself or to position itself intellectually with a particular school. Its leaders insist on defining their movement by denying any affiliation with the Syrian MB and having 'moved beyond' Salafi jihadism. I refer to this as post-jihadism.[10]

Jihadi movements are not concerned with non-violent politics as a process, a path, or a set of rules, instead adopting a violent revolutionary approach as the only way to establish a Shari'a government. The leadership of *Ahrar al-Sham* was no exception. During its early years it preferred to contain itself for fear of structural problems or internal divisions and the loss of fighters to more established jihadist movements.[11] This explains its refusal to join the *Jabhat Tahrir Suriya al-Islamiyya* (Syrian Islamic Liberation Front, SILF), founded in September 2012, which included what were then the largest Islamist factions.

The choice to affirm their independence and differentiate themselves from the Syrian Liberation Front led *Ahrar al-Sham* into a competition with the SILF to attract smaller Islamist battalions. This forced the leadership to adopt a broader and more flexible discourse, in order to find common denominators with the eleven other Islamist groups with which it formed the Syrian

Islamic Front (SIF or *al-Jabha al-Islamiyya as-Suriyya*) in December 2012. The SIF's charter incorporated an Islamist-Revivalist (*tajdidi*) rhetoric focusing on 'building a civilised Islamic society' instead of 'setting up an Islamist regime'. For the first time, it also addressed problematic issues such as religious minorities, moderation, alignment with Islam and women's rights. The addition of the word 'Syrian' was the most important, because it formally established the national dimension ('local-national') in Ahrar al-Sham's ideology.

The declaration of the Islamic State (IS) in Syria and the consequent shift in the Obama administration's priorities in Syria (and those of the Western countries more generally) away from regime change towards counterterrorism,[12] helped motivate the Ahrar's involvement in politics for fear of being listed as terrorists. The first step came with its transformation into a political movement (on 31 January 2013) following its full integration with the Dawn of Islam (*Fajr al-Islam*) movement, the Fighting Vanguard (*at-Tali'a al-Muqatila*) and the Faith (*al-Iman*) Battalions.[13] It renounced the name 'battalion' and redefined itself as 'a reformist Islamist movement working to build a civilised Islamic society governed by Shari'a law'. The institutionalisation of the movement contributed to its revitalisation, which in turn led to an internal debate regarding major objectives and priorities. This resulted in the emergence of a general orientation that made the achievement of major goals (such as establishing Shari'a rule) subject to capacity and community acceptance, with the possibility of accepting their non-implementation provided there is freedom to preach and practise politics.

The intellectual approaches above gave vague indications that *Ahrar al-Sham* had begun a process of radical intellectual review. But the rise of IS, its adoption of a discourse of total ideological warfare up to domination (*shawkat al-nikaya wa'l-tamkin*) and its declaration of a 'Caliphate' have had a great impact on the movement, especially given its fighters' hesitance to fight IS even after it assassinated military leaders of the Ahrar and expelled the latter from several areas. It was here that the movement realised the depth of the predicament facing it within its base: intellectual discussions had been confined to a particular elite, while its fighters had been given a heavy dose of religious encouragements and justifications framed within a Muslim-Infidel dichotomy to fight the regime and its allies, with no real doctrinal and intellectual preparation to fight outside this dichotomy.[14]

As a result, the movement's leadership decided that the best defence was a good offence, making a volte-face away from all previous ideological discussions as well as all the work done with other Islamist battalions on a political/ intellectual project. By doing so, they sought to prove to both IS and Ahrar fighters that they were not Islamist-coloured militias subordinated to the interests of others like the Iraqi *Sahwat* and that establishment of Shari'a rule was the main objective.[15] It was within this context that the formation of *al-Jabha al-Islamiyya* (the Islamic Front, IF) was announced in November 2013. Its charter, titled 'the *Umma* project', re-adopted the goal of 'establishing an Islamic state' as a local priority and rejected all other terms (democracy, secularism, civil state, nationalism) as incompatible with Islam.[16]

However, this charter, replete with official positions and normative provisions, did not last long after the Ahrar joined the fighting against IS in early 2014. Under the weight of internal debates and the presence of Arab and regional pressure, it abandoned the charter. Instead, it adopted a 'Revolutionary Code of Conduct' (May 2014), stipulating respect for human rights within the framework of the state of justice, law and freedoms and the maintenance of the diverse Syrian fabric with all its ethnic and confessional strata – and leaving the decision on the system of government, after the fall of the regime, to the Syrian people.[17]

Two Competing Currents

In late 2014, the movement faced an existential test after the death of its founder and thirteen senior and mid-ranking leaders (9 September 2014) in an explosion at the Safar headquarters in rural Idlib, during a meeting of the movement's Shura Council.[18] Despite the impact of the massacre, the movement succeeded in absorbing the first shock, and a solid organisational structure and unified legal position contributed to the rapid reconstitution of what remained of the Shura Council just one day later. Hashim al-Sheikh, known as 'Abu Jaber', was elected as the general commander of the movement. The 'massacre' and its victims were transformed into a heroic legend, evoking victimhood in life and death to solidify its internal structure.

At the beginning of his leadership, Abu Jaber took the same approach as his predecessor regarding the gradual move away from Salafi jihadism. The adoption of the slogan 'a people's revolution' rather than the '*Umma* project' was the first significant step towards a new flavour of political discourse, with new and unfamiliar expressions (such as 'a government emanating from the people', 'a mutual contract between the government and the people' and 'a constitution that guarantees the participation of religious minorities') as was evident in Abu Jaber's interview with *Al-Jazeera* in April 2015.[19] The movement also tried to open up to public opinion and decision-makers in the West. Labib al-Nahhas, a former member of the Political Bureau, published an article in the *Washington Post* in which he presented the movement as a 'moderate Sunni' party fighting IS, a party that 'believes in moderation and seeks to play a positive role in a pluralistic state that balances the legitimate aspirations of the majority in Syria and the protection of minority rights'.[20] In another article in the British newspaper *The Daily Telegraph*, al-Nahhas described the future strategy of the movement as establishing a 'representative' government for all Syrians, taking into account the identity of the absolute majority.[21] On another level, the movement has been open to discussion with opposition political bodies (the Syrian National Coalition [SNC], the Syrian Interim Government) after years of refusing to recognise or cooperate with them; this has been taken as an indicator of behavioural change.[22] This approach remained prominent until the end of Abu Jaber's term, when internal divisions began to appear under different names, presenting themselves as intellectual disputes but representing a struggle for power and influence within the movement.

Contrary to outward appearances, during his leadership Abu Jaber tightened his grip on the movement by appointing radical figures who held strongly to the movement's Salafi jihadist identity and rejected its liberalisation to important leadership positions. These figures include Abu Saleh Tahan, commander-in-chief of the military, and Abu Muhammad al-Sadiq, the senior judicial official (*shar'i 'amm*). While the former leadership enjoyed direct contact with the fighters and took the largest share of funding by virtue of the military effort, some figures such as Labib al-Nahhas were given a degree of relative freedom abroad to present an image of the sort of 'moderate', 'centrist' and 'open' movement on which the West was focusing. Accordingly, two currents have emerged within the movement at that time: a 'conservative' current on the ground represented by the tripartite leadership (Abu Jaber, Abu Saleh, al-Sadiq), and a more 'liberal' (*infitahi*) current abroad, represented by the Political Bureau and the Office of Foreign Relations in Turkey.

With the end of Abu Jaber's term and the election of his deputy Mohannad al-Masri (Abu Yahya al-Hamwi) in September 2015, internal conflict began to rise to the surface.[23] Al-Masri gradually reduced Abu Jaber's power by isolating 'conservative' figures in leadership positions loyal to him before distancing the former leader himself from any real executive role.[24] Abu Jaber and his allies opposed the new leadership by emphasising the movement's Salafi identity, exploiting al-Masri's lack of direct contact with fighters. On the other hand, the émigré (or 'liberal') current hoped that al-Masri would bring about intellectual changes within the movement. Although al-Masri was closer to the latter current, 'the movement did not witness any new intellectual changes in al-Masri's era'.[25] The fear of being outflanked by the other current's discourse and al-Masri's lack of personal charisma prevented this.

Split

Abu Jaber, who established his own personal military force within the movement under the name *Jaysh al-Ahrar* ('Army of Free Men') on 12 December 2016 after being excluded from leadership positions, had every hope of returning to the leadership.[26] But the election of Ali al-Omar as the new leader of the movement – succeeding Mohannad al-Masri, who was able to engineer his succession from within the Shura Council – destroyed all hopes of reducing, and attempts to reduce, internal conflicts. On the justification of the leadership's refusal to integrate with the *Jabhat al-Nusra* ('Nusra Front', JN) within a single military and organisational body, the former tripartite leadership (Abu Jaber, al-Tahan, al-Sadiq) broke away with thirty military and judicial leaders and around 1,500 fighters. The defectors now joined with the Nusra Front in a new organisation named *Hay'at Tahrir al-Sham* ('Committee for Liberation of the Levant', HTS), whose establishment was announced publicly on 9 February 2016, under the leadership of Abu Jaber al-Sheikh.[27]

This new body implicitly regarded *Ahrar al-Sham* as an enemy since it was the only surviving competitor on the Islamist scene, and thus attempted – through leaders who had broken with the movement – to try and turn *Ahrar* fighters against their own leaders, using the sort of outbidding discourse at which jihadist organisations are so fluent. While the *Ahrar* leadership them-selves were focusing on fundamental issues concerning the future of the Syrian conflict, especially after the defeat of the opposition in Aleppo and the start of the Astana process under Turkish-Russian-Iranian sponsorship, the dissidents succeeded in creating a gap between the leadership and the fighters. The fight-ers refused to carry out instructions from the leadership to counter the attack led by JN against the *Ahrar* in mid-2017, leading to the loss of most of the regions under their control along with the Bab al-Hawa border crossing (the most important strategic point of the areas under opposition control).

Jaysh al-Islam: From Salafism to Free Syrian Army

Jaysh al-Islam (Army of Islam, AoI,) belongs to the so-called 'Scholarly Salafist' (*al-salafiyya al-'ilmiyya*) current, which originated in Syria in the late 1950s.[28] This current has historically been politically quietist, emphasising moral and religious education. Its founding father – in its Wahhabi form – is generally held to have been Nasiruddin al-Albani. Al-Albani's students Sheikh Abdul Qader Arnaout and Mohammad 'Aid al-Abbasi were active in the Shari'a colleges and mosques of Damascus. They succeeded in finding a foothold in an environment full of contradictory currents and schools of thought.[29] The father of AoI's founder Zahran Alloush, Sheikh Abdullah Mohammed Alloush, was one of the most important Scholarly Salafist preachers in rural Damascus, particularly in Douma, Syria's only Hanbali stronghold.[30]

The Revolutionary Test

The revolution was a 'test' of Scholarly Salafism in Syria, whose sheikhs and preachers had to provide pressing and urgent answers to the questions that it posed outside the principles and boundaries of their previous activities. In a time of widespread revolutionary foment, it was no longer attractive or con-vincing to define it exclusively as a matter of religious education. Scholarly Salafism's refusal to engage in politics and political work, and its belief that to rebel against a ruler was impermissible, were no longer realistic in communi-ties that had been politicised horizontally and vertically during the revolu-tion. As a result, it reassessed its position in politics, joining opposition to the Syrian regime and citing religious justifications for the deposition – in the Syrian case only – of what it called the 'infidel ruler' (*al-hakim al-kafir*).[31]

With the support of Salafi clerical circles in Douma in which he was a familiar figure, on 14 September 2011 Zahran Alloush announced the establishment of the 'Brigade of Islam' (*Liwa' al-Islam*), which at its founding consisted of a small group of eager non-ideological youth (fourteen people), who followed Alloush as their source of ideological and financial support.[32] It was not long before dozens of smaller national battalions joined the Brigade of Islam in both eastern and western Ghouta and the southern suburbs of Damascus, bringing the total number after the first restructuring in mid-2012 to some 1,500 fighters.[33]

The Brigade of Islam initially declined to launch its own political project, instead focusing on organising military action while restricting the intellectual aspect to the narrow Salafi preaching elite.[34] By emphasising the popular dimension ideologically and addressing local communities in simple, easy-to-understand language suitable to their situation, they created a 'solid' popular base for the Brigade of Islam, particularly in Douma and its environs. They also earned their leader Zahran Alloush a high standing among his fighters, who he fought alongside, avoiding the dilemma of the hidden commander addressing fighters from above through direct announcements or audio messages.[35] However, the intellectual and ideological fluidity associated with the 'populism' of the leader also led him to political sectarianism.[36] In other words, in its early days the Brigade was an extension of its leader in both discourse and praxis.

Beyond rhetorical 'populism' and intellectual fluidity, Zahran Alloush aspired to reproduce the experience of the Lebanese party of Hezbollah.[37] The most obvious points of similarity are the desire to build a micro-state with administrative and organisational independence from its surroundings, the discourse of sectarian injustice, and the symbolic standing and jurisprudential authority (*marja'iyya*) of the leader.

The Test of Politics

The existence of a solid intellectual core based on regional popularity, in addition to organisational cohesion, helped AoI to carry out bold changes on the scale of other Islamist factions without fear of disintegration or internal dissent. Alloush was able to convince his fighters and followers that his decisions were reasonable, even if wrong,[38] and to find Islamic legal justification for them from the Salafist leadership in Douma.[39]

Fighting IS at the start of 2014 was AoI's first step towards entering politics. The old dispute between salafism and jihadism based upon accusations of being 'Kharijites'[40] (equivalent to 'heresy' in the Sunni world) served as a justification for confronting IS, eradicating it from eastern Ghouta, and isolating it within the southern neighbourhoods of Damascus.[41] AoI acted as an impenetrable barrier between IS and the capital, which placed it in the spotlight in the West as an organised force near Damascus that could be a partner in the fight against IS. Indeed, it opened channels of communication between the US and British officials, which effectively granted AoI limited military support from the United States.[42] Alloush subsequently realised the difficulty of continuing his experiment with an isolationist approach based on a totalitarian ideology centring on the goal of implementing Shari'a. This approach provided no satisfactory answers to questions of governance and the state and forbade cooperation with other political and military forces.[43]

Alloush's visit to Istanbul (April 2015) marked a new approach in terms of political practice. On the one hand, he showed a new openness to other political and military opposition groups, including competitors and those explicitly against him, and committed to their collective stance on various political and military issues pertaining to the Syrian crisis. On the other, he was also more open to the outside world. In this context there was a qualitative shift in AoI's discourse, which emerged in its leader's interviews with American and Western newspapers. It gave up its old populist rhetoric ('fight the Zoroastrians [i.e. Iranians] and the Shi'a', 'disregard democracy' and 'establish an Umayyad [i.e. Syria-based] Caliphate'), and spoke about the existence of a calculated plan complying with the need for security and order, the protection of public facilities and state institutions, and the right of the people to choose the form of their governmental system and state. Showing a more sophisticated position than the other Islamist battalions, he expressed his desire to be part of a 'Syrian army that takes on responsibility for security and order and disarmament and fights IS' ideological project, and the Iranian project, until they are expelled from Syria'.[44]

As a culmination of this approach, AoI was entered into the Syrian opposition's High Negotiations Committee (HNC) to represent it in the negotiating process. Its founding statement (10 December 2015) affirmed the establishment of a democratic, pluralistic civil state based on the principle of equal citizenship and human rights. *Jaysh al-Islam* made no specific demands of its own during the negotiations, except to maintain the constitutional clauses regarding the Arab and Muslim identity of Syria.[45]

The Sham Legion: Multiple Identities and Changing Alliances

It is difficult for scholars to deal with the Sham Legion separately from the Syrian MB for several reasons, including its leaders' (previous) ideological and organisational affiliation with the Brotherhood (Nazir al-Hakim, Haitham Rahma, Monzer Saras) and the support it enjoys from that organisation,[46] which has made it the best-financed and best-armed group relative to its numbers in comparison with other factions.

The Dialectic of the Relationship with the Syrian MB

The Syrian MB, as a result of its weakness and limited activity within Syria, was unable to adopt a clear strategy towards the revolution and the regime. However, a more daring faction in both its intellectual discourse and political ambition emerged from the Brotherhood and developed independently. A 'new Islamic youth' emerged from the Brotherhood's families abroad, which were very active at the beginning of the revolution, especially on social media. Elsewhere, former members of the group tried to form a bloc outside the framework of the Brotherhood but in coordination with it. It was in this context that in mid-2011 the establishment of a political body called the 'National Coalition for the Syrian Revolution' (NCSR) was announced, a body dominated by Islamists from Brotherhood families and headed by Nazir al-Hakim, a former member of the group.[47] Likewise, in August 2011 another political body was established, the 'National Action Group' (NAG). The NAG was led by figures from the (ostensibly more moderate) 'Aleppo faction' of the Brotherhood, most notably Ahmad Ramadan and Obeida Nahhas. In cooperation with Islamic academic figures (Imad al-Din al-Rashid and Abdul Rahman al-Haj), it sought to establish a body representative of the Syrian revolution under the name 'Syrian National Council'.[48]

All this activity was a subject of great discussion among the Syrian opposition. The opinions of interested parties and researchers were divided into two trends. The first saw it from the perspective of the 'generational divides' often noted in the study of Islamist movements; this tendency is represented by Rafael Laufer, who considered it a new movement led by Brotherhood 'youth' resentful of traditional sheikhs and aspiring to play a future political role via the revolution. The second, represented by figures like Aron Lund, saw it as an extension of the internal policy of the group which wanted from the outset to lead revolutionary and oppositional action without openly adopting it.[49]

A Revolutionary 'Democratic' Organisation

The Civilian Protection Commission (CPC), established on January 2012, is considered the first organised incarnation, or 'revolutionary incarnation' of *Faylaq al-Sham*. As indicated by its name, the CPC's founding reflected the end of the stage of peaceful protest in the Syrian Revolution, and the beginning of armed action. Accordingly, the Commission – headed by Haitham Rahma – presented itself as a revolutionary political-military body whose aim was to provide financial and military support to the battalions fighting under the name of the Free Syrian Army.[50] Early in its establishment, the Commission tried to differentiate itself from Islamist factions and put forward a revolutionary identity focusing on the national 'inclusive' dimension of the Syrian revolution and its slogans of freedom, dignity and the 'democratic state'. It thus expanded its political and military activity within the opposition Syrian National Coalition (SNC) and its military councils.[51] Despite their Islamist intellectual tradition, the leaders of the CPC were keen to avoid the religious-ideological nature that began to dominate armed action at the time. Moreover, compared to the rest of the factions, they took a bold stance against jihadi groups that included 'non-Syrian fighters' in direct reference to the JN.[52] However, the CPC did not achieve its desired goal of providing a political umbrella for civil-military action within a well-coordinated framework that might have produced a military leadership representing both the armed revolution and opposition political bodies. This was for several reasons, such as the loss of its local popularity, its ambiguous relationship with the Syrian MB and its selective way of providing military support.

The 'revolutionary' identity that the CPC projected during 2012 and 2013 was not so much an authentic part of the thinking and convictions of its leaders as much as it was a pragmatic response to the domestic and international context. Faced with this reality, especially after the failure of

Geneva 2 to find a political solution to the Syrian crisis, the Commission began to look for another way outside its revolutionary path, choosing to put greater emphasis on their Islamist identity – especially after absorbing *Hay'at Duru' al-Thawra* ('Shields of the Revolution Committee'). A new name was required better suited to this orientation, hence the rebranding as *Faylaq al-Sham*.

Faylaq al-Sham was established in Aleppo on 9 April 2014 from some nineteen brigades and battalions that had been operating under the CPC banner in the governorates of Aleppo, Idlib and Hama. In order to avoid repeating the mistakes of the CPC, officers who had defected from the regime army were appointed to the military leadership, most notably Yasser Abdel Rahim, who served as the military commander. These officers set about creating a 'disciplined' military model based on rules similar to those found in regime's army: focusing on the quality of fighters rather than quantity, providing them with sophisticated weapons, forming a Shari'a legal office to prepare them ideologically, organising fighters into fast-moving units and forming a 'central force' like the special forces able to move according to demand.[53]

In a subsequent transformation, *Faylaq al-Sham* adopted an Islamist approach in its rhetoric, symbolism and political alliances. Many years after its adoption by the CPC, it abandoned the flag of the revolution and replaced it with a white Islamist flag emblazoned with the declaration of faith (*la ilaha illa'llah*, 'there is no God but God'). Likewise, it came to issue statements unilaterally and separately from other FSA factions, flavouring them with Islamic vocabulary and Quranic verses.[54] Unlike the Civil Protection Commission, which refused to cooperate with jihadist groups and issued statements against both the JN and IS, on 30 April 2015 *Faylaq al-Sham* entered into a strategic military alliance with JN and *Ahrar al-Sham* in what is known as *Jaysh al-Fateh* ('Army of Conquest-AoC'), after the constituent factions succeeded in gaining control of the city of Idlib in northern Syria.[55] This alliance continued for about a year and a half despite the great ideological gap between *Faylaq al-Sham* – dominated by elements of popular religiosity close to the Brotherhood's school of thought – and the other factions in Jaysh al-Fateh, which belong to the Salafi jihadist movement. *Faylaq al-Sham* announced its withdrawal from this alliance on 3 January 2016 on the justification that with the defeat of regime forces in Idlib, AoC's mission was complete and there was a need to devote all efforts to supporting opposition forces in Aleppo, facing a fierce attack from the regime and its allied militias.[56]

Faylaq al-Sham passed itself off as an Islamist group in both discourse and praxis, arguably for functional purposes. The aim was to find common denominators with the Salafist factions to work together towards a common goal with Arab and regional forces (Qatar, Turkey and Saudi Arabia) who had agreed at that time in 2015 to provide the opposition with the military support necessary to expel the regime's forces from the northern provinces, upset the military balance in favour of the opposition, and stymie direct and indirect Iranian military intervention in Syria – similar to developments in Yemen after the Saudis' Operation Decisive Storm. And this was indeed what happened in mid-2015, pushing Russia to intervene to save the regime.[57]

With AoC's mission in Idlib complete, *Faylaq al-Sham* began to step back from its Islamic persona, returning to its 'revolutionary' identity both intellectually and in its behaviour. After its withdrawal from AoC it joined the Aleppo Operational Command (*Ghurfat 'Amaliyyat Halab*) which comprised the FSA battalions active in Aleppo. *Faylaq al-Sham* refused to join its former allies (the JN and Ahrar al-Sham) in their own coordinating body (the Ansar al-Shari'a Command). Instead, it readopted the flag of the revolution before joining the Military Operations Centre (MOC) in 2017 and participating in the negotiation process in Astana and Geneva.[58]

Determinants and Mechanisms of the Transformation Process

One clear conclusion that can be drawn from the experience of these three armed Islamist organisations is the absence of any one single variable or sole determinant leading to these changes. Rather, there is a set of interrelated variables, which this chapter has attempted to trace and deconstruct. These determinants can be divided as follows:

Internal Determinants

By this, I mean factors associated with the movement itself and its interactions that affect in some way the direction of its members' behaviour and the coalescence of their intellectual vision. The most prominent in the Syrian case-studies are explained below.

Charismatic Leadership

The leader occupies a great place in radical movements established during times of war and civil strife, sometimes to the point that these movements are conflated with their leaders and vice versa. The sudden absence of the leader may thus lead to the collapse of the movement or the decline of its influence. The Syrian case is full of many examples of radical Islamist movements that have been completely disrupted by the killing of their leaders. With *Ahrar al-Sham*, the movement's leader and founder, Hassan Abboud, played a pivotal role in the course of its transformations until his assassination, starting with the dissociation from global Salafi jihadism and ending with his central role in the transition from combat battalions to a movement presenting more realistic political visions and programmes. As a result of weak leadership, or lack of consensus on the choice of the leader after his assassination *Ahrar al-Sham* went through a series of splits that eventually led to its easy defeat or 'humiliation' by the JN. *Ahrar*'s leadership realised this point and addressed it by entering into prisoner exchange negotiations with the regime, which eventually led to the release of Hassan Soufan from Sednaya prison. He took command of the movement in August 2017 until March 2019, and managed to reorganise it, making bold decisions such as the declaration of *Ahrar al-Sham* as a 'revolutionary' movement and the adoption of the revolutionary flag for the first time, without this resulting in a major conflict.

The same applies to Zahran Alloush, commander and founder of Jaysh al-Islam, regarding the identity and nature of his movement and his role in the developments that have taken place in its political and intellectual trajectory over the past years. However, the deaths of Abboud and Alloush did not lead to the collapse or disintegration of the two movements but created a dynamic which led to the emergence of hidden conflicts and clashes, resulting in the division of the movement as happened with *Ahrar al-Sham* and the decrease of its military power as was the case with *Jaysh al-Islam*. As for *Faylaq al-Sham*, which was also known for its leaders (Nazir al-Hakim and Haitham Rahma), its leadership were behind all of the changes since its establishment as the CPC in early 2012: its adoption of a revolutionary identity, its posing as an Islamist group to humour the Salafist 'high tide' in the revolution and its ultimate return to a revolutionary character after its withdrawal from *Jaysh al-Fateh* and its participation in the political negotiation process.[59]

Internal Interactions: Conflicts and Balances

Comparing the three movements, there is not much information about the internal interactions within the *Faylaq* and the *Jaysh* factions (especially after the death of Alloush) and the impact of this on their overall transformational trajectory. It was, however, a major determinant in the transformations within *Ahrar al-Sham*. The struggle over the leadership of the movement and the new leaders' domination of the decision-making process created confrontational dynamics between the two rival factions, factions that have progressively positioned themselves within a radical-moderate intellectual dichotomy originating not within the movement but as one of the tools of the conflict. This ended with the partial division of the movement and the exit of the so-called 'conservative current' in February 2017.

Generational Divisions

The *Ahrar al-Sham* and *Jaysh al-Islam* movements, their cadres and their leaders are all considered part of the new generation.[60] Hence, there is no significant difference between the temporal age (the age of the movement) and the generational age (the succession of leaders)[61] in these two movements. The establishment of the Civilian Protection Commission (2012) and *Faylaq al-Sham* (2014), however, did to some extent reflect a generational polarisation between the Syrian MB sheikhs who dominated the leadership of the group and the subsequent generations that had grown up outside Syria. The latter exploited the opportunity of the revolution to engage in political activity independently or without direct organisational affiliation with the Brotherhood, as is the case with Haitham Rahma and Nazir al-Hakim, the founders of *Faylaq al-Sham*.[62] Their freedom from organisational ties, and their eagerness to assume a prominent political position in the revolution and the Syrian opposition, contributed to their adoption a pragmatic reformist approach that had a profound impact on the intellectual transformation of *Faylaq al-Sham* and on the nature of its political practice, as well as on its relationship with other factions with their differing intellectual and ideological orientations. The same applies to its social base, which extends throughout the areas of northern Syria outside the control of the regime.

External Determinants

By this I mean the factors related to the external environment in which these factions operate, and which played a role in shaping their transformations during the timeframe of this study. They can be divided into three contextual levels as follows:

A local context: The expansion of armed action placed various administrative burdens on Syrian Islamist groups, who were left to make up for the absence of the state. They were thus forced to interact closely with local communities and identify their demands and priorities and compare them with their own current and future goals. It is true that the inhabitants of the regions rebelling against the Syrian regime (Damascus countryside, Hama, Idlib and Aleppo) formed a local base for the armed Islamist factions and influenced their ideas and views. Due to daily communication and the differences between theory and practice, this influence was reciprocal in that it pushed the Islamists to set out their intellectual and political views based on what is existing and not what should be existing.[63]

A regional context: Since the spread of armed resistance to the regime's forces, armed action of opposition has become increasingly dependent on the regional and international forces supporting it. This has given these forces the ability to exert pressure and influence on the Syrian political and armed opposition, including the Islamist factions. The Revolutionary Code of Conduct, which was signed by all Syrian armed factions, including Ahrar al-Sham, and includes a new and more flexible political language compared to the 'Umma Project' charter, remains one of the most striking examples of the regional context's influence on intellectual and behavioural transformations within Ahrar al-Sham and Jaysh al-Islam.[64] Similarly, continued Turkish pressure was one of the factors that led armed Islamist organisations – except Ahrar al-Sham – to participate in the Astana negotiations after the fall of Aleppo in late 2016, despite the fact that these negotiations were overseen and dominated by Russia.[65] Faylaq al-Sham's political tone, on the other hand, was always kept in line with that of their supporters, and they willingly showed great flexibility in changing their behaviour to correspond with their supporters' positions.[66]

In short, the abovementioned Islamist organisations found themselves forced either by their need for support or by their geographical proximity to broker an unequal relationship with the regional powers. This gave the regional powers the ability to influence them. In the same context, other interactions in the region associated with the Syrian crisis have had a relatively significant impact on the Syrian Islamist factions, especially after the military coup in Egypt in 2013, when the aspirations and goals of the Islamists collided with the interests of some regional countries active in the crisis. This led them to reconsider some of their behaviours and ideas to avoid entering into a marginal conflict that distracts them from their real struggle with the regime.[67]

An international context: The international context is influential in two main ways. The first relates to incentives granted by the international forces – the most important being military support – and the second to restrictions they may impose. Western support is a criterion for classifying factions as 'moderate' with military and logistical support from both the international coordination bodies based in Turkey (MoM)[68] and Jordan (MOC), as distinct from other factions that are not supported but not included in the list of terrorist organisations.[69] Until the end of 2016, all three factions fell under the second classification, which does not qualify for qualitative military support, prompting some, especially *Faylaq al-Sham* and Jaysh al-Islam, to make changes to their discourse and practice to attract supporters of international forces to cooperate with them and provide military support. *Faylaq al-Sham*'s withdrawal from *Jaysh al-Fateh* (Idlib), the largest alliance of armed Salafi factions in Syria, can be understood as the step that allowed them to enter the MOC.

The change in *Jaysh al-Islam*'s discourse occurred in the same context, as it sought to present itself as a party that believed in 'pluralism' and that could be a partner against IS and part of a future Syrian national army. By contrast, the restrictions imposed by international forces on Islamist factions are of great importance in pushing them to make changes to suit reality. For example, since its establishment, *Ahrar al-Sham* has been preoccupied with the avoidance of international classification or being placed on the terrorism list like the JN or IS.[70] Within this framework, the movement has always emphasised its 'national' affiliation and its break with internationalist orientations, which undoubtedly served as an entryway to the process of transformation witnessed by the movement.

Intra-Jihadists Conflict and Rivalry

Radical movements usually define themselves as antagonistic, whether in terms of intellectual propositions or political perceptions, hence the 'others' do not matter much. On the other hand, they attach great importance to models that are intellectually and ideologically similar that force them to compete for their social base. Over the past few years, the Syrian conflict has been fertile ground for intellectual and behavioural developments among Islamist movements, which had direct consequences for the process of transformation and its outcomes – especially ideologically.[71] Since its establishment, rivalry has been the most prominent determinant controlling the relationship between the JN and Ahrar al-Sham. This rivalry went as far as armed clashes and deadly confrontations.

Ahrar al-Sham has always distinguished itself from traditional jihadism. Until the end of 2012, its political discourse continued to be influenced by Salafi jihadism, one of the movement's tools in the face of JN's attempts to upstage them. From this point, *Ahrar al-Sham* was unable to affirm this distinction until after the establishment of the Syrian Islamic Front in late 2012. The SIF was presented to fighters as an alternative to al-Qaeda and the FSA, which maintained the major aims while simultaneously taking into account actual conditions on the ground. This granted the leadership of the movement greater confidence and a wider margin of freedom to show greater flexibility at the level of intellectual debate and behaviour.[72] But the alternative model presented by the movement was shaken after its 2014 defeat by IS, who successfully outflanked them and neutralised many of their fighters.[73] In order to counter this, the movement issued the *Umma* Project charter in cooperation with other Islamist factions. As noted above, this was viewed as a retreat from the revisions and the transformations witnessed by the movement.

In contrast to Ahrar, the jihadi inter-generational rivalry gave *Jaysh al-Islam* a positive impetus to draw closer to the revolutionary path, since its leaders have been convinced that dialogue with IS is futile. *Jaysh al-Islam* moved towards opposition with IS early on, adopting the same tactic of ideological outbidding by describing ISIS fighters as Kharijites. They then set about eradicating them completely from the Ghouta and the surroundings of Damascus, which provided them with incentives to open up to the opposition and to foreign states.[74]

In a similar context, the establishment of *Faylaq al-Sham* reflected Islamist-jihadist rivalries. The decline in the presence of the FSA and the increasing domination of the armed opposition movement by Islamists was one of the factors that pushed the Civilian Protection Commission to abandon its 'revolutionary identity' and replace it with an 'Islamist' one, allowing it to enter *Jaysh al-Fateh* at the end of 2014.[75]

Conclusion: Dimensions of Collective Transformations

Syrian armed Islamist movements went through complex processes of ideological, behavioural and organisational transformations that led to the following fundamental changes. These transformations have been determined by four main variables: charismatic leadership, internal interaction within the group, intra-jihadists conflict and rivalry, and the external political environment.

The ideological changes in *Jaysh al-Islam* and *Ahrar al-Sham* were more radical than those of *Faylaq al-Sham*, whose own ideological transformations can be understood within the framework of its leaders' political pragmatism rather than profound ideational transformations.

After becoming involved in politics, *Jaysh al-Islam* joined the HNC and participated in the political negotiation process. It adopted a bold new vision and ideas accepting the civil state and a democratic system of government.[76] Indeed, for the last three years its leadership have been consistently promoting an alternative model that sees the AKP experience in Turkey as a source of inspiration to be applied in Syria, with minor differences that would give Islamic law a greater role and importance than it has in the Turkish case.[77] In addition, since participating in the negotiating process, it has officially adopted the revolutionary flag after disregarding it for about six years. The only thing distinguishing *Jaysh al-Islam* from FSA units today is its name.[78] Nonetheless, these transformations did not prevent Russia from continuing its military operations and ultimately defeating *Jaysh al-Islam* in April 2018, forcing it to sign a document of surrender guaranteeing its transfer from its stronghold of Douma to the Euphrates Shield areas controlled by the opposition and the Turkish army. This has plunged *Jaysh al-Islam* into a maze of division, with most of its political leaders resigning, the last of them being Mohammad Alloush, the former representative of the delegation of the HNC.

After long discussions, *Ahrar al-Sham* also arrived at a conciliatory understanding of its intellectual transformations, preserving its original slogans and its ultimate goal of establishing the Islamic state as a fixed ideology for the movement. However, its implementation is no longer considered a priority, and is made dependent on social acceptance of the idea. In this case, the movement is willing and able, with other models, to accept governance and authority provided that it guarantees public freedoms and the right to preach in society, and that its constitution does not contradict the principles and values of the Shari'a.[79]

In terms of behavioural transformations, the revolution forced Syrian armed Islamist movements to turn their political conceptions for the first time into solid organisational frameworks or military-political blocs providing a comprehensive vision for the future. In other words, while the revolutionary frame of most protesters and Syrian opposition bodies was based on a dichotomy of 'democratic' and 'authoritarian', most Islamists tended to frame their collective action within different polar narratives (Sunni/Alawite), which justified using violent means and waging war against the 'infidel' and corrupt regime. Although this narrative was initially put forward as 'sacred' or 'Quranic' and taken to reflect irreversible distinctions between 'us' and 'them', many event-initiated and agent-initiated frame transformations have since occurred, making the previous frame irrelevant to changing political circumstances.

In terms of organisational transformations, engagement in politics and political activity led to remarkable developments in the organisational and administrative structure of the majority of the armed Islamist movements, especially *Ahrar al-Sham* and *Jaysh al-Islam*. *Ahrar al-Sham* began its revolutionary journey as an armed group, and soon transformed into a movement with a bureaucratic administration, social services, political and media branches. In the same way, *Jaysh al-Islam* began its journey by establishing an armed group of just fourteen fighters. It later transformed into battalions and eventually into an 'army' of 10,000 fighters. The organisation ultimately held sway over the lives of around one million people crowded into the cities and villages of eastern Ghouta before its military defeat by the Russian-led forces. This defeat is likely to have a major role in shaping the characteristics and the transformations of Syrian armed Islamist movements.

Notes

1. Lisa Wedeen, *Ambiguities of Domination: Politics, Rhetoric, and Symbols in Contemporary Syria* (Chicago: The University of Chicago Press, 1999), p. 32.
2. Raymond Hinnebusch, 'Syria: From 'Authoritarian Upgrading' to Revolution?', *International Affairs*, vol. 88, no. 1 (2012), pp. 95–7.
3. Khader Zakaria, al-Mu'aradat al-Hizbiyya at-Taqlidiyya fi Suriya: al-Mawaqif wa'l-Ittijahat', in: *Khalfiyyat ath-Thawra: Dirasat Suriya [Backgrounds of Revolution: Syrian Studies]* (Doha and Beirut: The Arab Centre for Research and Policy Studies, 2013), p. 257.
4. Azmi Bishara, *Suriya: Darb al-Alam Nahw al-Hurriyya: Muhawala fi't-Tarikh ar-Rahin* (Doha and Beirut: The Arab Centre for Research and Policy Studies, 2013), p. 44.
5. For a longer discussion of this topic, see: Hamzah Almustafa, *al-Majal al-'Amm al-Iftiradi fi'th-Thawra as-Suriyya: al-Khasa'is, al-Ittijahat, Aliyyat San' ar-Ra'y al-'Amm [The Virtual Public Sphere in the Syrian Revolution]* (Doha and Beirut: The Arab Centre for Research and Policy Studies, 2012), pp. 14–15.
6. For more details see: Omar Ashour, 'Post-jihadism: Libya and the Global Transformations of Armed Islamist Movements', *Terrorism and Political Violence*, vol. 23, no. 3 (2011), pp. 379–80.
7. 'Hal Ataka Hadith al-Kata'ib', *YouTube*, 4/1/2012, accessed on 3/4/2017, at: https://goo.gl/zPMFQ5.
8. Guido Steinberg, 'Ahrar al-Sham: The "Syrian Taliban"', German Institute for International and Security Affairs, *SWP Comment*, 27/5/2016, accessed on 10/4/2017, at: https://goo.gl/TvuxvR
9. Personal interview with Eyad Shaar, Adviser to the Political Bureau and its former military commander, Turkey, 25/2/2017.
10. For the term and its definitions see: Ashour.
11. Personal interview with Eyad Shaar, Adviser to the Political Bureau and its former military commander, Turkey, 25/2/2017.
12. Policy Analysis Unit, 'Tatawwur al-Mawqif al-Amriki min an-Nizam as-Suri: Min Da'wat al-Islah ila't-Tafawud', Arab Center for Research and Policy Studies, *Policy Analysis*, 2/4/2015, accessed on 3/4/2017, at: https://goo.gl/MnVzie

13. 'Bayan al-'Alan 'an Harakat Ahrar ash-Sham al-Islamiyya', *YouTube*, 31/1/2013, accessed on 2/4/2017, at: https://goo.gl/iLN5Ep.

14. Personal interview with Ammar al-Ahmad, former fighter in 'Ahrar al-Sham', Turkey, 1/3/2017.

15. Personal interview with Ahrar leader (did not wish to reveal his name), Turkey, 26/2/2017.

16. To read the full *Umma* Project charter see: al-Jabha al-Islamiyya, 'Mashru'at Umma: an-Nass al-Kamil li-Mithaq al-Jabha al-Islamiyya', 26/11/2013, accessed on 10/4/2017, at: https://goo.gl/JvJ5ww.

17. Ratib Sha'bo, 'Harakat Ahrar al-Sham al-Islamiyya: Bayn al-Jihadiyya wa'l-Ikhwaniyya', *Democratic Republic Studies Center*, 15/4/2016, accessed on 10/4/2017, at: https://goo.gl/i95rpb

18. Personal interview with Abdulrahman al-Kilani, Syrian activist and director of the film 'Ahrar al-Sham', in Safar headquarters, Turkey, 28/2/2017.

19. 'Liqa' al-Yawm – Hashim al-Sheikh: Iran Intashalat an-Nizam as-Suri', *YouTube*, 17/4/2015, accessed on 3/4/2017, at: https://goo.gl/kZNEAN

20. Labib Al-Nahhas, 'The Deadly Consequences of Mislabeling Syria's Revolutionaries', *Washington Post*, 10/7/2015, accessed on 3/4/2016, https://goo.gl/hwWvvN

21. Labib Al-Nahhas, '"I'm a Syrian and I Fight ISIL Every Day. It Will Take More than Bombs from the West to Defeat this Menace"', *The Daily Telegraph*, 21/7/2015, accessed on 3/4/2016, at: https://goo.gl/ZBmHUc

22. Personal interview with Burhan Ghalyoun, Syrian thinker and previous President of the Syrian National Opposition Council, Doha, 25/12/2016.

23. Abu Yahya al-Hamawi, a leader of Ahrar al-Sham, *al-Hayaa*, 14/9/2015, accessed on 2/4/2017, at: https://goo.gl/fFccgh

24. 'Ahrar al-Sham: Taghyirat w Tahawwulat Shar'iyya', *al-Sharq al-Awsat*, 20/6/2016, issue 13719; and personal interview with Ahmad Moussa.

25. Personal interview with Mohammed Jalal.

26. Personal interview with Osama Abu Zeid.

27. Personal interview with Eyad Shaar; and personal interview with Mohammed Jalal.

28. Hamzah Almostafa, 'The al-Nusra Front: From Formation to Dissension', Arab Center for Research & Policy Studies, *Policy Analysis* (February 2014), pp. 1–2.

29. Ibid.

30. Personal interview with Mohamed Bayrakdar, head of the Jaysh al-Islam political bureau, Turkey, 23/2/2017

31. Policy Analysis Unit, 'Jaysh al-Islam: al-Bahth 'an Dawr fi Mustaqbal Suriya', Arab Center for Research and Policy Studies, *Case Analysis*, 7/7/2015, accessed on 9/4/2017, at: https://bit.ly/33SKoW9

32. Personal interview with Mohamed Bayrakdar.

33. 'Jaysh al-Islam fi Sutur', *official website of Jaysh al-Islam*, accessed on 9/4/2014, https://goo.gl/mC8QaJ

34. Personal interview with Islam Alloush.

35. Skype interview with Ahmad Hussam (*nom de guerre*), one of the fighters of Jaysh al-Islam, 5/3/2017.

36. "Awdat al-Majd al-Umawi ila Rubu' ash-Sham', *YouTube*, 4/1/2015, accessed on 9/4/2016, at: https://goo.gl/vZDZyL

37. Personal interview with a leader of Jaysh al-Islam (preferred not to disclose his name), Turkey, 23/4/2017.

38. Personal interview with Mohamed Bayrakdar.

39. Personal interview with Ahmad Abazid.

40. According to Oxford Bibliographies, the Kharijites (Arabic: *khawarij*; sing. *khariji*) were the first identifiable sect of Islam. Their identity emerged as followers of Muhammad attempted to determine the extent to which one could deviate from ideal norms of behaviour and still be called Muslim. The extreme Kharijite position was that Muslims who commit grave sins effectively reject their religion, entering the ranks of apostates, and therefore deserve capital punishment. This position was considered excessively restrictive by the majority of Muslims, as well as by moderate Kharijites, who held that a professed Muslim could not be declared an unbeliever (*kafir*).

41. Hamzah Almostafa, 'Ab'ad min Mukhayyam al-Yarmuk', *al-Arabi al-Jadid*, 21/4/2015, accessed on 10/4/2017 at: https://goo.gl/eeC1uT

42. Personal interview with a leader of Jaysh al-Islam (did not give his name), Turkey, 27/2/2017.

43. Ibid.

44. Policy Analysis Unit, 'Jaysh al-Islam', pp. 11–12.

45. Phone interview with Riyad Hijab, 10/4/2017.

46. Phone interview with Haitham Rahma, 13/4/2017.

47. Aron Lund, 'Struggling to Adapt: The Muslim Brotherhood in a New Syria', *Carnegie Middle East Center*, 7/5/2013, accessed on 13/4/2017, at: https://bit.ly/303GOr3

48. Personal interview with Abdulrahman al-Hajj.

49. Lund.

50. Phone interview with Haitham Rahma.
51. Ibid.
52. 'Hay'at Himayat al-Madaniyyin al-Muqarraba min al-Ikhwan al-Muslimin Tutalib al-Muqatilin al-Ajanib bi'r-Rahil,', *al-Quds al-Arabi*, 10/1/2014, accessed on 28/4/2017, at: https://bit.ly/3hYPllf
53. Phone interview with Ibrahim Abd al-Jabbar, a Faylaq al-Sham Central Forces fighter, 10/4/2017.
54. Personal follow-up by the student.
55. 'Jaysh al-Fatah', *al-Jazeera net*, 30/4/2015, accessed on 28/4/2016 at: https://goo.gl/pEkcKU
56. Anas al-Kurdi, 'Suriya: 'Faylaq ash-Sham' yansahibu min 'Jaysh al-Fatah' li-Da'm Halab', *al-Araby al-Jadid*, 3/1/2016, accessed on 28/4/2017, at: https://goo.gl/kFwT5Q.
57. Will Todman, 'Gulf States' Policies on Syria', *Center for Strategic and International Studies*, 18/10/2016, accessed on 24/9/2020, at: https://bit.ly/33TJRDj
58. Personal interview with Osama Abu Zeid.
59. Skype interview with Mohammed al-Dogheim.
60. Ahmad Abazid, 'Abu Khalid as-Suri: al-Jil al-Awwal fi Muwajahat al-Inhiraf al-Akhir', *Zaman al-Wasl*, 26/4/2014, accessed on 26/4/2017, at: https://goo.gl/rPCJ82
61. Yumna Soliman, 'al-Bunya al-Mu'assasiyya li'l-Ikhwan al-Muslimin: Iqtirab Tahlili', *Egyptian Institute for Political and Strategic Studies*, 4/2/2014, accessed on 26/4/2017, at: https://bit.ly/2EBqfer
62. Lund.
63. Personal interview with Ahmad Moussa.
64. Personal interview with Ahmad Abazid.
65. Personal interview with Osama Abu Zeid.
66. 'Ma'rakat 'Dir'a al-Furat' al-Ahdaf wa'l-Su'ubat', *Orient News*, 27/8/2016, accessed on 29/4/2017 at: https://goo.gl/4yNQGh
67. 'Amr Mashwah, 'Ikhwan Suriya: Arba'at Istratijiyaat li-I'adat at-Tamawdu,', *al-Jazeera net*, 5/12/2016, accessed on 24/9/2020, at: https://bit.ly/2RVVfsE
68. Known by its Turkish initials MOM.
69. Policy Analysis Unit, 'Syria's Armed Uprising: The Status Quo', Arab Centre for Research and Policy Studies, *Situation Assessment*, 15/6/2016, accessed on 27/4/2017, at: https://bit.ly/2ECfgl0
70. In the end, the movement commissioned a team of lawyers to defend it before a German local court in the state of Stuttgart, to overturn the ruling

finding it to be a terrorist organisation. Personal interview with Mohammed Jalal.

71. Charles R. Lister, The *Syrian Jihad: Al-Qaeda, the Islamic State and the Evolution of an Insurgency* (Oxford: Oxford University Press, 2015), pp. 260–69.

72. Personal interview with Ahmad Moussa.

73. Personal interview with Ahmad Abazid.

74. Personal interview with Osama Abu Zeid.

75. Personal interview with Mohammed al-Dogheim.

76. Personal interview with Ahmad Abazid.

77. Personal interview with Mohamed Bayrakdar.

78. Personal interview with Islam Alloush.

79. Personal interview with Mohammed Jalal.

5

THE MAHDI ARMY AND THE SADRIST MOVEMENT IN IRAQ: THE STRUGGLE FOR TRANSFORMATION

Haider Saeed

Introduction

The Mahdi Army (*Jaysh al-Mahdi*) is typically described as the armed wing of the Sadrist Movement (*al-Tayyar al-Sadri*).[1] In this sense, it seems to represent a paradigmatic model no different from many ideological mass parties worldwide whose structure is rooted in a particular brand of leadership, a clear ideological framework, a wide-reaching popular base and, in many cases, an armed wing/militia. This model appears frequently throughout the modern history of Iraq, from traditional parties like the Communists and the Baath, which established their own armed wings, to the Kurdish Peshmerga – which, despite its separate establishment as an ethnonational liberation movement, has become part of the organisational structure of the most prominent Kurdish party, the Kurdistan Democratic Party (KDP).

While armed wings of political parties perform many functions,[2] in Iraq they have served most clearly as a 'tool' by which parties can take power – meaning that, in an Iraqi context in which the prevailing political paradigm is that of the military coup, they have generally played supportive roles to cells established within the military establishment itself. Indeed, traditional ideological parties' focus on this notion of controlling the army has seriously limited both the experience and the organisational development of their armed wings *per se*.

The phenomenon discussed in this chapter differs somewhat from these classical cases. Firstly, the Sadrist Movement bears no resemblance to traditional parties: it is an organisation that works at the intersection of the political and the religious, based not on a specific roster of members but instead upon an open pool of followers and seekers (in the religious sense). Secondly, the Sadrist Movement and its armed wing(s) developed simultaneously, the political organisation emerging by way of infighting between competing factions to rein in the armed wing. In other words, the formation of the political organisation's identity and character was always defined by its fighting alongside or against the armed wing. We will thus discuss the extent to which the party's atypical emergence and makeup impact the general rules governing how militias make the transition to de-radicalisation and non-violent political activism.

The Mahdi Army on the Desks of Think-tanks

The literature on Iraqi armed groups states that the two largest Shiite Islamist armed groups are the Badr Corps and the Mahdi Army.[3] A comparison of these two groups is a good starting point for any attempt to understand the nature and the transformation of the Mahdi Army: if we move beyond the sort of general (often nebulous) criteria favoured by quantitative statistical analysis, we find that they have very little in common. Whereas the Badr Corps began to emerge in the context of the Shiite Islamist opposition to the Saddam Hussein regime in the 1980s, the Mahdi Army was established in the context of the emergent post-Saddam regime state. While the Badr Corps has a thoroughly traditional relationship with its parallel political organisation – having emerged as the armed wing of the Supreme Council of the Islamic Revolution in Iraq and having retained relatively limited manpower as a result[4] – the Mahdi Army is a much bigger organisation with a much more complex social and political structure that has birthed and transformed almost all the contemporary Shiite armed factions.

In 2008, following the major defeat sustained by the Mahdi Army during Operation Charge of the Knights (*Sawlat al-Fursan*), Muqtada al-Sadr announced that the militia's activities had been suspended and that its membership would subsequently be limited to a small core of fighters who would carry out armed activities only at the direction of the Movement's leadership (an issue that I will later return to and place in its historical and structural context later). In the months that followed, many studies were published on the Mahdi Army itself and the Sadrist Movement. Many of these originated from American think-tanks, who put forth the assessment that the Mahdi Army was one of the three greatest threats – if not the greatest threat – facing Iraq, alongside al-Qaeda and ethno-sectarian tensions.[5] This assessment matched that of the American military establishment, which by summer 2007 had taken the position that 'Shiite militias' (read primarily as the Mahdi Army) now posed a greater danger than the so-called 'Islamic State of Iraq'.[6]

This glut of new literature on the Mahdi Army and the Sadrist Movement in Iraq dwarfed similar efforts made before 2008, overshadowing even the output of 2004, the year that the organisation first started launching attacks on US troops. Of course, this can be attributed in part to the much greater danger the Mahdi Army now seemed to pose. However, it is also closely connected to the crisis of the Sadrist Movement between early 2007 and mid-2008 and to the increased deployment of US troops (the 'surge') ordered by President George W. Bush in January 2007. While the surge initially targeted al-Qaeda and a nascent ISI, it was ultimately extended to include the Mahdi Army after its role in the 2006 Civil War, a logical consequence given that the 'surge' essentially sought to address the Sunni community and enlist its support in the fight against al-Qaeda.

The central question for these think-tank studies was thus: how will the Sadrist Movement, as well as the Mahdi Army, develop and transform?[7] But while these reports and analyses did include information and important details about the Mahdi Army, they were governed by three key assumptions: that it was a militia group loyal to a political organisation; that its function was to gain influence within the state for that political organisation; and that the model through which all this could best be understood was that of the Lebanese Hezbollah. This last point was particularly prominent,[8] with numerous studies pointing out various perceived similarities between the two.[9] The studies thus logically concluded, in answer to the question given above, that the Mahdi Army and the Sadrist Movement would develop according to the Hezbollah model.[10]

In fact, we have no evidence that Sadr had the Hezbollah model in mind. Nonetheless, his unique position within the Shiite Islamist scene has continued to invite comparisons with the Lebanese organisation, and he has never shaken off the assumption that the Mahdi Army will develop in the same way as Hezbollah has (sometimes from forces outside the Movement which have pinned their hopes on such a development).

New Functions: The Mahdi Army and the Shiite Clerical Establishment

Generally speaking, the Mahdi Army's trajectory differs from the model governing relations between traditional populist parties and their armed wings. It was not established as the armed wing of an existing political organisation and traditional parties. Its founders were a movement or a group of young mid-ranking clerics within the Shiite religious establishment in Najaf – who, it is worth noting, did not represent the main school of thought even among Shiite clerics – led by Muqtada al-Sadr. Its stated duties as of its establishment were very broad ones, those of an 'army in waiting', and did not as yet include resistance to the US occupation (a task to which the organisation would later dedicate itself to enthusiastically). It was intended as a loose framework for various parastate functions the religious establishment might arrogate to itself as part of its attempts to compensate for state failure: simultaneously a militia, a political organisation and a mechanism for the provision of social services.

Various writers have argued that the establishment of the Mahdi Army was a reaction to the formation of the Iraqi Governing Council (IGC), announced just five days before. In fact, Sadr had already made it very clear that he was unwilling to engage with the US-backed political process.[11] But irrespective of the relevance of the IGC to the date of the announcement, the Mahdi Army represented a different kind of politics to that pursued within Shiite circles at the outset of the US occupation. A Shiite political elite made up of those who had remained in the country were squaring off against the traditional émigré opposition to the Saddam Hussein regime (the largest Shiite political bloc) and the US vision for Iraq. This approach, and the various conflicts it catalysed within the religious elite, culminated in an armed clash with the Americans. It cloaked itself in a particular ideological guise, presenting itself as a natural extension of the movement begun by Sadr's father (who coined the slogan 'No, no, America' [kalla kalla amrika]) – a more traditional position that has left its impression on Shiite elites across the region since the Islamic Revolution of Iran.

Despite the immediate context of its establishment, the Mahdi Army was not a centralised armed wing in the traditional sense of the term. Rather, it more closely resembled a general mobilisation force than an organised militia: a mobilisation of the Shiites allowing them to contend with the massive transformation ushered in by April 2003 occupation. Sadr's speech announcing its foundation made it clear that the Mahdi Army was the first step toward a state whose establishment, with this major turning point, had now become conceivable – not only an Islamic state but a state rooted in deference to the guidance and supervision of the Shiite religious authority: he was seeking to lay the foundation for 'the most important component of the state, namely an Islamic army that answers to clerical authorities as well as its commanders . . . It shall be the first seed of the independent Muslim state'.[12] This could be a Shiite state, a well-deserved victory after years of political exclusion.

During his first press conference after the US invasion,[13] Sadr rejected comparisons between the Mahdi Army and the Badr Corps, which he dismissed as a mere armed faction made up of 10,000 or 12,000 men – whereas 'Sadr's troops' accounted for 'three quarters of Iraq'. Despite the controversial figures, there was some shades of truth underpinning these claims: Sadr's movement benefitted both from the wide-ranging social networks his father constructed and its unique cachet within the clerical establishment in Najaf, which was unavailable to the Shiite Islamist resistance-in-exile. More importantly, however, his phrasing reflected a desire to mobilise the public at a pivotal historical moment; indeed, the Mahdi Army's formal creation, less than three months later, was both the product and a central vehicle of this mobilisation.

Even though the Sadrist movement was once widely regarded as the foremost Shiite opponent to the nascent political regime post-2003,[14] I would argue that militant Iraqi Shiism and its principal manifestation in the form of the Mahdi Army do not, ultimately, differ from other contemporary initiatives originating within the Shiite religious establishment in Najaf that sought to redefine the relationship between the religious establishment and the state. The militant Shiism that emerged just after 2003, for example, was not majorly different from Ayatollah Sistani's constitution-drafting efforts. Despite differences in (armed versus unarmed) tactics, both initiatives were launched in response to the power vacuum in an attempt to secure the collective interests of Iraq's Shiites and reshape the relationship between state and clerical establishment.

The Mahdi Army as an Embodiment of the Sadrist Movement

Within hours of the fall of the Saddam regime, a massive Shiite reaction had begun, a reaction that would launch Muqtada al-Sadr to the forefront of Iraqi politics and take control of the sprawling suburb of Saddam City (quickly renamed 'Sadr City' by its inhabitants in honour of Muqtada al-Sadr's father).[15] The Sadr phenomenon took both the US and the Iraqi émigré opposition completely by surprise. But although Sadr's political ambitions were obvious, it was not so immediately clear what exact role he was going to play. Only with the establishment of the Mahdi Army did a distinct political organisation linked to Sadr and his allies come into being.

Many questions have been raised about how the Sadrist Movement was able to affect such a meteoric rise at a time when it was sorely lacking in senior figures with the necessary religious credentials or personal qualities. Indeed, its rise is not explained by the personality of Muqtada al-Sadr himself or the circle of young clerics that surrounded him. In large part, it can be attributed to the activities of his father, Muhammad al-Sadr (d. 1999).

In a sense, the spread of the Sadrist phenomenon in post-Saddam Iraq represents an extension of the struggle launched by Sadr *père*, a well-regarded theologian and scion of one of the most prominent clerical families who broke with the traditions of the Najaf Hawza (seminary) to engage in broad-base political and social activism. Muqtada al-Sadr and his father's students presented themselves as the heirs to this vision of the Hawza's role. The rise of the 'Sadrist bloc' thus reignited much the same conflicts that had dogged Najaf in the 1990s – conflicts that looked very much like a struggle for control over Najaf and its spheres of influence in the power vacuum left by April 2003. They were also a continuation of the internecine conflicts between and within the major clerical families (Sadr, Hakim, Bahr al-Ulum and Kashif al-Ghita),[16] among whom the Sadrs felt themselves to be a perennial underdog.

For a while, the Sadrist Movement continued to develop and theorise the Hawza's political role. It accused traditionalists unwilling to play a political role of making Najaf into a 'silent seminary' (*hawza samita*), advocating instead a 'speaking seminary' (*hawza natiqa*) that would take an activist role in society. After 2003, however, this dichotomy appears less and less frequently in the Movement's literature. A total paradigm shift occurred in 2003, including in how the Hawza understood itself. Indeed, for both sides of the conflict, things were no longer as they had been before or even immediately after Saddam's fall. For the Sadrists, it was no longer just a matter of defining the Hawza's relationship with society – they now needed to work out how their political organisation was to relate to the new state. The traditionalists, meanwhile, found themselves suddenly involved in the creation of this new state, forcing them to confront a traditional approach to the secular power that was more than eighty years old.[17] Both the 'speaking' and 'silent' Hawzas found themselves suddenly in the same position *vis-à-vis* the 2003 state, forcing them both to consider what this moment meant for the Shiite community in Iraq and for their duties to their constituency.

Sadr's rise to prominence also created several other divisions, in the form of challenges and conflicts facing Shiite political society, that had a major impact upon Iraq as a whole. Most important was the domestic/ émigré dichotomy: while the bulk of the Iraqi political elite were returning from abroad, first among them the Shiite Islamist opposition, Sadr represented forces that had developed and grown quietly and invisibly within Iraq. Another major dichotomy was opposition or support for the post-2003 process, which Sadr openly rejected as the product of a foreign military occupation. The Arab/Iranian dichotomy, dominant in the older Sadr's rhetoric, was less noticeable in that of his son.

Another factor in the Sadrist Movement's rapid rise to prominence was the vast network built up by Muhammad al-Sadr and subsequently mobilised in the 1990s.[18] This network consisted of an army of deputies, orators and young clerics in addition to the mosques and libraries these officials oversaw. After 2003, the network began to take on a political character within areas of intense Sadrist influence. These areas are, of course, not simply 'Shiite' areas – Iraqi Shi'a support many different political parties, and there are other factors, yet to be identified by sociologists, driving support for Sadrism. The literature tends to characterise it as a movement of the marginalised Shi'a in general. But it is clear that it is above all else a movement of the Shiite suburbs of Baghdad and Basra (and Najaf to a degree). It was these suburbs that saw major uprisings after the elder Sadr's assassination.

One of Muhammad al-Sadr's projects was to establish a 'morality of obe-dience' (*akhlaq al-ta'a*) to Shiite scholars among the Shiite community more broadly (or at least among his own followers), expected to replace loyalty to any other political or social authority. His 1997 pamphlet *The Jurisprudence of Tribes* is arguably indicative of this, showing a hostility to the rising power of tribal forces empowered by the weak state of the 1990s. It is true that this effort was an engagement with tribal issues unprecedented among the schol-ars of Najaf, and that some contemporaries interpreted it as an effort to curry favour with the rural tribesmen of southern Iraq.[19] But the intention of the booklet was to expose the ways in which tribal elders' authority ran contrary to Islamic law, thereby reinforcing clerical power.

However, this morality of obedience was only one part of an interac-tive relationship between Muhammad al-Sadr and his followers. Sadr com-manded obedience not only for traditional religious reasons but also because of the symbolic role he played, creating a window of expression for margin-alised communities (to the point of socio-political revolution). Moreover, he was able to offer social services and economic support crucial in an Iraq buck-ling under the weight of international sanctions.[20] With his death in February 1999, he became a revolutionary martyr – an icon of social revolution. It is no surprise, given the general Shiite emphasis on inherited sacred qualities, that Muqtada was able to appropriate this symbolism.

In the days directly following the American invasion, a number of Muhammad al-Sadr's pupils, along with his son Muqtada, carried out an initial operation to lay the groundwork for the movement's emergence in the follow-ing months, reactivating the socio-religious network his father had built. They reopened mosques formerly overseen by Sadr's subordinates, reconstructed the network of deputies across the movement's areas of influence and opened new libraries. At the same time, the Sadrists rapidly deployed social services to these regions, including much-needed security, which was in short supply due to the power vacuum at the time.[21] This paved the way for the movement to spread its authority across these areas,[22] including Sadr City, which came under Sadrist control almost immediately – something that would have been impossible were it not for the network established by Sadr *père*.

It has been claimed that a leading committee of five young clerics closely associated with the older Sadr – Mustafa al-Yaqoubi, Muhammad al-Tabtaba'i, Riyadh al-Nuri, Qais Khazali and Jaber al-Khafaji – ran the movement in secret from Muhammad al-Sadr's assassination until the US invasion, when they handed over power to Muqtada. According to this narrative, Muqtada was not part of the committee due to a general lack of confidence in his leadership qualifications and his being under house arrest.[23] My interviews have not confirmed these claims, which are often cited to explain the rapid resurgence of the movement after 2003. But regardless of whether or not they are true, I do not imagine that it was difficult to revive the network of preachers, deputies and mosques directly following the American invasion.

It does, however, seem that Sheikh Muhammad al-Yaqoubi, Sadr *père*'s right-hand man, was initially set to take leadership of the movement, with Muqtada willing to fall in behind him so long as he did not claim *marji'* status – that is, a supreme religious authority, of equivalent rank to Muhammad al-Sadr – and thereby side-line the Sadr family name (and forsake the symbolism associated with it). In this account, Muqtada only took the definitive decision to act in his own name when Yaqoubi declared himself a *marji'*.[24]

In any case, the formation of the Mahdi Army in July 2003 was the Sadrist Movement's first systematic step forward in organisational terms, its huge efforts to revive its social network notwithstanding. Even from the perspective of registration, the Mahdi Army provided the first formal list of members: the day after the announcement saw a large influx of volunteers signing up to join. The relationship between the two organisations thus did not resemble that of a traditional ideological party and an armed wing established subsequently. Nor did it resemble an armed movement that subsequently develops into a political party. Both groups, in fact, emerged together: the armed wing and the political organisation (with all its social functions). If we assume that the structure of the post-2003 Sadrist Movement goes back to the 1990s, the Mahdi Army was both capstone and foundation stone: it served as the nascent movement's administration and the link between its components and its establishment.

The relationship between the military and political organisations remains crucial, and there is an inverse correlation between the strength or weakness of the Mahdi Army on the one hand, and the Sadrist Movement's organisational dynamism and desire to act like a political party on the other. The key moment in this regard was the defeat inflicted on the Mahdi Army by state forces during Operation Charge of the Knights (March 2008). This moment raised serious questions about whether the Sadrist Movement would be able to become a traditional political party, questions we will discuss in more detail later.

The Conflict within the Sadrist Movement

The years 2006–8 were decisive for the history of the Sadrist Movement, witnessing sizeable transformations in its relationship to the Mahdi Army and in the conflict between its wings. Although the Sadrist Movement participated in the December 2005 parliamentary elections and in the first Nouri al-Maliki government formed in May 2006, this coincided with a civil war – having escalated following the February 2006 al-Askari mosque bombing – in which the Mahdi Army played a central role as the primary Shiite faction to carry out sectarian reprisals. As such, it was regarded as a driver of Iraq's instability.

The Sadrist Movement's relationship with Maliki began to sour by the end of 2006, when Maliki decided to confront the Shiite militias (part of a broader strategy, coordinated with the USA, of tackling sectarian violence by taking on its main perpetrators). In early 2007, many of the Movement's political and military leaders were arrested and Sadr fled to Iran. The Mahdi Army then launched a series of major operations, including the infamous storming of the Karbala governorate building and the killing of five US soldiers who were holding a meeting there. In August 2007, during a Shiite holiday, pro-Sadr forces clashed with troops from the Holy Site Protection Force (an official detachment) and the Badr Corps in the vicinity of the tomb of Imam Hussein at Karbala, leading to hundreds of deaths.[25]

In the course of 2007 and 2008, the Mahdi Army's operations were suspended twice by its commanders. On the first occasion, in August 2007, Sadr announced a six-month suspension of activity after the armed clashes in Karbala; suspension, in this case, meant an end to violence against other groups (including US forces). At the end of the six-month period in February 2008, Sadr extended the suspension by six months, and in August 2008, following Operation Charge of the Knights and the new Law Enforcement Plan, he extended it again, this time indefinitely. The Mahdi Army's operations had come to an end, and it was subsequently split into two organisations: one of a cultural character entitled *al-Mumahhidun* (the vanguards); the other, *al-Mujahidin* (the mujahids), resembling special forces at the command of Sadr himself.

At the time, few parties to the conflict expected the better part of the rank and file of the now defunct Mahdi Army to abide by the cease-fire order, but in fact there was widespread compliance. Even among experts who dispute that the subsequent fall in violence can be attributed to the Mahdi Army, there is a general understanding that, beginning in the autumn of 2007, Sadr's cease-fire order played a major role in deescalating violence,[26] an indication of the authority the Sadrist leadership (and particularly Muqtada al-Sadr himself) held over the organisation's fighters. This is something of a puzzle: an armed group on the verge of dissolution, whose leadership was nonetheless able to keep its subordinates under control and force an end to hostilities. The Mahdi Army thus makes for a crucial case study.[27]

While fighters' compliance might be explained by the leadership's skilful management of the Sadrist Movement's social networks (not only senior commanders but also secondary and regional leadership, who formed the basis of this network), these networks are only generally useful so long as they can manage and distribute social and monetary resources among militants.[28] It is difficult to imagine the Sadrist Movement effectively obtaining resources at a time when it was under such colossal pressure. Iraqi political organisations at this point could only acquire resources via engagement with rentierism (i.e., by securing a share of state resources through participating in government) and its attendant clientelist networks. If the Sadrist Movement ever sought to engage with this regime, its unsteady situation during that period would have prevented it from so doing.

It is possible that the religious authority the movement's leadership enjoyed, especially the figure of Muqtada al-Sadr, was an essential factor. Once again, however, religious authority does not appear to me capable of providing a comprehensive explanation in isolation from its interactions with its social environment. We must return to the functions and roles of religious leadership within the marginalised communities or suburbs which represent the Sadrist Movement's primary base of support, given that, as previously noted, spiritual leadership of this variety develops a redemptive dimension and becomes an instrument of social revolution.

Regardless of the explanation, all this produced an axiom of contemporary Iraqi politics: that the Sadrist Movement's popular base is consistently and unswervingly loyal to the leadership. But we must not allow the success the leadership enjoyed in bringing an end to hostilities to distract from two central points. Firstly, this move was the result of a complicated array of military and political developments and was likely connected to the political leadership's desire to redefine its relationship to (or, perhaps, to exercise control over) an armed 'wing' to which it had no formal connections – an armed wing that had shown a certain degree of recklessness, with a number of its members becoming caught up in criminal activity. This created space for internal conflicts to push the organisation closer to the brink of dissolution.[29] Secondly, this very relationship with the Mahdi Army may itself have been the product of conflicts within the organisation's political wing. The Mahdi Army's suspension and the general compliance of fighters with the orders of the leadership thus do not negate the resultant fractures in the wake of the 2008 defeat, which placed it in a position similar to that of other armed factions in the wake of military setbacks.

Unlike the academic approaches mentioned above, which fixate on the Mahdi Army's 'coherence' and its fighters' obedience to leadership so as to imply that it had not suffered any notable schisms (or, at least, none of actual value), I argue that the Mahdi Army, as with any other armed faction in a similar position, did indeed experience fractures, and that it is of paramount importance to take note of these rifts so as to understand the relationship between the political organisation and its armed counterpart. These two points are closely interlinked: the leadership's attempts to gain control over the Mahdi Army were closely connected to the political conflict taking place between the movement's wings. Comments made by Sadr at a press conference regarding the suspension of operations provide some hints of this: without saying so explicitly, he alluded to the corrupt and arrogant behaviour on the part of individuals within the movement which had begun to reflect poorly on the Mahdi Army's reputation.[30] It is most likely that Sadr was here referring to senior figures in the armed wing who were promoting acts of violence, some of whom were beyond his authority. Thus, the militia's suspension became a tool that Sadr leveraged in the conflict, snatching it away from adversaries seeking to do so.

This conflict was a struggle to escape the amorphous situation the Mahdi Army had created, whether manifested in Muqtada's endeavour to formulate an organisation of many names – the Mujahids, the Brigade of the Promised Day (*Liwa' al-Yawm al-Maw'ud*) and, most recently, the Peace Companies (*Saraya al-Salam*) – or in Khazali's desire to establish 'Special Groups' from which the League of the Righteous (*'Asa'ib Ahl al-Haqq*) would later develop.

The formation of a professional militia organisation loyal to a higher leadership performed a separate role of critical importance. Its activity limited to its regions of influence; the Mahdi Army evolved along the pattern of local organisations.[31] The struggle to establish a more professional organisation thus helped shift the scope of these groups from local to national.

The struggle to establish a professional militia group within the Sadrist Movement was secondary to a broader conflict within the movement about its nature and character – was it an armed group or a political organisation, a militia or a party? This conflict over the movement's identity can likely be traced back to the very beginning of its operations, or perhaps shortly afterward. It was a conflict between two expansive wings,[32] each of which was rooted in a different understanding of the movement's identity and its relationship to the militia organisation. Indeed, the question of armed struggle was the central axis of this conflict.

The first of the two wings, which included Sadr and other clerics, believed that the movement should focus on social work and education, bringing an end to armed activity or turning the armed organisation into a specified, functional element within the movement. Therefore, the steps Sadr was taking in 2007 and 2008 (the August 2007 cease-fire, followed by the suspension of the Mahdi Army's activities and, eventually, its transformation into a social institution of religious morality and the distinction between the Vanguards and the Mujahids) appear to match this wing's inclinations.

The second wing understood the organisation as an armed resistance movement, determined to maintain armed activity in opposition to the ongoing American presence in the country. This wing, which later adopted the name 'League of the Righteous', was led primarily by Qais Khazali, one of Muhammad al-Sadr's disciples and a co-founder of the movement alongside Sadr *fils*; it defined itself as a part of the so-called 'Islamic Resistance Front', a regional and multinational organisation.

Some scholars trace the direct cause of this split to the fractures within the leadership that resulted from the two battles between the movement and American forces in 2004, the lack of financial resources, and opposition on part of some leaders (including Khazali) to Muqtada's decision to suspend military operations.[33] Khazali and his troops, therefore, continued fighting. Gradually, this organisation began operating with a degree of independence from the Mahdi Army's leadership. This conflict later extended beyond the question of whether to continue fighting the Americans or to stand down, and into the decision to participate in the 2005 elections and enter the political process. Competing desires and narratives as to the movement's future constantly dogged its leadership. For one group, the decision over whether to enter the political process led inexorably to the pruning of the militant wing, whereas the other adopted a new name and ostentatiously ignored Sadr's call to suspend military operations. Despite Khazali's arrest following the Karbala Governorate attack in January 2007, after which he remained in prison until 2010, the group remained committed under the leadership of Khazali's comrades.

In its official formation narrative, the League of the Righteous neglects to mention that it broke away from the Mahdi Army, or even developed from it at all. Rather, the group's history is considered to have begun with the Mahdi Army's formation, mentioning the first operation it carried out in mid-August 2003 when, on Khazali's orders, it struck an American encampment in Baghdad after the latter took down banners bearing the standard of the Imam al-Mahdi in Baghdad's Sadr City.[34] The League narrative focuses on two points: that it evolved from a group of Muhammad al-Sadr's disciples, and that it was founded in response to the American occupation.[35] Though it operated as part of the Mahdi Army for a period, it developed from the 'Special Groups' that served as elite forces within the militia. The Mahdi Army, on the other hand, took the front lines of the battles of 2004 against the American occupation, waging what resembled a war of attrition between rival gangs.[36] Later, the Special Groups took up a more specific course of action with a higher degree of independence from the Sadrist Movement. At that point, its founders renamed it the League of the Righteous, in reference to the Mahdist tradition of the group of fighters who come to the aid of the Imam al-Mahdi immediately following his reappearance, paving the way for the establishment of his state.[37]

The US Army came across the term 'special groups', the name adopted by Khazali's wing, and began to apply it within intelligence circles in July 2007 in reference to Iran-backed Shiite militias who were targeting American forces and institutions of the nascent Iraqi state. As far as American forces were concerned at the time, these were former Mahdi Army fighters who had disobeyed Sadr's cease-fire order in August 2007 and subsequent suspension of the militia's activities in the summer of 2008 to break away from his movement – particularly in the wake of Operation Charge of the Knights – and continued fighting American troops and the Iraqi security forces. The American army has used the term 'League of the Righteous' since August 2008 to describe a subset of the Special Groups. Thinktanks that analyse American intelligence data arrived at the very same conclusion.

The position on Iran was certainly a component of the conflict between the movement's wings. Although there was a consensus that Iran was providing the Mahdi Army with training and funding, Sadr worked to ensure there was space between Iran and the movement. It is possible that his decision to enter the elections came without Iranian approval, given that Iran sought to ensure the presence of an armed Shiite faction – despite having supported several Shiite Islamist outfits vying for power – that would remain susceptible to Iranian influence in one way or another. Therefore, some scholars argue that Iran focused on supporting Khazali's wing following the 2004 battles, given that he rejected the ceasefire and had begun laying the groundwork for a special position within the Mahdi Army;[38] indeed, when the Quds Brigade of the Iranian Revolutionary Guard decided to restructure its support of Shiite militias in Iraq in 2006, it selected Khazali to lead the network of 'Special Groups'.

As a result, the fractures within the Mahdi Army since 2008 and prior must be understood as a product of foreign intervention on the behalf of a foreign power (Iran) without whom these splinter groups would not have had any meaningful impact. In other words, the fractures were an attempt by Iran to compensate for the Mahdi Army's absence or refusal to act as Tehran wanted it to. It is possible, therefore, to understand these splinter factions' rapid absorption within the Iranian-led Islamic Resistance Front, which has played a role in many parts of the region (especially post-2012 Syria), as the route the Mahdi Army ought to have taken.[39]

In summary, the rift between the two wings allowed the first (that of Muqtada al-Sadr) to take clearer steps toward political organisation in the wake of the tumultuous years of transition from 2006 to 2008. The year 2009 saw two important developments in this matter. The first was the movement's participation in provincial council elections (January 2009) during which it achieved notable victories, having entered the elections not in the name of the Sadrist Movement but in the name of a closed, exclusive electoral organisation known as the Freemen (*al-Ahrar*), as a tradition the movement would repeat in each parliamentary or local election to come: deriving a closed parliamentary bloc designated as something other than the 'Sadrist Movement'. In May 2009, the movement organised the first extensive conference of the 'General Committee' in Istanbul, during which the essential question was that of the Movement's future and the possibility of it becoming more like the political organisation.[40]

Given the persistence of comparisons to Hezbollah, I would like to reiterate here that the Sadrist Movement developed in the opposite direction from Hezbollah. Its political ambitions did not develop into a strengthening of its armed wing nor did the party grow stronger through its military might, as did Hezbollah. Rather, the militia was isolated to the party's benefit. The Mahdi Army's division into the Vanguards and the Mujahids was a technique aimed at weakening, rather than strengthening, the armed wing – in other words, bringing it under control. In fact, it is the League of the Righteous that most closely resembles Hezbollah, having leveraged the strength of its armed faction to secure a sizeable parliamentary bloc and government positions.

Conclusion

This case study of the Mahdi Army is not so much ground-breaking as theory-confirming – even with regard to the organisation's relationship to the Sadrist Movement, which as we have shown bears little resemblance to traditional party structures. The decisive transformation of the Sadrist Movement toward non-violent activism and the establishment of a political organisation did not begin until 2009, after two years of transition during which the movement and the Mahdi Army experienced significant disturbances in the form of large clashes with American and Iraqi forces, beginning with the 'surge' of American troops into the country in January 2007; followed by the law enforcement plan launched by Prime Minister Nouri al-Maliki in February of that year, of which the Mahdi Army was a central target; and, lastly, the 'Charge of the Knights' battles of March 2008 during which the militia suffered a staggering defeat.

During this period, Sadr announced multiple initiatives to avoid armed activism. Therefore, the Sadrist Movement's transition from armed conflict to political work was subject to the classical model governing armed factions that undergo this sort of transition after a decisive defeat.[41] In other words, state repression was critical and so was the charismatic leader. This transformation also meant the victory of one wing over another, within a movement that has perennially experienced an identity crisis split between two wings. One wing sees the organisation as an armed movement whose objectives were not limited to resisting the American occupation, but also included supporting 'the Shiite community' in achieving what it stood to gain at the critical turning point initiated by the fall of Saddam; the other considers it possible to transform into a political party like all others. The course of the movement from 2003 to 2008 exhibited a dynamic of push and pull between the two wings, at times calling for armed activism and at times embracing the idea of a non-violent political organisation. At many points, each party attempted to impose their vision upon the other in an undeclared conflict, even if this meant using external support to overpower the other.

This complicated moment, one of simultaneous victory and defeat, was to cause the movement to come to terms with the transformation into a political party – not as a decision imposed from outside, but as a transformative strategy. This strategy would entail not the dissolution of the armed wing but instead its restructuring to transform it into a small part of the movement, under the control of its charismatic political leadership. This armed wing has taken various names within the movement since the initial choice of the Mahdi Army, including the Brigade of the Promised Day and the Peace Companies.

The victory of the movement's pro-transformation wing did not mean the end of armed activism or a comprehensive de-radicalisation. In fact, pro-violence factions would later break off into a separate organisation – the League of the Righteous. This model of fragmentation is also traditional in cases of defeat, where factions within the armed organisation generally come out against the transformation towards unarmed activism in a classic substantive/factional de-radicalisation. However, what is novel in the case of the Mahdi Army is that its fragmentation was supported by an outside party (Iran) who had been involved since the beginning of the inter-factional conflict and internal interactions within the organisation, supporting one faction over the other. Therefore, the dynamic of this transformation from violent to non-violent activism and the fragmentation that precipitated it, cannot be understood as a merely internal phenomenon in isolation from the role of external actors.

Notes

1. See: Anthony H. Cordesman and Jose Ramos, 'Sadr and the Mahdi Army: Evolution, Capabilities, and a New Direction', *Center for Strategic and International Studies (CSIS)*, 4/8/2008, accessed on 22/10/2020, at: https://bit.ly/3jnfTgu; Marisa Cochrane, *The Fragmentation of the Sadrist Movement*, Iraq Report 12 (Washington, DC: Institute for the Study of War, 2009); Phil Williams and Dan Bisbee, 'Jaish al-Mahdi in Iraq', in: Michelle A. Huges and Michael Miklaucic (eds), *Impunity: Countering Illicit Power in War and Transition* (Washington, DC: National Defense University/ Center for Technology and National Security Policy/ Center for Complex Operations and Peacekeeping and Stability Operations Institute, 2016), p. 233; Bruce R. Pirnie and Edward O'Connell, *Counterinsurgency in Iraq (2003–2006)* (Santa Monica: National Defense Research Institute (RAND), 2008).
2. Richard Gunther and Larry Diamond, 'Types and Functions of Parties', in: Larry Diamond and Richard Gunther (eds), *Political Parties and Democracy* (Baltimore and London: The Johns Hopkins University Press, 2001), p. 20.
3. Michael Freeman et al., 'Insurgent and Terrorist Finances in Iraq', in: Michael Freeman (ed.), *Financing Terrorism: Case Studies* (London and New York: Routledge, 2012), p. 33.
4. For more on the Badr Corps (later Badr Organisation), see: 'Badr Organisation', *Counter Extremism Project*, accessed on 22/10/2020, at: https://bit.ly/34kDE4N; 'The Badr Organisation of Reconstruction and Development', *Center for International Security and Cooperation (CISAC)*, accessed on 22/10/2020, at: https://stanford.io/36MJU6A
5. Cordesman and Ramos, p. 2.
6. This is based on the fact that, according to Gen. Ray Odierno, commander

of coalition forces in Iraq, 73 per cent of attacks targeting American forces that involved casualties were carried out by these militias; see also: Michael R. Gordon, 'U.S. Says Iran-Supplied Bomb Kills More Troops', *New York Times*, 8/8/2007, accessed on 22/10/2020, at: https://nyti.ms/34kN3Jx

7. Cordesman and Ramos, p. 23.

8. Ibid., p. 3; Cochrane, p. 6; Pirnie and O'Connell, p. 32.

9. Cordesman and Ramos note that, based on American intelligence sources, the Mahdi Army fighters received training in Iran and used Iranian weapons; see: Cordesman and Ramos, p. 3.

10. Ibid., pp. 3–4; Cochrane, p. 13.

11. Nir Rosen, 'Shiite Contender Eyes Iraq's Big Prize', *Time*, 3/5/2003, accessed on 7/12/2020, at: https://bit.ly/3otzBdx

12. See the full text of the speech: 'Establishment of the Army of the Imam al-Mahdi in Iraq in 2003', Grand Mosque of Kufa, *YouTube*, 16/9/2015, accessed on 22/10/2020, at: https://bit.ly/3jmriNy

13. Rosen.

14. Andre Krouwel, 'Party Models', in: Richard S. Katz and William Crotty (eds), *Handbook of Party Politics* (New York: SAGE Publications, 2006).

15. Faleh A. Jabar, *The Shiitete Movement in Iraq* (London: Saqi Books, 2003), pp. 25–6; Nir Rosen, 'Iraq's Shiites Under Occupation', *Middle East Briefing*, International Crises Group (ICG), 9/9/2003, pp. 15–17. The last two articles document the massive shock created by Muqtada al-Sadr's emergence in the days after Saddam's fall, using the term 'Shiite surprise'.

16. Jabar, p. 31; Williams and Bisbee, p. 44.

17. These specifications particularly concern Ayatollah Sistani and the political role he took up, in order to discredit his status as the Najaf *Hawza*'s public face, as its leader and most senior scholar.

18. Cochrane, p. 10.

19. Ibid.

20. Some studies go so far as to suggest that the senior al-Sadr established a wide-reaching charitable network in poor Shiite neighbourhoods, particularly in Baghdad and Basra during the embargo period in the 1990s, to offer social and economic support to the needy; see also: Jabar, pp. 272–3; Eli Berman, *Radical, Religious, and Violent: The New Economics of Terrorism* (Cambridge, MA: The MIT Press, 2009), p. 133. Berman believes that the Sadrist movement and the Mahdi Army are representative of what he calls the 'Hamas Model', which includes – along with the Sadrist movement and Hamas – Hezbollah in

Lebanon, the Taliban and the Muslim Brotherhood. According to this model, radical political Islam is linked to the provision of social services. Although I agree with this in principle, Sadr *père*'s activities require more investigation in order to establish the extent of his charitable work and whether this aspect has been exaggerated.

21. Cochrane, p. 6.
22. Williams and Bisbee, p. 44.
23. Anthony Shadid, *Night Draws Near* (New York: Henry Holt and Company, 2005), p. 172.
24. Interview with Dia' al-Asadi, the head of the Al-Ahrar Bloc in Iraqi parliament (Sadrist Bloc), 2014–18, Baghdad, 2 January 2019.
25. For further details, see: Cochrane, p. 6.
26. David Petraeus, senior commander of US forces in Iraq, stated that Sadr was particularly effective in reducing violence in Iraq. See: Dan Murphy, 'General Petraeus Says Violence Is Down in Iraq, But Warns Continued Success Is Not Guaranteed,' *The Christian Science Monitor*, 6/12/2007, accessed on 7/12/2020, at: https://bit.ly/39Vy77I. See also: Anthony Cordesman (with assistance from Emma R. Davies), *Iraq's Insurgency and the Road to Civil Conflict* (Washington, D C and London: Center for Strategic Studies (CSIS)/ Praeger Security International, 2008), pp. 595–600.
27. Alec Worsnop, 'Who Can Keep the Peace? Insurgent Organizational Control of Collective Violence', *Security Studies*, vol. 26, no. 3 (2017), pp. 483–4.
28. Ibid.
29. Williams and Bisbee, pp. 42–3.
30. Muqtada Al-Sadr, *Al-Huda Magazine Interview* (Booklet) (2016), pp. 15–17.
31. David E. Johnson, M. Wade Markel and Brian Shannon, *The 2008 Battle of Sadr City: Reimagining Urban Combat* (Santa Monica: RAND Corporation, 2013), p. 23.
32. Cochrane, pp. 15–18.
33. Ibid., p. 6.
34. The League published a booklet which can be considered an official history: Siraj Centre for Composition (Fulfilment and Translation), *League of the Righteous: Information Booklet* (D. M. Iraq: Dar al-Kafeel), pp. 12–15.
35. Ibid., p. 12.
36. Ibid., pp. 15–16.
37. Ibid., pp. 16–17.
38. Cochrane, p. 6.

39. Siraj Centre for Composition, pp. 51–5.

40. Interview with Dia' al-Asadi.

41. Omar Ashour, 'From Militias to Political Parties: How and Why Do Armed Organizations Take up Non-violent Activism?', *Siyasat Arabiya*, vol. 8, no. 44 (2020), pp. 10–11; David Close and Gary Prevost, 'Introduction: Transitioning from Revolutionary Movements to Political Parties and Making the Revolution "Stick"', in: Kalowatie Deonandan, David Close and Gary Prevost (eds), *From Revolutionary Movements to Political Parties: Cases from Latin America and Africa* (New York: Palgrave Macmillan, 2007), pp. 4–6.

6

A DRAW OR A DEFEAT?
HOW THE IRA TRANSITIONED FROM
BULLETS TO BALLOTS

Gordon Clubb

Introduction

The Provisional Irish Republican Army's armed struggle began in 1969 in the context of the Catholic civil rights movement's perceived marginalisation within Northern Ireland. Initial demands for 'British Rights for British Citizens' quickly gave way to more traditional Republican demands for an end to the partition of Ireland and the removal of British troops. 'The Troubles' in Northern Ireland, involving several non-state actors of which the Provisional IRA was the largest and most active, continued for almost three decades and claimed the lives of around 3,600. In this period, numerous attempts at ending the conflict met with little success, but in 1994 the Provisional IRA announced a ceasefire and signalled a willingness to negotiate. The resultant 1998 Good Friday Agreement marked the beginning of the end of the Provisional IRA's campaign, which by 2005 had officially disarmed and de-mobilised, with its key figures occupying positions of political power in a new Northern Irish assembly. While Brexit introduces uncertainty over the legacy of the peace process, especially given the important role the European Union has played in resolving the conflict, the Provisional IRA's disengagement from violence (or more accurately behavioural and organisational de-radicalisation/pragmatic de-radicalisation) still represents an important example of how armed non-state actors can successfully transition from bullets to ballots.

The following chapter has been tasked with explaining the Provisional IRA's transition away from armed violence and whether this can be explained as a draw or defeat. To answer this question, the chapter draws upon a book by the author which detailed the transformation of the Irish Republican movement away from violence.[1] The following chapter updates this work for a wider audience, situating the discussion more broadly within debates on transitions, specifically approaching the question of intra-group inter-play from the perspective of framing. Interviews quoted in the chapter were conducted in 2013 in Belfast. The chapter focuses on the period prior to the 1998 peace process in order to account for what led the Provisional IRA to disengage. The chapter begins by examining why discussing transitions in terms of 'draw or defeat' does not fully capture the drivers behind the end of the Provisional IRA's campaign.

Draw or Defeat? How Neither Captures the Provisional IRA's Pragmatic De-radicalisation

There are several reasons why it is inadequate to analyse the Provisional IRA's campaign in terms of victory or defeat. Practically, publicly framing the out-come of negotiations as a 'defeat' for one side undermines attempts by this side in negotiations to encourage its membership to support a shift away from engagement in violence; in contrast, the framing of the conflict as being stuck in a stalemate (or draw) was precisely utilised to facilitate a face-saving end to the conflict. Some scholars in the Northern Irish context have been critical of academics reproducing 'terroristic narratives',[2] and while academics ought to be normatively reflective upon these issues, particularly in a post-conflict setting, there are other limitations with seeking to study transitions in terms of victory and defeat.

Conceptually, discussions of the end of armed violence in the terms of defeat are closely linked to the literature on whether 'terrorism works'. One of the consistent findings in terrorism studies is that groups which use terrorism rarely achieve their strategic goals or substantial concessions (4–10% depending on the study) yet equally rarely are such groups defeated through military means (7%).[3] If 'success' (and defeat) are then understood in terms of achieving a group's primary and original goals, rather than achiev-ing concessions such as hostage exchange, minor territorial withdrawal, or organisational survival,[4] using terrorism does not work.[5] Thus from this perspective, advocated predominantly by Max Abrahms, terrorism is an invariably self-defeating strategy with little evidence that the use of terrorism can help to achieve a group's main strategic and ideological objectives. Thus, contrary to the perspective that the Provisional IRA's campaign ended through partial success as a result of the tactics it deployed, for Abrahms the measure of success or defeat should be whether it achieved its original and primary objectives of ending partition, which the Good Friday Agreement clearly did not. However, several other problems emerge from the 'does terrorism work' literature: (1) the finality of the term 'defeat' does not correspond to the continuity of activism among former Provisional IRA members, and it is therefore impossible to say that they will not achieve their strategic objectives and that prior uses of violence contributed to that, or that the movement will not in the future draw upon the legacy of the Provisional IRA to take up arms and be successful; (2) many Provisional IRA members were willing to continue using violence regardless of no immediate or realistic hope of strategic success, which underlines the importance of their decision to disengage independently of any perception or material reality of being defeated; (3) the rationalist assumptions underpinning the 'does terrorism work' discourse present a narrow view of why groups engage in violence, of which victory/ defeat may not necessarily constitute the main driver,[6] neglecting the potentially immense agency for social change that may derive from using violence and may factor in its use regardless of victory; and (4) while groups may no longer exist, their discourse can and does; the pragmatic de-radicalisation[7] of the Provisional IRA has largely normalised the Provisional IRA's narrative of the conflict. Thus, labelling the Provisional IRA's transition from violence in terms of a 'defeat', whether descriptively or by linking it to the associated body of research on the subject, does not advance the discussion.

Another way of conceptualising the Provisional IRA's transition away from violence has been in terms of a 'draw', or more specifically, that the stalemate within the conflict had presented a ripe moment which enabled and facilitated the peace process.[8] The theory of ripeness has been influential in explaining transitions from bullets to ballots. In short, this approach contends that continued Provisional IRA violence, despite combined successful military and policing repression by the state, led both sides to view the conflict as a stalemate. Electoral success by Sinn Fein – the Provisional IRA's political wing – in the 1980s, illustrated the opportunities presented by a non-violent approach. Thus, according to this theory applied to Northern Ireland, the existence of a mutually harmful stalemate and mutually enticing opportunities drove both sides to the negotiating table and, with the help of international intermediaries, culminated in the 1998 Good Friday Agreement and the official disbandment of the Provisional IRA in 2005. However, at least in the Northern Ireland context, the draw/ripeness/stalemate narrative is not an entirely convincing explanation for several reasons. First of all, the conditions in which the Good Friday Agreement was born was not overly different from the conditions in the last two decades, with the content of the agreement being similar to previously rejected peace proposals.[9] Even given the tautological claim that for ripeness to lead to a peace process the stalemate needs to be perceived,[10] key figures within the Provisional IRA had arrived at this position earlier yet it was still not sufficient on its own and while Pruitt's adaptation of the theory captures the importance of interaction between movements to develop a central coalition for peace he does not focus on 'the how and why' of dynamics within movements.[11] Therefore the perception that the two sides were in a stalemate – a draw – does not hold much weight in regard to the Provisional IRA's case, and to understand the transition to non-violence it is also important to look at processes within the Provisional IRA.

Theorising Structure, Interplay and Pragmatic De-radicalisation Framing

This chapter explains the Provisional IRA's transition by building upon work that emphasises the importance of intra-group interaction (or 'interplay') as a factor in driving pragmatic de-radicalisation. In his study on the de-radicalisation of once armed Islamist groups, Omar Ashour highlights several critical variables that facilitate a transition away from violence: the role of leaders and charismatic authority; the pressure on movements, including repression; interactions and debates within the movement and interaction with external actors, including 'the other'; and inducements such as power-sharing as provided in a peace treaty and the provision of amnesties to prisoners.[12] All of these factors were present in the case of the Provisional IRA's transition. The Good Friday Agreement made provisions for power-sharing and cross-border institutions. External actors played an important deal in brokering this peace deal, from the intervention of the US President Bill Clinton to other intermediaries including the African National Congress. Socio-economic factors were also important – greater British involvement in the province from the 1970s saw an improvement in the economic fortunes of the region, including for the Catholic population, and the European Union has been significant in softening the border in Ireland and investing in peace building activities. These factors have been important in the transition, however this chapter focuses specifically on the role of interplay because it was the final piece in the jigsaw – for all the significance of structural factors, the final arbiter in the transition was the Provisional IRA themselves. The importance of interaction and interplay has also been highlighted as a significant factor in the Northern Irish context elsewhere.[13] This research has shown, for example, how debates within prisons in Northern Ireland and former prisoner activities upon release were important in facilitating the peace process.[14] More generally, Ed Moloney details the extensive work done by the Provisional IRA leadership (including Sinn Fein) to prepare its membership for negotiations, often through deception and intimidation.[15] The purpose here then is to build upon this literature in order to advance our understanding of transitions in relation to ideology.

Transition from violence has been referred to as 'disengagement' and/ or 'de-radicalisation' – 'Pragmatic de-radicalisation' or 'disengagement' have also been used to designate behavioural and organisational change regardless of ideological change/maintenance, whereas de-radicalisation predominantly refers to ideological change alongside behavioural change.[16] The relationship between these two processes has been heavily debated – a debate beyond the scope of this chapter – however the concept of de-radicalisation is important insofar as it highlights ideational factors in transitioning away from violence. Nevertheless, de-radicalisation is limited, particularly in accounting for the Northern Irish case, because it erroneously assumes that an *abandonment* of ideology provides a better quality of disengagement. However, the scepticism of using de-radicalisation to account for transition risks neglecting the significance of ideological innovations as a cause and manifestation of successful transition. Hence the use of the concept of disengagement framing is to provide a focus on the role of ideology in the disengagement process without the linear and dyadic assumptions associated with de-radicalisation. Thus, this chapter seeks to emphasise the importance of processes of framing disengagement as a dimension of interplay.

Just as political entrepreneurs construct frames to identify grievances and solutions to grievances as a means of mobilising sections of the population,[17] so do militant group leaders construct a frame to disengage their membership. Despite the obvious nature of this point, a framing approach has not been significantly applied to understanding disengagement, even though understanding frame dynamics of disengagement can provide insights into disengagement which other approaches may not. For example, whilst de-radicalisation emphasises ideological abandonment, a framing approach focuses on how ideological components are socially reconstructed to take on different meanings – as a result, it occupies a middle ground between disengagement and de-radicalisation because it shows how ideological adaptation occurs and can shape behaviour. The contentious part of this process is that the framing of disengagement is constructed in the context of the mobilising frame so that in order to be accepted there is an incentive to maintain narrative fidelity to the initial goal, from which the causal dynamics emerge. The process of interplay in disengagement is specifically directed toward re-framing the position of violence within the movement's ideological framework – it is this process of re-negotiation, which is specifically important in accounting for the Provisional IRA's move away from armed struggle. Furthermore, interplay is a distinct element in transitions because several factors shape whether it occurs and whether it is successful – there is no inevitability that interplay will lead to disengagement because groups need to address ideological constraints before interplay can lead to a successful transition from violence. Thus, interplay is theorised as a (re)framing process within a movement which is shaped and constrained by the structures of the movement and the ideological architecture of the movement.

The Importance of Interplay and Framing Disengagement

Transition was not an inevitable outcome of interplay, as the advocates of the peace process faced considerable opposition within the Provisional IRA, specifically in having to overcome decades in which the conflict was framed as justifying the use of violence. Interplay and framing disengagement were important for the group's transition. Because 'stalemate' is a social construction, many members were unmoved by community pressure or repression and the importance of unity incentivised addressing disagreements rather than splitting. Framing the conflict as being stuck in a stalemate was important for the Provisional IRA's transition because it saved face, whilst also feeding into a developing narrative of 'changing conditions' which justified the abandonment of violence. External factors very clearly impacted upon the movement and provided the motivation to disengage, however there was also still an internal pressure to maintain commitment to violence in the 1980s onwards which had to be overcome. Thus, regardless of any perceived stalemate or public backlash, many within the Provisional IRA during this period were committed to the armed struggle. One influential Provisional IRA member rejected the idea that increased community opposition to violence was a factor in disengagement:

> Community revulsion to the armed struggle had been present throughout the conflict and it did not have an impact, although if there were problems with tactics, then you would just change it ... There was no straw that would have broken the camel's back. There was always latent support which could not be affected. The Brits could curtail armed action, but it would have no effect on community support.[18]

Consequently, for some Provisional IRA members, the chances of success or increased repression was not the primary motivation for disengaging – there were intervening factors which resulted from interplay within the movement. Interplay is important for changing the perspective of a movement and leading them to accept disengagement. Disengagement frames do not necessarily draw upon one singular narrative, but the gradual acceptance of a disengagement frame within a movement can encourage others to adhere to the disengagement framing even if they do not fully believe it. Furthermore, interplay was also important in this instance because for many in the Provisional IRA disengagement was contingent on bringing the majority of the movement along as far as possible within the Provisional IRA:

> We wanted the debate to take place in the room, so it wasn't going to take place in the street. Because the one thing, probably the most important

thing to us was, what we have learnt from our history, was that once we lose our unity, then it's over. And every successive rebellion has been defeated by the split . . . And we were determined to avoid that because we needed our unity, we needed our strength, we needed the cohesiveness of the comradeship that we had built up over many, many years, in two decades. We wanted to have our debates, and our arguments, and our disagreements, and our resolutions, within the confines of the army.[19]

Movements can often have an excessive commitment to maintaining unity. Elsewhere, under Yasser Arafat's leadership, the Palestine Liberation Organisation's prioritisation of Palestinian unity presented many problems for Arafat's efforts in negotiations. A commitment to bringing along the movement, which is embedded in a movement's ideology as much as a manifestation of organisational pragmatism, makes interplay increasingly important for transitioning from bullets to ballots. One Provisional IRA member claimed that this interplay was also occurring within the 'community', which can be taken to refer here to the radical milieu that was traditionally supportive of the armed struggle:

It was a central tenet that we all had to move, we all had to go forward, or we weren't going for it. And that meant the community because we are the manifestation of the community, we are not separate from it. The community is me and my family and my neighbours and my friends, so, of course, it was everybody you were talking about. You wouldn't talk about everything to everybody but within the wider community of course there had been the debate there at the townhall meetings and the clubs all over the place. And people would say 'just because you are in the IRA doesn't mean you get to make the decision, you are only a part of the community'. So it was the community that had to understand it and a very very important sector of our community was the dead volunteers' families . . .[20]

Of course, the Provisional IRA's disengagement did lead to several splits, however it is widely accepted that it managed to avoid a larger split which could be detrimental to the transition to peace and it is unlikely it would have occurred if there was no internal support. This could reflect a readiness within the Provisional IRA to negotiate, a readiness which emerged from a perceived stalemate.[21] However, a focus on interplay better accounts for why they were ready to disengage. Of course, whilst the point being made here is that the creation of intra-movement legitimacy – interplay – is emphasised as important in the Provisional IRA's disengagement, this is not to ignore the more coercive elements in this dialogue or that the process was driven by an elite influenced by a perceived stalemate in the conflict.

Framing the End of the Armed Struggle

The period of interplay began in the 1980s but intensified within the movement from the 1990s onwards, culminating in the Provisional IRA's official disbandment in 2005. Throughout this period the discussions on disengagement and the peace process were multifaceted, however it is retrospectively possible to identify several themes which here constitute a disengagement frame. The 1980s was marked by internal reflection on the armed struggle within the Provisional IRA and the dialogue within the movement was a considerable factor in ensuring the majority of the movement supported the transition to peace. Perhaps the reason the stalemate thesis has been so persuasive is that some within the Provisional IRA framed disengagement in such terms:

> [The Hunger Strikes] period made it much harder to have the debate [on disengagement]. But I do remember the day when [the British Secretary of State] made an aside that the British couldn't defeat the IRA. And that was the one-liner that opened [things] up, and thinking 'that's very interesting'. And I remember phoning people up and asking, 'did you hear that statement?' Some people were going 'well they have been saying that for ages', and you were going 'no, they haven't, they haven't ever said that'. So that perhaps was an open, throwing the door open to see if we would come through it or an invitation.[22]

Ripeness theory is criticised because it construes 'stalemate' as an objective state of being, which, upon its perception by actors, can facilitate negotiations. The quote above illustrates that the idea of a stalemate did feature in the framing of disengagement, and therefore ripeness cannot be entirely dismissed, however on the other hand it is important to situate 'stalemate' as just one part of how disengagement was justified. In other words, the stalemate discourse did play a role in the Provisional IRA's disengagement. However, this should be seen as subordinate to the overarching process of internal interplay and that it is not necessary for 'stalemate' discourses (or even realities) existing in other transitions. A practical objection to the stalemate/ripeness thesis is that the conditions in the 1990s were broadly similar to the conditions in the 1970s, however the Provisional IRA's framing of stalemate was utilised more to emphasise the changing conditions, which provided the agency for transitioning away from violence. One former Provisional IRA member commented on the differences between the failed 1975 ceasefire and negotiations and the 1990s peace process:

> Well the difference was you were politicised, you were far more mature and your politics was far more mature. Back in your mind, even back in 1975, in the back of your mind you knew there had to be political dialogue to resolve this thing. Back in '75 it was there, but it didn't really click on, it didn't kick in. In the later stages, '94 and '98, it was well and truly in the front, it was your vision. Number one for us was we looked at the military situation and we were in a stalemate: the British army weren't beating us, and we weren't beating them. We could carry on if we wanted to, the end result of that was going to be a vicious circle of people going to jail, people losing their lives. And somewhere, someplace there was going to be political dialogue . . . Someone has to break out of the circle and get something moving.[23]

Despite framing disengagement in relation to a stalemate, the combined pressures of military, police and paramilitary repression is not sufficient to explain the Provisional IRA's transformation. The quote above highlights how whilst the perceived stalemate provided agency for alternatives, it was not an inevitable outcome. A key part of the Provisional IRA's framing of disengagement was to re-frame the position of the armed struggle within the movement ideologically. Armed struggle was emphasised as a tactic towards achieving an end rather than a principle itself.[24] The logical consequence of reframing the armed struggle in this way is that it opens up alternative forms of behaviour, namely engagement in politics and the abandonment of armed struggle. The advocacy of the 'armalite and ballot box' strategy in the 1980s, which emphasised a more expansive role in politics, provided an alternative to armed struggle and strengthened the rationalisation of violence as a means to an end. *Without this re-framing of armed struggle as a relative means to an end, a stalemate makes little sense.* One former member reflected upon the type of debates and the topic of discussions, highlighting how such dialogue was aimed at framing disengagement:

> I was doing a lot of travelling with her and her husband, and she said: 'see since you two started travelling together, my marriage has improved 100%, because when he comes in, he is exhausted arguing with you', and he was like 'I can't do it anymore', because he was very opposed to the cessation of the armed struggle. We'd be [in the car] from Cork to Belfast, and we would have talked about nothing else, and there would have been scream-ing matches. It was not always comradely and 'let me hear your opinion', it was screaming: 'are you stupid! Think it through, think it through, it's not about the armed struggle, it's about the objective and how best to get there.' And once you have that in your head, it opens the possibilities: this is the best way forward, and nobody is going to die.[25]

The Provisional IRA's re-framing of armed struggle as one of many means to its objectives was also accompanied by a reframing of its objectives to justify disengagement. The Provisional IRA emerged in the context of a civil rights campaign for equality and rights for the Catholic population of Northern Ireland and an end to discrimination and violent state repression. Yet the Provisional IRA's diagnosis of the problem emphasised traditional Republican goals of ending partition and re-uniting Ireland through armed struggle. Many of the generation who joined the Provisional IRA in this period were initially motivated by the former, but it was the latter that became the justification and objective of violence. The Provisional IRA's mobilisation of the population built upon fusing these two issues together, but the latent tension between them existed insofar as the civil rights issues had been broadly addressed by the 1970s and continued violence was not productive to further addressing such issues. Consequently, when the leadership sought to move away from violence it exploited the tensions between the two to frame disengagement whilst maintaining narrative fidelity to the group's objectives. The framing of disengagement from the 1990s onwards involved an amplification of the grievances and objectives of the 1960s civil rights movement in order to justify the shift away from violence:

> The thing young people throw back at you is 'you done it, you fought the Brits, and you did this and you did that'. And I say, 'yep, in them circumstances, where I was growing up, the influences, the politics of the day and all of that stuff, that all influenced me to respond in a certain way'. The next big question is, 'would you go back to it?' 'If I lived in the circumstances then, I would go back to it because it is justified, because nobody has the right to treat me or my family like a second-class citizen' . . . nobody has right to deny me a job or treat me like dirt like the Orange Order or the Unionists did, and nobody again will, because what we've done is stop that, we have cut that off. Didn't achieve a united Ireland. Still not going to stop trying to achieve that, but it stopped that happening again . . . we have created a level playing field to talk.[26]

Thus, the Provisional IRA framed disengagement in three ways. Firstly, armed struggle was reframed as a tactic rather than as a principle, which was accentuated by the 'armalite and ballot box' strategy insofar as it put violence on an equal footing with political activism and consequently removed the unique historical justification of armed struggle. Secondly, the rationalisation of armed struggle as a means to an end, alongside other possible tactics, was logically consistent with the idea of a stalemate insofar as it represented trading violence/weapons for concessions. Thirdly, disengagement could be justified without wholly rejecting the basis of the Provisional IRA's legitimacy by amplifying the civil rights movement's goals as an objective. Analysing group transitions in terms of a perceived stalemate obfuscates that the framing of disengagement may not always or solely be constructed around the idea of a stalemate – the fact the Provisional IRA did justify it in this way does not mean it was the main factor, especially where we see a re-framing of objectives to also justify disengagement.

Resonating Factors: Consolidating the Disengagement Frame Stick

The section above outlined key themes in the Provisional IRA's disengagement framing; the following section discusses several structural and ideational factors which facilitated the resonance of this frame within the movement, specifically the role of prisoners and (charismatic) leaders. Yet more broadly speaking, changes within the Provisional IRA's organisational structure in the 1970s which followed the Northern leadership beginning to dominate the movement helped to solidify the position of the leadership.[27] The culmination of these changes and the ongoing pressure placed upon the Provisional IRA placed the leadership and upper echelons within generational hegemony – in other words a specific generation dominated the movement which entrenched the position of the leadership. It facilitated resonance insofar as there was a rough coherence in the perceptions of members and their experience in the 1960s civil rights movement provided shared experiences, which made their claims of conditions changing more resonant than the generations who joined the Provisional IRA after this period. Therefore, there are deeper structures which can account for why interplay manifested as it did but also why it was broadly successful, nevertheless a more significant factor was that some within the leadership were utilising these structural factors to construct and disseminate a disengagement frame.

The Provisional IRA's disengagement largely emerged from a prison setting and filtered outwards into the movement. Several factors made prisons an ideal setting for discussing and framing disengagement. Prisons were divided into wings where each of the groups had its members based, including the Provisional IRA, who still adhered to group's chain of command. Prisons were therefore sites of continued activism which gave prisoners experience in negotiating with the prison system, and an emphasis on education exposed members to the group's ideology and meant prisoners had extensive time to debate, albeit under the watchful eye of the Provisional IRA Officer commanding in prison (later selected by the Provisional IRA leadership). One senior Provisional IRA prisoner stated that 'anyone could say what they wanted. In the main, there was one or two in every wing who were opposed [to disengagement]. A lot of them found it difficult to articulate why'. Another Provisional IRA prisoner also stated how the prison environment provided a space to rethink the direction the movement was going in:

> I think there was a whole thing within prison where people had the ability to . . . that final stage of conflict would always have to be political engagement, and for me the end game was always going to be discussion and

negotiation. Those kinds of discussions developed in prison where people would say 'well I do agree with you'; outside it would have been heresy but inside you were allowed to have that thing going on.[28]

Thus, the prison system allowed for a managed dialogue which favoured the Provisional IRA leadership's agenda – dialogue did emerge from prisons which could not occur elsewhere, however the overall trajectory of dialogue favoured support for disengagement. Prisoners were important in convincing the movement outside of prison to support the strategy and a similar internal process of debate occurred on the outside. Several former Provisional IRA members refer to ongoing debates throughout the 1990s onwards, which aimed at assessing the mood of members but also very clearly at convincing them of the peace process. Furthermore, it is important to keep in mind that the interplay within the movement was clearly directed in favour of disengagement and was helped extensively by the utilisation of individuals who had credibility within the movement, especially those who were former prisoners:

> There was people in the middle tier there, people like Paddy McGeown, who could walk into a room full of IRA volunteers and had that respect, former hunger striker, former-prisoner, IRA volunteer himself, who was so well-respected and . . . people like Brian Keenan, prominent Republicans, so they had so much respect from the IRA volunteers on the ground that they were able to go into a room full of those people and say 'look, we need to change'. And people would challenge that and question that, and they would get a logical reason used for doing that, then people could buy into that. In the main, the IRA volunteers on the ground did buy into that and trusted them. It was about trust as well because there is the context of whenever Republicans move out of armed conflict immediately all the words of sell-out, traitors, it all flies.[29]

The role of charismatic authority has been identified by Omar Ashour in accounting for the transition of Islamist movements from violence to non-violent approaches and the Provisional IRA's example also illustrates the role of charismatic figures throughout the levels of the organisation. The Provisional IRA also utilised leading figures from the African National

Congress (ANC) in discussions with members, both inside and outside prisons, which sought to draw upon their credibility to assuage the concern of members. The Provisional IRA example also highlights structural factors that can generate charismatic authority – activism within the prison system gave some prisoners skills in negotiations and practice in debating which, alongside the standing of prisoners within the movement, placed certain prisoners in a special position to persuade other members of the merits of disengagement. Thus, the role of charismatic authority in transition is a resource that can be constructed and is not necessarily restricted to the upper echelons of the movement.

In sum, a key factor in the Provisional IRA's transition was the interplay which occurred within the movement. In this process, a framing of disengagement was constructed through a reframing of ideology. Importantly, successful disengagement depends upon building on mobilising frames and, while this constrains and shapes the types of disengagement which can manifest, it also maintains a degree of narrative fidelity which makes the framing resonant. Piecemeal adaptations in the Provisional IRA's thinking had a structuring effect, facilitating changes toward supporting disengagement. In addition to the content of the framing, several factors helped the frame resonate through internal discussion. One of the most important and counter-intuitive factors was the prison system's role in freeing up discussion (albeit within parameters) and bestowing skills and credibility upon (some) prisoners which put them at an advantage in advocating for disengagement. Changes in the Provisional IRA, such as the shift in the balance of power internally from south to north, the shift away from mass mobilisation and the general ageing of the movement created a 'generational hegemony'. This generation was rooted in the experience of the 1960s civil rights movement and the violence of the 1970s. Therefore, attempts by the Provisional IRA leadership to convince the membership of disengagement had latent shared experiences from which to build an alternative framing, which (1) resonated with sections of the movement and (2) which helped to marginalise traditional voices in the process. Interplay therefore explains why the Provisional IRA were able to transition from bullets to ballots, whilst these structural factors – ideational and material – shaped the interplay and facilitated its success.

Conclusion: Theorising Ideology and an End to Violence

This chapter set out to discuss the Provisional IRA's transition from armed to unarmed activism and whether this could be explained through the prism of 'draw or defeat'. It has critiqued the extant literature on this subject and its applicability to Northern Ireland, particularly the influential theory of ripeness, which highlights the role of stalemates in creating the conditions for negotiations. Instead, the chapter has argued that interplay within the movement was a more important explanation for the transition than stalemate on its own. Others have argued persuasively on the role of internal dialogue within the Provisional IRA and the role of prisoners in the peace process. This chapter has sought to understand interplay as a framing process, identifying how attempts to reconcile and adapt ideology to justify disengagement shape the course of transitions from violence. Stalemate was a feature of the Provisional IRA's framing of disengagement, yet this does not necessarily prove the theory but rather underpins the importance of interplay in constructing the existence as significant and justifying disengagement, at least for some members. Without ideological innovations within the Provisional IRA, such as amplifying the civil rights grievances as an objective or the reframing of armed struggle, the notion of stalemate makes little sense, particularly as a motivation for the type of disengagement the Provisional IRA undertook. The 1960s IRA recognised the limitations of armed struggle, but the nature of their transition is wholly different from the Provisional IRA in the sense that the former was seeking opportunities to return to violence whereas the same cannot seriously be said about the latter.

An undercurrent of this argument is that ideology – or rather ideas – play a role in collective disengagement. Of course, the dominant understanding of ideology is in the context of radicalisation and de-radicalisation, where the assumption has been that the potential abandonment of ideology (de-radicalisation) can lead to disengagement, and moreover, a better quality of disengagement than that by which groups/individuals remain committed to violence. However, extensive research on this subject has challenged this linear assumption, often showing that the opposite is in fact the case and that in many cases, such as those studied by Omar Ashour, disengagement can occur while ideology is maintained. The preceding chapter approached the matter of ideology, radicalisation and de-radicalisation in a different manner, which has hopefully provided some insights into the complex causal role ideas have regarding violent behaviour. In other words, the case of the Provisional IRA shows how ideology can facilitate ending violence. The Provisional IRA cannot be described as having de-radicalised, at least as the term is commonly understood, yet the focus on ideas as grand narratives, which the concepts of radicalisation tends to maintain, obfuscates the nuanced role of framing and reframing. The Provisional IRA's case shows how the ideas underpinning a movement are constantly under construction, but also how certain arrangements of ideas can present opportunities for agents.

Notes

1. Gordon Clubb, *Social Movement De-Radicalisation and the Decline of Terrorism: The Morphogenesis of the Irish Republican Movement* (London: Routledge, 2016).
2. Aaron Edwards and Cillian McGrattan, 'Terroristic Narratives: On the (Re) invention of Peace in Northern Ireland', *Terrorism and Political Violence*, vol. 23, no. 3 (2011), pp. 357–76.
3. Seth G. Jones and Martin C. Libicki, *How Terrorist Groups End: Lessons for Countering al Qa'ida*, vol. 741 (Santa Monica: Rand Corporation, 2008); Audrey Kurth Cronin, *How Terrorism Ends: Understanding the Decline and Demise of Terrorist Campaigns* (Princeton: Princeton University Press, 2009).
4. Robert A. Pape, 'The Strategic Logic of Suicide Terrorism', *American Political Science Review*, vol. 97, no. 3 (2003), pp. 343–61.
5. Max Abrahms, 'Why Terrorism Does Not Work', *International Security*, vol. 31, no. 2 (2006), pp. 42–78.
6. Peter Krause, 'The Political Effectiveness of Non-State Violence: A Two-Level Framework to Transform a Deceptive Debate', *Security Studies*, vol. 22 no. 2 (2013), pp. 259–94.
7. For the definition of the types of de-radicalisation, see: Ch. 1, this volume.
8. William Zartman, 'Ripeness: The Hurting Stalemate and Beyond', in: National Research Council, *International Conflict Resolution After the Cold War* (Washington, DC: The National Academies Press, 2000).
9. Jonathan Tonge, Peter Shirlow and James McAuley, 'So Why Did the Guns Fall Silent? How Interplay, Not Stalemate, Explains the Northern Ireland Peace Process', *Irish Political Studies*, vol. 26, no. 1 (2011), pp. 1–18.
10. Eamonn O'Kane, 'Decommissioning and the Peace Process: Where Did It

Come from and Why Did It Stay So Long?', *Irish Political Studies*, vol. 22, no. 1 (2007), pp. 81–101.

11. Dean G. Pruitt, 'Readiness Theory and the Northern Ireland Conflict', *American Behavioral Scientist*, vol. 50, no. 11 (2007), pp. 1520–41.

12. Omar Ashour, *The De-radicalization of Jihadists: Transforming Armed Islamist Movements* (New York and London: Routledge, 2009).

13. Eamonn O'Kane, 'When can Conflicts Be Resolved? A Critique of Ripeness', *Civil Wars*, vol. 8, nos. 3–4 (2006), pp. 268–84.

14. Peter Shirlow et al., *Abandoning Historical Conflict? Former Political Prisoners and Reconciliation in Northern Ireland* (Manchester: Manchester University Press, 2010).

15. Ed Moloney, *A Secret History of the IRA* (New York: W. W. Norton & Co., 2003).

16. Daniel Koehler, *Understanding Deradicalization: Methods, Tools and Programs for Countering Violent Extremism* (London: Routledge, 2016).

17. David Snow and Scott Byrd, 'Ideology, Framing Processes, and Islamic Terrorist Movements', *Mobilization*, vol. 12, no. 2 (2007), pp. 119–36.

18. Interview by author, Former Provisional IRA Member 2, Belfast, 2/9/2013.

19. Interview by author, Former Provisional IRA Member 5, Belfast, 3/9/2013.

20. Ibid.

21. Pruitt, pp. 1520–2.

22. Interview by author, Former Provisional IRA Member 5, Belfast, 3/9/2013.

23. Interview by author, Former Provisional IRA Member 4, Belfast, 3/9/2013.

24. Interview by author, Former Provisional IRA Member 5, Belfast, 3/9/2013.

25. Ibid.

26. Interview by author, Former Provisional IRA Member 4, Belfast, 3/9/2013.

27. Moloney; Michael Lawrence Rowan Smith, *Fighting for Ireland? The Military Strategy of the Irish Republican Movement* (London: Routledge, 2002).

28. Interview by author, Former Provisional IRA Member 1, Belfast, 22/8/2013.

29. Interview by author, Former Provisional IRA Member 4, Belfast, 3/9/2013.

7

TRANSFORMATIONS AND DEFEATS: ETA AND THE END OF THE ARMED CAMPAIGN

Nick Hutcheon

Introduction

In 2018, the Basque armed organisation, Euskadi Ta Askatasuna (Basque Country and Freedom [ETA]), announced its dissolution, concluding a chapter in Basque history spanning almost sixty years. That ended any doubt about the organisation's commitment to unarmed activism, having already declared a 'definitive ceasefire' in 2011. This elusive moment was profoundly significant for Basque society and politics, but it was not instantly transformative, nor was it unanticipated. In fact, socially and politically, the Basque Country was already well adjusted to life after ETA and the organisation's militants were also, in many respects, well prepared to de-radicalise both behaviourally and organisationally. ETA did not achieve its main political objectives (the establishment of a socialist and Basque-speaking Basque state) and it never seemed likely to do so in the context of an insurmountable political stalemate with the Spanish state. Accordingly, popular support for ETA diminished throughout the post-dictatorship period and the view that the goals of the Basque nationalist left (Izquierda abertzale[1], IA) could be achieved through armed activism became an increasingly marginal one. Despite that, it took time for the grassroots and political leadership of the IA, to which ETA belonged, to break the taboo and articulate that view openly and assertively. Although multiple rounds of negotiations between the Spanish state and ETA had taken place since the end of the dictatorship, the government during the period of ETA's decisive transformation rejected the possibility of a bilateral peace process, unwilling as it was to recognise a political dimension to the conflict, or even the existence of a conflict. Instead, the Spanish government focused its efforts on counter-terrorism measures, which, by implicating the entire IA, put pressure on ETA from within its own community. Indeed, as discussed in detail in this chapter, the incentives to end the armed struggle came primarily from within, focused as they were, on the achievement of tangible political goals, most importantly, the decriminalisation and political legitimisation of the IA. Thus, the decision to end the armed struggle was a unilateral one, driven by the political leadership of the Basque nationalist left and necessarily validated by prestigious political figures – and external interactions with them[2] – from outside the Spanish state. This chapter elaborates on those points, describes the process leading to ETA's dissolution and discusses certain elements of that process that explain the reasons how and why the organisation dissolved when it did.

A Disputed Conflict

In both scholarly and political spheres, the definition of the relationship between ETA and the Spanish state as a conflict is disputed. In academia, on the one hand, there are those who approach studies of ETA from the perspective of a political conflict[3] and, on the other, there are those who treat ETA as a purely criminal organisation.[4] The latter tend to disregard the possibility that ETA saw armed struggle as a politically expedient strategy[5] and, therefore, they also overlook the political logic of the organisation's end.[6] With that in mind, this chapter recognises that ETA had political objectives which were opposed by the Spanish state, and that the organisation sought to achieve its aims through armed struggle, to which the state responded using various methods, including violence.[7] In this sense, a conflict between ETA and the Spanish state did exist. Politically, left-wing Basque nationalists quite obviously recognised the end of ETA as the end of a conflict. However, this view is shared by very few other political parties or organisations in the Spanish state. Instead, the dominant view, shared by both the main parties of government since the transition from dictatorship to democracy, the Popular Party (PP) and the Spanish Socialist Workers' Party (PSOE), is that there was no conflict and therefore no political dimension to the relationship between the Spanish state and ETA.

The intransigence of the Spanish state on this matter is rooted in its determination to uphold the 1978 constitution. Refusing to recognise a conflict with ETA is not only because of the organisation's use of violence, but also because of its main political objective: Basque independence. Secession from the Spanish state is illegal, as enshrined in Article 2 of the constitution, which protects the 'indivisible unity of the Spanish nation'. Therefore, the Spanish state does not formally define or recognise itself as multi- or plurinational, nor does it define or recognise the Basque Country, Catalonia or Galicia as nations with the right to self-determination. Seeking to secede from the Spanish state is anti-constitutional and, as such, illegal, which, effectively, criminalises the aims of sub-state nationalists.[8] This has been explicitly exemplified in Catalonia since the Catalan government held a consultative referendum on Catalan independence in 2017. The imprisonment of Catalan nationalist leaders on charges including treason and sedition demonstrated the severity with which the Spanish state is willing to uphold the constitution, even in a context in which political violence is not present. At least rhetorically, the Spanish state governed by either the PP or the PSOE, there are no conflicts to negotiate with sub-state nationalists: there is constitutional law, and the role of the state is to uphold it, while citizens must abide by it. Thus, to breach constitutional law is, logically, to engage in criminal activity.

Seeing ETA's political objectives in such terms, Spanish governments have been reluctant to facilitate solutions to the conflict which could be construed as legitimising them. Although, perhaps because, negotiations between ETA and Spanish governments, led by both the PP and the PSOE, had taken place on multiple occasions since the end of the dictatorship, there was no appetite on the part of the PP-led Spanish government to enter dialogue with the armed organisation after it announced its intentions in 2011. In 2013, the Scottish Green Party MSP,[9] John Finnie, met the Spanish state's representative in Scotland, whom he commended for engaging in what he described as the 'peace process'.[10] The Spanish diplomat responded by saying he had no knowledge of any such process and concluded that, in any case, 'we don't deal with criminals'.[11] This attitude is characteristic of the Spanish state, particularly when governed by the PP, with regard to its relationship with ETA. This being the case, ETA sought external interactions to validate the so-called peace process unrecognised by the Spanish state. Consequently, in 2011, a group of prestigious political figures, including Kofi Annan, Bertie Ahern, Gerry Adams and Jonathan Powell, came together and produced the Declaration of Aiete (17 October 2011), in which they urged the French and Spanish governments to engage with ETA and negotiate a lasting peace. It suited ETA, but not the Spanish government, who rejected the declaration and quite aggressively discredited those who produced it. Whitfield described this as a virtual peace process and, indeed, it was unconventional and quite bizarre when compared to other comparable situations within Europe, such as Northern Ireland. However, three days after Aiete, on 20 October 2011, ETA announced a definitive ceasefire, in which they echoed the words of the declaration '[calling] on the governments of France and Spain to open a process of direct dialogue which aims to resolve the aftermath of the conflict and overcome the armed confrontation'.[12] Needless to say, the dialogue ETA asked for in that statement did not materialise. However, this outcome may actually have suited both sides: on the one hand, ETA could claim to have made a unilateral decision to bring an end to the armed struggle without being seen to have conceded to demands made by the Spanish government or to have been defeated; and, on the other hand, the Spanish government could claim its uncompromising approach had been vindicated, as ETA received no political concessions in return for ending its armed struggle. That is how it played out, meaning that the end of ETA produced competing and conflicting narratives on the reasons and consequences, bringing no collective sense of achievement, nor a bilateral project to consolidate the end of the conflict and secure its permanency.

ETA: 1959–2018

Before continuing to discuss the end of ETA, it is first helpful to step back and describe the organisation's beginnings and how it maintained one of the longest running armed conflicts in modern European history. The organisation was formed in 1959, at which time the Spanish state was a dictatorship ruled by General Francisco Franco. Franco seized power in 1939 after a three-year civil war with the democratically elected government of the Second Republic and those who defended it (predominantly the left and sub-state nationalists, such as the Basques and the Catalans). Franco's victory led as many as half a million people to flee the Spanish state, around 150,000 of whom were Basque.[13] Clark stated that it 'would be impossible to exaggerate the importance of the Spanish Civil War for Basque national identity'[14] since for the Basques it was 'one of those rare psychological moments in history when an entire culture passes through an experience of the deepest signifi-cance, and is never quite the same again'.[15] And so it was. Franco singled out the most populous, and most Basque nationalist, Basque provinces, Bizkaia[16] and Gipuzkoa,[17] for condemnation as 'traitorous provinces', for which they suffered more states of exception than anywhere else.[18] Symbols of Basque nationhood were erased from sight, use of the Basque language was prohib-ited and prominent Basque nationalists were exiled and executed. In this way, Franco uncompromisingly set about the task of homogenising the population of the Spanish state culturally and linguistically, which previous incarnations of Spanish nationalism had failed to achieve.

The regime's emphasis on language had a profound impact on the ideo-logical and strategic transformations in Basque nationalism from this period onwards. 'If a language is lost traumatically, there is an increase in conscious awareness of the loss of its use'.[19] And indeed the oppressive measures of the regime to suppress the Basque language generated real fears among Basque nationalists that its continued existence was in doubt, which in turn led to a reinterpretation of the role of language in defining Basque national identity. The shift from ancestry to language as the defining trait of Basque national identity was accompanied by internal tensions regarding the politi-cal direction of Basque nationalist opposition to the regime. The victory of the Allies in World War Two raised belief in the Basque Country that, with Nazi Germany and Fascist Italy defeated, a similar fate would soon befall Francoist Spain. However, the onset of the Cold War impeded any such possibilities, as the US courted Franco as a useful ally against the Soviet Union, dealing a fatal blow to any hopes of Allied intervention in Spain. Indeed, confirmation came in the form of the 1953 Defence Pacts signed between Franco and the USA, allowing the stationing of American military bases in the Spanish state. This, combined with the rising strength of the dictatorship, led to the emergence of a youthful and more radical strand of Basque nationalism.[20]

Until 1959, the main vehicle for clandestine Basque nationalist activity had been the Partido Nacionalista Vasco (Basque Nationalist Party [PNV]), the party formed in 1895 by the founding ideologue of Basque nationalism, Sabino Arana. The PNV leadership pinned its hopes on external intervention against the dictatorship and did not consider direct action as an alternative strategy. The forlorn approach of the PNV frustrated younger Basque nationalists and that would eventually lead to one particularly active group of young intellectuals, who were writing essays and publishing newsletters about Basque culture and nationalist politics, to form ETA in 1959. The group promoted the establishment of an independent Basque-speaking republic and believed that direct action was required to achieve those aims. Heavily influenced by anti-colonialism and the armed struggles in decolonising nations such as Algeria, ETA's young activists concluded that, in the circumstances they found themselves in, the use of violence was both morally justifiable and strategically imperative. Thus, in 1961, ETA initiated its armed campaign when the group attempted to derail a train carrying Franco loyalists to Donostia.[21] Few could have imagined at the time that ETA's armed activities would continue for another fifty years and escalate as dramatically as they did.

From its roots as a non-violent group primarily concerned with the survival of Basque nationhood and culture, ETA turned into a revolutionary socialist and nationalist armed organisation campaigning for the creation of a socialist and Basque-speaking state comprised of the seven Basque provinces in the French and Spanish states. The convergence of nationalist and socialist ideals synchronised the organisation's founding ideology with the contemporary socio-political reality of the Basque Country. In the 1960s, the Basque Country was a hive of heavy industrial activity, built on metallurgy and shipbuilding, which attracted hundreds of thousands of immigrants from other areas of the Spanish state. Internal debates in the 1960s and 70s centred on the strategic role of armed struggle in achieving ETA's political objectives and how the organisation could mobilise the working classes and engage with the immigrant population.

At the beginning of the 1970s, ETA incorporated four main factions: the Red Cells, who stressed the need to shift the priority of the movement away from nationalism and the national struggle towards the workers' movement and the social revolution; the ETA leadership, whose fundamental objective was to create a working-class led struggle towards both the national and social liberation of the Basque people; the defenders of the anti-colonial theses; and the *milis*, who considered the armed struggle to be the driving force of Basque nationalism.[22] The *milis* became the dominant faction in the 1970s, which shaped the ideological and strategic trajectory of ETA's armed struggle throughout the proceeding decades. The *milis* were committed to the armed struggle and focused on strategy and political tactics. This led to the most significant split in the history of ETA, in 1974, which resulted in the formation of ETA Military (ETA-m) and ETA Political-Military (ETA-pm). ETA-pm favoured a combined military and political strategy and believed the organisation should focus on mobilising the working classes, while ETA-m upheld the primacy of the armed struggle. The two factions effectively operated as distinct organisations, until September 1982, when ETA-pm announced its dissolution. In return for renouncing the use of violence, around 300 members of ETA-pm in prison and in exile were amnestied by the Spanish state and allowed to dedicate themselves to conventional political activism, primarily through ETA-pm's political wing, Euzkadiko Ezkerra (The Left of the Basque Country [EE]). This left ETA-m as the sole heir of the historic organisation until its own dissolution thirty-six years later. ETA-m assumed all military responsibilities while new political organisations, most significantly Herri Batasuna (Popular Unity [HB]), were formed to operate on the political front, but not to entice ETA-m militants away from armed militancy. This hierarchical restructuring, headed by ETA-m, laid the foundations for the Basque nationalist left movement.

The Gradual Appeal of Unarmed Activism

When ETA announced its dissolution in 2018, it was a diminished organisation, militarily, socially and politically. In each of those aspects, the prospect of recovery was minimal and very obviously so. Militarily, ETA activities peaked in the period 1978–80 and, from then on, the intensity of ETA's armed activities decreased, and its methods provoked increasing levels of discomfort within its traditional support base and intensifying public opposition.[23] The bombing of the Hipercor supermarket in Barcelona in 1987, in which twenty-one civilians died, and the kidnapping and assassination of the PP councillor Miguel Angel Blanco in 1997 are often cited by left-wing

Basque nationalists as turning points in their attitude towards ETA and the armed struggle. That can be seen in the polling data on support for ETA: in the early 1980s, support for ETA was high, but, by 1999, polls showed that support for ETA among the Basque population was 2%, ten years later it was 1% and in a poll conducted in 2018, 4% considered that the impact of ETA over the last forty years was positive, compared to 81% who considered it negative.[24] After the establishment of the autonomous communities in 1980, popular support for ETA dwindled and members of the organisation could not count on the levels of social support they had previously in the 1960s and 70s.

One reason for that was that the experience of state repression that affected the entire population of the Basque provinces in the Spanish state during the dictatorship became more individualised.[25] When Franco singled out Bizkaia and Gipuzkoa for especially severe treatment, he collectivised the experience of state repression and inadvertently brought disparate sections of Basque society together (e.g., the left and Basque nationalism and ethnic Basques and intra-state immigrants). There is a pro-ETA slogan which can still be seen in the Basque Country: *ETA herria zurekin* (ETA the people are with you). Certainly, at the very least, people in the 1960s and 70s knew what ETA stood for and why it did what it did and, given the social and political circumstances of that era, it is obvious that many people were able to empathise with their friends, family, neighbours and work colleagues who became active members of the organisation. Because of that, ETA militants were able to swim like fish in the sea, as the saying goes. But, post-Franco, as Spanish democracy established itself and, collectively, the experience of state repression against Basque culture and Basque nationalist politics diminished, the sea ETA members swam in began to dry up. But, that said, in a small country of 3.5 million people (including all seven provinces in the French and Spanish states), a third of whom live in the greater Bilbao[26] area, a substantial proportion of the Basque population has been affected in some way by the conflict and, with hundreds still in prison for their involvement with ETA and the IA, that remains true today. The difference in recent years was that feelings of empathy for friends, family, neighbours and colleagues who were members of ETA did not necessarily extend to the organisation itself as once might have been the case.

The absence of ETA as an active presence in Basque society and politics means activists of the IA can feel slightly more at ease, knowing that accusations of supporting and promoting ETA are more difficult to uphold. For families, friends and communities connected to those individuals, there is also obvious relief; likewise, of course, for everyone. More than 800 people died as a result of ETA actions, affecting families and communities all over the Basque Country and the Spanish state: it is uncontroversially true that opposing ETA was dangerous, especially so for politicians, police and military. But the violence extended much further and the fear and anxiety it caused spread much more widely than only those targeted by ETA. Being an activist of the IA was, and to some extent still is, a hazardous lifestyle choice. Statistics compiled by *Euskal Memoria Fundazioa*[27] give an indication of the risks of being engaged in left-wing Basque nationalist activism. According to their data, between 1980 and 2012 there were 16,569 arrests recorded of individuals associated with left-wing Basque nationalist activities. In the same period, they recorded 314 deaths, 3,371 cases of torture and 638 injuries.[28] The conflict has taken its toll on the Basque population and its end hopefully ensures that it can shake off the heavy burden of violence it has carried for decades.

Letting go of the past is no easy task as long as the perception of the Basque people as perennial recipients of Spanish oppression persists. However, the very obvious cultural, political and social advances made in the Basque Country since the end of the dictatorship made it increasingly difficult to justify armed struggle as a means of expressing the legitimate criticisms of Spanish democracy made by Basque nationalists. The Basque provinces in the Spanish state have a very substantial degree of political autonomy, the Basque language has flourished and Basque nationalism is well-established as the dominant political tendency – the PNV has governed the Basque Autonomous Community (BAC) for all but three years (2009–12) since 1980. Thus, the armed struggle came to be seen as anachronistic and ultimately, counterproductive, by increasing numbers of those who were once inclined to sympathise with ETA. What took time was for that view to be expressed by the IA openly and, crucially, with confidence that the political leadership had superseded ETA as the vanguard of the movement. These internal interactions were a key factor in the process towards ETA's dissolution.

ETA was formed to provide the radical political leadership its founders believed Basque nationalism lacked at that time. Consequently, ETA was the catalyst for the emergence of a vibrant political movement which has endured to the present day. From the beginning, the armed organisation was the vanguard of that movement, but, gradually, especially since the establishment of the autonomous communities, it was superseded by the political leadership of the IA.[29] That transformation was explicitly confirmed in 2010, when the social base of the IA concluded several months of internal debate on the future of the armed struggle by proposing its end. The debate was initiated by the political leadership of the IA, who, for the first time, deviated from the command structure of the movement, which had until then been heeded by the military leadership.[30] As part of the movement, ETA was obliged to follow the will of the majority. The abandonment of armed activism was a politically expedient move,[31] and the decision to end the armed struggle was a utilitarian one, just as it was in the 1960s when ETA militants began using violent methods. Material changes in the cultural, social and political circumstances since then undermined the case for armed activism, and by 2010 it was clear to a majority of the IA that armed activism was a hindrance to political progress.

The political advantages of unarmed activism became apparent almost immediately after ETA announced the definitive ceasefire in October 2011. In the Basque parliamentary elections almost exactly twelve months later, Euskal Herria Bildu (Basque Country Unite [EH Bildu]), a coalition of left-wing Basque nationalist parties, won 25% of the vote and the PNV reached 34%. In 2016, EH Bildu and the PNV won 21% and 37% of the vote respectively and in 2020 the figures were 28% and 38%. Thus, combined, Basque nationalists accounted for at least 60% of the vote share in all three parliamentary elections following the ceasefire, more than in any election that took place during the armed struggle. Further evidence of political progress as a result of the end of the conflict can be seen in Navarra, the most conflicted province in the Basque Country, where pro-Spanish Navarran regionalism has dominated the autonomous government since 1980. In the 2015 and 2019 elections to the Navarran parliament, two Basque nationalist coalitions, the centre left Geroa Bai (Future Yes), which incorporates the PNV and only exists in Navarra, and the left wing EH Bildu, which is present throughout the Basque provinces in the Spanish state, won 30% and 31% between them, enough to lead a coalition government on both occasions. Such a scenario would have been unthinkable in Navarra during the armed struggle, and for those who advocated for its end, developments in what Basque nationalists consider to be the cradle of the Basque Country vindicated the argument for a strategic change.

At the same time, the IA remains a radical political movement; thus, for former ETA members, behavioural and organisational de-radicalisation can be separated from ideological de-radicalisation. The political leadership of the IA advocates civil disobedience as an addition to mainstream political activities and an alternative to armed struggle. One example of how this non-violent radical activism has been put into practice is found in the *Aske gunea* (Free Place) mobilisations. These involved hundreds of activists gathering in public places to surround fellow activists as they resisted arrest by the police. Having to wade through hundreds of activists to reach their targets provoked the police to use force. Contrasted with the passivity of the activists, the symbolic value of this was obvious, as the scenes reinforced the portrayal of the Spanish state as oppressive and authoritarian. At the same time, these mobilisations gave the IA an opportunity to channel any residual enthusiasm for armed activism and recover some of the moral high ground it had lost during the years of the armed struggle. In these mobilisations, and others, there has been no trace of dissident factions seeking to continue the armed struggle, as is evident for example in Northern Ireland with the various splinter groups of the Irish Republican Army (IRA).[32] Instead, the IA has adapted strategically to make political progress in the post-conflict scenario. This, after all, was the objective of the movement when it called on ETA to end the armed struggle.

The End of ETA

Clearly, on the part of the IA and ETA, the reasons for ending the armed struggle were political and strategic. Strategically, ETA had two main aims: to form a Basque nationalist alliance and, through attrition, to force the Spanish state into making political concessions. As the organisation was weakened by the counter-terrorism strategies of the Spanish state, its leadership became less experienced and less effective in making armed activism work. At the same time, the Spanish state adopted the so-called 'everything is ETA' approach, believing that without the support of the IA, both in terms of recruitment and political legitimisation, ETA could not survive.[33] This resulted in political parties being banned, newspapers shut down, bars closed and hundreds of activists being arrested, all because of their alleged association with ETA. The perpetual cycle of violence, repression and renewal had no end in sight, and this concerned the more experienced and politically savvy leaders of the IA who could see that the armed struggle was a dead-end strategy and that ETA had become an obstacle to progress.[34] As long as ETA was on the scene, there was no prospect of a Basque nationalist alliance and even less chance of the Spanish state entering into discussions with ETA or the IA that could lead to successful political outcomes. On both matters, efforts to make progress failed precisely because the PNV and the Spanish state refused to cooperate with ETA, or the IA, while armed activities continued.

Negotiations between ETA and the Spanish state went nowhere in the past, most notably in Algiers in 1989 and from 2005 to 2007 with the government of Prime Minister José Luis Rodríguez Zapatero, so the IA and ETA adopted an approach that bypassed the state, which they called unilateralism. This was initiated by the political leadership of the IA, driven by the internal debate that took place within it between 2009 and 2010 and consolidated by the involvement of external actors. This final stage in the process was crucial, as it validated the conflict narrative and allowed ETA to end its armed activities without being seen to have been defeated. It is hard to see how the impasse could have been overcome without external interactions, yet those involved were shunned by the Spanish government, who stuck to the line that any form of engagement with ETA was, in effect, collaboration. The limited engagement of the Spanish government in the post-2011 process towards the dissolution of ETA makes the Basque–Spanish context markedly different to the processes which led to the end of the armed organisations that ETA most closely identified with, namely the Fuerzas Armadas Revolucionarias de Colombia (Revolutionary Armed Forces of Colombia [FARC]) and the IRA. After the failed negotiations in 2007, the Spanish government's involvement in the process became more antagonistic. In 2009, Arnaldo Otegi, who was the leading figure in the debate within the IA that led to the end of the armed struggle, was imprisoned for nine years accused of attempting to re-establish an illegal party, Batasuna (Unity). This frustrated the internal interactions that were crucial for establishing the route map towards the end of the armed struggle, but, ultimately, it did not derail the so-called 'peace process'. Otegi remained in prison until 2016, five years after the definitive ceasefire, by which time ETA was in the final phase of its existence. The motives behind Otegi's imprisonment are not for this article to discuss, though others have begged the question: was it *because* he forced ETA to stop?[35] The absence of ETA obliges the Spanish state to re-examine its approach to containing the aspirations of Basque nationalism and creates new opportunities for Basque nationalism to pursue them. Accordingly, it is notable that the Basque nationalist media welcomed the definitive ceasefire in 2011 as good news while much of the Madrid-based media treated it as bad news.[36]

There are conflicting narratives regarding the manner of ETA's end.[37] From the perspective of the Spanish state, the preferred view, held by politicians, media, academics and the general public, is that ETA was defeated. The orthodox position in the Spanish state is that this was a criminal rather than a political matter, which was resolved because the state refused to deal with ETA as an organisation with legitimate political aims. Without a doubt, the 'everything is ETA' approach had an impact on the IA and contributed to the movement's collective decision to openly disapprove of ETA's use of violence. In such a small country and upon such a close-knit movement, the heavy crackdown on the IA took its toll on its activists and those close to them, generating a collective fatigue with the perpetual cycle of violence, repression and renewal. In that sense, it could be said that militarily, through the Spanish state's counter-terrorism policies, ETA was defeated. Nonetheless, until its final days ETA maintained its organisational structure and its ability to recruit new members and operate militarily, albeit in a diminished capacity. Furthermore, politically, ETA's objectives continue to be pursued by the IA, even by the PNV to some extent, and, arguably, there is now more chance of their being realised. Therefore, characterising the end of ETA in terms of defeat does not sufficiently describe the outcome of its dissolution. To be clear, nor can it be described as a victory. Although ETA's political aims have not been defeated, they have certainly not been achieved. It is especially noteworthy that there is still no democratic means of achieving Basque independence, as the Catalan crisis resulting from the non-state-sanctioned referendum in 2017 exemplified. Despite certain obvious advances since ETA came into being in 1959, the armed campaign did not succeed in forcing the Spanish state into constitutional reform which could facilitate Basque independence. Politically, then, this represents the failure of ETA to achieve its goals through armed activism.[38] The dissolution of ETA was the result of a protracted, strategically motivated transformation from armed to unarmed activism, which, on the part of the armed organisation, reflected the evolution of its status from the creator and vanguard of a political movement to an obsolete faction.

Post-conflict

In ETA's final public statement, a militant described the organisation as if it were an organic entity, unique to the Basque Country: 'ETA arose from this people and now it dissolves back into it'.[39] It was a curious phrase that could be interpreted in many ways. However, one element of particular relevance here is that it very clearly projected a desired outcome with regard to the reintegration of ETA militants in the aftermath of the conflict. This remark suggested that ETA militants would naturally make the transition from being actively involved in the organisation to life outside it. Despite the hostility that existed towards ETA in Basque society and the marginalisation of ETA within the IA, it is also evident that there is a hospitable environment within which ETA militants are able to adjust to life after the armed struggle. At the very least, the community of the IA offers former ETA militants social spaces and political structures to fit into and, without ideologically de-radicalising, continue campaigning for a Basque-speaking and socialist Basque state – as they surely will. Politically, former ETA militants have a vibrant, ready-made movement within which they can dedicate themselves to unarmed political activism. There is no need for them to set up new political structures, since ETA was always part of a movement which still includes political parties, trade unions, youth groups, feminist groups, student groups and media. In addition to that, the IA is a social community that has a presence in every corner of the Basque Country, in the form of bars, social clubs and Basque cultural groups. It is easy to be entirely immersed in the activities associated with the IA; it is, to use a cliché, a way of life. Many former ETA militants are already active figures in the community of the IA and those who are disengaging from the armed struggle can now be confident of being able to do the same. The IA is a radical political movement, and this means former militants can behaviourally and organisationally de-radicalise without doing so ideologically. Framing the transformation from armed to unarmed activism in that way (i.e., as a strategic move) was undoubtedly part of the reason the Basque nationalist left movement was successful in guiding ETA towards dissolution and why there is little concern about a return to armed struggle by ETA or dissident former members.

Thus, on the part of disengaging ETA militants, behavioural and organisational de-radicalisation is facilitated by the security of knowing that they are acting in a way that fellow militants and the wider movement consider consistent with advancing the aims of the movement to which they belong. In September 1982, ETA-pm announced its dissolution and, in return, around 300 members of ETA-pm in prison and in exile were amnestied. Unlike the post-2011 situation, the state was heavily involved in the dissolution of ETA-pm and went to remarkable lengths to facilitate that process. But the cost that ETA-pm members paid for clemency from the state was hostility and excommunication from sections of the Basque nationalist community – two were assassinated by ETA-m. For ETA militants leaving the armed struggle now, such concerns do not exist, in the first place, because the wider movement is entirely supportive, but, also, because they did not receive any reward from the state, unlike ETA-pm members in 1982. This evidently facilitates the transition from armed to unarmed activism and the social and political integration of former militants in the post-conflict era.

Generally, the social conditions in the Basque Country for former ETA militants are favourable. The Basque Country is not as divided as it is often portrayed to be in academia, the media and by political opponents of Basque nationalism. Basque society is diverse, in terms of origins, national identities, linguistic practices, class and political options and, while the conflict has undeniably intensified some of those differences, the lived experience of cultural, political and social difference in the Basque Country is incomparable to many other conflict zones, of which Northern Ireland, where communities are arranged and segregated according to religion, identity and politics, is the most obvious example. ETA members, like Basque nationalists generally, reflected the Basque social reality; many were not born in the Basque Country, many more were the offspring of intra-state immigrants and many could not speak the Basque language (though this became gradually less true following the introduction of Basque-medium education in the 1980s).[40] Bilbao does not resemble Belfast, there are no physical barriers in residential areas separating one community from another and although certain voting trends are detectable, Basque political parties do not represent identity-based communities in the same way as Nationalist/Republican and Unionist/Loyalist parties do. To make that point, if consociationalism was introduced in the Basque Country, who would that be designed to accommodate? In this sense, the Basque Country is not a typical post-conflict society that requires the type of cross-community peacebuilding seen in markedly divided societies such as Northern Ireland. Thus, the immediate social impact of ETA's dissolution is limited and the reintegration of ETA militants into social as well as political life is less complicated than it would be in a more socially divided conflict, which, again, reflects the primarily political nature of the conflict between ETA and the Spanish state and the reasons they both have such conflicting narratives of the nature of their relationship between 1959 and 2018.

Conclusion

It took a long time, but in 2018 ETA finally announced its dissolution, ending nearly sixty years of armed struggle. From a Basque nationalist perspective, culturally, politically and socially the Basque Country has advanced beyond recognition since the period in which ETA was formed. However, despite that, ETA has not achieved its main political goal, Basque independence, and still there remains no democratic means of making that happen. This would suggest that ETA was defeated. But, as discussed in this chapter, that would be an inadequate way to describe ETA's dissolution. Instead, it is clear that ETA's end concluded a long period of transformation, during which the organisation's position within the IA evolved from being its creator and vanguard to becoming a faction which was eventually responsive to the political leadership of the IA, which grew in influence during the period following the creation of the Basque autonomous communities. Gradually, it became increasingly clear that armed activism could not succeed in forcing the Spanish state into making political concessions, nor could it bring about a Basque nationalist alliance. Instead, ETA's armed activities were a hindrance to progress and, ultimately, to break the perpetual cycle of violence, repression and renewal, the political leadership of the IA initiated an internal process of debate that for the first time in the history of the movement displaced ETA as its ultimate decision-maker. ETA emerged because of a lack of radical political leadership and it ended because that leadership existed and, eventually, asserted itself as the vanguard of the left-wing Basque nationalist movement that ETA created.

Notes

1. *Izquierda* is the Spanish word for 'left' and *abertzale* is the Basque word for 'nationalist', which literally translates as one who loves the patria.
2. On the role of external interactions with non-liked minded figures and organisations, see: Ch. 1, this volume.
3. Imanol , 'No More Bullets for ETA: The Loss of Internal Support as a Key Factor in the End of the Basque Group's Campaign', *Critical Studies on Terrorism*, vol. 10, no. 1 (2017), pp. 93–114; Teresa Whitfield, *Endgame for ETA: Elusive Peace in the Basque Country* (Oxford: Oxford University Press, 2014); Julen Zabalao and Mikel Saratxo, 'ETA Ceasefire: Armed Struggle vs. Political Practice in Basque Nationalism', *Ethnicities*, vol. 15, no. 3 (2015), pp. 362–84; Joseba Zulaika and Imanol Murua, 'How Terrorism Ends–and Does not End: The Basque Case', *Critical Studies on Terrorism*, vol. 10, no. 2 (2017), pp. 338–56.
4. Rogelio Alonso, 'The Madrid Bombings and Negotiations with ETA: A Case Study of the Impact of Terrorism on Spanish Politics', *Terrorism and Political Violence*, vol. 25, no. 1 (2013), pp.113–36; Florencio Dominguez, *La agonia de ETA: una investigacion inedita sobre los ultimos dias de la banda* (Madrid: La esfera de los libros, 2012).
5. Zabalo and Saratxo, p. 362.
6. Zulaika and Murua, p. 339.
7. Paddy Woodworth, *Dirty War, Clean Hands: ETA, the GAL and Spanish Democracy* (London and New Haven: Yale University Press, 2002).
8. Ioannis Tellidis, 'Peacebuilding Beyond Terrorism? Revisiting the Narratives of the Basque Vonflict', *Studies in Conflict and Terrorism*, vol. 43, no. 6 (2020), pp. 529–47.
9. Member of the Scottish Parliament.
10. John Finnie, 'Violence by Spain is Not Just Limited to Catalonia', *The National*, 4/1/2019, accessed on 28/10/2020, at: https://bit.ly/31MCdKv

11. Ibid.
12. 'ETA anuncia el cese definitivo de su actividad armada', *GARA*, 21/10/2011, accessed on 23/4/2012, at: https://bit.ly/31QqV88
13. Cameron Watson, *Modern Basque History: Eighteenth Century to the Present* (Reno: Center for Basque Studies, 2003).
14. Robert P. Clark, *The Basques: The Franco Years and Beyond* (Reno: University of Nevada Press, 1979), p. 76.
15. Ibid., pp. 76–8.
16. Vizcaya in Spanish and Biscay in English.
17. Guipúzcoa in Spanish.
18. Diego Muro, 'The Politics of War Memory in Radical Basque Nationalism', *Ethnic and Racial Studies*, vol. 32, no. 4 (2009), pp. 659–78.
19. Benjamín Tejerina Montaña, 'Language and Basque Nationalism: Collective Identity, Social Conflict and Institutionalisation', in: Clare Mar-Molinero and Angel Smith, *Nationalism and the Nation in the Iberian Peninsula: Competing and Conflicting Identities* (Oxford: Berg, 1996), p. 225.
20. Diego Muro, 'Nationalism and Nostalgia: The Case of Radical Basque Nationalism', *Nations and Nationalism*, vol. 11, no. 4 (2005), pp. 571–89.
21. San Sebastián in Spanish.
22. Antonio Elorza et al., *La Historia de ETA* (Madrid: Temas de Hoy, 2000).
23. Benjamín Tejerina Montaña, 'Nationalism, Violence and Social Mobilization in the Basque Country: Factors and Mechanisms of ETA's Rise and Fall', *Papeles del CEIC*, vol. 3, no. 136 (2015), pp. 1–19.
24. 'Oleadas Euskobarómetro', *Euksobarometro*, accessed on 4/1/2019, at: https://bit.ly/3jDsUCK
25. Montaña, 'Nationalism', p. 15.
26. Bilbo in the Basque language.
27. 'Centro documental – bases de datos', *Euskal Memoria Fundazioa*, accessed on 13/2/2015, at: https://bit.ly/3oxpaXf
28. Ibid.
29. Zulaika and Murua.
30. Ibid.
31. Zabalo and Saratxo, pp. 362–4.
32. Muru, pp. 341–2.
33. Elorza et al.
34. Muru, pp. 341–2.
35. Zulaika and Murua, pp. 351–2.

36. Imanol Murua & Txema Ramírez de la Piscina, 'Ceasefire as Bad News: The Coverage of the End of ETA in the Basque and Spanish Press,' *Revista Latina de Comunicación Social*, vol. 72 (2017), pp. 1453–67.

37. Zulaika and Murua, pp. 356–7.

38. Murua, pp. 338–40.

39. 'Comunicado integro de ETA para anunciar su disolucion,' *Euskal Irratia Telebista (EiTB)*, 3/5/2018, accessed on 14/1/2019, at: https://bit.ly/34F4Tr0

40. See: Nick Hutcheon, *Intra-State Immigrants as Sub-State Nationalists: Lived Experiences in the Basque Country* (London: Routledge, 2020).

8

THE AFGHAN TALIBAN AND THE PEACE NEGOTIATIONS: ARE THE TALIBAN 'DE-RADICALISING'?*

Thomas H. Johnson

Introduction

While sporadic efforts to end the conflict in Afghanistan via negotiations have taken place since soon after the US intervention and eventual occupation of the country, in February 2018 serious negotiations[1] began between the United States, led by Zalmay Khalilzad and Taliban representatives. These negotiations eventually led to a 'peace agreement' between the US and the Taliban, referring to itself as the Islamic Emirate of Afghanistan, signed in Doha, Qatar. This agreement will be discussed below.

The primary purpose of this chapter is to discuss the implications for the Taliban of participating in and signing this agreement with the US. Some of the explicit questions that will be addressed by this chapter are:

1. Whether or not these negotiations been accompanied by explicit transformations of the Taliban and, especially, their leadership;
2. Whether the talks caused or resulted in disagreements within Taliban leadership;
3. What the role has been of external actors in these negotiations;
4. Whether we have witnessed any state-level structural reforms (political, constitutional, security sector or civil-military related, transitional justice issues or any other relevant reforms to encourage the initiation

and/or the continuation and sustainability of the transformation) in Afghanistan;

5. Whether the 'negotiations' have suggested any significant events or policies to indicate that the Taliban may be de-radicalising.

Hence, the purpose of this chapter is how the Afghan Taliban have transformed, if at all over the years, especially in view of the 'peace negotiations'. An additional research objective is to explore why and how the inclination towards these negotiations happened.

Before explicitly addressing these explicit research questions, it is useful to briefly discuss the background of the Taliban and the Afghan conflict to lay a context for the research that follows.

The Taliban's Origins and Background

The *Talib* ('seeker of knowledge or student' in Arabic) has been an important fixture in society ever since Islam was introduced in the seventh century to the area of present-day Afghanistan.[2] For centuries Talibs travelled the countryside as ascetics, often living off the land and tithing's from Afghan villagers, in search of religious 'truth'. The *Taliban* (plural of Talib) would later became an extremely important part of the Afghan social fabric running religious schools (*madrassas*), mosques, shrines and various religious and social services, and serving as *mujahideen* when necessary.

The political foundations of the Afghan Taliban were directly related to the Soviet invasion (1979), occupation and anti-Soviet *jihad* (1979–89) and the basic inability of former Mujahideen commanders to unify and stabilise Afghanistan's post-Soviet withdrawal in 1989. After the withdrawal of the Soviet Union from Afghanistan, the United States also withdrew nearly all support for the Mujahideen (US support, aimed at 'bleeding' the Soviets to the maximum extent, represented the most expensive covert action in US history).

The Mujahideen were successful in overthrowing the Afghan communists in 1992, but, shortly after, a violent Civil War erupted amongst various Mujahideen groups, and especially commanders, seeking power in Afghanistan.

The violence and criminality of supposed Mujahideen-turned-warlords who raped, plundered and extorted the war-weary Afghan population between 1992 and 1994 resulted in the political formulation of the Taliban that was not only a reaction to the criminal warlords, but also represented a reactionary *Deobandi* (a revivalist movement within Sunnism – primarily *Hanafi*) Islamist movement. Many of the early Taliban leaders and soldiers had fought the Soviets in the Yunas Khalis' Hezb-e-Islami (Party of Islam) party (HIK) or *Harakat-i-Inqilab-i-Islami* (Islamic Revolution Movement) led by Mohammad Nabi Mohammadi.

One of these Jihadists, who had his own madrassa in Maiwand, Kandahar, was Mullah Mohammed Omar Mujahid (or simply Mullah Omar), who either because of piety, adept politicking, or the fact that he was descended from a major regional subtribe, soon became the leader of the Taliban. Although the Taliban were able to use their Pashtun ethnicity to rally many Pashtun tribes, the initial basis of the Taliban leadership core was Hotaki Ghilzai Pashtuns, Mullah Omar's tribe.

The Taliban was a unique political organisation in Afghan history, because its leaders were almost exclusively clerics and many of its members, especially foot soldiers, were Afghan refugees from Pakistan. While the Pashtun areas had seen charismatic cleric-led uprisings in the past, none were imbued with the same unique backstory of the Taliban. The radical ideology of the Taliban, in part, was birthed in the refugee camps on the Pakistan side of the Durand Line – as was the desire to transform a lost, Godless Afghanistan into a land sanctified by the effort of Afghan jihadists.[3]

While living as rebels and refugees, the young men that became the Taliban foot soldiers were significantly influenced by their madrassa teachers whose educations were entirely grounded in the ultra-fundamentalist Wahhabi and Deobandi ideologies. In their madrassas, the Taliban had been taught jihad and a narrow, rigid, orthodox interpretation of Islam that did not value extortive and criminal behaviour; therefore, though many fought against the Soviets, the Taliban were sheltered from becoming pawns for the Mujahideen warlords. Instead, due to the excesses of the early 1990s, the Taliban grew increasingly angry at the extortive and extractive nature of the warlords working in and around Kandahar and Helmand provinces.

Like other Afghan groups at the time, the Taliban appear to have taken whatever support Islamabad would give, but the Taliban remained independent and, according to Antonio Giustozzi, reflected a peculiar Afghan genius.[4]

To argue, as some have done, that the Pakistanis completely controlled the Taliban just does not stand up to the empirical data.

Taliban Organisation

After taking control of Kabul from the Mujahideen in 1996, Mullah Omar slowly learned the importance of organisation and structure in managing his widespread insurgency. In 2003, Omar worked to prevent similar issues and created a council of confidants to help supervise the growing arms of the Taliban. In *On Guerilla Warfare*[5] Mao highlights the importance of divisional structure, writing:

> In guerrilla warfare, small units acting independently play the principal role, and there must be no excessive interference with their activities . . . Only adjacent guerrilla units can coordinate their activities to any degree. Strategically, their activities can be roughly correlated with those of regular forces, and tactically, they must cooperate with adjacent units of the regular army.[6]

Omar's council appointed leaders for matters regarding finance, military operations, governance, religion and other important divisions, but allowed basic forces to work somewhat independently.[7] The new organisation allowed Omar to oversee the movements of the insurgency whilst also giving him the freedom to focus a majority of his attention on overall strategy.

The US invaded Afghanistan following 9/11 on 7 October 2001. From 2001 to 2004, the Taliban utilised a trial-and-error method as they worked to revolutionise their insurgency. Taliban leadership found tactics and methods that worked with the ideological goals of the insurgency, and then adapted them to ensure optimal success. This period of experimentation was integral in the success that the Taliban enjoyed from 2005 to 2020.

Taliban forces were initially outnumbered in Afghanistan, but they were experts of the Afghan landscape and found new ways to exploit their knowledge effectively against counterinsurgents. As Mao advises, the Taliban began to move quickly through the mountainous territories of the country and planned attacks and ambushes that they could control. Meanwhile, US conventional forces moved sluggishly, weighed down by heavy equipment, hindered by poor roadways, and slowed by constant sweeps for IEDs. The slow movements of the counterinsurgents allowed Taliban units to trap conveys, retreat and quickly move insurgents to their next location for preparation of continued attacks.

Again, following the guidelines set forward in Mao's *On Guerilla Warfare*, the Taliban transformed their organisation to meet the growing needs of the insurgency. Mao advises:

> The soldier must be educated politically. There must be a gradual change from guerrilla formations to orthodox regimental organisation. The necessary bureaus and staffs, both political and military, must be provided. At the same time, attention must be paid to the creation of sustainable supply, medical and hygiene units.[8]

While the government of Afghanistan attempted to modernise and liberalise, the Taliban also set out to revolutionise their structure and ideologies. Organisational alterations that began in 2008 transitioned the Taliban away from a patrimonial structure and towards a more centralised structure.[9] This substantial change paved the way for more uniformed and effective Taliban political divisions. Additionally, the Taliban began to adopt new ideologies in matters such as governance, technology and public services that would allow them to undermine progress made by the central government in Kabul. These changes, when compared to the Taliban of 1994, illustrate the ideological and political ingenuity of the Taliban from 2005 to 2020.

Ideology and Domestic Policies under Taliban Rule

Regardless of their intentions to create an Afghanistan devoid of ethnic division, the original Taliban were primarily Pashtuns who saw all other Afghan ethno-linguistic groups (e.g., Tajiks, Hazaras, Uzbeks) as their enemies. The village mullahs and clerics, who became the leaders of the Taliban, rebelled not only against urban modernity but also conflicted with many of the tenets of *Pashtunwali* (literally the 'way of the Pashtun' – the unwritten rules that drive and significantly influence a Pashtun's life, honour and conflict resolution, especially in rural Afghanistan).

An early tactic of the Taliban was to attack their enemies' arms depots. Shortly after their formation, Pakistan gave a massive arms depot near Spin Boldak which had originally 'belonged' to HIG to Mullah Omar's Taliban.

The Taliban used the heavy weapons from this depot to attack their enemies (Afghan Northern Alliance, officially known as the United Islamic Front for the Salvation of Afghanistan, and HIG). Importantly, the Taliban also used demonstrations of power that had significant psychological impacts on the war-weary Afghan population. Throughout 1994 and 1995, the Taliban rapidly gained control or made significant advances in much of south, southwest, central and eastern Afghanistan. While much of this could be attributed to military abilities, their success also came from early domestic policies. Not only in the south or southwest but also throughout the nation, Afghans were tired of the warlords' greed and violence, so they gravitated towards the hope and security offered by the Taliban. The Taliban became an almost mythical group as it quickly and clearly defeated Afghanistan's most powerful warlords, often without firing a weapon. And the Taliban developed a brilliant narrative campaign to gain the allegiance of rural Afghanistan via a series of resonating stories.[10]

At some point in time, prior to capturing Kabul, the Taliban changed their stated objectives from bringing peace and stability to establishing a 'pure Islamic state', which included the creation of a religious police force (the Committee for the Promotion of Virtue and the Prevention of Vice), appointing only 'pious' Muslims to government positions, the establishment of Sharia law and an economy based solely on the Quran and Sunnah. They also strictly enforced the burqa – head to foot hijab – for women, prohibted any 'alien cultural influences' and enforced education that encouraged jihad for all Afghans.

Initially after taking Kabul in 1996, the Taliban created an inner council (the Inner Shura) that maintained primacy, and an outer council (or Central Shura) for foreign relations and administrative purposes. This structure proved cumbersome and ineffective for managing a modern nation state, so in 1999 the Taliban re-established many of the administrative practices of the previous Afghan governments. It's important to note that Mullah Omar was bequeathed the title *Amir al-Mu'minin* ('Commander of the Faithful') after he donned the alleged cloak of Muhammad that was held inside the Mosque of the Cloak of the Prophet Mohammed in front of 1,500 Afghan religious leaders in Kandahar on 4 April 1996. He only travelled to Kabul – the traditional Afghan capital – on a couple of occasions during Taliban rule of

Afghanistan. He ruled the country from Kandahar in a complex built for him by Osama bin Laden. It is also important to note that the five person Shura that was in charge of the administration of Kabul consisted of Taliban who only spoke Pashto in a city that was primarily Dari-speaking. Quite simply, the Taliban proved to be extremely inept administrators.

The Taliban strictly segregated sexes (known as *purdah*). While this is an established practice throughout much of rural (particularly Pashtun) Afghanistan, Afghan urbanites, especially Kabulis, were extremely concerned when the Taliban pushed the practice onto the entirety of the country.

Even after the change of government structure in 1999, which the Taliban intended in part to enhance foreign relations in a bid to gain international recognition, the Taliban's foreign policies remained woefully amateurish. While only three countries formally recognised the Taliban Regime – Pakistan, Saudi Arabia and the UAE – Mullah Omar's government, shortly after obtaining control of the nation, realised foreign aid was necessary if the Taliban was to retain its power. Hence, the Taliban government did not reject foreign relations, however their rigid application of Sharia, often violent and draconian domestic policies, and threatening postures to many regional neighbours made contacts with the rest of the world difficult and unpractical. Nevertheless, the Taliban in Kabul, even over the protests of those in the Taliban heartland of Kandahar, worked to obtain United Nations' and other foreign aid.

A central aspect of the Taliban's domestic policy was to provide a haven for many international and regional jihadi groups. Unlike al-Qaeda (AQ), most of these groups were not global in either structure or ideology, rather they were mostly insurgent organisations looking to the Taliban for tactics, techniques and procedures in overthrowing their own repressive, un-Islamic, Western-influenced governments. Still, though providing a haven was part of Taliban practice and policy, the organisation never indicated or behaved in any manner that suggested the Taliban were overly interested in international jihad or terrorism. Rather they were primarily interested in fighting to gain total control of Afghanistan and impose an Islamic Emirate.

From 1997 to 2001, as the Taliban further consolidated control from the Northern Alliance, they simultaneously failed to achieve international recognition while increasing their radical behaviours. By March 2001, and increasingly influenced, but not controlled, by the most radical of Salafis (al-Qaeda), the Taliban rid the country of non-Muslims (excluding Afghan Sikhs and Hindus who the Taliban forced to wear special badges) and destroyed the Buddhist statues of Bamiyan. Military and political success only further motivated the Taliban to push Afghanistan into a state of 'pure Islam' grounded in the Wahhabi and Deobandi teachings of their youths (and reinforced by their Salafist allies, al-Qaeda).

By 2001, while the Taliban were successful in pushing their stated policies onto Afghans, they were never successful in creating jobs, infrastructure, or institutional development, or bringing security to the entire nation. Moreover, the United States and their allies would destroy the Taliban regime in November 2001 because they 'harboured' the architects (bin Laden and AQ) who planned and executed the 11 September 2001 attacks.

In his statement to the nation on the night of 11 September 2001, President George W. Bush outlined US strategy emanating from the 9/11 attacks: to capture or kill those responsible for the attacks – including nation states providing safe-haven. In his post-attack address to the nation, Bush stated, 'We will make no distinction between the terrorists who committed these acts and those who harbour them'.[11]

On Sunday, 7 October 2001 the United States, with the support of the United Kingdom, commenced its Operation Enduring Freedom (OEF) air campaign against AQ and the Afghan Taliban. Within four days the US had exhausted its initial target set. During his announcement on the commencement of operations in Afghanistan, President Bush again reemphasised the multi-national aspects of the coalition.

While there is no doubt that the Bush administration was successful in creating a coalition to initially support President Bush's metaphorical 'Global War on Terrorism', this coalition has, quite frankly, not been successful in Afghanistan. While all the specifics of this failure are beyond the scope of this chapter, one thing is clear: coalitions should not be viewed as a panacea that can solve all of the problems facing the United States and the West. After nineteen years, Afghanistan continues to be at war with itself, a corrupt economic basket case and, most importantly, the Taliban has not been defeated, whilst ISIL is also conducting operations in the country. Many have argued that Afghanistan has become another Vietnam for American foreign policy, and prominent to this argument is the proposition that the US coalition in Afghanistan has proven to be an interesting alliance, to say the least.[12]

President Obama, who greatly increased US involvement in Afghanistan during his tenure, claimed during his West Point 'Afghan surge' speech of December 2009 that Afghanistan was different from Vietnam because it was conducted by a 'coalition' of forty-three countries (during the 'height' of international involvement in Afghanistan). We would suggest, however, that the coalition has *not* had an overly significant impact on military or political results in Afghanistan and the coalition in Afghanistan was quite different quantitatively as well as qualitatively when compared to the US coalition in Vietnam. As I have argued elsewhere, the US Afghan coalition was basically a throwback to President Bush's 'Iraq coalition of the willing' mathematics. The truth is that significantly more foreign troops fought alongside the United States in Vietnam than actually fought with the Americans at the height of their involvement in Afghanistan.[13]

President Trump greatly reduced the US presence in Afghanistan and wanted to leave the country completely.[14] During much of the latter part of his administration, Trump pursued negotiations with the Taliban. In July 2018 US officials met secretly with the Taliban in their new office in Doha Qatar.[15] Shortly after this meeting, Trump appointed Zalmay Khalilzad to lead efforts to negotiate with the Taliban. These negotiations eventually led to the February 'Peace Agreement' with the Taliban that included clauses specifying that all NATO and US forces be withdrawn from Afghanistan within fourteen months and that the Taliban would prevent terrorists, especially al-Qaeda, from operating in Afghanistan and that the Taliban would conduct intra-Afghan talks with the Kabul regime.

The Taliban had risen to power in Afghanistan based on their ability to adapt, innovate and overcome seemingly insurmountable obstacles.[16] An additionally important factor was the Afghan population's extreme resentment after decades of war. It's also very important to recognise that the Taliban versions of 1996, 2001, 2006 and 2020 actually have little in common except for certain major political goals.

Analysis

Having so far focused on the history, organisation and ideology of the Taliban, and introduced the peace negotiations between the United States and the Taliban, we will now explicitly focus on the Taliban's approach to the negotiations[17] and their implications for the transformation of the Taliban into a political party. Here we will explicitly focus on the research question presented in the chapter's introduction in addition to examining why and how the inclination towards negotiations/compromise has happened. These questions will be assessed relative to what the Taliban has overtly stated through the media. Specifically, we will focus on the Taliban's statements from Twitter.[18]

While we have gathered reams of data from the Taliban's official website – Voice of the Jihad – and Taliban media statements, only the Taliban's Twitter statements will be assessed here. We are well aware that these tweets can be interpreted in a variety of fashions and can represent perceptions rather than reality. It remains to be seen what actual level of sincerity the Taliban have professed in their desire for the peace and freedom of all Afghan citizens. Nevertheless, we believe that the mere size of data collected will, in part, present Taliban peace negotiation narratives and associated stories.[19] Before assessing these data, let us first make some general comments concerning the Taliban and the peace negotiations.

First, one could forcefully argue that real and sincere negotiations have historically been accompanied by a ceasefire between warring parties. While there have been a variety of ceasefires between the Taliban and Kabul, especially around Eid, the end of Ramadan, in recent years (2019, 2020), these have usually been limited to three days and after its end the Taliban immediately returned to combat. Why didn't Khalilzad demand a ceasefire during the negotiations? It is not hard to argue that peace negotiations without a ceasefire are an in fact an oxymoron.

Second, these may be the first peace negotiations, signed on 29 February 2020,[20] in history that did not included the participation of one of the major warring parties – the Kabul government. The Taliban have long viewed the Afghan government in Kabul as merely a 'puppet' of the US and refused to have Kabul at the negotiating table with the US. The Taliban held brief conversations with former President Karzai in Moscow in February 2019, but these talks again did not involve the Afghanistan government.[21] As with the lack of a demand for a ceasefire during the talks, it is hard to understand why Khalilzad did not raise the issue of having Kabul participate in the negotiations, even just to be at the table so that Kabul could have exact knowledge of how the US was negotiating Afghanistan's future. While the February 2020 agreement did include a stipulation that intra-Afghan negotiations were scheduled for 10 March 2020 in Oslo, Norway, the disrupted nature of the 2019 Afghan presidential election did not allow for the creation of a Kabul negotiation team.[22] The US also agreed to the Taliban demand that 5,000 Taliban prisoners be released and the Taliban would in turn release 1,000 Afghan prisoners before intra-Afghan talks could commence. Ghani, who had absolutely no involvement in this agreement, initially rejected it. Direct negotiations were expected in March, according to the US–Taliban deal, but the start had been delayed by disagreements over the swap of 5,000 Taliban prisoners for 1,000 Afghan security forces. The Afghan government initially opposed the plan, saying that they had played no part in the negotiations, but conceded after much pressure from the Trump administration.[23] On 1 March 2020, Ghani stated that he would reject the prisoner exchange:

> The government of Afghanistan has made no commitment to free 5,000 Taliban prisoners . . . the release of prisoners is not the United States authority, but it is the authority of the government of Afghanistan.[24]

On 1 April 2020 Kabul and the Taliban had face-to-face talks concerning the prisoner release under the auspices of the International Committee of the Red Cross (ICRC) but nothing concrete resulted from this meeting. After Ghani and Abdullah Abdullah signed an agreement on 17 May 2020 'resolving' the highly contested 2019 presidential election results,[25] creating a power-sharing agreement and somewhat national unity government, peace negotiations were primarily made the responsibility of Abdullah Abdullah. By August, Kabul started to release Taliban prisoners, but it was a highly contentious move. On the surface it appears that the Taliban basically defined the parameters of the negotiations. One could also argue that the mere fact that the Taliban was able to hold initial negotiations based on their demands, suggest that they are not necessarily interested in holding impartial negotiations with the Afghan government to end this nineteen-year conflict.

Third, there are a variety of narratives and associated stories either presented or mentioned by the Taliban over the period of this study (2018–present) that deserve comment:

- Since early 2018, when violence or military operations have been announced by the Taliban it seems to largely coincide with rounds of peace talks. One interpretation of this could be that it makes perfect sense for the Taliban to post such accounts to suggest that they are coming to the negotiating table from a position of strength (albeit real or perceived), rather than from of position of weakness.
- The Taliban often post messages, especially recently, focusing on both the military and civilian population 'realising the truth' and abandoning their government posts to join with the Taliban, whereby the Taliban suggests such figures are always welcomed graciously, given gifts and are able to return to a 'normal' life.
- Since early 2020, definite effort has gone into projecting unity amongst the leadership and particularly the cohesion of political and military aims and goals. As will be suggested below, the Taliban have found it advantageous to appear as a united front. But certain events suggest that the Taliban is facing explicit factional problems that Kabul believes could impact on 'peace negotiations'.[26]
- The Taliban have also recently placed considerable emphasis on the Islamic Emirate of Afghanistan. The actual level of sincerity the Taliban have professed in their desire for the peace and freedom of all Afghan citizens remains to be seen.
- IEA's support of education and infrastructure as evidenced in their various Commissions that are publicised on the Official Website.
- The Taliban have also focused many posts on the COVID-19 pandemic and how it has obviously disrupted all facets of both US and Taliban operations. They have also focused on what they view as poor efforts by Kabul to protect the people from the pandemic.

In an effort to develop a more systematic understanding of the Taliban's position and their views concerning the negotiations and associated issues, we have collected data concerning Taliban statements (2018–20) from:

- The official Taliban Website – The Voice of Jihad (Arabic: صوت الجهاد Ṣawt al-Jihad);
- The Taliban's official Twitter site, most of the tweets are attributed to the official Twitter account of the Spokesman of the Islamic Emirate of Afghanistan, Zabihullah Mujahid, and;
- A wide variety of media sources reporting on the Taliban.

Because of the vast amount of data that we have collected, our analysis here will focus exclusively on Taliban statements from Twitter as suggested above.

In order to collate the massive amounts of Taliban Twitter statements from 2018 to 2020 that present their explicit views on the peace process, we will summarise the data through a series of bar charts. The bar charts that follow were created by sourcing the archived Twitter posts of Islamic Emirate of Afghanistan spokesman (name or alias) Zabihullah Mujahid; @Zabehulah_M33. They reflect the number of instances that an individual post was made regarding:[27]

1. Offensive attacks or successful defensive encounters by Taliban forces.
2. War crimes perpetrated by coalition forces or Afghan gov't forces.
3. Afghan gov't or military who defected to join the Taliban insurgency.

The charts only reflect the number of times in any given month from 2018 to the present; only one of these three events was tweeted about by @Zabehulah_M33 and not raw numbers of individuals in any case. It is also important to remember that these are claims made via Twitter by the IEA spokesman(s) and have not been verified for accuracy. They are presented to provide a visual representation of where the emphasis has been placed by the Taliban through social media propaganda in any given month starting in 2018. We will assess this data for each of the three years the US has negotiated with the Taliban.

2018

As suggested by Figure 8.1 below, during the initial months of negotiations the Taliban originally refused to admit to the authenticity of war claims attributed to their organisation. However, the Taliban claimed a wide number of

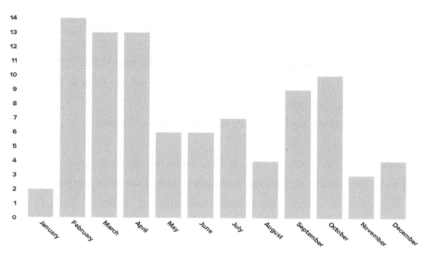

Figure 8.1 War crimes claimed by the Taliban in 2018

war crimes by Kabul and NATO. And these claims significantly increased in the following months of the beginning of US–Taliban negotiations.

There are a variety of ways to interpret this data. First, claiming an increasing number of war crimes by their enemies could be viewed as a justification of their entering talks with these 'criminals of the Afghan people'. By participating in negotiations with the 'crusaders' (US) the Taliban might be seen to spare the Afghan people from mass-casualty attacks. The data reinforces the Taliban narrative trope that only they can bring security to the Afghan people. For all practical purposes, the Taliban's central military strategy is to force their opponents and especially the US into making mistakes. For example, the Taliban as an insurgency has no great incentive to explicitly hold land. Hence this weakens attacks from the US' formable Air Force. In fact, because the Taliban do not have to hold specific land, they want the US to resort to high altitude air strikes knowing that if a 500 bomb goes astray and kills Afghan innocent civilians, especially children and women, it greatly enhances their cause and helps create new members for their movement.

For the last two years ANSDF, US and NATO forces have killed more Afghan civilians than the Taliban for the first time since the war began:

From 1 January to 30 September 2019 UNAMA documented 8,239 civilian casualties (2,563 deaths and 5,676 injured), similar to the same period in

2018. Anti-Government Elements continued to cause the majority of civilian casualties in Afghanistan and also caused slightly more civilian deaths than Pro-Government Forces in the first nine months of 2019, contrary to the first half year of 2019 when Pro-Government Forces caused more civilian deaths. Forty-one per cent of all civilian casualties were women and children. Civilians living in the provinces of Kabul, Nangarhar, Helmand, Ghazni, and Faryab were most directly impacted by the conflict (in that order).[28]

The Congressional Research Service puts it this way:

U.S. air operations have escalated considerably under the Trump Administration: the U.S. dropped more munitions in Afghanistan in 2019 than any other year since at least 2010. These operations contributed to a sharp rise in civilian casualties; the U.N. reported that the third quarter of 2019 saw the highest quarterly civilian casualty toll since tracking began in 2009, with over 4,300 civilians killed or injured from July 1 to September 30, though 2019 overall saw a slight decrease in civilian casualties. In the first two months of 2020 alone, U.S. forces conducted 1,010 strikes in 27 of Afghanistan's 34 provinces. In May 2020, U.S. Air Forces Central Command stated it would no longer release monthly reports on the number of airstrikes and munitions released, citing how the report could adversely impact on going discussions with the Taliban regarding Afghanistan peace talks.[29]

It should also be mentioned that the United States has conducted what appears to be a concerted effort through social media/internet channels to downplay overt offensive violent acts committed by the US and Afghan government forces over the last two and a half years.[30]

This is exactly what the Taliban desires and works to achieve. Nothing helps them more than when an air strike or indirect fire goes astray and kills Afghan civilians. This not only reinforces their narrative that their enemies care nothing about the lives of Afghans, but also serves as a recruiting poster in this honour/revenge society.

Figure 8.2 presents data concerning Taliban claims of GoIRA of

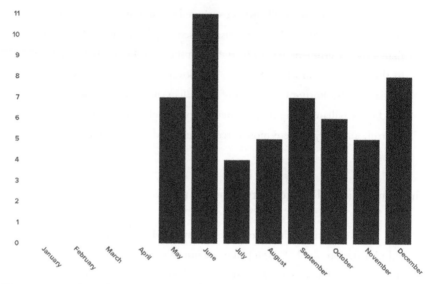

Figure 8.2 Military/govt employee defections claimed by the Taliban in 2018[31]

defections. This is also an important dynamic for Taliban's political strategy. Historically, changing alliances have been a regular phenomenon in Afghanistan and more times than not reflects the belief that one side is winning thus people want to defect to it. A review of the media will suggest that recent years have witnessed numerous defections to the Taliban not only OF citizen groups but also ANA soldiers and ANP police. This data also includes individual senior leaders. Moreover, it gives them considerable flexibility in negotiations by claiming that the Afghan people believe they are winning the conflict.

A review of the 2018 Twitter data also suggests that in early 2018, especially in January, the IEA Twitter feeds as well as IEA official website focused heavily on attacks, especially martyrdom attacks (suicide bombings) carried out by Taliban forces. Such attacks have much greater importance than the number of people killed; in fact, we believe that is possibly ancillary to the information operation component of such attacks. That is to suggest that such attacks are telling the Afghan people that the Taliban can operate when, where and how they desire and neither the ANDSF nor their US and NATO forces can stop them. This would seemingly put them in a strong negotiating position especially when the actual intra-Afghan negotiations began.

The February 2018 Taliban tweets contain numerous links back to the official IEA Website containing propaganda videos of intense Taliban military operations and training. This again could be intended to communicate that the Taliban are a force to be dealt with; the recognition that they represent an existential threat to the ANDSF. It is interesting to note that in September 2018 both the Pentagon and Kabul classified the size of the ANDSF and their causality rate;[32] this must be viewed as a 'tell' that things were not going the way that Kabul and the US had expected. A few weeks later it was reported that the Taliban had 65,000 fighters in Afghanistan. For years this figure was usually presented as being between 25,000 and 30,000. Soon after this report, the Taliban started their campaign against Afghan urban areas. A review of the Twitter data also suggests that in early June the Taliban started denouncing 'war crimes' by the enemy during ceasefire events. These pronouncements again presented the Taliban with fodder for their negotiations with Khalilzad. Also, it is interesting that late in 2018, the Taliban began tweeting about larger military operations especially aimed at Bagram Air Force Base. In late 2018 the Taliban were killing roughly fifty-seven soldiers and police a day.[33]

2019

Figure 8.3 presents the number of Taliban offensive and defensive operations in 2019. The data of this figure suggest that the Taliban conducted numerous military operations during their negotiations with the US. In most years, the Taliban ceased significant operations during the winter months and started their new year's military operations in spring (usually April); this surely was not the case in the winter of 2018–19. This could be an indicator of a variety of things pertinent to the research presented in this chapter. First, it could suggest that the negotiations were viewed as of secondary importance relative to their continuing pursuit of militarily destroying the Kabul regime. Second, it could suggest that the Taliban were willing to negotiate with the US based on their terms, because they believed that this was not going to impact on their military operations. As suggested earlier, we have always been amazed that Khalilzad did not demand an end to all military actions (a ceasefire) while the negotiations were being conducted. The Taliban took full advantage of his silence and his inaction.

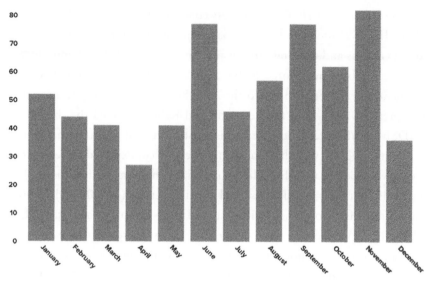

Figure 8.3 Attacks/defensive engagements claimed by Taliban forces in 2019

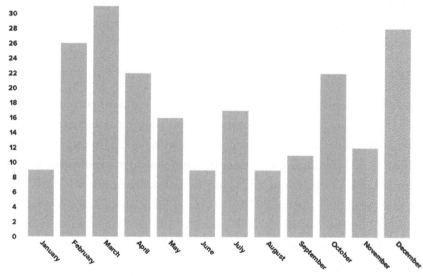

Figure 8.4 War crimes claimed by the Taliban in 2019

Figure 8.4, like Figure 8.1 for 2018, presents war crimes that the Taliban claimed that Kabul and its allies, especially the US, committed in 2019. Here again, the Taliban are exploiting the fact that during 2019 Kabul and its allies were responsible for more civilian deaths than the Taliban, for the first time

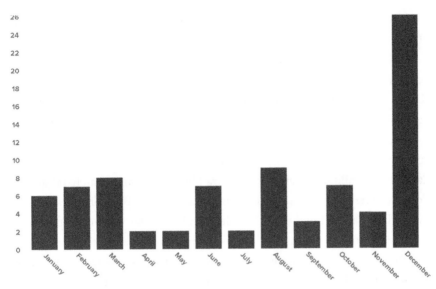

Figure 8.5 Military/govt employee defections claimed by the Taliban in 2019

since the beginning of the war in 2001. This was partly because of a change in types of operations. This again supports their key narrative that only the Taliban can provide security for the Afghan people.

Figure 8.5 presents the number of Afghan military and government employees the Taliban claim are defecting. This data also supports the Taliban claim that they are winning the conflict, and this is critical because historically Afghans like to be associated with victorious alliances and groups. This also suggests that 'jihad' is central to their activities. This would seem to be in direct contradiction with the Taliban holding 'peace' negotiations with the United States.

Further analysis of the 2019 Taliban tweets found in early 2019 a plethora of tweets concerning negotiations, whereas previous tweets had contained denials about IEA delegates even participating in any such negotiations. In late 2018 Mullah Abdul Ghani Baradar was released from a Pakistani prison and become the leader of the Taliban negotiating team.

It is claimed that Baradar actually sheltered fellow Popalzai Durrani Hamid Karzai in 2001 and possibly saved his life after an errant US bomb in Uruzgan Province killed several men on the Special Forces team that was escorting him. Baradar later became a confidant of the ex-president's brother, paid CIA informer Ahmed Wali Karzai, (assassinated in Kandahar on 12 July 2011).

The early core of the Ghilzai leadership of the Taliban had long suspected Baradar of being too willing to negotiate and too partial to his kinsmen – Karzai – in making field appointments. Indeed, this suspicion led to the creation of the Quetta Shura's Accountability Council in late 2009, whose job apparently included removing many of Baradar's excessively Durrani and Karlani appointments. This partially explains why Mullah Zakir, the hard-line ex-military chief of the Quetta Shura, was immediately released in Peshawar after being captured in Karachi, along with Baradar, in early 2010 by the Pakistani ISI and the CIA. Meanwhile Baradar was put in prison for eight years until his release to lead the Taliban negotiating team in 2018,[34] a position he presently shares with Mohammad Abbas Stanikzai. Before his capture, the Pakistani were extremely concerned that Baradar was apparently secretly negotiating with then President Karzai over the war, rathen tan following their directions or negotiation goals.[35]

While Baradar, before his capture, had been wary of the Pakistanis and their specific positions relative to peace talks, eight years in prison might have influenced his views. A question that should be asked is how swayed Baradar was by the Pakistanis while he was in prison, and how much of Pakistan's bidding he is willing to do, if at all.

As Giustozzi suggests:

> Mullah Barader was the best known of the Taliban political leaders and the de-facto head of the Quetta Shura; technically he was Mullah Omar's deputy, but Omar appeared only rarely at meetings and Baradar took almost all the key decisions.[36]

2019 also saw the Taliban relate many of the positions presented in their tweets back to the Taliban leadership and the IEA official website, where critical points could be covered in more depth.

It is also interesting to note that by mid-2019 we begin to see many more tweets regarding armed opposition and government officials realising the 'error of their ways' and joining sides with the Taliban. As suggested above, defections became fairly common in this period. Also, in June 2019, there were numerous tweets concerning large-scale Taliban military operations and offensives, a reflection, in part, that the Taliban had thousands more foot soldiers in the country than at any time since the outbreak of the war. In the midst of the negotiations, it appeared that the Taliban were burning the candle at both ends.

There were also tweets from the Taliban in July 2019, where the Taliban's delegation can be seen meeting with delegations outside of Afghanistan, such as Indonesia. One view of this could be that the Taliban was reaching out beyond its borders in a bid for international legitimacy.

January to July 2020

The next three figures display the same variables as have already been presented for Taliban tweets from 2018 and 2019.

Figure 8.6 presents the Taliban's tweets up to July 2020 focusing on Taliban military offensive and defensive military actions. What is interesting about this graph is that there were a significant number of Taliban military actions in the month before they signed a conditional peace agreement with the US – January – and also considerable such events in February, before the signing of the conditional agreement on 29 February 2020. After the signing one can see a significant drop in the reportage of Taliban military actions in March and April, followed by an increase in May. From 1 to 10 April we could not find one tweet from a Taliban spokesperson regarding offensive

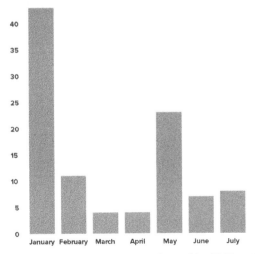

Figure 8.6 Attacks/defensive engagements claimed by Taliban forces in 2020

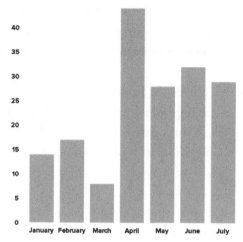

Figure 8.7 War crimes claimed by the Taliban in 2020

attacks by the Taliban. The first period in all the archival research assessed here that this happened. This clear movement away from claiming attacks and casualties to a focus on those joining the cause and the denial of hostilities by Taliban forces is pertinent. The Taliban also heavily emphasised an image of a more modern and well-equipped military. June and July also find a smaller number of tweets describing Taliban military operations. June continued with an emphasis on those joining the cause of jihad as well as Yweets in mid-June regarding the Taliban ability to preside over judicial matters and govern fairly.[37]

Figure 8.7 presents the number of tweets wherein the Taliban attributed war crimes to Kabul and its allies – the US and NATO. One can see while there was an initial drop in the number of war crimes claimed by the Taliban after signing the conditional peace agreement, these numbers increased significantly in April and the following months. Some of this may represent the Taliban's frustration at what they viewed as the Kabul Government of not fully honouring the agreement for a prisoner swap. While Ghani eventually signed a partial swap of prisoners on 10 March, undoubtedly after being pressured by the US, and released 1500 Taliban prisoners on 14 March, on the very same day the US announced that they had no plans for a full withdrawal of troops – A *major goal* of the Taliban. Their demand for the release of more Taliban prisoners were threatened by

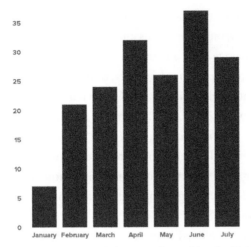

Figure 8.8 Militay/govt employee defections claimed by the Taliban in 2020

Kabul's position and eventually in April the Taliban withdrew from additional talks concerning a prisoner swap. This may reflect the reason that the Taliban claimed many more war crimes by Kabul and the US in April and the following months.

Finally, Figure 8.8 represents the number of Taliban tweets involving Afghan government and military desertions to assist them in their Jihad. In early February the Taliban posted numerous tweets referencing war crimes by US and Afghan government forces as well as tweets regarding military and administration personnel 'repenting' and leaving their posts to join the Taliban side. This actually seems to reflect the kind of desertions that were presented in Western media over the same period.

Additional points that should be made concerning Taliban tweets as presented up to July 2020:

- January saw considerable attention by the Taliban on IEA social media given to peace talks.
- February saw a lot of discourse regarding the results of the 'fake' elections, and posts regarding the history of the Taliban and guidance on the principles of Sharia.
- March continued with guidance on Sharia; a 7 March tweet linked to the IEA website series on 'Sharia: Questions and Answers'.

- 2020 saw far more emphasis on Twitter and the IEA Website for the clarification and rebuttal of claims and accusations made by other entities that would disparage the Taliban's image.
- Many tweets/posts denounced other factions, especially ISIS.
- March also contained a good deal of Coronavirus information.
- As suggested above, early April was heavy on war crime posts as well as prisoner release information.
- Early May continued to rebut any offensive posturing; however, by mid-May tweets began to reflect a more attacking posture once again.
- May contained tweets regarding the relationship between the Afghan Government and ISIS.
- The end of May contained many tweets in response to media reports of illness, disagreements and chaos amongst the Taliban leadership.
- July again focused on those joining the ranks and war crimes of the enemy, while downplaying Taliban aggression.

Implications of this Research

As suggested in the introduction to this chapter, this study was interested in assessing the question of whether the Taliban's negotiations with the US were accompanied by any explicit transformations of the organisation or their leadership.

Have the talks caused or resulted in disagreements within the Taliban leadership?

Very recent unconfirmed information suggests that there have been a number of recent leadership changes:

1. Mulawi Ahmed Jan Bilal appointed as chief of staff for Haibtullah's office, replacing Amir Khan Mutaqi.
2. Mullah Daud Muzamil appointed as the head of the commission for civilian casualties, replacing Mullah Abdul Manan Omari.
3. Sheikh Noorullah Munir appointed judiciary head, replacing Abdul Hakim and Mulawai Abdul Hakim Sahrai, appointed as a deputy to Munir.
4. Qari Fassihuddin, the Taliban shadow governor of Badakhshan, appointed as deputy to Zakir.

5. Mulawi Qudratullah Jamal appointed administrative head of the military commission for the Eastern zone replacing Mulawi Faiz Ullah.

6. Mulawi Abdul Hakim Sharai appointed as a deputy judiciary head for the Eastern zone.[38]

While it is still too early to fully understand the implications of these changes, two things seem to be true. These changes were made before intra-Afghan dialogue and there will probably be more changes in the near future. We would not be surprised if other senior members of the Taliban's First Deputy Council of Ministers are changed prior to the intra-Afghan negotiations.

It is also important to recognise that Mullah Baradar was released from prison in Pakistan, at the request of the US government,[39] ostensibly to lead the Taliban negotiations in Doha. However, there have been no significant changes over 2019–20 in senior Taliban leadership. Malawi Hibatullah Akhundzada, who was elected in May 2016, a few days after the US drone killed Mullah Akhtar Mansour, remains the leader of the Taliban.

Kabul's release of Taliban prisoners should perhaps be considered as a critical part of its agreement with the United States. As suggested by a recent article,

> Taliban prisoners released by the Afghan government as part of a deal brokered by the United States aimed at ending almost 20 years of war are returning to the battlefield as commanders and fighters, in direct contravention of pledges made by the insurgents to the White House.
>
> The Taliban – which styles itself as the government-in-exile of the Islamic Emirate of Afghanistan – refuses to recognize the legitimacy of Ghani's government.
>
> Since Feb. 29, Taliban violence has escalated – with a brief ceasefire to mark Eid at the end of July.[40]

It has also been reported that Kabul is going to demand a cease-fore before the intra-Afghan talks begin.[41]

Finally, important US military leaders such as the Central Command chief General Kenneth McKenzie suggested in June that the Taliban's enduring links with al-Qaeda have continued and 'that the Taliban had not 'fully met' the conditions of the Doha deal.[42]

Two key issues for the intra-Afghan talks are: first, a lasting ceasefire as an estimated 35,000 civilian lives have been lost during the conflict. Second, the make-up of the post-negotiations government, little is specifically known about the Taliban desires for a government, but the resurrection of the Islamic Emirate of Afghanistan seems to be central government. Some observers have argued that the Taliban 'does appear to want an inclusive, Islamic political system in which sharia laws are enforced – possibly akin to the theocratic government in Iran'.[43] The Taliban have also suggested that they will demand and require significant changes in the Afghanistan constitution.

A recent article suggests that, 'the Taliban is stronger now than at any point in the last eighteen years. With an estimated sixty thousand fighters, it controls many districts throughout the country and continues to launch major attacks'.[44] There has also been speculation that Taliban foot soldiers, especially the younger and more radical, do not agree with the peace negotiations. But there has been little significant evidence of *major disputes* concerning the peace agreement within the Taliban leadership, however as suggested above we have recently witnessed changes in Taliban leadership. Few differences, however, have been found in Taliban posted tweets or on their official website.

In fact,

> Mohammed Arif Rahmani, a member of the Afghan Parliament's security committee, said the Taliban had been emboldened since striking an agreement with the United States in February that began the withdrawal of American forces and largely ended the use of US air power crucial to keeping the insurgents at bay. But with repeated delays in the next steps of the peace process – a ceasefire and direct negotiations between the Taliban and the Afghan government – the Taliban have turned to smaller-scale operations meant to show a presence deep inside the capital and wide around it.[45]

At the same time, the Taliban continue to project strength through brutal violence around the country and increased activity in and around the capital. Afghan officials acknowledge that in districts surrounding the capital the Taliban has a small presence to carry out hit-and-run attacks. Reports of government employees being targeted in outlying districts are an almost daily occurrence.[46] Indeed, confidential research obtained by *Foreign Policy* shows that the majority of Taliban prisoners released under an agreement signed by insurgent leaders and the Unit ed States are taking up arms to fight Afghan forces and continue their 'jihad' to overthrow the US-backed Afghan government and replace it with an Islamic emirate.[47]

Meanwhile,

The United States has ramped up pressure on Afghans on both sides of the conflict to open up negotiations over what a postwar Afghanistan might look like, how the rights of women and minorities would be protected, and how the tens of thousands of Taliban fighters and pro-government militias are disarmed and reintegrated.[48]

How the Taliban will react to these 'demands' is unknown.

Another explicit question examined by this chapter was the role of external actors in these negotiations. Regional dynamics and outside actors have played a role in the conflicts in Afghanistan ever since the mid-1970s. Qatar, for example, has hosted, supported and skillfully meditated the negotiations between the US, the Afghan government and the Taliban. Pakistan has also tried to play a particular role in the peace negotiations, having already played an active, and by many accounts negative, role in Afghan affairs for decades. Pakistan's security services maintain ties to Afghan insurgent groups, most notably the Haqqani Network.[49] Pakistan has always believed that they must have a friendly regime in Kabul that they could influence. Much of Pakistan's positions on Afghanistan relate to the fact that there are more Pashtuns in Pakistan than in Afghanistan, especially in the FATA and Khyber Pakhtunkhwa Province and thus it has always been weary of any negative positions emanating out of Afghanistan that could influence their large Pashtun population. India has also played a role in Afghanistan, which greatly concerns Pakistan, and it is quite interested in the peace negotiations as are Russia and Iran who both have provided material support to the Taliban. Afghanistan may also represent a growing priority for China in the context of broader Chinese aspirations in Asia.[50]

Finally, have we witnessed any state-level structural reforms (political, constitutional, security sector or civil-military related, transitional justice issues or any other relevant reforms to encourage the initiation and/or continuation and sustainability of the transformation) in Afghanistan? The greatest state-level structural reforms we have seen in Afghanistan since the beginning of the negotiations has been the presidential election of 2019, which initially resulted in both Ghani and Abdullah Abdullah declaring victory and establishing their own governments with separate inaugurations. This resulted in a serious crisis that was eventually 'resolved' in May when a 'power sharing agreement'[51] was negotiated that basically represented a second 'National Unity Government' with both Ghani and Abdullah controlling 50 per cent of the government ministries and Abdullah being placed in charge of peace negotiations with the Taliban. This unity government almost immediately broke down and the future of the government is highly contentious, which could have a significant impact on the peace negotiations.

Conclusions

It is very clear that the Taliban of 2020 is not the Taliban of 2001, in fact it appears and can be persuasively argued that the Taliban are at a crossroads. Do they really want peace or are the negotiations merely a strategy to get international actors and especially the United States to withdraw from the country? The Taliban seem very confident that, as in Vietnam, once the US leave the country the present Kabul regime will quickly fall as the ANDSF disappears. Over the last twenty years they have managed to win the war of attrition, in the opinion of most, and have forced the hand of the US to come to the negotiating table. This is especially true under the Trump administration, which has recognised that Trump desperately wants to get the US out of Afghanistan. While their focus is now and always has been the country of Afghanistan, the US is faced with concerns and expenditure of resources on a global scale. However, the challenges they now face are manifold. The world in which their message and ideology was formed in the 1990s and even the early twenty-first century is a far cry from the one they find themselves in today. Furthermore, after twenty years of messaging that has focused primarily on war, the occupation of the West and the corruption of the Afghan people by outside entities, they must now fill the potential vacuum that peace creates with a narrative that resonates with the people they seek to lead.

It must also be noted that the major Taliban tweets in 2018 and 2020 suggest that their political and ideological goals are the re-emergence of the Islamic Emirate of Afghanistan and the institution and operation of the view of Sharia law. Does anybody seriously think that the Kabul regime will accept these two major, non-negotiable demands of the Taliban? We believe that the only permanent solution to this political and military conflict and crisis in Afghanistan is for the formation of a true and sincere coalition government, but we can find no significant evidence that either of the sides to this conflict would accept or adhere to such a solution. And there is no convincing evidence that the Taliban is willing to voluntarily de-radicalise in any significant way. Indeed, one of the Taliban interviewees from the Queens University's Afghan Project led by Semple and Kuehn, suggested that the 'public pledge that released prisoners would not resume fighting was seen by many of the interviewees as meaningless, with one [Taliban] saying it was "simply a deception, as part of a trick that we are playing on the foreigners".'[52] Indeed a recent United Nations' senior official has recently suggested that 'with the formal launch of direct peace negotiations imminent, near-record violence in the country is creating an atmosphere of mistrust that risks derailing long-sought talks between the Government and the Taliban'.[53]

Notes

* The views expressed in this chapter are the author's alone and should not be construed as an official position or policy of the U.S. Government, Department of Defense, or Naval Postgraduate School. The author would like to thank Nathan Herbert for his invaluable research assistance on this chapter. It should also be noted that chapter was written during March and April 2020.

1. Susannah George, 'U.S. Signs Peace Deal with Taliban Agreeing to Full Withdrawal of American Troops from Afghanistan', *Washington Post*, 29/2/2020.

2. For example, see: Thomas Barfield, *Afghanistan: A Cultural and Political History* (Princeton: Princeton University Press, 2010); Peter Tomsen, *The Wars of Afghanistan* (New York: PublicAffairs, 2013); Robert D. Crews and Amin Tarzi (eds), *The Taliban and the Crisis of Afghanistan* (Cambridge, MA: Harvard University Press, 2008); William Maley (ed.), *Afghanistan and the Taliban* (New York: New York University Press, 1998); Antonio Giustozzi, *Decoding the New Taliban: Insights from the Afghan Field* (New York: Columbia University Press,

2012); Antonio Giustozzi, *Afghanistan's Endless War: State Failure, Regional Politics, and the Rise of the Taliban* (Seattle: University of Washington Press, 2001(; Thomas H. Johnson, *Taliban Narratives: The Use and Power of Stories in the Afghanistan Conflict* (Oxford: Oxford University Press, 2018); Thomas H. Johnson and W. Chris Mason, 'Understanding the Taliban and Insurgency in Afghanistan', *Orbis*, vol. 51, no. 1 (2007), pp. 71–89; William Maley (ed.), *Fundamentalism Reborn? Afghanistan and the Taliban* (New York: New York University Press, 1998); Ahmed Rashid, *Taliban: Militant Islam, Oil, and Fundamentalism in Central Asia* (London: Yale University Press, 2000); Riaz Mohammad Khan, *Afghanistan and Pakistan: Conflict, Extremism, and Resistance to Modernity* (Baltimore: Johns Hopkins University Press, 2011); Peter Marsden, *The Taliban: War and Religion in Afghanistan* (New York: Zed Books, 2002); Hassan Abbas, *The Taliban Revival: Violence and Extremism on the Pakistan-Afghanistan Frontier* (London: Yale University Press, 2014); Thomas H. Johnson and W. Chris Mason, 'Refighting the Last War: Afghanistan and the Vietnam Template', *Military Review* (November, 2009), pp. 2–14. Some of the Taliban historical background information contained here can be sourced to Thomas H. Johnson and Ludwig Adamic, *The Historical Dictionary of Afghanistan* (Lanham: Rowman & Littlefield, 2021).

3. For an outstanding analysis of the present Taliban consult, See: Antonio Giustozzi, *The Army of Afghanistan: The Political History of Fragile Institution* (New York: Oxford Univeristy Press, 2015); and especially: Antonio Giustozzi, *The Taliban at War: 2001–2018* (New York: Oxford University Press, 2019).

4. Giustozzi, *Afghanistan's Endless*.

5. According to a Senior US Afghan analyst and manager, while in exile in Pakistan, 2002–4, Taliban leaders and commanders read Mao and Che Guevara in their effort to prepare for a guerrilla insurgent war in Afghaniastan.

6. Mao Tse Tung, *Mao Tse Tung on Guerrilla Warfare* (Hawthorne: BN Publishing, 2007), p. 52.

7. Anotonio Giustozzi, *Koran, Kalashnikov, and Laptop* (Oxford: Oxford University Press, 2009), pp. 89–90.

8. Tse Tung, p. 113.

9. Antonio Giustozzi, 'Military Adaptation by the Taliban: 2002–2011', in: Theo Farrell, Frans Osinga and James A. Russell (eds), *Military Adaptation in Afghanistan* (Stanford: Stanford University, 2013), pp. 259–60. And Thomas H. Johnson, 'Taliban Adaptations and Innovations', *Small Wars and Insurgencies*, vol. 24, no. 1 (2013), pp. 3–27.

10. Johnson, *Taliban Narratives*.

11. Kathleen T. Rhem, 'Bush: No Distinction Between Attackers and Those Who Harbor Them', *DoD News*, 11/9/2001, accessed on 17/9/2020, at: https://bit. ly/3c7MRzz

12. Johnson and Mason, 'Refighting the Last War'.

13. Thomas H. Johnson and W. Chris Mason, 'Obama's Indecent Interval', *Foreign Policy*, 10/12/2009, accessed on 17/9/2020, at: https://bit.ly/33ANbmB

14. 'Trump Says He Wants Full Afghanistan Pullout but Sets No Timeline', *Al Jazeera*, 26/5/2020, acceseed on 17/9/2020, at: https://bit.ly/2ZL0FLu

15. Taimoor Shah and Rod Nordland, 'U.S. Diplomats Held Face-to-Face Talks with Taliban, Insurgents Say', *The New York Times*, 28/7/2018, accessed on 17/9/2020, at: https://nyti.ms/3kpYbKh

16. Johnson, 'Taliban Adaptations and Innovations'.

17. While there have been attempts at negotiations especially during the Karzai negotiations, our analyses will focus primarily on the negotiations starting in 2018 culminating with the peace agreement signed between the US and Taliban in February 2020. Afghanistan even held a Peace Jirga in June 2010, but the Taliban refused to participate.

18. These data will eventually be published.

19. See: Johnson, *Taliban Narratives*.

20. The actual agreement was the result of nine different rounds of negotiations involving Khalilzad and Taliban representatives recently lead by Mullah Abdul Ghani Baradar, head of the Taliban's office in Qatar.

21. Andrew Higgins and Mujib Mashal, 'In Moscow, Afghan Peace Talks Without the Afghan Government', *The New York Times*, 4/2/2019, accessed on 17/9/2020, at: https://nyti.ms/3kqGSc9

22. Secunder Kermani, 'Afghan Conflict: What Will Taliban do After Signing US deal?', *BBC News*, 1/3/2020, accessed on 17/9/2020, at: https://bbc.in/3hEOiH5

23. Mujib Mashal, Fatima Faizi and Najim Rahim, 'With Delay in Afghan Peace Talks, a Creeping Sense of "Siege" Around Kabul', *The New York Times*, 23/8/2020, accessed on 17/92020, at: https://nyti.ms/3c7He4o

24. 'President Ghani Rejects Peace Deal's Prisoner Swap with Taliban', *Al Jazeera*, 1/3/2020, acceseed on 17/9/2020, at: https://bit.ly/2ZH0kJG

25. For an analysis of the election, see: Thomas H. Johnson, *The 2019 Presidential Election: A Continuation of Problematic Processes and Results*, Constitutional and Political System Reform Studies, Series VI (Kabul: The Afghanistan Institute for Strategic Studies, 2020).

26. Lynne O'Donnell, 'Factional Struggles Emerge in Virus-Afflicted Taliban Top Ranks', *Foreign Policy*, 9/6/2020, accessed on 17/9/2020, at: https://bit.ly/32DlFFN

27. See: Johnson, *Taliban Narratives*.

28. 'Quarterly Report on The Protection of Civilians in Armed Conflict: 1 January to 30 September 2019', *UNAMA*, 17/10/2019, accessed on 17/9/2020, at: https://bit.ly/3hETj27

29. Clayton Thomas, 'Afghanistan: Background and U.S. Policy: In Brief', *Congressional Research Service*, 25/6/2020, accessed on 17/9/2020, at: https://bit.ly/3c5vcsp

30. See: Emran Feroz, 'Death by Drone: America's Vicious Legacy in Afghanistan', *Foreign Policy*, 27/3/2020, accessed on 17/9/2020, at: https://bit.ly/2Ftk6BH; Elian Peltier & Fatima Faizi, 'I.C.C. Allows Afghanistan War Crimes Inquiry to Proceed, Angering U.S.', *The New York Times*, 5/3/2020, accessed on 17/9/2020, at: https://nyti.ms/3mxgsXS

31. January–April were missing in the Taliban Twitter archives.

32. Rod Norland, 'The Death Toll for Afghan Forces is Secret: Here's Why', *The New York Times*, 21/9/2018, accessed on 17/9/2020, at: https://nyti.ms/3hFUoXo

33. Ibid.

34. Thomas H. Johnson and W. Chris Mason, 'Down the AfPak Rabbit Hole', *Foreign Policy*, 1/3/2010, accessed on 17/9/2020, at: https://bit.ly/32EvKCh

35. Ibid.

36. Giustozzi, *The Taliban at War*, p. 63.

37. The data and tweets are collected up to mid-July 2020.

38. Information from Bilal Sarwary Twitter account (@bsarwary), 7 September 2020.

39. Mujib Mashal and Taimoor Shah, 'Taliban Deputy is Released Amid Push for Afghan Peace Talks', *The New York Times*, 25/10/2018, accessed on 17/9/2020, at: https://nyti.ms/35HCp0A

40. O'Donnell.

41. 'Kabul to Push for Ceasefire in the Talks with Taliban: Afghan Official', *Al Arabiya*, 6/9/2020, accessed on 17/9/2020, at: https://bit.ly/2E9KGz3

42. O'Donnell.

43. Kaweh Kerami, 'Afghanistan's Future: The Core Issues at Stake as Taliban Sits Down to Negotiate Ending 19-Year War', *The Conversation*, 8/9/2020, accessed on 17/9/2020, at: https://bit.ly/3iG5ahE

44. Lindsay Maizland, 'U.S.-Taliban Peace Deal: What to Know', *Council on Foreign Relations*, 2/3/2020, accessed on 17/9/2020, at: https://on.cfr.org/2RwIrJ4

45. Mashal, Faizi and Rahim.

46. Ibid.

47. O'Donnell.

48. 'Khalilzad Departs for Qatar, as Afghan Government, Taliban Exprs Readinessfor Talks', *RFE/RL's Radio Free Afghanistan*, 5/9/2020, accessed on 17/9/2020, at: https://bit.ly/2FOmPFG

49. Cited in Ibid. See: Clayton Thomas, 'Al Qaeda and Islamic State Affiliates in Afghanistan', *Congressional Research Service*, 24/6/2020, accessed on 17/9/2020, at: https://bit.ly/3krLdvO

50. See, for example: Barbara Kelemen, 'China's Economic Stabilization Efforts in Afghanistan: A New Party to the Table?', *Middle East Institute*, 21/1/2020, accessed on 17/9/2020, at: https://bit.ly/3c4RkTM

51. 'Afghanistan: Rival Leaders Ghani and Abdullah in Power-sharing Deal', *BBC News*, 17/5/2020, accessed on 17/9/2020, at: https://bbc.in/2ZJoWBw. Also see: Johnson, *The 2019 Presidential Election*.

52. O'Donnell.

53. UNAMA, 'Afghanistan: Near-Record Violence Risks Derailing Imminent Talks Between Government and Taliban', *UN News*, 3/9/2020, accessed on 17/9/2020, at: https://bit.ly/3hE14W4

9

TRANSFORMATIONS AFTER 'DEFEATS': THE CASES OF THE TUPAMAROS AND THE ARMED LEFT IN LATIN AMERICA

Aldo Marchesi

Introduction

During the first decade of this century José Mujica and Dilma Rousseff were elected as democratic presidents of Uruguay and Brazil representing two important political parties: the Frente Amplio (FA, 'Broad Front') and the Partido dos Trabalhadores (PT, 'Workers' Party') respectively. However, five decades ago both were members of guerrilla groups that claimed political violence was the only way to achieve social change during the Latin American cold war. What happened during the intervening decades that can explain these radical changes of behaviour? The changes were not only related to the historical experience of these armed organisations but also to the political opportunities created by the geopolitical possibilities of the post-cold war order.

Mujica and Rousseff belonged to a generation of political activists that emerged in a context marked by increasing social protests, the rise of authoritarian regimes (Brazil, 1964; Bolivia, 1966; Argentina, 1966; Bolivia, 1971; Uruguay, 1972–3; Chile, 1973; Argentina, 1976) and growing expectations fuelled by the social alternatives demonstrated by the Cuban Revolution. In an earlier work,[1] the author of this chapter analysed this political generation – composed primarily of young people who in the late sixties had not reached their thirties – that challenged the traditional ways of doing politics and proposed new forms of social, political and cultural mobilisation. The activists of this 'new left' criticised the legalism and reformism of the communist and socialist parties – the parties of the traditional left. They proposed new, more radical methods, which they viewed as more effective for ensuring the social changes demanded by popular sectors. Armed organisations gradually became the leading players in this wave of 'new left' movements that spread across the region.

The exchanges among these organisations spanned over the course of more than ten years. They began in Uruguay as a result of the rise of authoritarianism in Brazil and Argentina and were furthered by Che Guevara's Bolivia campaign in 1966. They became formal exchanges in Chile under the Unidad Popular (UP, 'Popular Unity') government, where a number of groups started considering the possibility of creating a new regional organisation. This organisation would be called *Junta de Coordinación Revolucionaria* (JCR, 'Revolutionary Coordination Board'), formed by Bolivia's ELN (Ejército de Liberación Nacional – National Liberation Army), Chile's MIR (Movimiento de Izquierda Revolucionario – Leftist Revolutionary Movement), Argentina's ERP (Ejército Revolucionario del Pueblo – People Revolutionary Army), and Uruguay's MLN-T (Movimiento de Liberación Nacional: Tupamaros – National Liberation Movement: Tupamaros). These coordination efforts reached their highest point in Buenos Aires from 1973 to 1976, the year in which the coup d'état in Argentina eliminated the last 'refuge' of these groups. The region was subsequently dominated by brutal military dictatorships that destroyed these armed organisations and other leftist groups. These groups faced intense repression that included torture, imprisonment and exile.[2]

After being defeated, some groups were able to adapt their strategies to the new political circumstances offered by the re-democratisation context of the eighties and nineties. For instance, the Tupamaros were able to regroup and develop a successful political strategy that turned them into the largest political force within Uruguay's majority party in 2010. The Chilean MIR and the Argentinian PRT-ERP entered a period of successive divisions and factionalisation from which they would not recover. However, the memory of these groups was part of new political movements, some of them established by former militants of these organisations, that emerged in Argentina, Brazil and Chile from the eighties up to the new century.

The process of adaptation to the new democracies implied a fragile balance among the survivors of the sixties and seventies. The way in which the tension between revolutionary political culture and the political strategies of the eighties was resolved depended on the feasibility and continuity of these political projects. The key to success lay in achieving some sort of balance in which certain aspects connected with that political culture, such as the militant ethics of the seventies associated with self-sacrifice, giving oneself to the cause and egalitarian notions, coexisted with a pragmatic and critical acceptance of the rules of democracy and the market.

This chapter analyses how some former guerrilla members were able to incorporate and take advantage of the new political opportunities of democratic transitions while others were unable to do so. The analysis starts by reviewing the main features of the political processes and some personal biographies, assessing the political and ideological adaptation of these groups to the new democratic context of the eighties and nineties, and evaluating the new democratic government policies toward these revolutionary organisations. The chapter reviews how the idea that these armed organisations were defeated and its different temporalities, might be rethought as a result of the political achievements[3] of recent decades. The chapter empirically reflects on the role of militant leadership in leading successful transformations, as well as the role of state repression and the costs of the armed path, interactions with human rights norms and non-like-minded organisations in reshaping the worldview of former militants as well as the inducements offered by the new democratic-transitional environment.

Political Processes and Individual Trajectories

This section reviews the main features of the political developments in Argentina, Uruguay and Chile to understand the ways in which the armed leftist organisations of the seventies tried to incorporate the transitions to democracies during the eighties. After the Argentinian coup d'état of 1976, when the southern cone was ruled by military dictatorships, the future of these leftist armed organisations looked bleak. Surviving militants fled to different parts of the world. Many found refuge in Europe, others in Mexico and Cuba, and a few groups ended up in North Africa and the Middle East.

Among the exiles many questions about the viability of armed struggle were raised. Some claimed that it was a necessary change of strategy, shifting from an approach that insisted on revolutionary violence to another one focused on the denouncement of dictatorships for their human rights violations. There were others that continued to support armed struggle and developed networks among exiled militants to return to their respective countries and reinitiate the armed struggle against dictatorships. The Uruguayan Tupamaros failed in their successive attempts to return to Uruguay from Argentina. The Chilean MIR and the Argentinean PRT meanwhile were able to organise return operations in 1978 and 1982 respectively, but they had different outcomes.

Although the MIR suffered defeats during the period of 1978–84, it was able to develop an armed organisation inside Chile and promoted insurgency tactics within social movements against the dictatorship during the eighties. Some members of the PRT-ERP tried to spark an insurgency in North Argentina in 1982, but they quickly reconsidered when the military dictatorship occupied the Malvinas/Falkland Islands, creating a new political landscape in which the nationalist cause strengthened popular support for the dictatorship. By the middle of the eighties, and in the context of democratic transitions, most armed organisations, with the exception of the Chilean MIR, had renounced armed struggle.

De-radicalisation Processes in Argentina

The transition to democracy in Argentina was marked by a fast and somewhat chaotic retreat by the military after the dramatic defeat of the Falklands War in 1982 and 1983. As they withdrew, they tried to impose a self-amnesty two weeks before the elections. That attempt was thwarted by the centre-leftist victory at the polls. In his campaign, Raul Alfonsín had shown his support for the cause of human rights. Upon taking office in December 1983, the new president called for the repeal of the self-amnesty law, ordered the arrest and prosecution of the members of the first three military juntas, reformed the military code, and convened a commission to investigate the crimes committed by the dictatorship in connection with forced disappearances. However, on the same day that the president issued Decree 158 ordering the arrest of the military junta members on charges of human rights violations committed under the dictatorship, he issued another decree ordering the arrest of the surviving members of the 'terrorist leadership' of the Montoneros and the ERP.[4] In the case of the PRT-ERP, Alfonsín specifically ordered the arrest of Enrique Gorriarán Merlo, as he was the sole surviving member of the group's historical leadership. In this sense, the discursive and political strategy on the issue of human rights, labelled by some as the 'theory of the two demons', had two clear targets: the armed left of the 1970s and the military juntas. Both belonged to a past that the new democracy wished to escape.

Another specific consequence of this policy was the delay in the release of political prisoners. Faced with increasing protests from human rights organisations and from the prisoners themselves through series of hunger strikes, the government proposed a law for the commutation of sentences that gradually secured the prisoners' freedom. Nonetheless, by 1987 thirteen of the 114 political prisoners who had still been in prison at the end of the dictatorship were still behind bars.[5] This also affected several exiled militants, who decided to remain abroad after seeing the situation the prisoners faced and worrying about detention upon return.[6]

A group of former PRT-ERP militants around the leadership of Enrique Gorriarán Merlolaunched its first press project as early as 1982, an initiative that anticipated the political stance that these militants would embrace in the coming years. The magazine *Frente* (published in 1982 and 1983) and the second publishing project called *Entre Todos* (a magazine published as of 1984) expressed the pluralist will of that new moment in the armed leftist experience of the sixties. Even the title – which translates to *All of Us* (with the subtitle *Who Want Liberation (Peronists, Radical Party Members, Intransigent Party Members, Christians, Socialists, Communists, Independents)* – expressed the aim of building a broad and plural political movement that would bring together the various progressive sectors of Argentine society in the context of re-democratisation. This aim was rooted in the realisation that in Argentina there was a powerful social movement with a variety of leftist political positions with which it was possible to build a new form of political movement.

Entre Todos gave clear expression to this form of coalition politics. Its pages showed a pluralist political approach that sought to unite all those who had an anti-imperialist discourse and an affinity with those sectors, regardless of their political affiliations. Moreover, the publication replaced the highly ideologically charged language of the PRT newsletters with a popular language closer to the rhetoric of Latin American nationalism. Great attention was paid in its articles to local social movements, culture and human rights. Also underlying these articles was the idea that the leading conflict was between authoritarianism and democracy.

In 1986 *Movimiento Todos por la Patria* (MTP, 'Everyone for the Homeland Homeland'), a movement connected with the journalistic project *Entre Todos*, would be created.[7] The magazine was connected to the elusive Gorriarán Merlo, wanted by the Argentine authorities, who from Nicaragua and Brazil – and in some cases entering Argentina clandestinely – met with the different leaders who would later form the MTP. The founding group included a hard-core group of militants of the PRT-ERP, who had been planning what can be termed a leadership-led process of de-radicalisation. However, Gorriarán's situation was a complicated one. He was the brains behind this de-radicalisation process and legal and political collective transformations. But he remained in the shadows, as it was not wise to have someone wanted by the law as the leader of a legal organisation. The activities carried out by the *Entre Todos* project gathered together old ERP militants who had survived repression, leftist Peronist activists, young people who identified with the experience of the seventies, several of whom had joined the Intransigent Party in the context of the transition, Catholic sectors that sympathised with liberation theology and activists and lawyers of the human rights movement, many of whom travelled to Managua to participate in the foundation of the MTP.

The first positions adopted by the MTP were featured in *Entre Todos* in May 1986.[8] The head of the movement had been one of the leaders of the PRT-ERP in the seventies, who had insisted on hard-line ideological rhetoric. Hence, the article presenting the movement's position was surprising. It had little to do with the old Marxist orthodoxy and much more to do with populist Latin Americanism that seemed to be connected with the traditions of the late fifties. Although this political strategy initially began to yield some returns, it was limited by the extent to which Gorriarán's circle remained committed to keeping the armed struggle as a viable strategy. Also, the transitional context and the popularity of the human rights policy of the new democratically elected President Raúl Alfonsín had put ERP militants, who continued to think of the armed struggle as a valid strategy, in a difficult position.

The fact that Gorriarán, who was among the 'demons' of the transition, was leading from the shadows, made it difficult to build the movement's identity. And it placed him and the MTP in a complicated position, as the most progressive aspect of Alfonsín's policy – his approach to the issue of human rights – rested on stigmatising the experience of the sixties. In 1988, speaking from an undisclosed site, Gorriarán declared that he would refuse an amnesty if that amnesty was in exchange for an amnesty for the military junta members.[9]

The threat of a possible military return also challenged the process of de-radicalising these old militants. During the Alfonsín government there were three uprisings by military forces opposed to the human rights policy implemented in the first years of the return to democracy. Several sectors of the Left, and even of the Radical Party, began to fear what they saw as the very real possibility of a military coup. They believed they needed to be prepared to resist such a threat. This idea had a greater effect on the MTP militants who had been linked to the official structure of the PRT-ERP. Very quickly the aim of building a great inclusive political movement was dropped, and the old issues and discourses of the seventies were picked up again. The key question was once again how to go about consolidating the revolutionary vanguard. This interpretation gained ground in 1987 and 1988 following the two military uprisings. In a document on the second uprising, the MTP noted with alarm that 'the military are advancing. What do we do?' And it declared: 'The people must take the defence of democracy into their own hands.'[10]

Internally, this debate over expanding the political movement or developing a military apparatus to prepare for an adverse situation, such as a military coup, aggravated the conflicts that were beginning to appear between Gorriarán and other political leaders of the MTP. Gorriarán, who remained in Nicaragua, was still very much defined by his revolutionary past. MTP leaders, who were more connected with political and social activism on the ground, realised how far the Argentine society was from the imaginaries of the 'revolutionary heroism of the seventies'. The two sides had very, very different ideas of how to deal with a possible military coup. This led to a series of internal fractures in the MTP that meant that by 1988 the group had been reduced to Gorriarán's inner circle.

This group began planning a military operation that was put into action in January 1989. The operation involved spreading the rumour that a coup was imminent, thus justifying an attack on a military barracks. There were actually no solid grounds for fearing such a coup. Although the possibility of a coup was not altogether unfounded in the summer of 1989, there was nothing specific that could have justified the belief that it was imminent. Subsequent events would prove that it was all part of a sham to prepare for the attack on the Cuartel de la Tablada military barracks.

The Cuartel de la Tablada assault featured gaining entry into the barracks by pretending to belong to a coup faction, throwing flyers in the air and chanting the names of the Carapintada (military mutineers) leaders and then seizing the barracks and the tanks.[11] Once the barracks had been seized, the people would be called on to defend democracy. A number of militants were prepared to surround the barracks and convene social organisations. Afterwards, they would head to Plaza de Mayo and call on the people to rise up in an insurrection to demand that a popular and revolutionary army be formed.[12]

The action was one of the most resounding failures in the history of Argentina's guerrilla organisations. Of the forty-six individuals who participated in the action, thirty-three died, some of them executed after they were taken into custody, four were seized by the military and disappeared, and in the days that followed several militants were captured and thrown in jail. The action failed to generate any of the effects sought. In the armed forces, it strengthened the officers' esprit de corps in the repression of social protests and by raising again the threat of subversion that gave legitimacy to their memories and their past and present actions. Social and left-wing organisations tried to distance themselves from the action, which they saw as absurd; they warned that it would have serious consequences for the political development of the Argentine left and that it would bring back the national security discourse that was re-emerging among the military and conservative civilian sectors. There were some exceptions, such as Hebe de Bonafini, a member of the Mothers of Plaza de Mayo, who on the anniversary of the coup, on 24 March 1989, in a rally convened under the slogan of 'to resist is to combat' warned of the characteristics of the military officers who had crushed the action in La Tablada. This disastrous action seemed to mark the end of a historical cycle.

De-radicalisation Processes in Uruguay

Ten days after Uruguay's return to democracy in 1985, a law granted an amnesty to prisoners of conscience and commuted the sentences of those political prisoners who were implicated in violent crimes, in consideration of the inhumane conditions they had suffered during their incarceration. As a result, all political prisoners were set free and a favourable climate was ensured for the return of exiles, as they would not be prosecuted on charges connected with the past.[13]

The Tupamaros' attempt at reorganising began on the same day, which was celebrated as a day of rejoicing. On the very day they were set free, the members of the old MLN-T leadership, who since 1972 had been held under hostage conditions marked by constant abuses and complete isolation, gave a press conference in which they acknowledged the new stage the country was embarking on. As a spokesman, Eleuterio Fernández Huidobro acknowledged that they were witnessing a unique moment in the history of the country:

> We believe that a stage of burgeoning democracy has opened up in our country. Democracy is a fact that is not to be found in votes. Nor is it to be found in the results of the elections. It is in the streets. Democracy in Uruguay, the democracy we have today, was forged by the Uruguayan people. And we understand that you would have to be blind not to see that reality, we would have to be blind not to see it; it has to be respected because it is an order of the people. So, we are going to abide by that order of the people . . . It is not a decrepit democracy like that of 1972 and 1971, in which the forces of reaction were trampling the people. A democracy with militarised workers and imprisoned comrades. This democracy is different, it is a democracy in which, as you can see, prisons have disappeared.[14]

That same day, the leader of the movement delivered a public document informing that they would respect the law and would enter a process of internal discussions among the members released from prison, those returning from exile, those who had survived in the country and the young people who had joined the movement. It was an official initiation into a process of behavioural, organisational and ideological de-radicalisation. However, after the initial idyllic moment in which hundreds of Tupamaro militants reunited, problems began to arise in the movement's reorganisation. The distance between those who had been exiled in different places, those who had been in prison and those who had remained in the country began to be felt. For almost a decade, numerous groups throughout the world, even inside various prisons and in the country, had developed different political interpretations of the defeat of the MLN-T, as well as of the events leading up to the process of democratisation.

Astrid Arraras, a political scientist who studied this process of reorgan-isation, identified at least four groups in 1985: the Tendencia Proletaria ('Proletarian Tendency') group formed in Argentina in 1974 during the exchanges with the ERP; the 26 de Marzo ('26 March') group in Uruguay, connected with militants who regrouped during the transition; the histori-cal leaders, who had remained in prison and had experienced abuse and severe isolation; and various groupings of exiles. The meeting of these groups sparked highly intense debates. Several of these debates had to do with the issue of self-criticism and referred back to old disagreements dating back to the seventies, which had not been openly expressed due to the persecution under the dictatorship. The diverse experiences of the exiled militants also affected how the old issues of the revolutionary aims and the new issues of democracy were analysed.[15]

However, despite disagreements, the organisation gradually regrouped, and the Tupamaros began to carry out social actions that had an impact at the popular level. In the first years, in certain districts of Montevideo, the organisation's influence grew as it focused on social work and engaged in a direct dialogue with the people through open meetings known as *mateadas* (named for the popular Uruguayan herbal tea, *mate*, shared at these sessions), in which MLN-T leaders gathered in neighbourhood plazas to talk with anyone wishing to meet the historical leaders who had been imprisoned for years. The Tupamaros were also particularly concerned with communica-tions, launching their weekly publication *Mate Amargo*, where in a renewed style they engaged in a form of political journalism that sought to appeal to popular sectors, alongside a radio station that achieved a significant audience and a publishing house, Tupac Amaru Ediciones, where Fernández Huidobro published a series of testimonials and historical books that became bestsellers in the eighties.[16]

Although initially the Tupamaros defined themselves as social activists, they would gradually move closer to the Frente Amplio, the left-wing coalition toward which they had shown their sympathy since its creation in 1971, but which they had never officially joined. In the new environment imposed by legal political life, joining the FA and aligning themselves with certain groups in the coalition seemed inevitable.

According to a testimonial biography of one of the historical leaders, Jorge Zabalza, who showed a greater inclination to maintaining the organisation's subversive practices and resisted the political adaptation process that would unfold in the nineties, a group was formed within the MLN-T, known as The Seventeen, which gathered most of the historical leaders outside the organisation's official governing bodies to determine its international relations with the revolutionary movement, sought forms of financing for the organisation's new communication projects and discussed security measures to adopt in the event of military threats. Zabalza reveals that the efforts to find forms of financing included contacts with Gorriarán and the Argentine MTP, ETA, and Peru's Movimiento Revolucionario Tupac Amaru (MRTA, 'Tupac Amaru Revolutionary Movement'). In that book, he also mentions robberies committed by Tupamaro militants in Uruguay with the purpose of obtaining funds for the organisation.[17] All of this shows how the tension between political and military aims still existed within the MLN-T. Although initially the more political side of the organisation had prevailed, the conflict was still latent.

This tension was aggravated in the nineties. As social mobilisation contracted and a neoliberal agenda emerged, the Fifth Convention of the MLN-T, held in 1991, leaned toward the views within the organisation that were closer to the path of armed radicalisation. Discussions at the convention pitted those who proposed building a political and military organisation (*Organización Político Militar*, or OPM), which would operate legally but would be prepared for future scenarios of armed violence, against those who stressed the need to focus on election-based politics and social mobilisation.

The defenders of the OPM made a negative assessment of the economy, which in their view would lead to an increased social response and state repression with predictable authoritarian reactions from the state. On the other side were those who, while sharing certain elements of that diagnosis, insisted on the need to further the work on the political front and who, in particular, wanted to move away from the conspiratorial and militarist practices of the past. However, internal discussions continued. Although the proposal to build an OPM was the majority position, it had different meanings for the various groups of militants that supported it. For some it entailed a path towards generating the conditions to take up arms again, while for others it was a sort of safeguard against a possible authoritarian resurgence.[18]

The year 1989 also brought positive developments for the Left. For the first time ever, the Frente Amplio won the municipal elections of Montevideo, the country's capital. The growth of the coalition showed that with each new election it was closer to the possibility of successfully disputing the national government. That year the MLN-T had formally become part of the Frente Amplio and joined other radical sectors of the Left in a sub-coalition known as Movimiento de Participación Popular (MPP, 'Popular Participation Movement'). The Tupamaro leaders refused to participate in the lists of candidates for parliament but enthusiastically supported the initiative.

After the Fifth Convention, the debate continued as to what the organisation's approach to the electoral process should be, becoming more heated as a result of an incident that, according to political scientist Adolfo Garcé, divided once and for all those who tried to keep an armed insurrection alive and those who were more in favour of electoral participation. Two months before national elections were to be held in 1995, a series of clashes between demonstrators and police forces in the vicinity of the Filtro Hospital caused a stir within the MLN-T. The clashes occurred when the police tried to remove three Spanish nationals who were accused of being members of ETA and were holding a hunger strike to protest their extradition to Spain. Several social and political organisations had convened a demonstration outside of the hospital to call for the Spanish nationals' asylum and to oppose their removal from the hospital. When the police arrived to take them to the airport, a number of demonstrators tried to stop the police from leaving the hospital. From its radio station, the MLN-T urged demonstrators to prevent the removal of the Basque prisoners. Some demonstrators were particularly defiant, throwing stones and Molotov cocktails at the police – actions very uncommon at the marches held during the transition, which had largely been peaceful. For their part, the police responded with clearly excessive force, firing their weapons directly at the demonstrators. The repression left two dead and approximately eighty wounded. The MLN-T's radio station was shut down, accused of inciting the clashes.

The Filtro episode, or 'Filtro massacre' as it would be known, was an issue of debate in the election campaign and within the Left. The right-ist National Party and the centrist Colorado Party took the opportunity to wheel out their old credos about the violent nature of the Left, in keeping with the national security discourse used by the army in past decades. On the Left, many organisations within the Frente Amplio questioned the role of the Tupamaros in that incident and the failure to reflect on how that event would be used against the Left in the election campaign. The Frente Amplio candidate Tabaré Vázquez lost by only 1.8 per cent of the votes in the 1994 national election. Several sectors of the Left were convinced that they lost the elections because of the Filtro episode.

In the MLN-T, the Filtro episode and the elections that year exacer-bated the conflict between those who presaged scenarios of greater repression and demanded the consolidation of a political and military organisation that would contribute to an insurrectional strategy, on the one hand, and those who focused on elections and had their hopes pinned on the electoral growth of the Frente Amplio. For both, 1994 had confirmed their intuitions. For the former, the Filtro massacre was a dress rehearsal for what was to come, of the way in which the dominant sectors would act in reaction to rising social mobilisation. For the latter, the takeaway from the events of that year was that a left victory at the polls was a real possibility in the medium term.

Moreover, for this second group there was a development that would have major consequences in the coming years. Although the Tupamaros par-ticipated in the MPP and backed its candidates, they had consistently refused to present the historical leaders of the MLN-T as candidates for legislative seats. In 1994, José Mujica ran for a seat in the lower chamber of parliament as an MPP candidate for the first time. His participation in parliament would have major consequences for both his future and the future of his organisation. During his term in parliament, he had a significant public impact. Various aspects of his work as legislator were highly valued. Mujica arrived to work on a Vespa motorcycle dressed informally. This was no demagogical gimmick but an attempt to retain a certain authenticity that politics, both to the right and left, seemed to distort. He also spoke in a clear, simple way, with a discourse that was not overly ideological but was based on certain left-ist principles and backed by much preparation that enabled him to give an opinion on the range of topics touched on by legislative activity. Lastly, his non-confrontational and conciliatory tone in legislative debates earned him the sympathy of some politicians from the traditional parties.[19]

Although some aspects of this success had to do with his charismatic personality, it was also linked to the historical experience he represented. Certain ideas and values of the sixties were translated into his work as leg-islator. Aspects of militant life such as self-sacrifice, giving oneself entirely to the cause and a militant ethics were reinterpreted in the context of the nineties in a national representative who donated a large part of his salary, had no material interests dictating his actions and engaged with common people in a direct way. With respect to his guerrilla past, Mujica expressed no regrets, although he did appear self-critical regarding various actions or ways of thinking from that decade.[20]

De-radicalisation Processes in Chile

Despite the persecutions and losses suffered in the years 1984 and 1985, the MIR tried to regain some initiative by furthering certain forms of vio-lent resistance within mobilised working-class neighbourhoods, as well as by participating in the human rights movement through the Corporación de Promoción y Defensa de los Derechos del Pueblo (CODEPU, 'Association for the Promotion and Defence of the Rights of the People') and at the polit-ical level in the Movimiento Democrático Popular ('Popular Democratic Movement'), the left-wing coalition that refused to negotiate with Pinochet for an end to the dictatorship.[21] The context within the Left had changed. The emergence of the Frente Patriótico Manuel Rodríguez (FPMR, 'Manuel Rodríguez Patriotic Front'), an armed group with connections to the Communist Party, transformed the traditional relationship between MIR militants and communists. This opened doors but also introduced a new competitor that challenged the MIR's leadership among certain sectors of the social movement. Despite these political efforts to remain standing, the military apparatus continued to sustain losses, and by 1986 the MIR no longer had the capacity to conduct any armed actions.[22]

The 1978 debates regarding the tension between more militarist options and more political options began to re-emerge in the face of the repeated defeats and the impossibility of reorganising. Although in this period the MIR had gained a significant presence in some of the organisations of the anti-dictatorship mass movement, the other part of the strategy of Operation Return that had to do with the MIR's military actions turned out to be impossible to carry out. This tension was evident at a meeting of the steering committee in which leaders who prioritised social work and believed that military action should come later as a result of social mobilisations came against those who saw this position as subordinating military aims to social aims.[23] In 1988 the two groups split into two factions: 'Political' MIR, headed by Nelson Gutiérrez and representing militants connected with social movements; and 'Historical' MIR, which was led by Andrés Pascal Allende and retained most members of the party apparatus.[24]

Once again, the problem of the Left's restructuring was linked to the military-political dichotomy and how even though in theory the two categories were not antagonistic, in the context of democratisation they appeared to be. This rift occurred in a particular context in which the transition was starting to change course. In 1986 the FPMR's failed assassination attempt against Pinochet unleashed a fierce wave of repression that affected the entire left. This created divisions between those who continued to wager on a revolutionary end to the dictatorship and the majority sectors of the Left that began to lean towards a negotiated solution in alliance with Christian Democratic sectors. The latter would emerge as the sectors with the greatest capacity for leadership and those which were to effectively guide the transition toward a negotiated end to the dictatorship, which finally arrived in 1990 with the Patricio Aylwin government.

The last years of the democratic transition were very difficult for the fragmented MIR, with Historical MIR suffering another schism in 1987 led by Hernán Aguiló, head of the military commission, followed by two further breakaways, and in 1990 two new rifts. Although the members of Political

MIR were still significantly divided over how to position themselves, the faction remained relatively stable behind its project of participating in the parliamentary elections along with the Partido Amplio de Izquierda Socialista (the 'Broad Socialist Left'). However, by 1990, Political MIR had splintered into four factions, resulting in practice in its virtual disappearance. By this point there were eight groups claiming the identity of the old MIR, spanning a wide range of positions with respect to the situation in the country. On one end of the spectrum were those who argued against a negotiated democracy and for the need to continue with armed struggle, whilst on the other were those who joined the Socialist Party amidst that party's process of reunification and would ultimately be appointed to government positions among the members of the governing Concertación de Partidos por la Democracia (Coalition of Parties for Democracy, or Concertación).[25]

This political fragmentation and uncertainty with which MIR met the new democracy was compounded by the legal situation in which several of its jailed militants found themselves. Although initially the new democratic government expressed its will to implement a broad amnesty policy for the 400 political prisoners who were still in jail, pressure from the opposition and the armed forces was too strong, particularly with respect to those imprisoned in the eighties for violent crimes. The fact that various groups, which supported MIR or FPMR, maintained or renewed their armed actions in the context of the nascent democracy further complicated the situation. The attempt on air force general and post-coup junta member Gustavo Leigh's life by FPMR militants just ten days after the inauguration of the democratic government generated a difficult situation for President Patricio Aylwin, with the media raising the spectre of leftist 'terrorism' again and the Concertación government resorting to harsh measures so as not to yield any space to the right. All of this slowed down the release of dictatorship-era prisoners, a process that involved long negotiations. By late 1992, after various proceedings that entailed studying case by case, 300 prisoners had been freed. The most problematic cases, those connected with the FPMR attempt on Pinochet's life, were settled in the last days of the Aylwin administration, by commuting the forty-year jail sentences of the militants involved with their exile in Belgium.[26]

The new government also developed a counterinsurgency strategy aimed at dismantling the armed leftist groups that were still active. That strategy was not entrusted to military officers trained under the national security doctrine but to old comrades who also belonged to the same ideological families of the Left, mainly members of the Socialist Party, who now took on the counterinsurgency tasks. To that end, in 1991 a Public Security Coordinating Council was formed to coordinate the intelligence tasks involved in the surveillance of these armed groups and to organise related police action. In addition to being headed by the socialist militant Marcelo Schilling, the council was assisted by other militants with insurgency and counterinsurgency experience trained in Eastern Europe, who participated as advisors. One of the legal instruments that played a key role in structuring the persecution of these militants was the Repentance Act, which exchanged denunciation for amnesty. In addition, the sentences established under earlier laws (the Interior Security of the State Act, the Weapons and Explosives Control Act, and the Anti-Terrorist Act) were toughened and a high security prison (Cárcel de Alta Seguridad, or CAS) was created, which would later be called into question because of the isolation and punishment mechanisms used against militants.[27]

This was the difficult context in which the MIR faced democracy. Even for those who had chosen to renounce armed struggle, it was very difficult to shed the stigma created under the dictatorship, which was now reshaped by the first democratic government with much greater legitimacy. All of this led to a complete fragmentation from which the MIR has yet to recover and which appears irreversible. The last two decades, however, have shown a particular presence of the Chilean left in different areas of the country's social and cultural life. The testimonial work produced in various formats, ranging from film documentaries to written memoirs, has found numerous militants from that experience contributing to a collective reflection that has to do with their own organisations but also with the country as a whole. In academic circles, a group of prominent historians with different historiographic approaches reference their MIR experience as a major part of their intellectual development. In the field of human rights, particularly with respect to memory policies, various groups have set out to tell the experiences suffered by MIR militants under state terrorism. The reflection generated by these multiple experiences of social and cultural activism is an open one has had a certain influence in youth movements that have taken a critical view of the experience of the Concertación in these past decades.

De-radicalisation Processes under Democratic Transitions

A number of studies have shown how the international context of the late seventies, marked by a new sensitivity toward the defence of a particular notion of human rights promoted by the Jimmy Carter administration, the efforts of international organisations such as Amnesty International and Human Rights Watch, and greater attention to these matters by international bodies such as the United Nations and the Organisation of American States influenced the way in which opposition movements positioned themselves with respect to the dictatorships of the Southern Cone.[28] The region's armed groups participated in these movements with a degree of ambiguity that allowed them to report human rights abuses to international bodies, while at the same time arguing in their publications that the only way of putting an end to such abuses was through revolutionary change that would bring down the dictatorship.

The language of human rights was accompanied in the Left's reflection by the idea of its renewal. Several intellectuals and militants in the exile diaspora who were in contact with other experiences proposed a variety of issues ranging from a re-valorisation of liberal democracy and human rights with respect to the views that had prevailed in the seventies more tied to a critique of liberalism, the acknowledgement of various emancipatory causes, such as the rights of women and indigenous groups, and, lastly, a more pluralist approach to social change incorporating Christian groups, democratic groups from the centre of the ideological spectrum and groups from Latin America's populist and nationalist traditions. In terms of theory, the renewal involved a reading of Gramsci that was closely linked to the issue of cultural hegemony and affected reflection on the forms of political action. This renewal was part of discussions in various cities, from Mexico City to Rome, but also in the Southern Cone countries where emerging social movements, much less ideologized than those of the seventies, were starting to strike a new tone in the way they approached political action.

The atmosphere of renovation put into question some of the principles on which the political culture of the armed groups had been built. Many associated this renovation with the end of the armed experience of the seventies. In a context of strong persecution of armed groups by the region's dictatorships, diminished support from the Cuban Revolution, as Havana aligned itself more closely with the Soviet Union, and the possibilities that were opened by the human rights movements, these discourses of renovation emerged as an alternative to previous revolutionary discourses.

Although the paths taken by each of these groups would gradually diverge and the elements that united their actions in the seventies grew less significant with time, those groups that attempted to act in the eighties faced the same dilemma, namely, how to balance an insurgent political culture tradition with the climate of renovation?

With the exception of Chile, none of the countries of the region – neither Argentina, with the exception of *La Tablada*, nor Uruguay nor Brazil – saw these militants resuming armed struggle with the return to democracy. All of the militants who remained organised into groups, however, viewed armed struggle as a possibility that could not be ruled out. Even those who became legally operating organisations maintained armed groups involved in security and finance issues. For instance, in 1992 the Brazilian police captured a group of Argentinean and Chilean leftist militants, with previous ties to armed organisations. They had previously kidnapped businessmen to obtain financial resources used to fund activities within their home countries.

By the early eighties neither the JCR nor the possibility of developing a regional project to promote armed struggle in the region was something envisioned by any of the survivors of the seventies, who were instead trying to reorganise old organisations hard hit by the dictatorships. The international context marked certain changes that had an effect on these militants. The shift in Cuba's foreign policy, with its alignment with the Soviet Union, its campaign in Africa and the end of its support to armed struggle in the Southern Cone, made it difficult for the region's organisations to resume certain initiatives. Also, the attention paid by certain international bodies to the reports of human rights abuses, connected with a renovation in left-wing thinking, opened up a different path for activism which seemed more effective in the struggle against dictatorships. Lastly, the anti-dictatorial social mobilisation that these militants were seeking to move closer to incorporated new issues such as the re-valorisation of democracy, human rights as well as gender and ethnic rights and a valorisation of cultural and ideological pluralism.

In all the groups there was a tension between the past of the seventies and the present of the eighties. For some, this entailed abandoning armed struggle for the time being, while for others it meant rethinking the ways in which armed struggle could be developed in a new context.

After the Malvinas/Falklands War, the surviving Argentine ERP members did not believe that conditions were ripe for resuming armed struggle, and therefore focused on building a political movement that was later embodied in the MTP and which represented the new historical moment. As the Tablada episode shows, for some the decision to abandon armed struggle was only temporary. In Uruguay's case, the defeated MLN-T, which began reorganising in 1985, also understood that conditions were not ripe for taking up arms again. In Brazil, some of the former guerrilla members that had first-hand experience of the Southern Cone from their time spent in exile in Montevideo and Santiago de Chile contributed to the PT.

The Chilean case was somewhat different. The decade began with MIR's Operation Return. While the MIR was not without internal conflicts, such divisions had not led to the levels of fragmentation that affected the organisations in Argentina or Uruguay. The MIR was also the only organisation that received the support of Cuba to carry out this project. Lastly, the scenario of Chile's transition, marked by Pinochet's victory in the 1980 plebiscite, left the country's political forces with much less room for political negotiation and encouraged a radicalisation of other parts of the Left, including the influential Chilean Communist Party, which also backed the idea of developing an armed strategy through the FPMR (Frente Patriotico Manuel Rodríguez – The Manuel Rodríguez Patriotic Front). All of this led to the emergence of a strong social movement between 1983 and 1986, where ideas of armed radicalisation propagated by MIR and by FPMR were somewhat appealing. MIR reassessed the military strategy it had followed in the seventies, with the aim of incorporating social mobilisation. After the movement began to wane in 1986 due to the increasing political repression and certain sectors of the Left's decision to negotiate, MIR had to face the dramatic choice of taking a political path or resuming a military path, a choice given expression by the factions that emerged at that moment.

In short, for all of these groups the tension between the revolutionary political culture inherited from the past and a social struggle linked to the social and political movements of the transition was the central element of this period. The experience of the Nicaraguan Revolution helped build a bridge between the old and the new. It was a revolution forged by militants who had been formed in the armed struggle of the seventies, to whom several Southern Cone militants were close as a result of their involvement in that process and who in the early eighties had an agenda with renewal-related issues, such as democratic pluralism, forms of mixed economy, and the relationship with social movements.

Abandoning subversive practices and armed struggle was in no case a decision brought on by a radical ideological transformation, rather it was the result of an assessment of the historical conditions that these actors were facing. For some it was the realisation that the development of the armed apparatuses of the state left guerrilla strategies little room for manoeuvre. For others, it had to do with the awareness that social movements' protest repertoires were proving more effective. Nonetheless, several practices were maintained. Generally speaking, success in overcoming that tension was not only a matter of the ability of the actors involved but also the structure of political opportunities that enabled the political process of each transition.

In her insightful study, Vania Markarian has shown how certain Uruguayan leftist militants gradually incorporated the human rights discourse developed internationally, as that language allowed them to effectively combat the dictatorship.[29] Building on Nancy Bermeo's notion of 'political learning', Astrid Arraras proposes something similar when she analyses the Tupamaros' incorporation into Uruguay's political system.[30] According to both approaches, it was not a sudden ideological conversion to liberalism (or ideological de-radicalisation) that led them to embrace certain political principles but rather the realisation that those strategies would allow them to move closer to attaining certain political objectives (pragmatic de-radicalisation).

But what were the key aspects that made this possible in Uruguay? The full answer goes beyond the scope of this chapter, but, allowing for the differences in more general aspects, such as national political culture and the degree of stability of each political system, there is a very specific aspect that can be observed in comparative terms. The amnesty and exile return policies can provide clues for understanding which strategies were most successful. In the cases of Chile and Argentina there were policies that hindered the integration of the groups that had engaged in armed struggle in the seventies. Chile's case was particularly complex because these groups continued to be active in the eighties. In Argentina and Uruguay, all armed groups had been disarmed by the time these countries returned to democracy.

The new democratic Argentinean government had a very active role with respect to disappeared militants, but the situation was somewhat more complicated when it came to the living revolutionary survivors. Political prisoners were not freed en masse, and the orders for the arrest of the Montonero and ERP leaders impacted the exile community. To a certain extent this made reorganising efforts and incorporation to the democratic process more difficult. For example, the MTP, whose main leader, Gorriaran, acted from the shadows due to an order for his arrest from Argentina's courts, reveals how the possibilities for integration in the new democratic climate were not just determined by the ideological mindsets that these militants brought from the seventies, but also had to do with the political opportunities and selective inducements offered by each transition.

Unlike in Argentina, in the Uruguayan democracy all political prisoners, among them the Tupamaros, were freed, and this made those who had taken up arms in the past more inclined to believe in the feasibility of operating under the new state of affairs. While there were also sectors that favoured a more militarist approach, they failed to take their proposals further, unlike what occurred in Argentina. Also, the case of Brazil appears to support the hypothesis that political amnesties enabled a greater integration of armed leftist groups into the new democracies (processes of selective inducements and incentives). The 1979 amnesty law that set off the process of democratisation in Brazil, the liberation of political prisoners and the return of exiles to the country helped dispel the doubts of those who were still considering the possibility of taking up arms again. Moreover, many of the actors involved in armed struggle joined the PT, successfully competing in elections, which led to former armed militant Dilma Rousseff being elected president in 2010.

Conclusion: Rethinking Defeat and De-radicalisation

In the second decade of the current century, significant sectors of the governing parties of Argentina, Bolivia, Brazil and Uruguay admit to having some kind of connection to armed activism. While the aforementioned former presidents of Uruguay and of Brazil were both former guerrillas, in Bolivia the surviving Peredo brothers who belonged to the ELN were important figures in the Bolivian MAS (Movimiento al Socialismo, 'Movement toward Socialism'), and in Argentina the sector headed by the former presidents Néstor and Cristina Kirchner have vindicated the experience of political struggle of the 1970s as a founding element of their political identity. Although Chile – at the time of writing – is governed by a right-wing party, some of the members of the left opposition vindicated the experience of the sixties and seventies radical left.

In a way, this resurgence of the experience of the 1960s and 1970s in the new century is connected with the memory struggles of the last decades. The denunciations of the human rights movements helped break down the stigmatisation of these left-wing organisations which prevailed during the authoritarian regimes. As Gilda Zwerman and Patricia Steinhoff have argued in their studies on new left activists in the United States and Japan, state actions have long-term effects, and what might initially be seen as a victory may be inverted in the long run if the state lacks sufficient legitimacy to sustain its actions.[31] The struggles for truth and justice and against the legacies of authoritarian states gave rise to questions that had been relatively silenced during the transitions to democracy. In the framework of these struggles, different left-wing political experiences from the 1970s were vindicated, both armed and legal. In the case of armed groups, this entailed a resignification that minimised aspects connected with violent practices and highlighted the supposed ethical integrity of the armed organisations and the final goals that guided their projects. In the current circumstances, then, the notions of short-term defeat and victory are generally being put into a broader context. The involvement of some activists from that period in politics today, as well as the sympathy of some groups among the voting public prompt a reassessment of these political experiences.

Notes

1. See: Aldo Marchesi, *Latin America's Radical Left Rebellion and Cold War in the Global 1960s* (Cambridge: Cambridge University Press, 2018).
2. On Argentina see: Richard Gillespie, *Soldiers of Perón: Argentina's Montoneros* (Oxford and New York: Clarendon Press; Oxford University Press, 1982); María

José Moyano, *Argentina's Lost Patrol: Armed Struggle, 1969–1979* (New Haven: Yale University Press, 1995); Pablo A. Pozzi, *Por las Sendas Argentinas: El PRT-ERP, La Guerrilla Marxista* (Buenos Aires: Eudeba, 2001); Vera Carnovale, *Los Combatientes: Historia Del PRT-ERP* (Buenos Aires: Siglo Veintiuno Editores, 2011). On Chile's case, see: Daniel Avendaño and Mauricio Palma, *El Rebelde de la Burguesía: La Historia De Miguel Enríquez* (Santiago, Chile: Ediciones CESOC, 2001); Francisco García Naranjo, *Historias Derrotadas: Opción y Obstinación de la Guerrilla Chilena (1965–1988)* (Morelia: Universidad Michoacana de San Nicolás de Hidalgo, 1996); Pedro Naranjo et al., *Miguel Enríquez y el proyecto revolucionario en Chile: Discursos y Documentos del Movimiento de Izquierda Revolucionaria* (Santiago, Chile: LOM Ediciones, 2004); Carlos Sandoval, *M.I.R. (una historia)* (Santiago: Sociedad Editorial Trabajadores, 1990). With respect to Uruguay, see: Clara Aldrighi, *La Izquierda Armada: ideología, ética e identidad en el MLN-Tupamaros* (Montevideo: Ediciones Trilce, 2001); Hebert Gatto, *El Cielo Por Asalto: el Movimiento de Liberación Nacional (Tupamaros) y la Izquierda Uruguaya (1963–1972)* (Montevideo: Taurus, 2004); Alfonso Lessa, *La Revolución Imposible: Los Tupamaros y el Fracaso de la vía Armada en el Uruguay del siglo XX* (Montevideo: Editorial Fin de Siglo, 2002).

3. See the first chapter for the theoretical framing. Also see: Omar Ashour, *The De-Radicalization of Jihadists: Transforming Armed Islamist Movements* (London and New York: Routledge, 2009) for a comparative dimension.

4. To understand the strategy of the government and its context, see: Claudia Feld and Marina Franco. *Democracia, hora cero: Actores, políticas y debates en los inicios de la posdictadura* (Buenos Aires: Fondo de Cultura Económico, 2015); Marcos Novaro and Vicente Palermo, *La Dictadura Militar, 1976–1983: Del Golpe de Estado a la Restauración Democrática* (Buenos Aires: Paidós, 2003). See: Emilio Crenzel, *La Historia Política del Nunca más: La Memoria de las Desapariciones en la Argentina* (Buenos Aires, Argentina: Siglo Veintiuno Editores, 2008), pp. 57–63; Marina Franco, 'La 'teoría de los dos demonios' en la primera etapa de la posdictadura', in: Feld and Franco.

5. Santiago Garaño and Werner Pertot, *Detenidos-Aparecidos: Presas y Presos Políticos desde Trelew a la Dictadura* (Buenos Aires: Editorial Biblos, 2007), p. 293.

6. Soledad Lastra, 'Los retornos del exilio en Argentina y Uruguay. Una historia comparada de las políticas y tensiones en la recepción y asistencia en las posdictaduras (1983–1989)', PhD Dissertation, Facultad de Humanidades y Ciencias de la Educación (UNLP), La Plata, 2014.

7. Samuel Blixen, *Conversaciones con Gorriarán Merl: treinta años de lucha popular* (Buenos Aires: Editorial Contrapunto, 1988), p. 355.

8. 'Una nueva propuesta política. Todos por la Patria', *Entre Todos*, no. 17 (May 1986).

9. The information on Gorriarán is based on Interviews with Enrique Gorriaran Merlo conducted by Archivo de Historia Oral, Instituto Gino Germani, 9/8/2005, 11/08/2005, 15/09/2005, 27/10/2005; Enrique Gorriaran Merlo and Darío Díaz, *Memorias de Enrique Gorriarán Merlo: de los Setenta a La Tablada* (Buenos Aires: Planeta, 2003).

10. MTP, 'Los militares avanzan. Que hacemos?'.

11. The carapintadas´ movement was an extreme rightist nationalist fraction within the army.

12. See: Claudia Hilb, 'La Tablada: el último acto de la guerrilla setentista', accessed on 29/8/2020, at: https://bit.ly/3hGOTbT; Felipe Celesia and Pablo Waisberg, *La Tablada: A vencer o morir: La última batalla de la guerrilla* Argentina (Buenos Aires: Aguilar, 2013). By way of example, see the coverage in the magazine *El Porteño*, February 1989, in particular: Eduardo Blaustein, 'Un alfiler menos', *El Porteño*, February 1989, p. 13; Eduardo Aliverti, 'Un comando de maniaticos', *El Porteño*, February 1989, p. 17.

13. María Allier Eugenia, *Batallas por la memoria* (Montevideo: Trilce, 2010), pp. 31–46.

14. 'Conferencia del MLN', *Las Bases*, 11/3/1985.

15. Astrid Arrarás, 'Armed Struggle, Political Learning and Participation in Democracy: The Case of the Tupamaros', PhD Dissertation, Princeton University, New Jersey, 1999.

16. See: Eleuterio Fernandez Huidobro, *Historia de los Tupamaros*, three volumes (Montevideo: TAE, Tupac Amaru Editores, 1986–8); Mauricio Rosencof and Eleuterio Fernández Huidobro, *Memorias del Calabozo* (Montevideo: Tae, 1988).

17. Federico Leicht, *Cero a la izquierda: una biografía de Jorge Zabalza* (Montevideo, Uruguay: Letraeñe Ediciones, 2009).

18. For an overview of that process, see: 'Resoluciones de la V Convención Nacional', *MLN-T*. Junio-Julio 1990. For ananalysis of the conflict, see: Adolfo Garcé, *Donde Hubo Fuego: el proceso de adaptación del MLN-Tupamaros a la legalidad y a la competencia electoral (1985–2004)* (Montevideo: Editorial Fin de Siglo, 2006), chapter 5.

19. See: 'El 'fenómeno Mujica': La seducción de un intruso', *Brecha*, 8/10/1999.

20. Andrés Danza and Ernesto Tulbovitz, *Una oveja negra al poder: Pepe Mujica, la política de la gente* (Barcelona: Debate, 2016).

21. On CODEPU's activities, see: Patricio Orellana and Elizabeth Quay Hutchison, *El movimiento de derechos humanos en Chile: 1973–1990* (Santiago de Chile: Centro de Estudios Políticos Latinoamericanos Simón Bolívar, 1991), pp. 34–6.

22. See: Hernan Aguiló, 'Inicio de un balance autocrítico de mi militancia revolucionaria', 2005, accessed on 29/8/2020, at: https://bit.ly/32H5t5o

23. For a review of Mir´s Return operation see: Comité Memoria Neltume, *Guerrilla en Neltume: Una historia de lucha y resistencia en el sur chileno* (Santiago de Chile: LOM Ediciones, 2003).

24. 'Contra la dictadura y por la liberación popular', *Comunicado del IV Congreso del MIR (Político)*, 1988, accessed on 29/8/2020, at: https://bit.ly/3b8RVTH; 'Única vía a la democracia', *El Combatiente. Periódico oficial de la Comisión Militar*, no. 1 (March 1988), p. 2. For descriptions of the political fragmentation, see: Verónica Valdivia Ortiz De Zárate, Rolando Alvarez Vallejos and Julio Pinto Vallejos, *Su Revolución Contra Nuestra Revolución: Izquierdas y derechas en el Chile de Pinochet (1973–1981)*, vol. 1, 2 (Santiago: LOM, 2006, 2008); Mario Garcés and Sebastián Leiva, *El golpe en La Legua: Los Caminos de la Historia y la Memoria* (Santiago: LOM Ediciones, 2005), pp. 125–36; Igor Goicovic Donoso, 'Transición y Violencia Política: En Chile (1988–1994)', *Ayer Revista de Historia Contemporánea* (2010), pp. 87–98.

25. Steve J. Stern, *Reckoning with Pinochet: The Memory Question in Democratic Chile 1989–2006* (Durham, NC: Duke University Press, 2010), pp. 36–7; Brian Loveman and Elizabeth Lira, *Las Ardientes Cenizas del Olvido: Vía Chilena de Reconciliación Política 1932–1994* (Santiago: LOM Ediciones / DIBAM, 2000), pp. 490–539.

26. Ibid., pp. 490–539; Stern, pp. 36–7.

27. See: CODEPU, *Informe de Derechos Humanos: 1990–2000* (Santiago: LOM, 2001), chapter 2; Donoso, p. 79; Pedro Rosas, *Rebeldía: Subversión y Prisión Política* (Santiago: LOM, 2004), chapter 4.

28. To understand the impact of human rights global discourse, see: Samuel Moyn, *The Last Utopia: Human Rights in History* (Cambridge, MA: Harvard University Press, 2010); Barbara J. Keys, *Reclaiming American Virtue: The Human Rights Revolution of the 1970s* (Cambridge, MA: Harvard University Press, 2014). To understand the impact of human rights discourse in Latin America See: Vania Markarian, *Left in Transformation: Uruguayan Exiles and the Latin American Human Rights Networks, 1967–1984* (New York: Routledge, 2005);

James Green, *We Cannot Remain Silent: Opposition to the Brazilian Military Dictatorship in the United States* (Durham, NC: Duke University Press, 2010); Kathryin Sikkink, *The Justice Cascade: How Human Rights Prosecutions Are Changing World Politics* (New York: W. W. Norton & Co., 2011).

29. Markarian, pp. 3–4.
30. Arrarás, pp. 10–14.
31. Gilda Zwerman and Patricia Steinhoff, 'When Activists Ask for Trouble: State-Dissident Interactions and the New Left Cycle of Resistance in the United States and Japan', in: Christian Davenport, Hank Johnston and Carol Mueller (eds), *Repression and Mobilization* (Minneapolis: University of Minnesota Press, 2005).

10

LEAVING THE WEAPONS WITHOUT LOSING THE WAR: UNDERSTANDING THE TRANSFORMATION OF THE FMLN

Alberto Martín Álvarez

Introduction

Between 1981 and 1992, El Salvador underwent a devastating civil war that killed more than 70,000 people and turned 25 per cent of the population into refugees or internally displaced persons. The roots of this conflict lie in the political and economic exclusion of a large majority of the population by the military regime established in 1932. The armed forces maintained an alliance, sometimes troublesome, with the small economic elite that controlled the country's main economic resources. This control translated into an enormous inequality in the distribution of productive resources and, in particular, of arable land, which at the height of the 1970s was still the main resource of a poorly diversified agro-export economy.

As Francis Steward observes,[1] political exclusion and socioeconomic exclusion are inextricably linked because the former ensures the persistence of the latter. In the Salvadoran case, the exclusion of the opposition from the political game prevented any variation in the patterns of land ownership and, in particular, the implementation of an agrarian reform that would reverse the unequal distribution of land.

The repression of the demands for democratisation and social justice made by organised sectors of the peasantry, urban workers and students led to their gradual radicalisation and the formation of armed left-wing groups from the early 1970s. The revolutionary movement expanded slowly from the cities to the countryside, relying on the organisational infrastructure previously created by the Catholic Church in rural areas of the north, centre and east of the country.[2]

During the war, left-wing armed groups depended heavily for their survival on a highly motivated and disciplined militancy. This was because the country lacked significant natural resources for the revolutionaries to appropriate, and also because they received only moderate foreign support. In this sense, the Salvadoran left-wing armed groups were clear examples of the kind of 'activist' movements described by Jeremy Weinstein.[3] Contrary to the findings of the 'greed approach' in the study of civil wars,[4] the thousands of Salvadoran peasants, workers and students who joined the revolutionary movement did so for moral or emotional reasons, as shown by Ellen Wood,[5] due to ideological convictions, or sometimes as a result of life-threatening events caused by the armed forces or paramilitaries as some of Jocelyn Viterna's informants explained.[6]

Although this social support remained significant throughout the years, it was gradually undermined by the prolongation of the war and the inability to defeat the regime's armed forces. The gradual liberalisation of the political regime, which opened up spaces for participation to the opposition, together with war weariness, prevented the armed left from enlisting broad sectors of the population beyond those already mobilised in the late 1970s or early 1980s.

The inability to defeat the government triggered internal conflicts over the definition of strategy and leadership within the armed left. These conflicts produced a change in the leadership of the most important armed organisations. In turn, this change prompted a gradual displacement of the most radical goals of the insurgent coalition – armed struggle, revolution – and the acceptance of polyarchy as a first step towards the end of the socioeconomic exclusion of the popular majorities. This process occurred in parallel to – and drew on – a gradual change in the political stance of the main allies of the revolutionary coalition, who by the late eighties faced increasing difficulties in maintaining their support.

Without the possibility of a military triumph and with an increasingly precarious foreign support, the cost of continuing the war for the insurgents was clearly greater than the achievement of a peace agreement that granted them the right to pursue some of their political goals by other means.

On the other hand, the economic changes produced by the war made the insurgency's demands for political participation or land distribution acceptable to the economic elite. Once leading businessmen received guarantees that peace would not produce substantial changes in the distribution of economic power, they became active supporters of the negotiations.

Finally, by 1990 and with the end of the Cold War already in sight, the US government, principal backer of the Salvadoran armed forces, began to exert pressure for a negotiated exit to the war and overcame the resistance and the fears of the Salvadoran military towards the consequences of a peace process. The result of these interconnected processes was the signing of the Chapultepec Peace Accords in 1992.

This chapter proceeds as follows. First, the causes that led to the war are briefly analysed, with an emphasis on the formation and expansion of the revolutionary movement. Secondly, the main transformations experienced during the war by the major political actors are explained. The focus here is on the changes within US policy on the conflict, the position of the allies of the armed left, the structural transformations of the economy and the interests of the Salvadoran elite and the internal dynamics of the armed left. The chapter ends with some concluding remarks.

The Road to War

Wave of Protests and the Emergence of the Armed Left

The Salvadoran revolutionary left emerged at the beginning of the 1970s in the context of a dual process of political liberalisation and economic modernisation implemented by Coronels Julio Adalberto Rivera (1962–7) and Fidel Sánchez Hernández (1967–72). The contradictions produced by both processes led to the mobilisation of different social sectors, which used political liberalisation to create a dense organisational network from the mid-1960s onwards. Industrial workers, students and state employees – especially teachers – whose relative importance had grown from strength to strength since the beginning of the 1950s as a result of the developmental policies of the period, were at the forefront of an important wave of protests between

1967 and 1972.[7] The various mobilised sectors demanded the democratisation of a political regime that had been controlled by the military since 1932.
In the context of an enormously unequal country, these democratic claims
were usually fused with demands for social justice, land distribution or with
basic corporate demands for higher wages or better working conditions.

In was within this wave of protests specifically that the organisations
of the armed left appeared. Their first militants were mostly young middle-
or lower-middle-class university students and, to a much lesser extent,
workers. Their participation in the protests helped to radicalise these young
people, most of whom had a background in the university student movement
or the militant sections of the Partido Comunista de El Salvador (PCS) or
the Partido Demócrata Cristiano (PDC)'s youth wings. The stance adopted
by these two parties against the war between El Salvador and Honduras in
the summer of 1969 caused many of them to abandon their organisations
and join the new armed revolutionary movements. Notwithstanding their
internal differences, the most radicalised militants of the student movement
shared the conviction that it was impossible to achieve social justice in the
context of capitalism, and assumed that the armed struggle spearheaded by
professional revolutionaries would be capable of defeating the regime's army,
seizing control of the state apparatus and guiding the country down the path
to socialism.[8]

However, the revolutionary left's diagnosis of El Salvador's reality was not
a mere ideological construct. Indeed, despite the military regime's attempts
to transform the economic structure, at the beginning of the 1970s the country was still fundamentally agrarian, dominated by a landowning elite closely
associated with the army, on whom they depended to guarantee the continued extra-economic coercion of the peasantry.[9] The regime's democratisation
implied organising the country's rural labour force in unions, and this would
pose a direct threat to the survival of the elite's vital interests, which in turn
explains the violent resistance of the landowners to any attempt at democratisation. There was some domestic and international pressure, as from the
mid-1960s the regime made some room for the opposition in the political
system, but this was to a limited extent and permitted only provided that
the social and political control of the peasantry by the landowners and the
military was not questioned.

Although its origins date back to 1970, the Ejército Revolucionario del Pueblo (ERP, 'People's Revolutionary Army'), mainly formed by former social-Christian and Christian-democratic student activists, appeared on the public stage in March 1972. They were joined soon afterwards by a number of militants from the youth organisation of the PCS and activists of the university student movement who had played a leading role in the Common Subject Areas Strike (*Huelga de Áreas Comunes*) at the University of El Salvador (UES) in February 1970.[10] In its early days, it should be noted that the ERP tended to give priority to armed actions and its military development at the expense of the task of organising the masses. This was in turn related to the predominance of an insurrectional strategy, according to which the conditions for a popular insurrection did indeed exist in the country. This approach coexisted inside the organisation with another strategy identified more closely with the protracted people's war. These different approaches led to a power struggle in the ERP, which ended in the murder of two prominent militants – Armando Arteaga and Roque Dalton – in May 1975, and the creation of a new organisation by the dissidents: the Fuerzas Armadas de la Resistencia Nacional (FARN, 'Armed National Resistance Forces'). Shortly before, at the end of 1973, another group of militants, who had abandoned the organisation due to similar disagreements over the armed group's strategy, formed the Organización Revolucionaria de los Trabajadores ('Revolutionary Workers' Organisation'), whose armed wing was the Fuerzas Revolucionarias Armadas del Pueblo (FRAP, 'People's Armed Revolutionary Forces').[11] Later on, its militants would end up either joining the FARN or contributing to the efforts to create a new organisation, the Partido Revolucionario de los Trabajadores Centroamericanos (PRTC, 'Central American Revolutionary Workers' Party'), founded in 1976.

The Farabundo Martí Popular Liberation Forces (FPL) claimed its first armed action in August 1972, however, its origins date back to 1 April 1970, the moment at which Salvador Cayetano Carpio, then secretary general of the PCS, and a small group of militants abandoned the organisation to create a new revolutionary group. Their reasons had to do with the diverging views in the party as regards the revolutionary strategy, plus its stance on the 'Soccer War' between El Salvador and Honduras in July 1969.

Inspired by the example of the Viet Cong, the FPL envisaged a 'prolonged popular war', whose main theatre would be the countryside. Unlike the ERP, the FPL was at first a very disciplined organisation with a personalist leader, Carpio. Together with the care with which the FPL trained and indoctrinated its militants, this reinforced the transmission of a well-defined organisational culture.

Finally, from March 1980, the Fuerzas Armadas de Liberación (FAL, 'Armed Liberation Forces'), the armed wing of the PCS, began to be organised in the context of a progressive rapprochement between all the factions of the revolutionary left.

Despite sharing ideological traits and political goals, during the 1970s relations between the different armed groups were characterised by mistrust and even confrontation. The lack of consensus on alliances and mobilisation strategy explain, in part, the revolutionary movement's lack of unity, although the hegemonic pretensions of the different revolutionary groups were just as decisive.

From Urban Guerrillas to Political-Military Movements

Between 1970 and 1973, the left-wing armed groups were small, militarised vanguard parties with a few dozen fully committed combatants operating largely in urban and suburban areas. In parallel, insurgents gradually forged clandestine links with the organisational structures of the social movements, above all those created since 1969 by networks of priests and laypeople committed to liberation theology.[12] The pastoral work of these networks led to the establishment of cooperatives, the creation of Christian base communities and the training of peasant leaders. While, in the cities and on the basis of a radical interpretation of the Gospels, Catholic Action groups contributed to the development of anti-authoritarian and anti-capitalist thinking among sectors of the country's middle- and upper-middle-class youth. It was thanks to the social work that they undertook in peasant communities and urban slums,[13] including literacy and education programmes, that it was possible to forge social links between peasant leaders and urban activists. A significant number of these urban Catholic activists joined – from university or secondary school – the guerrillas, placing the social networks that they had built up in the countryside and in the slums on the outskirts of San

Salvador at the service of the armed organisations. Moreover, in the cities, armed organisations infiltrated trade unions, neighbourhood organisations and student groups, through both the dual membership of their cadres[14] and the new organisations created by the guerrillas. From then on, the revolutionaries encouraged the creation of popular coordination committees with the purpose of pooling the efforts of the different organisations under their control or influence. Thus, from 1974 to 1979 the following groups came into being: the Frente de Acción Popular Unificada (FAPU, 'Unified Popular Action Front'), the FPL's Bloque Popular Revolucionario (BPR, 'Popular Revolutionary Bloc'), the ERP's Ligas Populares 28 de Febrero (LP-28, '28 February Popular Leagues') and the PRTC's Movimiento de Liberación Popular ('Popular Liberation Movement').

The authoritarian drift of the regime, first under Coronel Arturo Armando Molina (1972–7) and then General Carlos Humberto Romero (1977–9), was characterised by increased repression and election rigging on a massive scale to prevent the victory of a political opposition that now stood united. This led to a greater rapprochement between the popular movement and the guerrillas.

The Salvadoran political context reached a turning point on 15 October 1979, when a group of young military officers staged a coup that put an end to the authoritarian regime established in 1932. A civilian-military Junta then established a government with representatives from the centre and the centre-left of the political spectrum, together with progressive members of the military, and with the support of the PCS. Control over the army and police forces remained, however, in the hands of hard-line military officers. It was, in fact, the lack of control over the military and paramilitary apparatus that rendered the Junta's governing body unable to end repression, which peaked from this moment on. Due to this, the Junta's civilian members left the government in early January 1980, and installed a new government headed by the Christian Democrat José Napoleón Duarte and made up by representatives of the conservative branch of his party (PDC) and the armed forces with the support of the US government.

In mid-1979, with the mediation of the Cuban government, the armed left initiated a dialogue with the aim of establishing a coordinating platform. As a result of these negotiations, on 17 December 1979, the PCS, RN and

FPL established a new coordinating body, the Political-Military Coordination Body (CPM), which was made public on 10 January 1980. The following day, the social movement organisations controlled by the guerrilla groups announced the creation of the Revolutionary Coordinating Committee of the Masses (CRM) with the aim of implementing an armed insurgency as a means of solving the crisis faced by the regime. Afterwards, following the murder of the San Salvador archbishop, Monsignor Oscar Arnulfo Romero, on 24 March 1980, the centre-left opposition and the guerrillas converged under the latter's hegemony. One concrete outcome of this convergence was the creation of the Revolutionary Democratic Front (FDR) in April of that year. The FDR grouped together, among others, PDC dissidents now under the banner of the Social Christian Popular Movement (MPSC); the social-democratic National Revolutionary Movement (MNR); and the Jesuit Central American University (UCA) and the University of El Salvador (UES), alongside the coordinating structures of the social movement controlled by the guerrillas. The Unified Revolutionary Direction (DRU) was established on 22 May 1980, which grouped together the FPL, RN, ERP and PCS. Finally, on 10 October 1980, and after much hardship, the Farabundo Front for National Liberation (FMLN) was founded, to which the PRTC joined in December of that year. The establishment of the FMLN implied the creation of joint committees composed of representatives from the five armed groups, such as the General Command (*Comandancia General*) or various specialised commissions such as the Political-Diplomatic Commission, made up of representatives of the Front's five organisations and those of the FDR, which monitored the FMLN's relationship with foreign governments and political parties.

By late 1980, the FMLN and FDR had established a strategic alliance that was to last throughout the entire war. This alliance adopted a political programme (the Revolutionary Democratic Government) that included, among other demands, the dissolution of the army and security forces; agrarian reform; the dissolution of state powers, and the passing of a new constitution.

At this time it was obvious that the cabinet had no control over the radical far-right groups or over the intelligence and security services. In this context of mounting repression by death squads and police and military forces, and encouraged by the success of the Nicaraguan Revolution of July 1979, guerrilla groups launched a 'final' nationwide offensive on 10 January 1981. However, the lack of arms and training, as well as the lack of coordination among the different armed groups, stopped the FMLN from taking power.

After the failure of the 1981 offensive, guerrilla organisations retreated to the rural north and northeast areas of the country, and the conflict turned into a large-scale civil war that would last until January 1992. On that date the FMLN signed a peace agreement (the Chapultepec Accords) without being militarily defeated and retaining significant popular support.

The Transition to Peace

From late 1983 on, hopes for a speedy defeat of the government vanished, which along with a series of internal changes forced the Front to develop a new strategy of negotiation and armed struggle. In the end, following a second nationwide FMLN offensive in 1989, the insurgents, the Salvadoran government and their respective allies concluded that a military resolution of the conflict was not possible. The transition to peace was the result of a fortunate combination of variables: The impossibility of a military victory, the change in the positions of the strategic allies of the warring parties, the changes in the domestic political context and also in the leadership of the FMLN were, without doubt, the most salient factors. In this work all these variables will be treated separately with analytic purposes. However, all of them interacted and fed back each other resulting in the Chapultepec Peace Agreement.

Liberalisation of the Political Regime

The new regime inaugurated in January 1980 was built on an alliance between the PDC, the military and the US government, and had from the beginning two main objectives: the military defeat of the FMLN and the implementation of an agenda of economic and political reform. The strategic goals were both depriving the insurgency of its support base and undermining the economic foundations of the landowning elite's power. The cornerstones of this reformist project were the establishment of a polyarchy and the development of an agrarian reform. However, throughout the 1980s, the landed elite and the most conservative parts of the military continued to maintain enough power to impose severe limits on the democratisation of the regime. In fact, due to the autonomy of the armed forces, until the 1992 Peace Agreements the regime was a hybrid case: half-way between a collective military regime and an electoral democracy. A gradual liberalisation throughout this decade did provide a limited margin of freedom within the political system, as well as allowing for the holding of regular elections. Despite their obvious counter-insurgent purpose, and despite the fact that elections fundamentally sought a demonstrative effect, the electoral processes held in the 1980s served to legitimise the political system that had emerged from the coup of 1979. In parallel, the increasing legitimacy of the political system weakened the FMLN, which was unable to win the support of significant sectors of the population that became the basis for sustaining the PDC (1984–9), and later ARENA (1989–94), governments.

Also, some sectors, in particular from the middle class, progressively withdrew their support from the insurgency as its chances for victory vanished and the political regime showed signs of opening up. Particularly during the early 1980s, the PDC was the organisation that most directly contested popular FMLN support, through the aforementioned reformist agenda. These reforms went hand in hand with the creation of unions and organisations amongst their beneficiaries, especially those of the agrarian reform. These organisations provided crucial social support for the reformist model implemented by the PDC, thus contributing to its legitimisation.

The liberalisation of the political system also led to a relative reduction of repression in the cities. According to Charles D. Brockett,[15] the number of civilian victims decreased considerably between 1984 and 1988. While over 18,000 people were killed by the military and police forces in 1981, the yearly number of casualties went down to 6,000 from 1982 to 1983, and to less than 4,000 in 1984. It remained under 2,000 until 1989.

The decrease in repression from the mid-1980s on, together with some of the guarantees attached to electoral processes as a consequence of international pressure – in particular the Esquipulas II process – on the Salvadoran government, offered the guerrillas' civil allies the possibility of starting a legal political struggle. By late 1987, the FDR returned to El Salvador to participate in the March 1989 elections under the Democratic Convergence (CD) party's ticket. This participation proved that there were new guarantees to develop a left-wing political agenda peacefully. The greater transparency of electoral processes, the incorporation of the FDR into the political system and the new empowerment of political parties within the system, increased the appeal of the electoral path in the eyes of the armed left.

The existence of greater (although not full) possibilities for political participation made the FMLN's justifications for armed struggle, largely based on political exclusion, less and less credible.

Structural Economic Changes and the Transformation of the Country's Economic Elite

The Salvadoran landowning elite experienced a dual process of political and economic change throughout the war. The armed conflict produced an acute crisis in export agriculture, which was the traditional economic foundation of the Salvadoran elite. The agrarian reform and the nationalisation of banks and foreign trade launched by the reformist governments following the 1979 coup undermined the agro-export model that the Salvadoran economy had been rooted in, and thus the dominion of the landowners. Despite the great difficulties faced in applying the agrarian reform, and although its scope was limited, it strongly affected the elite's economic foundations, in particular coffee production. According to Ana Cardenal,[16] the 136 largest coffee producers were affected by the reform, including eight family groups who dominated production. Along with the reform, the impact of the war caused the abandonment of around 88,000 hectares – close to 43 per cent of the country's farming land. This, as well as the disappearance of infrastructure and the tax demanded by the guerrilla groups, contributed to a decrease in producers' earnings. Thus, both war and agrarian reform caused a strong impact on the land ownership structure, undermining the oligarchy's economic foundations. In addition, the nationalisation of foreign trade, whose aim was to earn an important income for the state, also affected coffee and cotton producers.

All these changes, in turn, produced a fragmentation and a transformation of the economic elite. The sector which was the most dependent on land ownership for the extraction of its wealth was strongly hit by the reforms implemented in the 1980s. A second group, made up of financiers, exporters and industrialists who had a greater capacity to sail through the crisis that derived from war, began to diversify its investments during this period with the help of the United States Agency for International Development

(USAID). The development of the services sector (including financial services), of the maquila industry and non-traditional agricultural exports were the mainstay of this productive diversification strategy. The modernisation of the Salvadoran economic structure through the creation of non-traditional exports was a fundamental aim of the US government, who found a useful partner in this modernising sector of Salvadoran entrepreneurship. The US also contributed to the political modernisation of this sector of the economic elite through promotion and consultancy services as well as through the creation of think tanks such as the Salvadoran Foundation for Social and Economic Development (FUSADES).[17]

The post-1979 reformist agenda encouraged the country's economic elite to move with the times. In this sense, the foundation in September 1981 of the ARENA party was an effort to adapt to a new political environment marked by electoral competition. The founders of the party came mostly from the oligarchic (landowning, industrial and financial) sectors, the armed forces and paramilitary groups. In its first years, the organisation was characterised by a belligerent style, the use of confrontational rhetoric and violent tactics. However, the aforementioned changes in the economic structure, the US support for the right's political renovation and the exile of some of the main representatives of the old landowning oligarchy helped increase the political influence of the modernising sector of the economic elite, which was also reflected in ARENA's internal balance. After its electoral defeat in the 1985 legislative elections, the radically anti-communist landowning sector that had dominated the party in its early years was replaced by a group of modernising businessmen. Alfredo Cristiani's 1988 nomination as presidential candidate for the 1989 elections exemplified the style and composition of the new dominant coalition that ruled ARENA from that moment on. The successive electoral victories of 1988 and 1989 strengthened this group's position and prestige within the party.

This sector of the elite, which now headed the party, had a greater interest in putting an end to war than in keeping it alive. The lengthening of the armed conflict made it impossible for them to fully engage in their financial and commercial activities while, on the other hand, the demands of the FMLN on land issues with the aim of ending conflict no longer posed a threat to their survival. The fact that land ownership and traditional agro-export had lost economic weight, as well as the fact that the nucleus of the creation of wealth had shifted towards the trade and service sectors, made it unnecessary to maintain the coercive structure which had formerly guaranteed control over the workforce since the 1930s. Also, in the scenario of the new polyarchy that was now established in the country, the modern entrepreneurial elite no longer felt the need to turn to the armed forces for the representation and defense of their interests. They now had their own instruments, such as ARENA and FUSADES, and they were better adapted to the new national and international political and economic environment.[18] As compared to their predecessors, Alfredo Cristiani and the forces he represented were structurally in a much better place in the government to engage in peace negotiations with the FMLN. Thus, when the circumstances were ripe following the 1989 offensive, this group was willing to make a series of political concessions that were under their control and did not contradict their core economic interests, which at the end of the day facilitated reaching an agreement with the insurgents.

Changes in US Policy towards El Salvador

Until the 1970s, the involvement of the US government in El Salvador was not very significant, however as the political crisis worsened, it increased and was more evident after the Sandinista victory in July 1979.

When Jimmy Carter took office, his administration (1977–81) adopted a new foreign policy, with defense of human rights becoming one of the premises of the United States' relationship with developing nations. However, it soon became evident in the Salvadoran case that the alleged moral commitment that was guiding the new US foreign policy was, in fact, a diplomatic tool that easily gave way to strategic interests. In 1978, the US government dispatched a 10-million-dollar financial aid package to General Carlos Humberto Romero's government, despite the abundant incriminating evidence of assassinations and disappearances perpetrated by the security forces and death squads since Romero's rise to power. Confronted by the boom of the revolutionary movement in El Salvador, and following the victory of the Sandinista Front in Nicaragua in July 1979, Carter chose to prioritise US security interests. In light of a likely revolutionary victory in El Salvador, the US administration backed moderates in the armed forces in an attempt to pry the most conservative groups of the military from the state's control. The goal of US foreign policy from that moment on was that of politically isolating both the armed left and the extreme right, and laying the foundations for the construction of a representative democracy aligned with Washington. The Revolutionary Government Junta that took power following the 15 October 1979 coup was, in the eyes of the US, an instrument that would allow it to meet both goals.[19]

When the first Junta resigned in January 1980, the US administration looked for a leading figure with democratic credentials that would also be acceptable to the Salvadoran military. This figure was Napoleón Duarte, the leader of the PDC's conservative wing, who would be promoted from that moment on by the Department of State as an image of moderation. The new Junta, controlled by the military and now exclusively supported by the PDC, would thus become the ideal platform from which to launch a series of structural reforms geared towards weakening the insurgency and undermining the economic foundations of the landowning oligarchy's power. Duarte's reputation as a democratic leader who had for years opposed the military dictatorship gave the US government the possibility to offer El Salvador enough military support to defeat the revolutionaries.

Facing the gradual rapprochement of the armed left towards the moderate left represented by the FDR, Carter chose to unreservedly support the military and the PDC. Neither the assassination of Archbishop Romero in March 1980,[20] nor that of three US nuns, or even the murder of the FDR's own leadership orchestrated by sectors of the security forces in that year were enough to cancel US military aid to the Salvadoran government, who received almost six million dollars from the US in early January 1981.

When President Ronald Reagan took office (1981), US foreign policy in El Salvador became militarised. For the new US administration, El Salvador was a proxy theatre for the East–West confrontation. It must be stated that Ronald Reagan's aggressive foreign policy found a certain counterbalance in the Chamber of Representatives, which was controlled throughout this period by the Democratic Party.[21] The Democrats criticised Reagan and his team's aspiration of escalating the Salvadoran conflict, which they refused to view as a product of the East–West confrontation.

The Reagan policy resulted in an exponential increase of US military aid to El Salvador throughout the 1980s. This aid was not restricted to providing

funding and arms, but also extended to CIA participation in covert operations in El Salvador, the deployment of military consultants and the training
of Special Forces. According to Knut Walter,[22] US military aid to El Salvador
surpassed 950 million dollars from 1980 to 1989. The tangible result of
this support was that the Salvadoran armed forces were able to resume the
military initiative from 1984 onwards – and up until the Front's offensive in
1989 – thus forcing the FMLN to give up on concentrating troops and to
utilise a 'hit and run' strategy, which decreased their chances of implementing large-scale offensives that could threaten the government's stability. In
the long run this resulted in a military stalemate, at high political cost for
the FMLN, as it became apparent over time that the insurgents were unable
to attain power, while growing war costs contributed to dwindling popular
support for the guerrilla organisations.

From June 1981 onwards, as a result of Thomas O. Ender's promotion
to Assistant Secretary of State for Inter-American Affairs, a new strategy was
added to the initial focus of the Reagan administration on the mass provision
of military aid to defeat the insurgency: the promotion of democracy. As per
Enders' strategy, if the left did not agree to take part in the political system,
it would show that they refused to renounce violence, as elections were the
only political exit from war. In doing so, they would negate the possibility
of negotiating with the insurgency, in which the latter might acquire what it
had been incapable of obtaining on the battlefield.[23] Despite its instrumental
goal, the holding of regular elections would open up political space, which
would in turn allow the FMLN's civil allies to be inserted into the political
system in 1988.

Parallel to this was another crucial aim of US economic aid: upholding
an economy that was being sorely weakened by war. Walter[24] believes this
aid was an estimated 2,685 million dollars from 1979 to 1989, and that it
stabilised a Salvadoran economy that would otherwise have collapsed in the
midst of conflict.

From 1987, Reagan's policy towards Central America was undermined by the Iran-Contra affair; by the Esquipulas II Agreement of August
1987, which indirectly condemned US support of the Nicaraguan contras;
and by the Democratic Party once again taking control of the US Senate.
Later, the dissension between the US and the Soviet Union (USSR), and

George H. W. Bush's arrival to the White House in January 1989, resulted in Central America having considerably less weight on the US security agenda. Unlike the Reagan administration, the Bush administration had a pragmatic vision of the conflict and was determined to decrease its costly involvement in the region. The USSR's position, which had since the mid-1980s been in favour of a negotiated solution to Central American conflicts, and the victory of Nicaragua's Violeta Chamorro in February 1990, also played a part in this.

Thus, following the assassination of six prominent Salvadoran Jesuit priests in November 1989, and the ensuing pressure on the US Congress to halve the military aid given to the Salvadoran armed forces, making it conditional on progress being made on investigating these murders, the US executive was able to change its standpoint on the conflict at no great political cost. Since 1990, the US government exerted pressure and favoured negotiations between the Salvadoran government and the FMLN.

Changes in the Position of the FMLN's Allies

The Cuban government remained committed to a position of promoting revolutionary internationalism, which translated into sustained support for the FMLN throughout the war. Contact between Salvadoran political-military organisations and Cuba went back to the early 1970s, but they had kept a low profile until 1979, largely because the preconditions for Cuban intervention agreed upon by Havana and the Latin American communist party in 1975 – high chances for success, Soviet consent and unified revolutionary forces – remained unmet.[25] These conditions came together in 1979.[26]

The example of the unification of the three trends of *Sandinismo* and the victory of the Nicaraguan Revolution, combined with the military weakness of Salvadoran political-military organisations, encouraged the latter to come together. Along with this, Fidel Castro's personal intervention made it easier to overcome distrust among the different groups, paving the way towards the attainment of the agreements that gave rise to the FMLN. From this moment on, Cuba became a logistical platform, training camp, hospital and political ally of the Salvadoran insurgency.

Although this support did not disappear at any time throughout the war, by 1982 it had taken on a lower profile. The North American threat to 'go to the source' of the Salvadoran insurgency,[27] the USSR's conservative position and the impossibility of the FMLN attaining a rapid military victory in El Salvador caused the Cuban government to become cautious. All this led the Cubans to recommend by late 1982 that the FMLN leaders promote a strategy for conducting armed struggle and negotiation in parallel.[28] It seems that the Cubans attempted to persuade Salvadoran revolutionaries of the convenience of reaching an understanding with their government as a way to placate the Reagan administration, seeking through this to guarantee the survival of the Nicaraguan Revolution.

With regard to Nicaragua, some parts of the Sandinista National Liberation Front (FSLN) leadership cooperated with the Salvadoran revolutionaries throughout the war. Like Cuba, Sandinistas prided themselves on their revolutionary internationalism, but they also contributed to paying the debt of solidarity they owed their Salvadoran companions.[29] Nicaragua served as a logistic corridor and warehouse of supplies, provided constant political support – even allowing the FMLN to openly set up office there for several years – and procured arms throughout the conflict. It must be noted that the hardening of the US position forced Nicaraguans to lower the profile of their official relationships with the FMLN from 1983 onwards. Proof of this lies in the fact that the support Salvadorans received from Sandinistas from then on came from parts of the party leadership and the army, but not from the Nicaraguan government as such.[30] The electoral defeat of the FSLN in February 1990 resulted in Salvadoran revolutionaries facing further challenges when it came to receiving supplies via Nicaragua.

As for the Soviet Union, the rise to power of Mikhail Gorbachev (1985–91) redefined Soviet foreign policy priorities, as it sought to reassign its already depleted economic resources and channel them towards meeting domestic needs.[31] Since 1988, it became clear that the Gorbachev administration changed Soviet third world policy by recognising that the US had legitimate national interests and that it was necessary for both powers to respect their given areas of influence. The USSR renounced its exporting of the revolution and stopped providing military solutions to the numerous regional crises developing at the time, and rather, they began a negotiated exit to armed conflicts within the scope of cooperation with the US. These changes had an important impact on the Central American crisis. In the case of El Salvador, in 1990 the Soviets repeatedly insisted on the FMLN negotiating with the government in the presence of the UN and suggested that if the US stopped supporting the Salvadoran government, the Front would need to abandon arms. In February of that year, the Soviets even seemed to have reached an agreement with the US on finding a negotiated solution to the Salvadoran conflict.

Internal Dynamics and Political Development of the FMLN

The defeat of the 1981 offensive showed that within the FMLN there were at least two different conceptions of the strategy and the goals of the revolution. The first was represented by the leader of the FPL, Salvador Cayetano Carpio. For him and his followers, the revolution was to be driven by a worker–peasant alliance, and victory would only be achieved by prolonged popular war. In practice, this translated into Carpio refusing to make alliances with other revolutionary groups, and considering negotiation with the government synonymous with betrayal of the revolutionary movement, which should only be used for tactical purposes. Besides this, Carpio had a deep-rooted distrust of all the other armed organisations and of the PCS and suggested that the FPL should have a presence throughout Salvadoran territory.

The other FMLN leaders, championed by the PCS Secretary-General Shafick Handal, sought closer relationships with the more moderate parts of the PDC and negotiations to end the war. Carpio's standpoint was rejected by the majority of the FMLN guerrilla commanders in the summer of 1982, who agreed instead to promote a dual strategy of armed struggle and negotiation with the government – a strategy to which Carpio was opposed, but that he was forced to accept given the pressure exerted by the rest of the FMLN.[32] The purpose of this dual strategy was for the FMLN to occupy positions in a future coalition government alongside the PDC, and from there, with the popular support the insurgents thought they would get, develop their own political project. The possibility of taking power and having exclusive control over the state apparatus via armed struggle was not ruled out, but a second route opened up that would put an end to the conflict in a scenario of shared power.

Carpio's position was rejected also by a majority of the commanders of his own organisation at a meeting of the FPL's Central Command held in Managua in January and February 1983,[33] where the position favouring a strategy that combined armed struggle and negotiation upheld by Mélida Anaya Montes (aka Ana María) and other commanders prevailed. This conflict was the trigger to the assassination of Anaya Montes in Managua, on 6 April 1983, and to Carpio's suicide a few days later, on 12 April.

The death of its Secretary General allowed for the FPL, now in the hands of a generation of younger and more pragmatic militants, to pursue greater political openness. As Facundo Guardado stated: 'all the debate that was created around Anaya's assassination in a large measure helped de-fanaticise the FPL'.[34] The new leadership, made up of Salvador Sánchez Cerén as Secretary General and Dimas Rodríguez and Salvador Guerra as numbers two and three respectively, had a greater capacity for articulation and rapprochement towards the rest of the revolutionary movement, as well as a more favourable position on political compromises.

The departure of Carpio, leader of the FMLN's most powerful organisation, made it easier to adopt the dual strategy of armed struggle and negotiation that the Front pursued until 1989. One of the first results caused by this strategic shift was the publication of the Government of Broad Participation (GAP) proposal on 31 January 1984, two months before the presidential elections. The GAP, which became the Front's official political platform, proposed creating a plural executive that was to include the 'non-oligarchic bourgeois' and holding elections in the shortest timeframe possible. In order to put this government together, the Front suggested starting a process of dialogue and negotiation and offered a ceasefire once the process was well underway. Despite its tactical motivations, this document demonstrated an important political change within the guerrilla organisations. The GAP proposal meant that the FMLN-FDR alliance was opting, from that moment on, for a negotiated solution if certain conditions were met, including the guarantees for its militants' physical well-being and official recognition of their representation as a political force.[35]

This new perspective, and the rise to power of the PDC, created the conditions necessary for the first public talks between the government and the guerrilla groups in La Palma in October 1984 and in Ayagualo in November of that year.[36] These talks ended due to the pressure exerted by the armed forces, who did not view a negotiated solution to the conflict as an acceptable option. In May and October 1987 there would be further contacts with a government drastically weakened by the prolonged war and the economic crisis and by its incapacity to assert itself over the armed forces, whose decision to seek a full victory over the insurgents was backed by the US. Some sectors inside the FMLN, in turn, were convinced that the masses were becoming radicalised and that a defeat of the government was a possibility in the near future. With these perspectives, the talks were merely tactical in nature for both parties and yielded no substantial results. This also happened in the talks between the FMLN and ARENA government representatives held in Mexico and San José in September and October 1989. For the Front, these talks were a part of a strategic counteroffensive in which the demonstration of military strength would be necessary to force the government to negotiate.[37]

The results of the November 1989 offensive backed the position of those within the FMLN who supported a negotiated solution to the conflict. The fact that no popular insurgency took place, as some commanders expected it would, showed that the Salvadoran people were tired of war, and that more than insurrection, what they craved was the end of the war at all costs. The population was exhausted after so many years of conflict, demonstrated by the increasing difficulty of recruiting combatants for guerrilla groups. Meanwhile, international solidarity was diminishing and changes in the Eastern Bloc raised serious questions about the future of national liberation struggles the world over. All of this contributed to the victory of pragmatism within the FMLN following the 1989 offensive.

The extension of the conflict and the inability to attain a definite military victory unleashed a gradual political and strategic change of the FMLN. Around 1983, the Front shifted from its initial political position, in which revolution and socialism were viewed as the only solution to the country's troubles, and armed struggle was seen as the only way to reach them, to a progressive recognition of political negotiation as an alternative option. A third approach sprung up in 1989, based on holding transparent elections, with the independent functioning of the judicial power and demilitarisation becoming the struggle's main goals – a struggle that was to combine negotiation with military pressure. In other words, implementing reforms within the framework of a representative democracy and market economy was identified with a revolution that was now termed 'democratic'. From then on, the Front's strategy would involve participating in elections as a means to take power, and to then begin the transition towards a new society. The 'Democratic Revolution' project was presented in several documents published between 1989 and 1990. In January 1989 the Front made public its proposal to turn elections into a step towards peace, in which it agreed to attend the presidential elections that were to be held in March if they were postponed for six months and as long as some minimal pre-requisites for assuring their transparency were met. Some months before, Joaquín Villalobos, the ERP leader, published a paper titled *Perspectives for Victory and the Revolutionary Model*.[38] This document posited the need for a revolution adapted to the Salvadoran reality, a revolution driven not only by workers and peasants, but also the middle class. It challenged the wisdom of adopting a one-party system and accepted elections as a valid means to attain political power, as long as they were held in a climate of equal opportunity for all contestants. Also, it accepted the existence of private property, political pluralism, press freedom and the role of the Catholic Church.

From 1990 onwards, the use of violence was subordinated to the progress of negotiations. The demilitarisation of the state, rather than socioeconomic transformation became the central theme of negotiations. The Front assumed the latter would take place once the revolutionaries had reached power through elections, although the guerrilla commanders did, during the negotiating process, seek landowning guarantees for the peasants who were the rank and file of their army or their support bases.

Disarmament of the FMLN was discussed from September 1991, when some of the most important agreements in the negotiations had been reached, as guerrilla groups were not willing to dismantle their armed structures without having secured solid commitments. In the same month, the FMLN adopted a unilateral ceasefire that would not be violated. The fact that the ceasefire and the discussions on disarming the Front took place at a very advanced point in the negotiations gave the guerrilla commanders time to discuss with combatants the decisions that were being made, and to gain the support of the militants in laying down their arms.[39]

Concluding Remarks

The Salvadoran revolutionary movement arose in response to an authoritarian political regime that kept the majority of the population in a situation of political and economic exclusion. Against the repression of the popular movement's demands for democratisation and economic improvements, some dissident members of the Communist Party and the radical Catholic youth opted for armed struggle as a means of achieving comprehensive political and economic transformation within El Salvador. The strong roots of the guerrilla organisations in the popular movement allowed them to develop into a broad revolutionary movement that faced the state in a civil war for almost twelve years.

To meet the challenge posed by the FMLN, the Salvadoran state, supported by the United States, launched a political reform strategy and an increase in military activity. Liberalisation of the political regime, agrarian reform, and the modernisation and expansion of the armed forces were the main elements of the government's strategy. Ultimately, this strategy prevented the military success of a revolutionary army whose external support was much lower than its opponent's, and which had failed to convince broad sectors of the population of the legitimacy of its political project.

The inability to defeat the government triggered changes in the balance of power inside the FMLN and ushered in gradual changes to the revolutionaries' strategy and political project. Over the course of the eighties the Front shifted from a position in which revolution, armed struggle and socialism were considered the only possible solutions to the national crises to a position in which holding clean elections, having an independent judicial power and demilitarising the state became the main goals of the struggle – a struggle that would combine negotiations with military pressure. This would be the agenda and the strategy that the FMLN maintained regarding the peace negotiations.

All this shows that in the Salvadoran case, armed organisations had to adapt their goals before they could transition to a political strategy. Despite the image of ideological rigidity that some of the Salvadoran revolutionary organisations projected, they were actually quite flexible and responded continuously by adapting their strategy and discourse to the changing political and military environment. The role of the leadership was crucial regarding this adaptation. Given the organisational features of these groups (clearly defined hierarchy, levels of authority and responsibility), the major strategic decisions and redefinition of the objectives of the fight were taken within small leadership groups and later accepted by a disciplined membership guided mainly by moral or ideological incentives.

The Chapultepec Peace Agreements proved very effective in incorporating the revolutionary left into the political system and demilitarising the state. In this sense, the transition to democracy in El Salvador, which was a result of the agreements, was the product of the challenge posed by the insurgency, although representative democracy was not part of the initial agenda of either the insurgents or the armed forces.

It was the promise of an end to political exclusion as a first step towards the end of socioeconomic exclusion that led the FMLN to reach an agreement with the government. However, this other objective would prove much more difficult to achieve. Acceptance of the rules of the political game also included acceptance of the power arrangements that govern Salvadoran society. Becoming a prospective government meant accepting the impossibility of a profound change in the economic structure or property relations. El Salvador today is a deeply unequal country in terms of the distribution of wealth and power and this is the main debt of a peace agreement that for many Salvadorans is already just a reminder of unfulfilled promises.

Notes

1. Frances Steward, 'Inequality in Political Power: A Fundamental (and Overlooked) Dimension of Inequality', *The European Journal of Development Research*, vol. 23, no. 4 (2011), p. 542.

2. Alain Rouquié, *Guerras y paz en América Central* (Mexico: Fondo de Cultura Económica, 1994), p. 232.

3. Jeremy M. Weinstein, *Inside Rebellion: The Politics of Insurgent Violence* (Cambridge: Cambridge University Press, 2007), pp. 9–12. This did not prevent, however, some of the armed organisations resorting briefly to forced recruitment at specific times in the mid-1980s, or, exceptionally, exerting violence on their support base, suspecting infiltrations by the armed forces.

4. Paul Collier and Anke Hoeffler, 'Greed and Grievance in Civil War', *Oxford Economic Papers*, vol. 56, no. 4, (2004), pp. 563–95.

5. Ellen J. Wood, *Insurgent Collective Action and Civil War in El Salvador* (Cambridge: Cambridge University Press, 2003).

6. Jocelyn Viterna, *Women in War: The Micro – Processes of Mobilization in El Salvador* (Oxford: Oxford University Press, 2013).

7. Paul D. Almeida, *Waves of Protest: Popular Struggle in El Salvador, 1925–2005* (Minneapolis: University of Minnesota Press, 2008).

8. Yvon Grenier, *The Emergence of Insurgency in El Salvador: Ideology and Political Will* (Pittsburgh: University of Pittsburg Press, 1999), p. 75.

9. Ana Sofía Cardenal, *La democracia y la tierra: Cambio político en El Salvador* (Madrid: CIS, 2002).

10. Alberto Martín Álvarez and Eudald Cortina Orero, 'The Genesis and Internal Dynamics of El Salvador's People's Revolutionary Army (ERP): 1970–1976', *Journal of Latin American Studies*, vol. 46, no. 4 (2014), pp. 663–89.

11. Francisco Jovel, former General Secretary of the PRTC and member of the FMLN's General Command., Interview by the author, San Salvador, 28/01/2011.

12. Joaquín Mauricio Chávez, *Poets and Prophets of the Resistance: Intellectuals and the Origins of El Salvador's Civil War* (New York: Oxford University Press, 2017), p. 88.

13. Nidia Díaz, former member of the Political Commission of the PRTC, Interview by the author, San Salvador, 5/10/1998.

14. Kristina Pirker, *La Redefinición de lo Posible: Militancia Política y Movilización Social en El Salvador (1970 a 2012)* (Mexico: Instituto Mora, 2017).

15. Charles D. Brockett, *Political Movements and Violence in Central America* (Cambridge: Cambridge University Press, 2005), p. 235.

16. Cardenal, p. 88.

17. William I. Robinson, *Transnational Conflicts: Central America, Social Change and Globalization* (London: Verso, 2003), pp. 217–30.

18. Cardenal, p. 111.

19. William M. Leogrande, *Our Own Backyard: The United States in Central America, 1977–1992* (Chapel Hill: The University of North Carolina Press, 1998), p. 41.

20. The intellectual author of the crime was Major Roberto D'Aubuisson, founder of the ARENA party and promoter of one of the death squads: the Uniòn Guerrera Blanca ('Union of White Warriors').

21. Knut Walter, 'Estados Unidos y El Salvador: la década de 1980', *Estudios Centroamericanos*, nos. 713–14 (2008), p. 201.

22. Walter, p. 202.

23. Leogrande, p. 127.

24. Walter, p. 203.

25. Jorge G. Castañeda, *La utopía desarmada: Intrigas, dilemas y promesa de la izquierda en América Latina* (Barcelona: Ariel, 1995), p. 101.

26. The need for unity was expressly transmitted by Fidel Castro at a meeting with FPL leaders as revealed by Ricardo Gutiérrez, one of the commanders who was part of the FPL delegation. Ricardo Gutiérrez, former member of the FPL Political Commission, Interview by the author, Ciudad de Guatemala, 24/10/2013.

27. Walter F. Lafeber, *Inevitable Revolutions: The United States in Central America* (New York: W. W. Norton & Co., 1993), p. 278.

28. Eduardo Sancho, former Secretary General of the FARN and member of the FMLN's General Command., Interview by the author, San Salvador, 27/01/2011.

29. Salvador Guerra, former member of the FPL's Political Commision, Interview by the author, San Salvador. 2/8/2008.

30. Ibid.

31. Danuta Paszyn, *The Soviet Attitude to Political and Social Change in Central America, 1979–90: Case-Studies on Nicaragua, El Salvador and Guatemala* (London: Palgrave Macmillan, 2000), pp. 88–107.

32. Eduardo Sancho, former Secretary General of the FARN and member of the FMLN's General Command, Interview by the author, San Salvador, 27/01/2011.

33. This meeting made it clear that Carpio could no longer impose his decisions on the FPL but had to undergo a collective decision-making process and that if he did not accept it, he would be replaced. Ricardo Gutiérrez, former member of the Political Commission of the FPL, Interview by the author, Ciudad de Guatemala, 24/10/2013.

34. Facundo Guardado, former member of the FPL's Political Commision, Interview by the author, San Salvador, 19/08/2008.

35. Alberto Martín Álvarez, 'De guerrilla a partido político: El Frente Farabundo Martí para la Liberación Nacional (FMLN),' *Historia y Política: Ideas, Procesos y Movimientos Sociales*, no. 25 (2011), p. 225.

36. This public negotiation had been preceded by several attempts at talks by the FMLN through intermediaries.

37. James Dunkerley, *The Pacification of Central America: Political Change in the Isthmus 1987–1993* (London: Verso, 1994), p. 68.

38. Joaquín Villalobos, *Perspectivas de Victoria y Modelo Revolucionario* (El Salvador: Sistema Radio Venceremos, 1988).

39. Cate Buchanan and Joaquín Chávez, 'Guns and Violence in El Salvador Peace Negotiations', *Negotiating Disarmament*, Country Study 3 (Geneva: Centre for Humanitarian Dialogue, 2008), p. 21.

11

NEGOTIATED REVOLUTION IN SOUTH AFRICA: 1990–1994

Thula Simpson

In speeches delivered over successive days on 17 and 18 January 1990, South Africa's state President F. W. de Klerk addressed the Police's top brass in Pretoria, and the African National Congress's (ANC) Acting President Alfred Nzo, his organisation's National Executive Committee (NEC) in Lusaka. De Klerk said the Police would no longer be used as 'instruments to attain political goals'. He added, 'We cannot become embroiled in an 80 Years' War', because they had to consider future generations:

> Do we want to leave them a future where revolution keeps on boiling below the surface? . . . Where the battle lines are being drawn for the great Armageddon? For if Armageddon takes place – and blood flows ankle-deep in our streets and four or five million people lie dead – the problem will remain exactly the same as it was before the shooting started.[1]

Nzo for his part mistakenly read a statement meant for the NEC's closed gathering, in an open session. Before a shocked media corps, he stated 'looking at the situation realistically, we must admit that we do not have the capacity within the country to intensify the armed struggle in any meaningful way', and that the main task faced by the movement may therefore be to build up its capacity to 'fight effectively should the need arise, and to have sizeable forces at the moment when a new South African Army is formed'.[2]

The statements reflected an understanding that the country's main liberation movement was incapable of waging an armed struggle, or the state of winning one. They also illustrated the polarisation that underlay the stalemate, in the sense that the state's military strengths were belied by its political weaknesses, while the opposite applied with the ANC. The political opprobrium directed at the apartheid system is well known, while the military asymmetry was attested to by the fact that from 1976 to 1988, the ANC's military wing, Umkhonto we Sizwe (MK), never managed to conduct more than 300 actions in any single year (and only managed more than 250 in one year), but it suffered a 'casualty ratio' of over two guerrillas killed or captured for every three operations.[3]

The two speeches were delivered as the struggle stood on the cusp of a shift towards negotiations. This shift was facilitated by the end of the Cold War, which deepened the apartheid regime's isolation and the ANC's military enfeeblement. When asked about the ANC's armed struggle, the spokesman of the Soviet Union's Foreign Affairs Department, Gennady Gerasimov, had responded on 14 March 1989: 'What armed struggle? How can one support something which doesn't exist?' South Africa's Foreign Minister Pik Botha hailed the statement a day later as evidence that 'the season of employing violence is over . . . Moscow is not interested in using these tools any longer'. Botha was speaking directly after a meeting with Margaret Thatcher, who told the Houses of Parliament the following day that she had told him Nelson Mandela had to be released, following which negotiations with the African and Coloured population needed to begin. Responding to these developments, the ANC's president Oliver Tambo encouraged an Organisation of African Unity (OAU) meeting on 22 March to develop a framework for negotiations to 'enable Africa to take the initiative and not respond to the strategies of those who have defended South Africa at every turn'.[4]

This chapter follows the course of the subsequent negotiations, from the initial attempts at peacemaking to the initiation of constitutional negotiations that enabled the non-racial multi-party elections in April 1994, which swept the ANC to power.

Talks about Talks

F. W. de Klerk informed South Africa's Parliament on 2 February 1990 that 'the prohibition of the African National Congress, the Pan Africanist

Congress [PAC], the South African Communist Party [SACP] and a number of subsidiary organisations is being rescinded'.[5] He justified the decision by citing war weariness among South Africans who had been 'embroiled in conflict, tension and violent struggle for decades'. The 'silent majority' was yearning to 'break out of the cycle of violence and break through to peace and reconciliation'. He emphasised that his goal was to 'normalise the political process in South Africa without jeopardising the maintenance of good order', and he pointed to the end of the Cold War as a factor that had weakened the organisations concerned to the point where the South African police felt confident of being able to contain them without needing outright proscription. Declaring 'the agenda is open' for constitutional negotiations, de Klerk added 'Nelson Mandela could play an important part', though he emphasised that 'I wish to put it plainly that the government has taken a firm decision to release Mr Mandela unconditionally'.[6]

Although de Klerk insisted that the reform package meant there was 'no longer any reasonable excuse for the continuation of violence', when Mandela was released on 11 February after twenty-seven years' incarceration, he used his first public address at Cape Town's Grand Parade that evening to say that the conditions that had led to the formation of MK (of which he had been the founding Commander from 1960 to 1962) 'still exist today'. Specifically, Mandela referred to the 'Harare Declaration' (a document drafted by the ANC in 1989 setting out its stance on negotiations), and called on the government to take the further steps of 'the immediate ending of the state of emergency, and the freeing of all – and not only some – political prisoners'.[7]

The initiation of constitutional negotiations in South Africa would be delayed by the sides having to reconcile these respective positions against the backdrop of numerous forms of violence inherited from the past.

That violence assumed three main forms. First was the conflict between the state's security forces and black communities, particularly in the townships. The first bilateral talks between the government and the ANC were scheduled for April 1990, but had to be postponed when the ANC pulled out following the killing of twelve black civilians at the hands of the police in the Vaal Triangle township of Sebokeng on 26 March.[8] The 'talks about talks' were rescheduled for 2–4 May, when the government and the ANC adopted the 'Groote Schuur Minute', committing themselves to combatting the 'existing climate of violence and intimidation from whatever quarter as well as a commitment to stability and to a peaceful process of negotiations'.[9]

The second major form of political violence was the ANC's ongoing armed struggle. The matter came to a head in July 1990 when the police uncovered 'Operation Vula', which was an ANC mission initiated in 1986 to establish underground politico-military command structures in South Africa. It was directed by seven men, namely Oliver Tambo, Joe Slovo, Alfred Nzo and Thomas Nkobi outside South Africa, with Ronnie Kasrils, Mac Maharaj and Siphiwe Nyanda the internal commanders. By July 1990, fifteen safe houses had been established in Johannesburg and Durban, and no fewer than seven double agents had infiltrated the security police. When the arrests were leaked to the media, Vula was framed as having involved around forty SACP members or supporters who had developed a contingency plan for armed insurrection should talks between the ANC and the Government collapse.[10] This police narrative collapsed when it was confirmed that the 'Comrade Joe' referred to in one of the captured transcripts was not the party's general secretary Joe Slovo as had initially been believed.[11]

Only a declaration from Mandela that the ANC still abided by the Groote Schuur Minute enabled the next talks to proceed in Pretoria from 6–7 August. The talks resulted in the 'Pretoria Minute', which saw the ANC compromise on the red lines offered in the Harare Declaration: it agreed to unilaterally suspend 'armed actions and all related matters', in return for the government merely consenting to 'consider' lifting the state of emergency in Natal (it had been lifted in South Africa's three other provinces in June); to give 'immediate consideration' to 'review' certain provisions of the Internal Security Act; and to offer a timetable for releasing categories of political prisoners and indemnifying exiles.[12]

Continued emergency rule in Natal reflected the third dimension of political violence, which was the conflict dating from the mid-1980s between the ANC and the Inkatha Freedom Party (IFP). By February 1990, deaths from the Natal conflict had passed the 5,000 mark.[13] The days before the Pretoria Summit had seen a dramatic geographical expansion of the Natal violence to the Transvaal when an IFP rally in Sebokeng on 22 July led to clashes with ANC-supporters, which spread across the Vaal Triangle.[14]

The Climate of Violence

A working group established under the Pretoria Minute had a deadline of 15 September 1990 to deliver a report clarifying the terms of the ANC's suspension of armed struggle. However, amidst the recriminations caused by the upsurge of violence in the Transvaal, it was only on 21 January 1991 that the Working Group reached an agreement.[15] The concord led to the DF Malan Accord of 15 February 1991 which clarified that the suspension involved ending all attacks and infiltrations, the creation of new underground structures and military training inside South Africa.[16]

It followed closely on a meeting between the ANC and IFP delegations in Durban on 29 January 1991, where a declaration was agreed commiting both signatories to establishing a joint peace committee to monitor violence on the ground and recommending 'appropriate action' against perpetrators.[17]

The meetings in Pretoria, Cape Town and Durban between August 1990 and February 1991 failed, however, to end the violence on the ground. Just two days after the 29 January meeting, ANC and IFP supporters clashed at Umgababa, a Natal township, causing six deaths.[18] While ANC–Inkatha follow-up talks on 31 March were presented by the media as positive progress in the peace process, it soon became clear that the ANC was dissatisfied with the rate of advance. On 3 April the organisation held discussions with the police about the need for action against the carrying of 'traditional' or 'cultural' weapons at IFP gatherings. When this yielded no result, the ANC NEC held a two-day extraordinary meeting from 4–5 April, at the conclusion of which Mandela read an open letter featuring seven demands for the government to meet by 9 May, failing which the ANC would withdraw from talks. The demands included the imposition of a ban on the carrying of *all* weapons at public gatherings; and for Law and Order Minister Adriaan Vlok and Defence Minister Magnus Malan to be dismissed.[19]

With the 9 May deadline approaching, de Klerk met the IFP's leader Mangosuthu Buthelezi on 7 May, and Mandela a day after. It enabled him to issue a statement on the 9th announcing new laws restricting the carrying of weapons in so-called 'unrest areas'. Crucially however, spears and traditional weapons were excluded, while the other six demands were not mentioned at all.[20]

When a week-long extension of the deadline expired, the ANC announced that it would refuse to partake in constitutional negotiations until progress was achieved on *all* its demands, while it announced a campaign of action to support them, including a consumer boycott, a general strike and mass demonstrations. The organisation also mentioned an immediate measure, involving it refusing to participate in a peace conference called by the government for 24–25 May. The ANC stated that it had instead approached the churches to convene a committee with business, union, party-political and governmental representation, to pave the way for a peace conference that would result in binding commitments including a code of conduct for all political actors.[21]

The ANC was not the only party absent from the government conference, as the PAC and the right-wing Conservative Party also boycotted the event. The government acknowledged the need for a broader-based participation, and at the summit's conclusion, de Klerk raised his left hand, urged all parties to take it in the search for peace. The attendees accordingly authorised Dr Louw Alberts to form a committee to broaden participation. This was significant because Alberts had co-chaired a national conference of church leaders that met in Rustenberg from 5 to 9 November 1990 to discuss reconciliation. The other chairman was Reverend Frank Chikane of the South African Council of Churches (SACC) which had also boycotted the May 1991 meeting,[22] and had strong connections with the ANC. It re-opened channels of communication, and the 'Rustenburg group of churches' managed to broker a fresh conference on 22 June where the Conservative Party and other right-wing organisations were the only major absentees.[23]

Inkatha only sent a small two-person delegation to the June meeting, but it would soon lose any claim it had to the moral high-ground on the issue of violence. On 19 July, revelations appeared in the *Weekly Mail* – based on security police documents, receipts and deposit slips – showing that the police had paid the IFP at least R250,000 to help it organise rallies and other anti-ANC activities shortly after Mandela's release.[24]

In the ensuing furore, President de Klerk announced a cabinet reshuffle on 29 July that saw Adriaan Vlok and Magnus Malan removed from their security portfolios. While this met one of the ANC's demands, observers noted that Pik Botha, who authorised the donation of secret funds to Inkatha, kept his position as foreign minister, while Malan, who was not named, was side-lined. The *Star* newspaper suggested that a likelier motive was a desire to demote the last of the hard-line 'securocrats' from the era of de Klerk's predecessor, P. W. Botha.[25]

The following weeks saw tripartite talks between the NP, IFP and ANC. The talks were sponsored by the 'National Peace Initiative', a mediating committee of leading church and business members. The discussions led to an agreement on 14 August to a draft accord to combat violence. It called for codes of conduct for political parties and the security forces, including restrictions on the carrying of weapons at political meetings, and a ban on private armies. The document called on groups from across the political spectrum to offer feedback by 9 September, prior to a national peace summit five days later.[26]

That peace summit in Johannesburg on 14–15 September 1991 saw a 'National Peace Accord' signed by over twenty political organisations. But there were important ommissions: one change from the August draft was that the stipulation 'No private armies shall be formed' was changed to 'No private armies shall be allowed or formed'. This was at the insistence of the IFP, who intended it to mean that MK should be disbanded. However, at a joint press conference with de Klerk and Buthelezi after the summit, Mandela said the ANC had 'no intention of dissolving MK, either now or in the future. It is a matter which is under discussion between the ANC and the government'. At the same press conference, Buthelezi was asked whether he believed the provision in the accord forbidding the carrying of weapons included cultural weapons. He answered, 'No. That is why I am carrying one'.[27]

CODESA

Despite its palpable weaknesses, the Peace Accord paved the way for agreement on 21 November 1991 by the government, the ANC and the IFP, for full constitutional negotiations on 20–1 December (the talks till then had been focused on clearing the largely violence-related obstacles to constitutional negotiations).[28] The negotiations were titled the Convention for a Democratic South Africa (CODESA). Before adjourning on 21 December, the delegates appointed five working groups to deliver reports on issues likely to impede progress when the next full session sat in 1992.[29]

That next session was scheduled for 15 May 1992, with the deadline for the working group reports falling two days prior to that that. Working Group Three reached agreement on 11 May on a particularly fraught question when it endorsed the creation of a transitional executive council with up to six sub-councils, whose members would be drawn from CODESA and would make decisions with 80 per cent support. With Working Groups One (on the creation of the right political climate and the role of the state media), Four (on the future of the independent homelands) and Five (on time schedules and the application of Codesa decisions) having also reported, Working Group Two was the only one to fail to meet the 13 May deadline.[30]

The opening of 'CODESA Two' on 15 May was delayed as negotiators attempted to resolve the issue that had caused the deadlock, namely the majority required to pass the eventual constitution. The differences were that the government wanted a 75 per cent majority, while the ANC wanted two-thirds and 75 per cent for the Bill of Rights. The Democratic Party (DP) fell between the two, demanding 70 per cent and 75 per cent for a Bill of Rights. The discussions on the 15th started with the ANC offering to embrace the DP position. The government countered with a revised 70 per cent on all issues except regional and local government where it demanded 75 per cent. Over the course of the discussions, further proposals were offered but none bridged the divide, and the teams walked out shortly before 3 p.m. with the matter postponed to the next round of talks, mooted for June.[31]

In practice, those talks would be delayed by almost a year. An ANC policy meeting in Johannesburg from 28–31 May 1992 discussed the constitutional deadlock and agreed a resolution attributing the failure of CODESA Two to the government's desire to lock the ANC 'into a permanent "power-sharing" arrangement in which the system of white minority domination will be largely intact'. The declaration set the ANC the task of defeating this object by ensuring 'the removal of the de Klerk regime from power and the institution of a democratic government', to which end it would be required to launch 'mass action' to secure the installation of an interim government whose composition would be negotiated by CODESA.[32]

Ronnie Kasrils was elected to head the committee responsible for coordinating the mass campaign. In an interview with the *Sunday Times* on 13 June, he outlined the specifics of 'Operation Exit', a four-phase campaign starting on 16 June with a day of protest including occupations, sit-ins, marches, boycotts and civil disobedience. That phase would end on 30 June, when a second stage would begin to coordinate campaigns on a national scale. Phase two would culminate with a national strike in mid-August. Phase three would see intensified civil disobedience targeting corrupt institutions with the aim of bringing the government to a standstill. 'Exit Gate' was the name given to the fourth phase, when the force accumulated since 16 June would force the government from power.[33]

On the same evening as the interview, ANC supporters moved through the township of Boipatong in the Vaal Triangle, seeking Inkatha members and 'sympathisers', who in many cases were merely ordinary Zulus wearing leather wristbands denoting veneration for the spirits of their ancestors. The rampage led to the death of a woman romantically involved with a Zulu hostel dweller, and two *bona fide* Inkatha members. The launch of 'Operation Exit' on 16 June would soon be overshadowed by events the following evening, when hostel dwellers in Boipatong launched a revenge attack on township residents that left over forty people dead.[34]

In Evaton (another Vaal Triangle township) on 21 June, Nelson Mandela said the ANC would not partake in the next CODESA talks, which were scheduled in two days' time. He announced that the ANC would instead seek foreign intervention. This included calling on the United Nations (UN) to convene a Security Council debate 'on the massacres committed by Mr de Klerk and his regime'. Mandela contacted UN Secretary General Boutros Boutros-Ghali on 22 June to request the debate.[35]

It marked the commencement of direct international involvement in the peace process, because the government proved amenable to the suggestion. On 27 June, Foreign Minister Pik Botha held three-hours of talks with Boutros Boutros-Ghali on the side-lines of an OAU meeting in Abuja, Nigeria. Botha announced afterwards that he had invited Boutros-Ghali to visit South Africa.[36]

The UN Security Council met on 15–16 July to discuss an OAU resolution calling on the Secretary General to send an envoy to investigate township violence. The meeting – which was addressed by Nelson Mandela and Pik Botha – concluded with the unanimous adoption of Resolution 765 which called for the Secretary General to appoint a special representative 'to recommend, after discussions with the parties, measures which would assist in bringing an effective end to violence and in creating conditions for negotiations leading towards a peaceful transition to a democratic . . . South Africa'.[37]

Cyrus Vance was the special envoy chosen by Boutros Boutros-Ghali. He arrived in Johannesburg on 21 July, and succeeded in brokering talks between the ANC and the government that were held on 28 July on releasing the remaining political prisoners (this last, most sensitive category of prisoners involved those responsible for civilian deaths during the struggle). The meeting re-established contact between the respective parties, and when Vance departed on 31 July he told reporters that 'the leaders on both sides have said they want to get back to the conference table. They hope it can be done soon'.[38]

UN monitors arrived in South Africa on Sunday 2 August 1992, just prior to a 'week of unprecedented action' that the ANC's National Working Committee had called for on 16 July to support its demands on the constitution and political violence.[39] The mass action commenced with a two-day general strike on 3 August. While the ANC estimated four million of seven million black workers had gone on strike, business estimated two million. An occupation of the Union Buildings – the seat of South Africa's government – followed on 5 August. While Nelson Mandela addressed supporters outside, de Klerk made a point of carrying on with business as usual in his office. He emerged later to tell reporters: 'certain discussions have been taking place' between government and the ANC, and he expected formal talks to resume shortly.[40]

Mandela and de Klerk shared a brief phone call on 7 August, which was the day on which Boutros Boutros-Ghali delivered a report to the UN Security Council in New York conveying Vance's findings. The key recommendations for ending violence and re-opening negotiations were for the government, as an immediate step, to release the remaining political prisoners in orderto build trust. In the longer term, the report called for broad investigations into violations by the security forces and liberation movements, but for this to be accompanied by a general amnesty.[41]

ANC Secretary General Cyril Ramaphosa met with the government's Minister of Constitutional Development and Communication Roelf

Meyer on 21 August, to discuss the removal of the remaining obstacles to negotiations.[42]

Historic Compromises

Following an incident on 7 September, when twenty-eight unarmed protesters were shot dead at an ANC organised march in the independent 'homeland' of the Ciskei,[43] President de Klerk issued an urgent call for a summit with the ANC. His call on 9 September was met with a response by Cyril Ramaphosa a day later, saying the ANC 'was prepared to participate in a summit', provided its demands were met for a comprehensive ban on displaying weapons in public; for action against migrant workers' hostels; and for the release of the last prisoners.[44]

Following further talks between Ramaphosa and Roelf Meyer, the government on 25 September began releasing hundreds of prisoners convicted for incidents that had caused civilian deaths during the struggle. It preceded an eight-hour meeting on 26 September between de Klerk and Mandela at the World Trade Centre (WTC) in Kempton Park, where the two leaders shook hands and announced that they had laid the basis for resumed negotiations. The basis was outlined in a Record of Understanding which affirmed, regarding the constitutional negotiations, the need for a democratically elected single-chamber constituent assembly that would serve as an interim/transitional parliament, while there would also be an interim/transitional government of national unity; on political prisoners, it set 15 November 1992 as the date for all to be released; while on violence, it announced that the government would fence off problematic hostels, and prohibit the carrying of dangerous weapons at all public occasions.[45]

There was no mention of disbanding MK, which was the IFP's key demand on violence. In a speech in KwaMashu on 27 September 1992, Mangosuthu Buthelezi announced the IFP's withdrawal from further talks with the government while he undertook consultations with other affected parties. He met with the Ciskei's Oupa Gqozo and Bophuthatswana's Lucas Mangope on 29 September where the three leaders rejected the Record of Understanding, while calling for an urgent meeting of parties sharing their concerns to 'discuss the way forward'. That discussion occurred outside Johannesburg on 6 October when Buthelezi, Gqozo and Mangope were joined by CP leader

Andries Treurnicht, and Andries Beyers (the leader of a new white right-wing movement, the Afrikaanse Volksunie). The quintet formed a 'Concerned South Africans Group' (COSAG) to take their concerns forward.[46]

In a press briefing on 29 September, Pik Botha emphasised that the Record of Understanding was merely in line with Boutros Boutros-Ghali's report on Vance's findings,[47] which had articulated a framework for restarting negotiations. Neither it nor the Record of Understanding offered any prescriptions on the content of the negotiations. Regarding the constituent assembly, the Record merely said it would be,

> bound only by agreed constitutional principles . . . have a fixed time frame
> . . . have adequate deadlock breaking mechanisms . . . arrive at its decisions
> democratically with certain agreed to majorities [and would] be elected
> within an agreed predetermined time period.[48]

The details regarding the principles, time frames, mechanisms and majorities remained to be established by negotiation. CODESA Two had collapsed on these issues; future talks would founder similarly without movement from the respective sides.

In the issue of the SACP's journal *African Communist* that was published in October 1992, Joe Slovo addressed the negotiations stalemate. Arguing that since neither side won the power struggle, neither could be expected to surrender at the negotiating table, he added that compromise was inevitable. He suggested a number of compromises the ANC could make, including 'a period of power-sharing – perhaps three to five years – after a new constitution was adopted', and for civil servants – including police and army officials – to be given guarantees that they could keep their jobs and pensions, and where necessary be granted amnesties.[49]

The idea was contained in a discussion document circulated within the ANC ranks later that month. The issue was raised formally when the National Working Committee (NWC – the organisation's highest policy making body) met on 18 November. The NWC approved a document which said that an interim government featuring a 'central role' for the ANC and the National Party during *and possibly after* the transition may be necessary, depending on 'the balance of forces, and the interests of the country as a whole'.[50]

The matter was then discussed by the NEC on 25 November. The meeting adopted 'Negotiations: A Strategic Perspective', a paper which addressed the 'balance of forces' issue. The critical considerations were identified as the ANC's weaknesses, which were defined bluntly as being that it 'suffers many organisational weaknesses . . . it does not command significant military and financial resources . . . it is unable to militarily defeat the counter-revolutionary movement or adequately defend the people'. On that basis the paper advocated a strategy involving 'a negotiations process combined with mass action and international pressure . . . to secure a thorough-going democratic transformation'. [51] Meanwhile, in keeping with the discussion initiated by Slovo's paper, it also considered *post*-election arrangements. It argued that the power balance 'may still require of us to consider the establishment of a government of national unity', and 'it may be necessary to address the question of job security, retrenchment packages and a general amnesty based on disclosure and justice, at some stage, as part of a negotiated settlement'. [52]

Bilateral talks between the ANC and National Party resumed on 2 December 1992 leading to an agreement on 12 February 1993 regarding power sharing. In terms of the accord, there would be an election by April 1994 for a 400-seat assembly that would act as parliament until 1999 and would be responsible for writing a new constitution. The president would be chosen from whichever party won the election, while any party that won 5 per cent or more of the seats in the assembly would have cabinet representation in a national unity government that would also last for five years. When the five years were up, a new government would be elected in accordance with the new constitution, and power sharing would end. In exchange for power sharing the government accepted a two-thirds majority for approving the final constitution. [53]

The Negotiated Settlement

The February 1993 agreement was a bilateral one between the ANC and NP. On 1 April 1993 South African groups from across the political spectrum met formally to discuss procedural matters ahead of fresh multi-party constitutional talks. 'CODESA' disappeared, but the delegates were unable to decide on an alternative moniker. [54]

The renewed negotiations were marked by increasingly desperate attempts by white right-wing paramilitaries to scupper a settlement. On 10 April the leading ANC and SACP figure Chris Hani was killed outside his Boksburg home by Janusz Walus, a member of the CP and the Afrikaner Weerstandsbeweging (AWB), a right-wing paramilitary group.[55]

Twenty-six delegations resumed full multi-party constitutional negotiations on 30 April 1993. Their focus was on setting a date for elections. Crucially, reflecting a general acknowledgement that the negotiations had reached make-or-break point, the PAC, the Conservative Party and Inkatha had joined the process. On 3 June, the negotiators set 27 April 1994 as the election date, but decided to meet again on 15 June to debate the matter afresh having consulted with their leaders. On 15 June, the IFP forwarded a motion to halt proceedings until the negotiations technical committee had reported on various constitutional alternatives. When this was rejected, the IFP and its COSAG partners walked out. Within minutes, the remaining negotiators endorsed the 27 April 1994 date, but decided to forward it to a larger sitting of the negotiating forum on 25 June for ratification.[56]

The scheduled vote on the election date had by 25 June actually been postponed for a week, but a demonstration organised by the Afrikaner Volksunie gathered outside the World Trade Centre nonetheless. Members of the AWB, which was a Volksunie constituent, were among those present. In violation of the police's refusal to allow them to rally on the WTC grounds, the AWB's leader Eugene TerreBlanche directed his followers – many of them armed – to advance. The approximately 600 on-duty police failed to obstruct them, and in fact many fraternised with the AWB members who burst past a security gate and entered the WTC building itself. For two hours they rampaged through the building, vandalising property and spray-painting racist slogans, leaving only when government negotiators offered assurances that there would be no on-the-spot arrests.[57]

In an emotional debate following the withdrawal, the negotiators resolved to accelerate the talks. On 2 July they officially approved the 27 April 1994 election date after which IFP and CP delegates walked out.[58] The negotiating council itself went into recess on 2 July, and on the weekend prior to their scheduled re-commencement on 19 July, the IFP and CP announced they were pulling out of the process for good.[59]

In September 1993, the negotiators reached a deal for a transitional executive council that would be entitled, with 75 per cent agreement, to override almost any Government decision in the run-up to the elections.[60] Then at fourteen minutes past midnight on 18 November, the WTC negotiators reached agreement on a Bill of Rights that provided for a 400-member national assembly and a ninety-member senate that would have two years to adopt a final constitution. The president would be elected by the national assembly, with the cabinet consisting of deputy presidents from any party with over eighty seats, and ministers from any party with over twenty seats.[61]

When the multiracial Transitional Executive Council took office in Cape Town on 7 December,[62] the negotiations per se came to an end, and the country entered fully into the transition to non-racial, multiparty elections.

Transition

In Pretoria on 7 October 1993, the five COSAG constituents reconstituted themselves as the 'Freedom Alliance' which committed itself to push for a strong federal state that would provide for ethnic homelands.[63]

On 7 March 1994, Bophuthatswana's cabinet announced that the homeland would *not* participate in the elections. From that point, civil service strikes that had disrupted the rural areas for weeks spread to the homeland's main cities of Mmabatho and Mafikeng. On 10 March Lucas Mangope telephoned General Constand Viljoen, the former chief of the South African Defence Force (SADF) appealing for military assistance for four days till the Bophuthatswana parliament next met.[64]

Viljoen promised to muster 3,000 men. They began massing at Cullinan at midday. That evening however, AWB members began to congregate in bakkies at the Protea Sechuba hotel outside Mmabatho. Bophuthatswana Defence Force commander Major-General Jack Turner met Eugene Terre-Blanche and told him the army and police were 'dead set against the presence of the AWB'. Terre-Blanche however ignored this and from about 3 a.m. on 11 March, over 400 vehicles containing armed AWB paramilitaries drove into Mmabatho. They surrounded the Mega City shopping complex and shot at looters, before driving around town, intimidating people on the streets, and harassing and beating up journalists. By mid-morning however, the Bophuthatswana army had rallied and driven the rightists out of town.

A five-minute firefight was captured on camera involving three AWB stragglers in central Mmabatho being shot dead execution style in what became a symbol of the military rout of the white right.[65]

On 22 March 1994 Oupa Gqozo announced he too would step down. It followed indications of policemen, soldiers and civil servants in the Ciskei stirring in a manner similar to their counterparts in Bophuthatswana prior to the uprising there.[66]

This left the IFP. The issue of the fate of the Zulu king had become part of the dispute in Natal. On 18 March, the Zulu King Goodwill Zwelithini declared in a prepared speech in Ulundi that: 'We here today proclaim before the world our freedom and sovereignty and our unwavering will to defend it at all costs'. KwaZulu government spokesman T.C. Memela clarified that while the king had 'claimed sovereignty' over the area controlled by Zulus in the last century, he did not 'declare independence'.[67]

Mandela, de Klerk, Buthelezi and King Goodwill met in the Kruger National Park on 8 April to try and resolve their differences. Mandela offered the King powers as a constitutional monarch over the whole of Natal. In response Zwelithini asked to be allowed to consult with his advisers, who included Buthelezi. After ninety minutes, the royal household member Prince Vincent Zulu returned saying 'The king has examined your proposals and finds them unacceptable'. The meeting continued, with Mandela asking repeatedly what further concerns the Zwelithini had, to which the monarch remained silent, leaving it to members of his delegation to respond that they refused to separate concerns about the king's position from the IFP's on the issue of federalism in the constitution.[68]

Attempts at international mediation launched on 12 April ostensibly failed two days later when Lord Carrington, Henry Kissinger and others packed their bags after the ANC and IFP failed to agree terms of reference for them. Washington Okumu, a Kenyan, decided to stay, and when Mangosuthu Buthelezi arrived at Johannesburg's Lanseria Airport on the 15th to catch a plane to Ulundi, he found a message from Okumu requesting a meeting. At the meeting Okumu sought to convey to Buthelezi the fact that time was *against* him, because after the election 'the new government would take over the running of KwaZulu'. The argument registered and Buthelezi flew back to Ulundi to consult. Discussions over the next few days led to an agreement signed by Buthelezi, Mandela and de Klerk in Pretoria on 19 April, providing for Inkatha's participation in the elections in exchange for a promise that 'Any outstanding issues in respect of the king of the Zulus and the 1993 constitution as amended will be addressed by way of international mediation, which will commence as soon as possible after the said elections'.[69]

The 1994 Elections

By April 1994, an estimated 20,000 South Africans had been killed in acts of political violence over the previous decade. March 1994 meanwhile saw 461 people killed, in a 103 per cent increase over the previous month.[70] It was therefore with foreboding that many looked upon the impending elections. At a press conference on 18 April, Thabo Mbeki read a statement on the ANC's behalf, noting reports of panicky shoppers clearing supermarket stores in order to stockpile essential goods; of other civilians setting up temporary home in Zimbabwean camp sites; of foreign governments drafting contingency plans to evacuate their nationals; and domestic servants picking out suburban houses to commandeer. He dismissed the rumours as part of a well-orchestrated campaign to spread panic and confusion and frighten people into not voting. Mbeki said the ANC would act firmly against looters, and he would personally head an 'emergency disciplinary structure' to investigate contraventions of the electoral code by members of the movement.[71]

But by then there were signs that the tide had turned in terms of political violence. On the day after the briefing, the *Star* noted a huge drop in both political and ordinary criminal violence over the past few days.[72]

The ANC's election manifesto was titled *A Better Life for All – Working Together for Jobs, Peace and Freedoms*. It committed the organisation to the constitutional principles agreed in the multi-party negotiations, but added that democracy meant more than the right to vote and should properly be measured by improvements in people's quality of life. Regarding the latter, the manifesto offered a broad-brush version of the 'Reconstruction and Development' programme (RDP) that was concluded at a conference in Johannesburg in January 1994 following consultations at branch and regional level after an NEC resolution in October 1992. It proposed levies on capital transfers, on land and luxury goods, and taxes on fuel and land, to finance initiatives including the electrification of 2.5 million new homes by 2000;

the provision of free healthcare for all children under six; the construction of 300,000 new houses per annum; and the extension of social insurance to all workers.[73]

With the polls scheduled to open on 26 April, there was a flurry of bomb blasts in the forty-eight hours preceding it. The targets were polling facilities and even just crowds of black people, and they resulted in at least nineteen deaths and about 150 injuries.[74]

The ANC held a victory celebration at the Carlton Hotel in Johannesburg on 2 May 1994 after it became clear that the party had an unassailable lead in the polls. On that evening, President de Klerk conceded the election. The full results were released on 6 May: the ANC received 62.65 per cent of the vote; the National Party 20.39 per cent; and Inkatha 10.54 per cent. No other party garnered over 2.5 per cent. On 9 May the new members of the national assembly were sworn in, and then on 10 May, Nelson Mandela was inaugurated the new state president.[75]

Lessons

In the second half of 1994, the journalist Patti Waldmeir conducted a series of interviews with key participants in the transition, which informed her book *Anatomy of a Miracle: The End of Apartheid and the Birth of the New South Africa*. One of her interlocutors was Gerrit Viljoen, who had been Minister of Constitutional Development from 1989 to 1992. She asked 'How late in the process did you accept black majority rule?' to which he answered 'I would still say that we haven't accepted black majority rule'.[76] It indicated that the government was simply overwhelmed at the negotiating table following the government's decision to no longer rely on the security forces to achieve political goals.

The October interview was sandwiched between two with Constand Viljoen in June and November. The former SADF chief recalled that during his time in the army, the military explored 'virtually every case study of revolutionary war in Africa' involving insurgency against white minority rule, from the Mau Mau in Kenya, the conflict in Portuguese Africa and the war in Rhodesia. It convinced them that the South African conflict would 'never be a military war alone', and that 'you have to do more on the political, economic and social aspects', because if those non-military factors remained unresolved they would ultimately erode the morale of the civilian population. Viljoen accordingly advised his political superiors that 'a long drawn out war from the military point of view is completely possible but from the country's psychological point of view it is not possible'.[77]

These ideas informed de Klerk's statements in January and February 1990. Domestic war weariness combined with the dynamics created by the end of the Cold War persuaded him to push for a negotiated settlement. The subsequent talks were bedevilled by the persistence of three main forms of conflict inherited from the past, namely that between the state and ANC-supporting communities; the ANC's armed struggle; and ANC–IFP violence. These interlocked conflicts delayed the onset of constitutional negotiations by almost two years. A decisive factor in determining the outcome of the South African negotiations was the fact that the two most important protagonists – i.e., the ANC and the National Party – were each committed for their own reasons to the success of the process initiated by de Klerk, and with the end of his five-year presidential term approaching (in 1994), the parties advanced in December 1991 to constitutional talks even though the issue of violence was far from resolved, as the Boipatong Massacre demonstrated.

It was ultimately the conclusion of the constitutional negotiations in 1993 that laid the basis for a termination of political violence, because they established 27 April 1994 as a date certain for elections. The approach of that deadline generated a momentum that would overwhelm the resistance of the 'Freedom Alliance': the prospect of being left out of the elections set people's power in motion in Bophuthatswana, while the right-wing fragmented on its failure to prop-up Lucas Mangope. Concerns over pensions led civil servants in the Ciskei to stir against Oupa Gqozo, while the imminent prospect of facing an ANC bolstered by the full power of the state brought the increasingly isolated IFP into line.

South Africa's experience ultimately highlighted a recurrent problem in the history of revolutionary wars against minority rule in Africa. Constand Viljoen told Waldmeir that a 'big problem' in the insurgencies he studied was that 'politicians always do too little too late'. He mentioned the example of Ian Smith in Rhodesia who settled for far less in 1980 than he could have got in the HMS Fearless talks a decade earlier. He contended that in modern insurgency the function of military force was to give politicians time to address the political, economic and social grievances fuelling conflict.[78]

He noted that as far back as the late 1960s he had advised parliamentarians to 'accommodate the political aspirations of the black people as far as the constitution' was concerned. He also made a specific proposal involving the creation of a 'federal' system that would dissolve the central white parliament and establish a network of black and white areas. Viljoen told Waldmeir this was 'in line with the thinking' of homeland leaders at the time such as Kaiser Matanzima and Mangosuthu Buthelezi, and he said the difference between his proposal and the policy of independent homelands pursued by the government in those years was that 'instead of going to total separateness we will go to a political federal type of system' where the homelands would be one of the 'building blocks'.[79]

It is worth noting that the reforms implemented by P. W. Botha (South Africa's President from 1978 to 1989, overlaping with Viljoen's term as SADF chief from 1980 to 1985) were substantial. Changes to citizenship and property rights rendered unworkable the principle of territorial separation on which apartheid rested. Yet one reform that Botha consistently baulked at was negotiating with the liberation movements over majority rule in a unitary South Africa. The political reforms that he made – involving separate parliamentary chambers for Indians and Coloureds, and executive powers for local authorities in the black townships – were marked by low popular buy-in, including low voter turnout, mass resistance and ultimately a nationwide insurrection that led to the imposition of a state of emergency that remained in force when F. W. de Klerk took over in 1989.

It was only de Klerk's preparedness to take the final step of negotiating with the ANC over majority rule that created the basis for a settlement. From the counterinsurgent's perspective, that was the problem, because politicians resort to military force to *avoid* political capitulation. To phrase the same point in terms of Africa's experience with revolutionary warfare: Ian Smith could have ended nationalist agitation in Rhodesia at any point by conceding majority rule; likewise, Portuguese colonialists could have terminated anti-colonial militancy in their dependencies in an instant by consenting to decolonise. They pursued military solutions to avoid such concessions. In the South African instance, de Klerk's predecessors explored various alternatives to majority rule. The failure of their numerous efforts at ethnic balkanisation poses the question of whether the homeland-based 'federalism' proposed by Viljoen and others had any realistic prospect of meeting black constitutional aspirations. Ultimately the onus falls on them to make the case – assertion is insufficient, given the historical record. What can be said with certainty is that it was de Klerk's willingness to pursue a settlement that responded to the basic political demands of the nationalists that enabled peace to be achieved.

That said, it would be wrong to conclude without emphasising the great achievement of the country's peace process. Professor Tom Lodge noted that political violence continued on a diminishing scale for about two years after the 1994 elections,[80] while Frederik van Zyl Slabbert (a liberal opposition leader during the apartheid era) was able to write in 2006 that if one considered the roots of any society's political stability on a continuum with state repression at one pole and voluntary consent at the other, South Africa's new dispensation should be considered as resting mainly on 'consensual consensus' in terms of both its system and how to seek change within it.[81] This categorisation remains valid over a decade later. Considered in the context of the clichés that it is impossible to legislate for all time, and that a week is a long time in politics, then the architects of the new South Africa can fairly be credited with having established a 'lasting' and 'durable' peace. As post-apartheid South Africa reaches the end of its third decade, no future twist of fate will be able to reverse that verdict.

Notes

1. 'Police Still Have to Enforce Apartheid', *The Cape Times*, 29/1/1990.
2. Thula Simpson, *Umkhonto we Sizwe: The ANC's Armed Struggle* (Cape Town: Penguin, 2016), pp. 453–4.
3. Howard Barrell, 'Conscripts to Their Age: African National Congress Operational Strategy, 1976–1986', PhD Dissertation, Oxford University, Oxford, 1993, pp. 452–4.
4. Simpson, pp. 436–7.
5. 'Text of President de Klerk's Address to the South African Parliament', *Independent*, 3/2/1990.
6. Ibid.
7. 'Text of Nelson Mandela's Speech Outside Cape Town's City Hall', *Associated*

Press, 12/2/1990; See texts of the 'Harare Declaration' and of Mandela's speech on the Grand Parade, in: Gail M. Gerhart and Clive L. Glaser, *From Protest to Challenge: A Documentary History of African Politics in South Africa, 1882–1990*, vol. 6: Challenge and Victory (Bloomington: Indiana University Press, 2010), pp. 702–4, 725–8.

8. Nelson Mandela, *Long Walk to Freedom: The Autobiography of Nelson Mandela* (London: Abacus, 1997), p. 691.

9. 'Text of Statement at South African Talks', *New York Times*, 5/5/1990; 'Relief as Talks Stay on Track', *Sunday Star*, 23/9/1990.

10. Oxford University, Bodleian Library, MSS. Afr. s. 2151 1/3, Howard Barrell interview of Mac Maharaj, 3/2/1991, pp. 527–9; 'Crackdown on Communists', *Sunday Star*, 22/7/1990; 'Mystery "Comrade Joe" Comes in from the Cold', *Star*, 7/8/1990; 'Safe as Houses', *Sunday Times*, 4/11/1990; 'Hunt for 7 ANC Moles', *Sunday Times*, 4/11/1990.

11. 'South Africa: The Wrong Joe', *The Economist*, vol. 316, no. 7666, 4/8/1990, p. 32.

12. 'Mandela Meets De Klerk to Defuse Crisis', *United Press International*, 1/8/1990; 'ANC Agrees to Suspend Armed Struggle', *The Financial Times*, 7/8/1990; 'ANC Report Back to the People of South Africa', *Weekly Mail*, 10/8/1990.

13. Tom Lodge, 'Resistance and Reform, 1973–1994', in: Robert Ross, Anne Kelk Mager and Bill Nasson (eds), *The Cambridge History of South Africa: volume 2, 1885–1994* (Cambridge: Cambridge University Press, 2012), p. 483.

14. 'Mandela Accuses Government of Waging War Against ANC,' *Associated Press*, 11/9/1990; 'Where Violent Conflict Has Become Way of Life', *Star*, 16/8/1990; '13 Killed in Black Township Violence': *Times*, 15/8/1990; 'South African Tribal Clashes Leave 16 Dead', *Toronto Star*, 15/8/1990; Saul Dubow, *The African National Congress* (Stroud: Sutton, 2000), p. 93.

15. 'Onderhandelingsknoop finaal deurgehaak', *Vrye Weekblad*, 25/1/1991.

16. 'South Africa, ANC Agree on Armed Struggle Details', *Associated Press*, 15/2/1991.

17. 'Mandela and Buthelezi Urge End To Strife', *Guardian*, 30/1/1991.

18. 'South African Rival Black Groups Renew Fighting', *Christian Science Monitor*, 1/2/1991.

19. 'Disarm Them!', *Weekly Mail*, 5/4/1991; 'ANC Puts Talks on Line', *Saturday Star*, 6/4/1991; 'Defiant ANC Will Form Defence Units,' *Sunday Star*, 14/4/1991.

20. 'No Press Conference after De Klerk and Mandela's Crucial Meeting', *Agence France Presse*, 8/5/1991; 'De Klerk Announces Ban On Most Weapons in Black Townships', *Associated Press*, 9/5/1991.

21. 'ANC to Give Government Another 10 Days to Ban All Weapons: Report', *Agence France Presse*, 10/5/1991; 'ANC: No Constitutional Talks Until Violence Resolved', *Associated Press*, 18/5/1991; 'Mandela's Group Quits Discussions on a New Charter', *New York Times*, 19/5/1991; 'ANC Dodges its Own Deadline', *Independent*, 19/5/1991.

22. South Africa conference on violence concludes; 'Broad Consensus', 27/5/1991, BBC Summary of SAPA dispatch, 25/5/1991; 'Zulu King Calls for End to Township Violence', *Times*, 27/5/1991; 'Breakthrough in Search for Peace', *Saturday Star*, 22/6/1991.

23. 'Far-reaching Plan to End Township Violence', *Agence France Presse*, 24/8/1991; 'Report to Congress on the Status of Apartheid', *US Department of State Dispatch*, 14/10/1991.

24. 'Police Paid Inkatha to Block ANC', *Weekly Mail*, 19/7/1991.

25. 'Vlok, Malan Resign from the Cabinet', *Business Day*, 30/7/1991; 'Shuffle Ends Reign of the Securocrats', *Star*, 31/7/1991.

26. 'Leading Parties Reach Agreement on Peace Accord', *Associated Press*, 15/8/1991; 'S. African Accords Advance Peace', *Christian Science Monitor*, 19/8/1991.

27. 'Peace Gets its Chance', *Sunday Times*, 15/9/1991; 'De Klerk Demands ANC Disband Military Wing', *Guardian*, 17/9/1991.

28. 'Pretoria and ANC Agree on Negotiations', *Independent*, 22/11/1991.

29. 'De Klerk Proposes Blacks Join Interim Rule', *Washington Post*, 21/12/1991; 'Talks in South Africa End Hopefully', *New York Times*, 22/12/1991.

30. 'Mandela Firm on Majority Rule', *Agence France Presse*, 14/5/1992; 'Constitutional Talks Break Down', *Agence France Presse*, 15/5/1992; 'South Africa is One Issue Away from Accord', *New York Times*, 15/5/1992.

31. 'Day of High Drama at Codesa', *Citizen*, 14/5/1992; '"No Breakdown" in SA Negotiations', *Independent*, 16/5/1992; 'South Africa Talks in Deadlock; De Klerk Confers with Mandela', *New York Times*, 16/5/1992; 'South Africa Talks: Rush to Impasse?',' *New York Times*, 18/5/1992; T.R.H. Davenport, *The Transfer of Power in South Africa* (Cape Town: David Philip, 1998), pp. 13–14.

32. 'ANC Focuses Ire on S. African President', *Financial Times*, 1/6/1992; 'Mandela Group Plans Mass Disruptions', *New York Times*, 1/6/1992; 'ANC Holds Policy Conference', *Facts on File World News Digest*, 4/6/1992; 'ANC Unveils Battle Plan', *Sunday Times*, 14/6/1992.

33. 'ANC Focuses Ire on S. African President', *Financial Times*, 1/6/1992; 'ANC Unveils Battle Plan', *Sunday Times*, 14/6/1992.

34. 'Boipatong's Necklace of Guilt', *Guardian*, 30/6/1992; Hein Marais, *South Africa: Limits to Change: The Political Economy of Transition* (London: Zed Books, 2001), p. 89.

35. 'As Black Anger Grows, Mandela Pulls ANC Out of Talks', *Associated Press*, 22/6/1992; 'Mandela Asks for United Nations Help', *Agence France Presse*, 22/6/1992; 'Mandela Attacks 'Faceless' Killers U.N. Urged to Investigate "Massacres"', *Toronto Star*, 22/6/1992.

36. 'U.N. Chief to Visit South Africa in Attempt to Solve Political Crisis', *Agence France Presse*, 28/6/1992.

37. 'Mandela Asks UN to Look into Violence', *Financial Times*, 16/6/1992; 'Botha Rejects Charges of Inciting Violence, Offers Talks', *Associated Press*, 16/7/1992; 'Vance Tipped to Lead UN Mission to End South African Violence', *Financial Times*, 18/7/1992.

38. 'Vance Aims to Broker SA Settlement', *Guardian*, 22/7/1992; 'Vance Optimistic Talks Will Resume', *Associated Press*, 31/7/1992; 'Hopes Rise of South African Breakthrough', *Financial Times*, 31/7/1992; 'ANC Reopens Talks with Government', *Guardian*, 31/7/1992.

39. 'ANC Gives Details of its Mass Action Programme', 20/7/1992, BBC Summary of SAPA PR wire service dispatch issued by the African National Congress, 17/7/1992; 'Nation Braces for Two-day Strike', *Associated Press*, 3/8/1992; Robert Harvey, *The Fall of Apartheid: The Inside Story from Smuts to Mbeki* (Basingstoke: Palgrave Macmillan, 2003), p. 237.

40. 'Nationwide Strike Cripples Industry', *Facts on File World News Digest*, 6/8/1992; 'Mandela Takes His Message to Apartheid's Citadel', *New York Times*, 6/8/1992; 'Stalemate in South Africa', *Financial Times*, 7/8/1992; 'South Africa: Mass Action Success Boosts ANC Position', *IPS-Inter Press Service*, 8/8/1992; 'Protests Underline South Africa's Hopes and Perils', *Associated Press*, 8/8/1992.

41. 'UN's Blue Print for Peace', *Sunday Times*, 9/8/1992; 'Mandela Talks to de Klerk in Hopeful Sign', *Toronto Star*, 10/8/1992 ; 'Boutros Wants to Boost Peace Accord', *Star*, 10/8/1992; 'Pretoria Accepts UN Report on Crisis', *Christian Science Monitor*, 14/8/1992.

42. 'ANC, Government to Discuss Resumption of Negotiations', *United Press International*, 21/8/1992.

43. 'Slaughter in South Africa', *Newsweek*, 21/9/1992; UWHP, 'A3345, E2.2.1,

Ronald Kasrils 'Affidavit', (March 1996); David Welsh, *The Rise and Fall of Apartheid* (Jeppestown: Jonathan Ball, 2009), pp. 453–4.

44. 'ANC Sets Conditions for Meeting with De Klerk', *Associated Press*, 10/9/1992.

45. 'Release of ANC Prisoners Helps Restart Reform Talks', *Times*, 26/9/1992; 'De Klerk Freeing Prisoners; Talks Today', *New York Times*, 26/9/1992; 'FW, Mandela Shake Hands and Get Talks Back on Track', *Sunday Times*, 27/9/1992; University of Oxford, Bodleian Library, MSS AAM 949, CODESA, 'Record of Understanding', 26/9/1992.

46. 'Zulu Leader Breaks off Talks with Government', *Associated Press*, 27/9/1992; 'Three S. African Homeland Leaders Oppose the Outcome of ANC-Pretoria Summit', *Xinhua General News Service*, 29/9/1992; 'ANC Says it Will Resume Constitutional Talks', *Associated Press*, 30/9/1992; 'President de Klerk and Foreign Minister Botha React to Homeland Leaders' Meeting', BBC Summary of a SAPA dispatch, 1/10/1992; 'Black, White Conservatives Condemn ANC-Pretoria Pact,' *Washington Post*, 7/10/1992.

47. 'President De Klerk and Foreign Minister Botha React to Homeland Leaders' Meeting', 1/10/1992, BBC summary of SAPA dispatch, 29/9/1992.

48. University of Oxford, Bodleian Library, MSS AAM 949, CODESA, 'Record of Understanding', 26/9/1992.

49. 'ANC Radical Softens His Line', *Independent*, 30/10/1992.

50. 'ANC Considering Joint Rule with National Party,' *Associated Press*, 1/11/1992; 'ANC Says Black-White Power Sharing Likely in Future S. Africa', *Associated Press*, 19/11/1992; 'South African Communist Sparks an Explosive Debate', *Washington Post*, 22/11/1992.

51. 'ANC's "Strategic Perspective" Paper on Negotiations', 28/11/1992, BBC summary of SAPA dispatch issued by the ANC titled 'Negotiations: A Strategic Perspective' – (as adopted by the National Executive Committee of the African National Congress on 25 November 1992), 25/11/1992.

52. 'ANC's 'Strategic Perspective' Paper on Negotiations', 28/11/1992, BBC summary of SAPA dispatch issued by the ANC titled 'Negotiations: A Strategic Perspective' – (as adopted by the National Executive Committee of the African National Congress on 25 November 1992), 25/11/1992.

53. 'South African Government, African National Congress Reach Power-sharing Deal', *Facts on File World News Digest*, 25/2/1993.

54. 'South African Talks Resume', *Guardian*, 2/4/1993; 'Pro-democracy Talks Resume in South Africa', *United Press International*, 1/4/1993.

55. 'Point Blank Shots Fired at Lifeless Body', *Sunday Times*, 11/4/1993.

56. 'Black, White Groups Hold Fresh Talks on Ending Minority Rule', *Associated Press*, 30/4/1993; 'Sorry, But New Dawn Has Planes to Catch', *Observer*, 2/5/1993; 'South Africa's Right Wing Circles its Wagons', *Christian Science Monitor*, 11/5/1993; 'Tentative Date Set for South Africa's First Non-Racial Elections', *United Press International*, 3/6/1993; 'Conservative Organizations Walk out of South African Talks', *United Press International*, 15/6/1993; 'South Africa; COSAG Members Walk out of Multi-Party Negotiations; to Return 17th June', 17/6/1993, BBC Summary of SAPA dispatch, 15/6/1993.

57. 'Front Split Looms as Viljoen Quits'm *Sunday Times*, 13/3/1994; 'White Militants Use Armored Truck to Crash S. African Talks', *Washington Post*, 26/6/1993; 'White Separatists Storm South African Negotiations', *New York Times*, 26/6/1993; 'Nazi-style Tactics May Backfire on White Extremists', *Observer*, 27/6/1993; 'Afrikaners Threaten Guerrilla Campaign', *Sunday Times*, 27/6/1993.

58. 'Death Blow to Apartheid', *Independent*, 3/7/1993.

59. 'Key Negotiations Resume Without Black, White Conservatives', *Associated Press*, 19/7/1993.

60. 'South Africa's White-dominated Parliament Passes Democracy Bill', *United Press International*, 23/9/1993; 'South Africa's Parliament Votes For a Black Role in Government', *New York Times*, 24/9/1993; 'Chronology of Politics and Violence', *Associated Press*, 23/10/1993.

61. 'Highlights of South Africa's New Constitution', *Associated Press*, 18/11/1993; 'Sekunjalo!', *Sunday Times*, 21/11/1993.

62. 'Low-key Start to New Order in S Africa', *Financial Times*, 8/12/1993.

63. 'New Political Movement 'Freedom Alliance' Formed; Government and ANC React', 9/10/1993, BBC summary of SAPA dispatch, 7/10/1993; 'South African Leaders to Meet November 17 to Endorse Draft Constitution', *Agence France Presse*, 11/11/1993.

64. 'It Started with a "No" and Ended in a "Yes"', *Sunday Times*, 13/3/1994; 'How Homeland Almost Fell to the Men of the Right', *Sunday Times*, 20/3/1994.

65. 'Events Day by Day' and 'Events Leading to 'Executions', *Star*, 14/3/1994; 'How Homeland Almost Fell to the Men of the Right', *Sunday Times*, 20/3/1994; Allister Sparks, *Tomorrow is Another Country: The Inside Story of South Africa's Negotiated Revolution* (Sandton: Struik, 1994), pp. 209–14.

66. 'Another Domino Falls', *Argus*, 23/3/1994.

67. 'Kingdom: ANC Threat', *Cape Times*, 19/3/1994; 'Confusion, Fear at Zulu King's Sovereignty Call', *Sunday Times*, 20/3/1994.

68. 'Royal Flush Beats ANC Ace', *Sunday Times*, 10/4/1994.

69. 'How Deal was Brokered', *Star*, 20/4/1994; 'Was Buthelezi Suckered?', *Sunday Times*, 16/4/1995.

70. 'Free and Fair . . . or Flawed?', *Star*, 19/4/1994.

71. 'Mbeki Dismisses Election Paranoia', *Business Day*, 19/4/1994.

72. 'Dramatic Decrease in Crime And Violence', *Star*, 19/4/1994.

73. Oxford University, Bodleian Library, MSS AAM 948, 'Statement of the National Executive Committee of the African National Congress at the Conclusion of the National Reconstruction and Strategy Conference, 23/1/1994; 'ANC Unveils Plan to Spread Wealth', *Star*, 15/1/1994; 'Populist Pull', *Financial Mail*, 4/22/1994.

74. 'Campaigns wrapped up,' *Star*, 25/4/1994; 'Bombs fail to stop poll,' *Star*, 26/4/1994.

75. 'There Just Has to Be a Morning After ... But Not Yet', *Weekend Star*, 7/5/1994; 'ANC 62,65pc in 'Substantially Free, Fair Poll', *Citizen*, May 7, 1994; 'The Night the Party Partied', *Sunday Times*, 8 May, 1994; 'The New Dawn', *Pretoria News*, 10/5/1994; 'The First Day of the Rest of our Lives', *Pretoria News*, 10/5/1994; Andrew Reynolds, 'The Results', in: Andrew Reynolds (ed.), *Election '94 South Africa: The Campaigns, Results and Future Prospects* (London: James Currey, 1994), p. 183.

76. UWHP, A2508, Interview of Gerrit Viljoen, 20/10/1994; Patti Waldmeir, *Anatomy of a Miracle: The End of Apartheid and the Birth of a New South Africa* (London: Penguin, 1998).

77. UWHP, A2508, Interviews of Constand Viljoen, 23/6/1994; 15/11/1994.

78. Ibid.

79. Ibid.

80. Lodge, p. 483.

81. Frederik van Zyl Slabbert, *Duskant die Geskiedenis: 'n persoonlike terugblik op die politieke oorgang in Suid-Africa* (Cape Town: Tafelberg, 2006), pp. 135–6.

12

TRANSFORMATIONS IN ETHIOPIA: FROM ARMED STRUGGLE TO THE POLITICS OF COALITION

Mehari Taddele Maru

O n 26 December 2019 a new party was formed in Ethiopia.[1] The Prosperity Party (PP) is reportedly a merger of three constituent parties – the Amhara Democratic Party (ADP), Oromo Democratic Party (ODP) and Southern Ethiopian People's Democratic Movement (SEPDM) – of the ruling, now defunct, Ethiopian People's Revolutionary Democratic Front (EPRDF).[2] Left out of the new party was the Tigray People's Liberation Front, which is credited with creating the EPRDF coalition in 1989, two years before the toppling of the Derg regime in 1991. Though described as a reform of the old EPRDF, PP is actually a new formation by the current Prime Minister Abiy Ahmed; the formation of the EPRDF in 1989 and its transformation to a nationwide party was the work of the late Prime Minister Meles Zenawi.[3]

An offshoot of the Ethiopian Student Movement, which played a key role in the 1974 Ethiopian Revolution, the EPRDF overthrew the Derg regime of Colonel Mengistu Haile Mariam in 1991 after years of armed struggle. Once it took power, the armed group transformed into a party that was to rule the country continuously until the events of last December.

This chapter examines the way in which Ethiopia's armed groups have been transformed into political or quasi-political organisations. It measures this development against four timelines: the imperial period up to 1974; the Derg period from 1974 to 1991; the period from 1991 to 2018 when the

EPRDF exercised a virtual monopoly on political power; and finally, the post-2018 period, marked by the end of the EPRDF's domination and the return of armed groups to Ethiopian politics. The chapter's main purpose is to examine the way in which the opposition armed factions transformed into unarmed political parties, the role of leadership, the military victory of the EPRDF in 1991 and the popular unrest in 2015, in particular the transformation that the EPRDF underwent from pre-1991 to 2018. It explores the role of the leadership, the significance of the military victory over Derg in 1991, and the incentives to reform from both foreign and domestic sources.

Armed Groups in Ethiopia

Since the 1960s, there have been more than twenty armed groups in Ethiopia (see table 12.1 below). Some do not exist anymore, but others still operate as wings of political parties.

The armed groups may be placed into four categories. First are the ideologically leftist armed groups founded on the basis of class struggle such as the Ethiopian People's Revolutionary Party (EPRP). Second are the community-based ethno-nationalist movements fighting for self-determination and equality between cultures. An example in this category is the Oromo Liberation Front (OLF). The third are groups, among them the EPRDF, that are ideologically leftist and also claim to represent cultural communities. The final category comprises those that are neither class-based nor organised on an ethnic basis, such as the Ethiopian Democratic Union (EDU) which fought as part of an armed struggle for the restoration of the imperial regime.

After the Ethiopia–Eritrean Border War of 1998, and the 2005 elections, which ended in violence, new armed groups such as the Tigray People's Democratic Movement (TPDM) and Ginbot 7 were formed. All the new groups had very limited military capabilities and were thus reduced to insignificant opposition factions.

The following is a table of some of the influential armed groups that have existed in Ethiopia:

In the next section, this chapter will examine the armed groups in Ethiopia under four timelines: the imperial era up to 1974; the Derg regime era (1974 to 1991); the 1991 to 2018 period; and the post-EPRDF 2018 era.

Table 12.1 List of Influential Armed Groups in Ethiopia

	Group	Transformation (Political Party, Splinter, Defunct)	Notes
1	The Afar Liberation Movement (ALF)	Turned into political party.	
2	All Ethiopia Socialist Movement (AESM, 'MEISON' in Amharic), 1968	Joined the United Ethiopian Democratic Forces.	
3	Amhara National Democratic Movement (ANDM)	Splintered from Ethiopian People's Revolutionary Party (EPRP), which turned into a political party in 1991 as part of the ruling EPRDF coalition.	ANDM has governed the Amhara Regional State since 1991 and is now the Amhara Democratic Party.
4	Coalition of Ethiopian Democratic Forces (COEDF)	Defunct	
5	The Eritrean Liberation Front (ELF)	Defunct	
6	Eritrean People's Liberation Front (EPLF)	Splintered from ELF, now ruling Eritrea as People's Front for Democracy and Justice.	
7	Ethiopian Democratic Union (EDU)	Merged with Ethiopian Democratic Party in 2003.	
8	Ethiopian People's Revolutionary Party (EPRP)	Split into political party in Ethiopia and abroad.	
9	Gambella People's Liberation Movement (GPLM)	Ruled Gambella, then turned into an armed group and transformed into apolitical party in 2018.	
10	Horyaal Democratic Front (HDF)	Merged into the Western Somali Democratic Front.	
11	Islamic Front for the Liberation of Oromia (IFLO)	Boycotted elections in 1995.	
12	Ogaden National Liberation Front (ONLF)	Transformed into a party in 2018.	
13	Oromo Liberation Front (OLF)	Co-established the Transitional Government and left it in 1992. Became active again in Ethiopia in 2018 and fights against the government in many parts of Oromia.	
14	Oromo People's Democratic Organization (OPDO)	Part of the EPRDF ruling coalition since 1991. Governed Oromia regional state. Changed its name to the Oromo Democratic Party.	

Table 12.1 (*continued*)

Group	Transformation (Political Party, Splinter, Defunct)	Notes
15 Tigray People's Liberation Front (TPLF)	Part of the ruling EPRDF coalition. Has governed Tigray since 1991.	
16 Western Somali Liberation Front (WSLF)	Swallowed into the ONLF.	
17 Afar Revolutionary Democratic Unity Front (ARDUF)	Joined the peaceful political competition with splints since 2002.	
18 Tigray People's Democratic Movement (TPDM) (1999), and Ginbot 7 Front (2005)	Has returned to Ethiopia, and renounced armed struggle in 2018.	
19 Red Sea Afar Democratic Organisation (RSADO)	Still continues armed struggle.	
20 Sidama Liberation Front (SLF)		

Armed Groups under Imperial Rule

From the fourth century CE until 1974, Ethiopia was a Christian monarchy. The common armed groups during the imperial regime were either those resisting colonial rule or else armed peasant revolts. There were also criminal bands called *shifta*s ('bandits' or 'outlaws'). In the final decades of Haile Selassie's regime, there existed a few peasant-based armed units from Oromia, Tigray and other regions. Additionally, active political agitation by nationalist peasant revolts and extremist factions among university students led to the formation of armed organisations. Most of these groups were leftist in ideology.

These groups represented various different agendas, ranging from secessionists (Eritrea being one example) to Marxists such as the EPRP. This period was characterised by divisions between and among revolutionary movements. What held most militias together were their common enemies – the imperial regime, feudalism and imperialism.

The 1974–91 Military Junta

After the last emperor, Haile Selassie I, was overthrown in 1974, 'anti-feudal' movements found that socialism as a creed was not sufficient to bind revolutionaries to a common cause. The army, under the name Derg and led by Colonel Mengistu Haile Mariam, set up a single-party state.[4] Thus, the revolution ended up in a military junta that had hijacked power from the revolutionary movements. Other forces consisting of student organisations were left out the new dispensation by the army – which was the best-organised segment of the revolution. In the struggle for control of government, the revolutionary student movements fragmented into factions which set up their own armed wings. Under the banner of revolutionary 'Red Terror' and its counter 'White Terror', Ethiopia's youngest and brightest fought in the capital city of Addis Ababa and in provincial towns.[5] The political battle between, on the one hand, the Derg and its Marxist-Leninist supporters from the All Ethiopia Socialist Movement (MEISON), and on the other, EPRP and other opposition groupings, led to the destruction of EPRP as a political party in the urban areas. During this period, ideologically based groups such as MEISON and EPRP, the latter with its military wing the Ethiopian Peoples' Revolutionary Army (EPRA), were significantly weakened by armed clashes both with the national army and with other non-state armed groups battling for control of territory and military bases. In keeping with the phenomenon of revolutions 'devouring their own children', the Derg later turned against and annihilated MEISON and some of its own internal dissenters. The struggle for power culminated into a two-decade civil war that ended in the secession of Eritrea from Ethiopia and the assumption of power by the EPRDF in Addis Ababa.

In this period, the non-state armed groups had five notable elements in common. First, most of them had originated in the student movement of the 1970s, which played a key role in the 1974 revolution. Second, in the early 1970s almost all of them supported the 'nationalities question' struggle (*Ye Biher Bihereseb Tiyaque*, a popular term for the 1960s struggle against ethno-linguistic domination in Ethiopia). Most of them also embraced the 'land question' (*Ye Meriyet Tiyaque* or *Meret La Rashu*, 'Land to the Tiller'). Unlike those groupings organised around purely ideological lines, ethnic-based operations such as EPLF, the Tigray People's Liberation Front (TPLF), Oromo Liberation Front (OLF) and the Ogaden National Liberation Front (ONLF) displayed a degree of resilience and were able to gain the upper hand in protracted conflicts. A third shared characteristic was that in general the political leadership of the armed groups was left leaning and ideologically driven. Early on, such groupings followed the Marxist-Leninist ideology.

Fourth, their political ideology was marked by an extreme intolerance of dissent. Fifth and most importantly, the armed movements were under the tight control of their respective political leaders. The organisational principle of democratic centralism was employed to ensure the suppression of dissent. Internal democracy was sacrificed for ideological unity under a rigid command, control and communication hierarchy. This organisational approach produced a concentration of force that compensated for their numerical (and other) military disadvantages.[6]

What, then explains the different outcomes – viz, the resilience and eventual victory for the ethnic-based armed groups? Many factors could here be cited. The first is the alien nature of class struggle and socialist ideology to highly religious, culturally conservative and economically underdeveloped Ethiopian communities. Identity politics under the banner of the 'nationalities question' was an effective basis for mobilising constituencies. The self-serving nature of the leadership of the student movement and the Derg contributed to the competition for power for private glorification rather than civic duty. While the leadership may have been self-serving, the rank and file displayed an extreme selflessness and a high commitment to public service. They saw resistance as a question of government power.

1991–2018: From Armed Liberation Movement to Dominant Ruling Party

When the EPRDF eventually took control in Addis Ababa in 1991, Ethiopia was home to more than a dozen ethnic-based secessionist groups. The interactions between various armed and civilian political forces with varied and sometime contradictory strands of political thoughts led to a formation of a big-tent Transitional Government of Ethiopia that ruled until 1995. During these transitional years, the rift between the EPRDF and some of the members of the Transitional Government such as the OLF and ONLF widened. Other armed groups such as ARDUF were also partially co-opted. Western countries, particularly the USA and EU, supported EPRDF rule as a reliable government that did not contradict their interests in the Horn of Africa. This position was further reinforced by the War on Terror.

The party held a peace conference to conclude hostilities soon after. Representatives from more than twenty parties were invited.[7] Some of these had been part of the fight against Mengistu.[8] In a sign of astute political manoeuvring, the EPRDF 'managed the conference and kept participation, the agenda, and therefore the eventual outcome firmly under their careful control'.[9] It formed a transitional government under a Transitional Charter with Meles Zenawi as the leader.

The EPRDF's transmutation into a governing party was rejected by some powerful sections of the Ethiopian elite, the effect of their opposition being to delegitimise TPLF and polarise the political landscape. Although politically controversial, the assumption of political power and the accompanying incorporation of the ERPDF armed wing into the national armed forces was not to be dismissed out of hand.[10] As is true of other armed movements which achieve political power after a military victory,[11] the ideologically driven ERPDF was ill-prepared for inclusive nation-building. Nonetheless, it was well organised and determined to deliver on its political-economic vision as source of legitimacy.

In the beginning, it had allies: the OLF and ONLF were active and significant participants in the transitional government. There were hiccups, however, in late 1991 and 1992. Disputes emerged between the EPRDF and the OLF, threatening a return to fighting by their armed wings.[12] They differences were partly about the role the OLF armed wing would take in the new dispensation and partly about political control ahead of elections to be held in 1992. However, through its sheer military might, and massive grassroots presence, the EPRDF was able to brush off competition from other parties.

Eritrea seceded in 1993 under the leadership of EPLF and remained a friend until the border war in 1998. Divergent views, previously subordinated to the sole common goal of removing the military junta, inevitably emerged soon after the common challenge was over.

The OLF opposed a monopoly of executive power by the EPRDF and requested that its leaders were allocated some ministerial positions. When this was rejected, in 1992, just one year after the formation of the transitional government, the OLF withdrew from it.

In May 1995, the EPRDF completed its transformation from armed group to political party. Having outfoxed the other political parties through its network of officials in all areas of Ethiopia and superior strategy, it took over the legitimate leadership of the country.[13] The only blot was that some parties refused to take part in the elections, raising queries of legitimacy.

Reform in the Security Sector

The EPRDF disbanded all elements of the existing security apparatus, including the military, intelligence and police and began building a new security sector through a process of demobilisation, disarmament and reintegration (DDR). As part of the process, the EPRDF's armed wing was turned into the national army. This root and branch strategy was the fruit of deep distrust of the previous regime and a different ideological approach to addressing the key questions facing the country. The change took place without a formal process of national reconciliation, but instead through unilateral imposition of a new political and economic order.

From the start, the EPRDF's attempt at nation and state-building faced strategic hurdles. The departure of the OLF and ONLF from the transitional government was evidence of the EPRDF's lack of will to transform itself into a democratic political party. It did however enjoy the capacity to remould that government into a more inclusive constitutive process. Such an undertaking required the EPRDF, as the ruling party with a monopoly on state power, to demonstrate a democratic propensity. For instance, it could have begun with some element of justice (in, say, the allocation of cabinet seats). In failing to do so, the EPRDF also failed to effectively address critical national questions or to manage differing aspects of public opinion. This was to prove a strategic mistake in the pursuit of the EPRDF's main political project of consensus-based federal democracy, political delivery and stability. The OLF and ONLF were forces for equality which shared the EPRDF's vision on consensus federalism and the need for economic delivery and stability. Therefore, the EPRDF's limited social base could have been expanded by drawing the OLF and ONLF, among other political groupings, into its project.

For the first time the armed forces were placed under the total control of the government. The EPRDF used its core political leadership and its former armed wings as the seedbed for a new security sector, including intelligence services. This move was attributable in part to the fact that the EPRDF was an ideologically driven liberation movement, the military wing of which was under the control of the political leadership. The ideology provided the basis for defence and security policy, and its doctrine determined the function, form and structure of the security sector and its relationship with government and society. In building the security sector from scratch, the EPRDF ensured that it was subservient to the civilian political wing of the ruling party, hence indirectly to the government.

Although some reform programmes were implemented in the security sector after 1991, they failed to change the behaviour of the EPRDF, the state, or its institutions. Democratic constitutional commitment from all the actors, especially the armed elements of the EPRDF, was essential for national stability – though not always forthcoming. However, perhaps one of the EPRDF's most enduring legacies was the establishment of an army that had no political ambitions.

Changes within the EPRDF – and thus in the government – in 2018, although not necessarily to the liking of most leaders of the military establishment, were nevertheless accepted by the army, which subordinated itself to the new government leadership. The total submission of the security sector, including the armed forces, to the new leadership in 2018 was more reflective of the acceptance of constitutionalism than any political endorsement of the new leadership.

Aversion to Change

The absence of internal democracy within the EPRDF was a crucial problem in its transmutation from an armed group to a ruling party claiming democratic legitimacy. The EPRDF remained enmeshed in its revolutionary culture throughout the 1990s. Its internal political dynamic was governed by the principle of democratic centralism, which ensured unified command, control and communication within the armed wing and between the political and armed elements of the party. This is hardly a viable approach to representative government. From Lenin to Putin, including Mao Zedong and Pinochet, such centralism has always been more about suppression of dissent for the sake of concentration of resources, than about responding to broad-based popular will.

Under such a principle, a regressive status quo prevails, and any progressive reform becomes almost impossible without resort to violence. It is common enough for former liberation movements finally holding political responsibility to find it difficult in practice to espouse a constitutional separation of powers between various state organs. In Ethiopia, this undemocratic tendency also manifested itself in the country's weak legislative, regulatory and enforcement mechanisms.[14] Rampant corruption also impeded political transformation. Institutions of state, including the judiciary and the legislature, fell under the absolute control of the EPRDF. With no military, legislative or other state institutions able or willing to resist the EPRDF abuses and misuse, autocratic elements captured the state.

Oversight by lawmakers remained a mere formality. The legislative body lacked the power or the institutional independence to monitor the overall political and constitutional accountability or budgetary duties of the executive. For all practical purposes, the judicial bodies were – and remain – almost non-existent in interventions on matters of judicial review concerning complaints about decisions and actions by the state and its security institutions. State institutions were more likely to get their instructions from the EPRDF's top leadership than from constitutional bodies such as the parliament and cabinet, and officials became more accountable to the party than to state decision-making bodies. As long as the security sector was politically supervised by the EPRDF, neither the cabinet nor the government exercised control over it. Officials in the security and military establishments regularly reported to individuals and rarely appeared in parliament or the courts to report and present evidence when relevant cases arose.

This fusion between the image of the state and practice of the EPRDF became the main obstacle to constitutional transformation. Any leadership crisis within the ERPDF immediately turned into state-wide governmental paralysis and in consequence, over time the party turned to authoritarianism. The root cause of the problem was the ERPDF's decision to monopolise power in all branches, which in practice equated the party with the state.

Corruption, Decay and Schism

The monopoly of power claimed by the EPRDF weakened national accountability, regulatory and enforcement mechanisms, with the result that corruption became so endemic that a majority of Ethiopians believed and acted as though malfeasance were normal practice. Power and corruption kept the regime intact over the short term, but rival groups emerged, vying for more power and more money. Further hampering progress towards any meaningful reform, clean officials, citizens and foreigners were either forced to leave the country or simply resign themselves corrupt practices.

The most significant outcome is that the line dividing the EPRDF and the state became so thin that continuous internal squabbles within the EPRDF morphed into state-wide crises. Its primary victims were usually from within its own ranks and quite often from the highest levels of its political leadership.

Like other liberation movements, in the early days of its assumption of power, the EPRDF faced internal divisions, including the loss of significant 'old guard' supporters. The leaders of the armed struggle also became insular and alienated some coalition partners.[15] Despite these cracks, administrative power, control over resources and the internal political system of democratic centralism all held the EPRDF together. And, even as its ideological underpinnings were eroded, the party moved towards promoting a commonly shared vision attending to economic development and poverty eradication in the country. Thus, transforming itself into a (civil) democratic political party fit to govern a country became less of a priority for an outfit aiming at revolutionary transformation of the political economy.

Elections 2020: Litmus Test for the EPRDF's Transformation

Since the end of the Derg's military rule in 1991, Ethiopia has conducted six nationwide elections.[16] After the transitional government was established in May 1992, elections of national, regional and *Woreda* (district) council representatives were held. Two years later, in May 1994, a constitutional assembly was elected. Under the federal constitution, four multiparty elections were then conducted at five-year intervals in 1995, 2000, 2005 and 2010.

The presence of dozens of political parties registered at federal and regional states ensured diverse participation but did not make the elections competitive. Fewer than half of the registered parties regularly contested elections. Moreover, the ruling party had its affiliated political parties in all the regional states and ethnic communities, which almost always rallied behind its policy and programmes. Considered to be the most competitive of those held so far, the 2005 elections led to disputed results and violence. By contrast, local elections in April 2008 and the 2010 and 2015 elections were generally peaceful but uncompetitive. Since 2005, EPRDF has emerged as the winner of all the contested parliamentary seats.

Transformation Post-2018: EPRDF's Self-immolation

Since 2015, the EPRDF has faced popular protests that began as leadership crises within the party. Currently, cracks in the system have widened, exacerbating these crises and leading to a paralysis in government. The changes are attributable to opposition not from outside, but from within the party itself. They have been accelerated by the rise of populism, against a backdrop of renewed geopolitical competition between global superpowers.

At the heart of the EPRDF's internal fractures is an ideological bankruptcy, facilitated by the absence of a unifying leader with a sense of responsibility, control and vision. As it is, the ideological kinship of the coalition members of the EPRDF does not appear to be equally distributed. The late prime minister Meles Zenawi held the EPRDF together as a coalition and since his death the party seems to have been left without an anchor. Above all, a dearth of competence in the EPRDF and its ultimate (non-ideological) internal power struggles have led to fissures and fragmentation. The chain effect began with the TPLF's inward-looking and internal leadership schism, and a failure on the part of the EPRDF leadership to repair that division proved fatal because it left the party with a sole shared vision: to cling to power (and – perhaps – to some developmental work as well). These perhaps, were the cause of the fallout that led to the dissolution of the EPRDF and the rise of the Prosperity Party.

Armed Groups in Political Transition

Since the change of government in April 2018, most armed groups have denounced violence and announced their readiness to participate in peaceful electoral politics. Some of them, for example the OLF, may participate in the next elections (in 2020) – even as elements of their armed wings are fighting the forces of the state. When political parties formed by armed groups have contested elections, they have influenced the level of participation, competition and electoral integrity (as happened in 1995 when the OLF and EPRDF traded accusations as a result of which the OLF boycotted the elections).

Ethiopia is entering a post-EPRDF dominated era with the possibility of coalition politics on the horizon. However, the kind of institutions that could regulate competitive coalition politics do not exist. The security sector, including its defence element, has shown itself to be more apprehensive than ever and remains prone to fragmentation unless it is insulated from schisms within the ruling party.

Nevertheless, recent crises should not overshadow the progress Ethiopia has made in recent decades under EPRDF, both in terms of economic development and political stability. Since April 2018, when a new administration took office, Ethiopia has taken drastic measures to address the problem of armed groups by removing them from its terrorist list. Partly as a result of rapprochement with Eritrea, many such groups, together with exiled opposition leaders, have been invited back into the country. Consequently, entities including the OLF, the ONLF, the Afar People Liberation Front (APLF), TPDM and Ginbot 7 are back in the country.

Current changes were designed to be less of a revolution than a reform and as a result may bring a degree of instability. Political leaders in both the ruling and opposition parties are pushing their luck by playing a waiting game, preparing to seize the initiative at the most opportune moment.

There still remain concerns as to whether or not the reform process is indeed informed by a conscious roadmap for the delivery of a new Ethiopia. Meanwhile a new EPRDF leadership is attempting to work out a compromise between demands for democratisation on the one hand and holding on to power on the other. Whereas the old EPRDF was allergic to protest and opposition, the new party seems to be in a hurry to adopt most of the positions advanced by protesters and opposition parties.

In consequence the official policy of the government is so muddled with that of the opposition that the differences between the social base and political constituency of the EPRDF and that of the various opposition groups are not clearly delineated. Some of the positions held by opposition parties such as the OLF are closer to those of the TPLF than to those of the latter's fellow coalition members, the ODP and the Amhara Democratic Party (ADP). Further complicating the issue, the current ODP leadership shares more political platforms with Ginbot 7 than it does with its old ally, the TPLF. All this makes for something of a political quagmire as it becomes difficult to differentiate the ruling party from its opposition. Against this background, the EPRDF leadership has two options. Either it can continue to focus on electoral reform regardless of its implications for the future of what is left of the EPRDF; or it can reconstitute the EPRDF based on a new social base and constituency before the next elections. Either course would have serious implications for various elements in the EPRDF (mainly for the ODP and ADP, which would be the most affected due to their facing stiff electoral competition in the Amhara, Oromia and SSNPR regions). The TPLF may face some competition in urban areas but this is likely to be so insignificant as to offer no serious challenge to its dominance.

Re-emergence of Armed Groups

Armed groups are widely seen as a danger to national stability. For this reason, the decision to allow political groupings such as the OLF and its armed wing OLA to return to Ethiopia without some arrangement for disarmament and demobilisation is puzzling. In a similar vein, recent clashes in parts of Oromia between the armed forces and OLA may be the result of a poorly-planned and implemented peace deal between the OLF and the Ethiopian army – a deal which defies logic and disregards lessons from history, including Ethiopia's own recent history. Peace cannot be expected to last when an armed group outside the purview of the state functions in parallel to the national army, the federal police and the regional state police. In this case, the government's logic is clear: the national army aims to quickly swallow the armed groups operating beyond its remit, either through integration into its own structures or by demilitarising and demobilising them. But the groups themselves invariably try to stay intact so as to enhance their clout and continue to deploy their armed wings as a political bargaining chip. One consequence has been that subsequent to some armed clashes, the OLF and its supporters have accused the leadership of the ODP, a part of the ruling coalition, of failing to honour an agreement signed with the ODF in Asmara before the latter's return to Ethiopia. The altercation between the OLF and ODP in the regional state of Oromia was symptomatic of a deep mutual distrust, mainly due to competition between the parties ahead of upcoming state elections.

Conclusion

The current crisis in Ethiopia and its security apparatus is an outcome of the EPRDF's inability to transform itself into a political party detached from challenges in the security sector. This can partly be attributed to the paralysis within the ruling party. Benefits and risks attach to the participation of armed groups in elections. However, the risks associated with exclusion outweigh those arising from participation. Inclusive processes have a better chance of success than do those with limitations on the participation of such disruptive elements in the political process, in particular in elections.

Since their return to Ethiopia and their engagement in peaceful political competition, armed groups and opposition parties have been given the chance to influence the national political process. If they remain within that process it should prove possible both to consolidate and extend political tolerance and to move toward constitutional democracy. Turning the highest commanders of guerrilla groups into party political leaders remains largely the responsibility of the state. In order to avoid a return of opposition parties to the armed struggle, some incentivised infrastructure and regulatory enforcement mechanisms should be set up well before the 2020 elections. The leaders of armed groups should be given a chance to appreciate the advantages of their peaceful participation in political contestation.

At the same time, rank and file members of armed groups should be offered adequate social and institutional incentives disassociated from political lines and loyalties. There could well be cases in which factionalism and new alignments may emerge in the electoral process, and such a development should not be condemned. As an example, the recent denunciation by the OLF's military wing OLA of one of the OLF's political leadership could cause its disintegration. Such cases demonstrate the fragility of an organisation in transition. A recognition that the leadership of a dissident group has no effective command and control in place (nor, perhaps, communications), shifts the responsibility for consulting with such factions on to the state. The groups themselves also have to understand the legal consequences of violating peace agreements and already-arrived-at constitutional arrangements.

Ideally there should be a cessation of hostilities on the part of the federal government and all regional states, political parties and armed groups. Such a ceasefire might include renunciation of violence, of possession and use of weaponry, of military training and of hate speech. Should the various interests cease hostilities, engage constructively and sign a transparent agreement inclusive of all political parties and armed groups, with robust and coercive compliance mechanisms, an arrangement could be arrived at that could ultimately end with the containment, registration, disarmament, selection and training of armed groups towards integration with statutory forces; and with the demobilisation of insurgents and their incorporation into regular regional police or the federal security sector.

More importantly, such a pact would move the country forward to a sustainable peace. Stability and legitimacy should be pursued together, without sacrificing legitimacy for the sake of stability. Such unfavourable circumstances would require the adoption of some positions that are less than ideal, and demand approaches such as the inclusion of ethnic and religious representatives with the vision and plan to move through time from sectarian representation to democratic citizenship. Only if the dialogue is reflective of the hopes and fears of all segments of the society can the national constitutive dialogue in Ethiopia enjoy any popular legitimacy through the constituent assembly. *Carpe diem*: if the moment can be seized, the current crisis of legitimacy can be turned into an opportunity to transform Ethiopia both politically and constitutionally.

Notes

1. Staff Reporter, 'The EPRDF Officially Ends; The Prosperity Party Begins', *Ezega News*, 26/12/2019, accessed on 6/9/2020, at: https://bit.ly/2Dy6cwY
2. Ibid.
3. Sarah Vaughan, 'Ethnicity and Power in Ethiopia', Ph.D. Dissertation, University of Edinburgh, Edinburgh, 2003.
4. 'Ethiopian Communist Party is Set up, with Mengistu at the Helm', *The New York Times*, 11/9/1984, accessed on 6/9/2020, at: https://nyti.ms/3lXgbNG
5. Forrest D. Colburn, 'The Tragedy of Ethiopia's Intellectuals', *The Antioch Review*, vol. 47, no. 2 (1989), pp. 133–45.
6. Mulugeta Gebrehiwot Berhe, *Laying the Past to Rest: The EPRDF and the Challenges of Ethiopian State Building* (London: Hurst & Company, 2019).
7. Terrence Lyons, 'Closing the Transition: The May 1995 Elections in Ethiopia', *The Journal of Modern African Studies*, vol. 34, no. 1 (1996), pp. 121–42.
8. Ibid.

9. Ibid., pp. 121–3.

10. Berhe.

11. See: Ch. 1, this volume.

12. Lyons, pp. 125–32.

13. Ibid.

14. Mehari Taddele Maru, 'In-depth Analysis: The Tigray Dilemma', *Addis Standard*, 23/9/2019, accessed on 7/9/2020, at: https://bit.ly/2GtYZPA

15. Tom Gardner, 'Will Abiy Ahmed's Bet on Ethiopia's Political Future Pay Off?', *Foreign Policy*, 21/1/2020, acceseed on 7/9/2020, at: https://bit.ly/3lXeq3b

16. Mehari Taddele Maru, 'A Basic Introduction to Ethiopian Electoral System', paper presented at the EU Delegation to Ethiopia, Addis Ababa, January 2014.

13

TRANSFORMATIONS OF ARMED NONSTATE ACTORS: ENDURING CHALLENGES AND STRATEGIC IMPLICATIONS

Omar Ashour

Comparative Pasts versus Uncertain Futures

The various chapters of this book have highlighted some of the challenges, complications and implications of initiating and sustaining collective transformations towards non-violent, socio-political activism. The first two chapters provided first-hand testimonies from co-leaders of transformation processes towards non-violence. These testimonies showed that the implications of the ANC's and IG's collective transformations are as different as their ideologies, behaviours and organisational structures and sizes. The ANC won its political war by ballots; the IG did not. The ANC is not a designated foreign terrorist organisation;[1] the IG still is.[2] Yet despite the major differences, the determinants causing their collective transformations were very similar: the critical roles of leadership, combat costs and pressures, interactions and inducements. The macro-level variables of democratisation and regional/international support had different values in these two cases. The degree of democratisation in Egypt was almost always well below that of South Africa, including high levels of state repression, a corrupt and unreformed security sector, unbalanced civil–military relations and the absence of a serious transitional justice process in Egypt (including the 2011–13 fragile democratisation period). The relatively progressive ideology and rhetoric of the ANC, its anti-apartheid cause, and some of its propaganda and tactics yielded major regional and international support. In comparison, the IG's overall ideology and the public upholding of terrorism both rhetorically and behaviourally during the 1980s and 1990s produced the exact opposite outcome: international condemnation and limited national support. To pursue collective de-radicalisation, the organisation had to primarily rely on its own resources and on relatively limited international and national support for its transformation, up to 2002 and after the 9/11 terrorist attacks. At the time of writing – and as detailed in the first two chapters – the transformations to non-violence are being challenged by social and political developments in both countries. The status of collective de-radicalisation is far from a *fait accompli* or an 'end of history'.

The cases of collective transformations in the Arab-majority world also highlight a few comparative nuances. In Syria, the three armed Islamist organisations examined in Chapter Four showed how ideological, rhetorical, behavioural and organisational transformations *below* de-radicalisation can happen *during* an armed conflict, as opposed to after its outcome (defeat, draw, or victory). In Iraq, meanwhile, the Mahdi Army exhibited various organisational, behavioural and contextual peculiarities even when compared with other Iraqi militias associated with political parties. The experience of the organisation's transformation and factionalisation show that a 'military defeat' – even state repression – remains essential to recalculations of the strategic costs of combat by a charismatic leader. In Egypt, the complex and dynamic relationship between the Muslim Brothers and political violence shows the nuances of this organisation, in contrast with some of the established patterns in the literature.[3] Sustained and reactive state repression – as exemplified by the 2013 military coup and its aftermath – did not yield a complete collective armed radicalisation of the movement, as in other cases examined in this book. The role of leadership and internal interactions – including factional infighting – has been critical in curbing a collective transformation towards upholding political violence.

The Western European cases of the Provisional IRA and ETA have also exhibited some important nuances. The Provisional IRA in particular was a part of a more sustained transformation over a longer period of time compared to the Middle Eastern cases. However, the challenges posed by Brexit, the relative decline of European liberal-centrism and the relative rise of right-wing populism serve as stark reminders of the political sensitivity of collective de-radicalisation and transformation processes. In such a context, regional support (in this case the EU's critical and sustained incentives for these trans-formations) can be undermined by political change. In the South Asian case of the (Afghan) Taliban, the outcome may be even bleaker. Whereas the Taliban has evidently changed some elements of its rhetoric, ideology and behaviour during its almost two decades of its insurgency, Johnson argues that there are no signs of a comprehensive de-radicalisation process. Ideologically, the local war remains between the Islamic Republic of Afghanistan (Afghan govern-ment) and the Islamic Emirate of Afghanistan (Afghan-Taliban insurgents); the local environment in which both sides operate have and will remain to have a major impact on their ideological transformations or lack thereof. Yet, regional support to peace and transformations – especially Qatari peace diplomacy and persistent mediation – has transformed and may continue to incentivise transformation of the behaviours and the organisational structures of the Taliban.

The cases of collective transformations – from bullets to ballots – in Latin America provide valuable lessons and empirical cases of how collec-tive de-radicalisation was initiated, sustained and undermined. As Marchesi's chapter and Rushdi's testimony have shown, the interactions of the unarmed traditional Left and the armed revolutionary Left in Latin American in the 1970s and 1980s are comparable to the interactions (and even to the out-bidding) between the status-quo-tolerating, gradualist Muslim Brothers and anti-status-quo radical Islamists in the same period. As Marchesi concludes, several governing parties in Argentina, Bolivia, Brazil and Uruguay were either connected or directly involved in armed activism. The two former presidents of Uruguay and Brazil were former guerrillas who led or supported the transformations and de-radicalisation of their own networks. Similar political profiles of leading politicians existed in Argentina and Bolivia. In Chile, Heraldo Munoz, who was a former member of the Socialist Party's armed apparatus, became the country's foreign minister in 2014 and – before that – represented Chile in the United Nations and presided over the U.N.'s al-Qaida/Taliban Sanctions Committee.[4] His insightful personal memoirs of the Pinochet years and its aftermath is by itself a story of Latin American indi-vidual and collective transformations towards non-violence.[5] In Colombia, between 2003 and 2014, over 60,000 combatants – at least 19,000 of whom were former guerrillas in the FARC – abandoned armed organisations, either as factions or as individuals.[6] The remaining guerrillas of the FARC (14,500 fighters approximately) demobilised between 2014 and 2016. Hundreds of ex-combatants sought to enter non-violent, constitutional politics, many of whom sought political party independence from their former commanders.[7] The collective transformations from bullets to ballots in Colombia yielded two tracks: non-violent political movements ideologically aligned with former armed groups and politically independent non-violent movements unaligned with (and even critical of) the former armed groups, whether left- or right-wing.[8] As elsewhere, collective de-radicalisation and transformations towards non-violence in Colombia face major sustainability challenges, including social and political reintegration,[9] collective recidivism and re-joining of armed groups,[10] continuous revenge-violence and vendetta assassinations,[11] and limited support and mixed messages among the current political leadership of the country (at the time of writing).[12]

Overall, although major progress has been made worldwide in terms of initiating, sustaining and understanding collective de-radicalisation and transformations towards non-violent activism – in both academic and practitioner circles – major challenges can still impede or even completely undo that progress. To highlight the challenges and opportunities in light of revising our understanding of collective de-radicalisation, this concluding chapter outlines summary reflections and remarks in following second section. In the third and final section, it proceeds to outline some of the strategic implications of the transformations from bullets to ballots.

Reflections on the Study of Collective De-radicalisation

From the chapters and the sections above, a few concluding thoughts can be deduced about the major variables affecting the initiation and the sustainability of de-radicalisation processes. The following subsections revisit each of the six meso- and macro-level variables and the complimentary synergy between them.

On Leadership

Leadership – whether represented by one charismatic leader or a central command structure – remains a decisive variable in the success or the failure of the initiation of the collective transformation processes examined. The authors of the previous chapters have shown different types and critical roles of leadership in transformation processes. These roles do not only include initiating and legitimating the collective transformation, but also creating a narrative for it, undermining spoilers, proffering hope and incentives as role models, and even directly engaging in counterterrorism and counterinsurgency policies.

In South Africa, both Kasrils and Simpson, despite their different assessments of the ANC and MK's trajectory, agree on the decisive role of Nelson Mandela's charismatic leadership. In Egypt, Rushdi's testimony shows a different type of leadership: the IG's central command structure – representing ideological leaders as opposed to organisational commanders – was able to bestow legitimacy on a multi-dimensional comprehensive de-radicalisation process and force it through the rank-and-file, having contained would-be spoilers as well as high-level organisational commanders and mid-rankers who opposed the transformation.[13] Spoilers can be internal or external to the transforming organisation. For example, Kasrils highlighted the role of external spoilers from within the status-quo's forces, as well as from the anti-status quo forces (IFP factions). Inaccurate and outdated intelligence reports could be manipulated to mislead the status-quo leadership (as was the case with the former South African President F. W. de Klerk) and thereby undermine or spoil support for the transformation process. Similar internal and external spoiling attempts have been demonstrated elsewhere, and either countered or foiled by the leadership. One violent example comes from Algeria. In the summer of 1997, negotiations were ongoing for a ceasefire that ultimately yielded a pragmatic de-radicalisation and a civil peace process. The negotiations were held between the former deputy head of the Department of Intelligence and Security (DRS), the late General Smain Lamari, and the commander of the Islamic Salvation Army (AIS), Madani Mezrag. While the negotiations were going on, several AIS detained affiliates and relatives of AIS guerrillas were summarily executed in the area of Umm al-Thalathin,[14] which is close to some of the hills controlled at the time by the armed organisation.[15] Mezrag interpreted this act as an attempt by rival factions in the military establishment to 'drive his followers crazy' before the talks: 'they wanted to tell us that the authorities have no intention to reach a resolution . . . and possibly drive one of our men to kill their delegate [General Lamari]', he recalled.[16] Due to this incident and others, the AIS leadership control was tested. It was relatively successful in limiting the spoilers' impact and in controlling its militiamen. In the case of the Provisional IRA, Clubb has shown how leaders can construct a framing narrative to foster both organisational and societal support for the transformation, just as radicalisers and political entrepreneurs construct frames to identify grievances and violent 'solutions' to these grievances.[17] On both the collective and the individual levels, leaders can serve as role-models incentivising non-violent transformations. As Marchesi has shown, the case of José Mujica of the Tupamaros serves as a contrast between rhetoric and behaviour: although he has not recanted his guerrilla past, he nonetheless fully endorses non-violent activism and a democratic status quo (including a free market). Like Mandela, Mujica represented a role model: donating a large part of his salary, with no material interests dictating his actions, and directly engaging with the common people and – perhaps most importantly for political activists – winning parliamentary and presidential elections via ballots, not bullets. Like in the Middle East, West Europe and Sub-Saharan Africa, former militants have also taken roles in counterterrorism and counterinsurgency in Latin America. This was represented by the Public Security Coordinating Council in Chile, which was headed by the former socialist militant Marcelo Schilling and assisted by other former militants.

The *sustainability* of non-violent transformation and collective de-radicalisation processes remains a different variable compared to *initiation*. The roles of leaders/leadership are crucial in both. Yet, in sustainability, these roles are likely to be diminished by time and socio-political developments. In addition to the cases discussed in the previous chapters, diminished influence is especially the case when the leadership of a de-radicalised organisation attempts to influence an armed, radical one during an ongoing insurgency. One example comes from the Sinai insurgency in Egypt during the fragile democratisation period of February 2011 to July 2013.[18] In 2012,

288 | OMAR ASHOUR

the IG leaders in Egypt attempted and failed to de-escalate the insurgency mainly because of their revisions and their de-radicalisation process. 'Those guys [specific IG leaders were named] signed the revisions [ideological basis for collective de-radicalisation/initiative for ceasing violence] and supported it. They are considered "snitches" by many jihadists', a former detainee from Sinai stated. [19] Despite their impact in the 2000s over the IG rank-and-file and other armed Islamist organisations, in the 2010s the IG leaders had limited influence over other violent Islamist organisations.

Finally, leadership remains only *one* crucial variable, whether on the state or the nonstate side(s). There are outliers, where charismatic leaders existed on both the incumbent and the insurgent sides, wanted a de-escalation process within a certain timeframe but other variables intervened to fail the initiation and/or the sustainability. De-radicalisation then never happened. Perhaps a good example of this would be the Turkey–PKK peace process of 2012/2013–15, which was initially supported by charismatic leaders on both the incumbent and the insurgent sides (the then Prime Minister Recep Tayyib Erdogan and the PKK founder Abdullah Ocalan, respectively). Yet, the process collapsed by 2015 due to other variables discussed below. [20]

On Combat Pressures: The Firefight Factor

Some elements of Edward Luttwak's controversial *Foreign Affairs* article titled 'Give War a Chance' do apply here. [21] In almost all cases discussed in this book, both the incumbent and the insurgent sides were bloodied and exhausted by firefights and other forms of armed confrontations. More interestingly, the combat costs and pressures have engendered behavioural, ideological, organisational-institutional and even legal-constitutional changes among the state and the nonstate sides, *regardless* of the insurgency outcome (defeat, draw or victory). In defeats or close-to-defeats, the cases of the IG in Egypt, the AIS in Algeria, the Mahdi Army in Iraq, ETA in Spain and all of the South American Cone armed leftist cases in Chile, Argentina, Uruguay and Brazil stand out in terms of the behavioural, ideological, organisational changes and transformations. In these same cases, however, despite the victory or the near-victory of the status-quo forces, armed state actors incurred costs, attempted to de-escalate and sometimes to reform, and – in multiple cases – attempted to shun a replay of the confrontations via deliberate policies and procedures. In draws, near-draws or 'constructed' draws,[22] such as the cases of the ANC-MK in South Africa, the FMLN in El-Salvador, and – arguably – the FARC in Colombia and the Provisional IRA in the United Kingdom, the impacts of violence costs and combat pressures on the collective state institutional and nonstate organisational behaviours were even clearer as outlined in the previous chapters. Even in some of the cases when the insurgents were victorious, either coalition politics (Ethiopia in 1991 and onwards) or electoral democratic politics (Nicaragua in 1990 and, arguably, up to 2014 or 2016)[23] had to be pursued by the victorious insurgents to either contain/de-escalate existing conflicts or to avoid future rounds of combat. Perhaps the Nicaraguan case clearly illustrates this. After the Sandinistas (SNLF) lost the elections in February 1990 to a coalition of parties known as the National Opposition Union (UNO) and led by Violeta Barrios de Chamorro, the then SNLF leader and Nicaraguan President, Daniel Ortega, accepted the defeat and handed over power. Combat costs and pressures (and regional and international support for a non-violent transition) were at the heart of this outcome.[24] Chamorro's promise to end the unpopular military draft and bring about civil reconciliation, alongside her warnings that the Contra insurgency and combat operations would continue if the SNLF remained in power, contributed to getting the UNO 54.7 per cent of the popular vote against the SNLF's 40.8 per cent. Finally, the three cases examined within Syria's armed Islamist opposition and the case of the Afghan Taliban have demonstrated nuanced ideological, rhetorical and behavioural changes, all relevant to collective de-radicalisation but still below it. These changes were engendered, evolved and continued to develop *during* combat, under its ongoing pressures and before the combat finally concludes with an outcome.

On Interactions: Messages, Messengers and Mediums

As shown in the previous testimonies and chapters, combat pressure was not the only factor that impacted both nonstate and state leadership and forced them to politically learn, strategically recalculate and ideologically update. Interactions with non-like-minded organisations and individuals (external) and between the layers of same organisations (internal) had a clear impact as well. As shown, the impacts of the interactions were maximised under the pressure of combat and/or other pressured environments, such as prisons or exiles. Whether it was the negotiation within the framework of the 'Convention for a Democratic South Africa (CODESA)', prison talks with the IG leadership to debate the 'theological legitimacy' of the 'Initiative for Ceasing Violence', or intense debates between civil society leaders and leftist guerrillas in Latin America; internal and external interactions under pressure were crucial in shaping the updated ideology, rhetoric, behaviour and organisational transformations. The cases of the IG in Egypt and the Provisional IRA have shown different types of interactions in the aftermath of abandoning arms. In terms of inter-organisational external interactions, the IG leaders attempts to influence other armed Islamists, including attempts to deradicalise factions and individuals from the Egyptian Jihad Organisation and even al-Qaida.[25] In terms of organisational–community interactions, former combatants in Northern Ireland played an important role in the transition to peace, particularly at the community level as demonstrated by Clubb in Chapter Seven.

Generally, former leaders and mid-ranks in organisations such as the MK, the IG, the LIFG, the AIS, the Provisional IRA, ETA, the Tupamaros, the FMLN and others represented credible messengers to new generations and communities who may underestimate the costs of political violence or overvalue the legitimacy and/or the allure of it. The 'messages' conveyed in these interactions varied, depending on the audience, ideology, ethnicity, religion and other peculiarities of the context (perhaps most importantly the *very* local one; sometimes as local as the town, the neighbourhood or the village level). The credibility and the impact of the message partly depended on the identity of the message-bearers. One example from an internal organisational interaction in Egypt may illustrate the importance of the 'messenger' as opposed to the 'message'. As the former commander of the IG's armed wing put it,

> hearing the [theological/moral/instrumental] arguments directly from the Sheikhs [IG leaders] was different . . . do you think I did not hear this [the tailored message] before? . . . we heard those arguments from the [nonviolent] Salafists and from al-Azhar [official religious institution in Egypt] . . . we did not accept them . . . we accepted them from the Sheikhs because we knew them and we knew their history.[26]

While the identity and the background of the 'messenger' is critical in these interactions, it is also important that the 'messages' are tailored for both the audience and the local context. Both internal and external interactions usually involve a new/updated narrative with a message(s) that has – at least – five dimensions: political, historical, socio-psychological, instrumental and moral-religious (religious interpretations are involved if the organisation employs/employed theological foundations for its ideology such as the IG, the Lord's Resistance Army, Aum Shinrikyo and others). To legitimate violence, the political dimension emphasises the various types of grievances which a particular group can suffer, while clearly identifying the culprit(s). To root that dimension further, specific historical episodes are selected to give the political part a historical legitimacy. This is usually emboldened by a socio-psychological dimension to empower the armed challengers of the existing status-quo, with a focus on the glorification of violent acts, including terrorism, and their perpetrators. The violent acts are usually directly linked to the political and historical grievances. The instrumental dimension promotes the effectiveness of violent methods in achieving social and political goals and alleviating the grievances. Finally, the moral-religious dimension emphasises the moral-religious 'legitimacy' and even the moral-religious 'duty' to react to the socio-political and the historical grievances. Any ethical or moral issues are addressed within that dimension as well. During the interactions to de-radicalise/transform, both the message(s) and the messenger(s) challenge and/or offer nuances to all of the aforementioned dimensions. This includes undoing any ready-made, swift and easy pro-violence ideological answers to complex questions and valid grievances. The edge some of these 'messengers' may have is that they hold a very good understanding of the peculiarities of the ideology and the ontology, the internal factional maps of the organisations or the communities/audiences with which/whom they are interacting, and the nuances of the context(s) in which they operate. The validity of some or all of the grievances (depending on which case) is usually recognised and upheld with an offer of an alternative unarmed methods to address those grievances, in addition to highlighting the legitimacy and the effectiveness of non-violent social and political activism. Finally, the mediums within which these interactions occur, through which the messages are conveyed and where the messengers are operating are also important for the impact/effectiveness and propagation/dissemination. *Pressured environments* (such as prisons, exiles and rugged strongholds), state and nonstate sponsored talks within *safe environments,* online *virtual environments* and other media platforms have all been used during these interactions and had varying impacts. Lessons learned from online and other interactions models, successes and failures of prison and exile interactions and other forms of interaction in different mediums and environments remain one area of research that still merits further investigation.

On Inducements

As a reminder, selective inducements are any explicit or implicit socio-political/socioeconomic incentives proffered by local, regional or international actor(s) to the transforming organisation in exchange for behavioural, ideological and/or organisational changes towards non-violence. The quantity and the quality of the inducements are related to the combat effectiveness/performances of the incumbent and the insurgent forces, as well as to the conflict outcomes.[27] As a result, they can range from enhancing prison conditions (usually if the status-quo forces are effective and dominating the combat) to a power-sharing formula for participation in the government or a negotiated transition of power (if the anti-status-quo forces are dominating the combat or effective enough to reach a draw or a victory). A good contrast would be the IG in Egypt or the AIS in Algeria versus the FARC in Colombia or the Taliban in Afghanistan. Despite this conclusion, in almost all cases discussed in this book incentives were proffered to the organisations, factions or individuals who de-radicalised regardless of the conflict outcome. The Middle Eastern and the South American cases may further illustrate the latter observation. In Egypt, Algeria and Iraq, despite the failures of the insurgencies of the IG, the AIS and the Mahdi Army to achieve their strategic goals, the status-quo forces had to offer either socioeconomic and/or political incentives to induce, incentivise and support collective de-radicalisation. In South America, the post-authoritarian elected governments in Chile, Argentina and Uruguay offered compensations, as well as the opportunity and the legitimacy for social and political activism of former guerrillas despite their previous defeats. Overall, the selective inducements bolster the position of leaders who support collective de-radicalisation relative to those who oppose the process within a once armed organisation. If sustained, these inducements also serve as disincentives to reversals towards violence. In many instances however, reversals did occur when either the expectations were not met or agreements were not upheld in classic 'commitment problems' and 'security dilemmas'.[28] Perhaps, the most recent example of these 'commitment problems' shown during the writing of this chapter is that of the FARC in Colombia.[29]

On Democratisation and Security Sector Reform (SSR)

If selective inducements incentivise transformations towards non-violence at the organisational level (meso-level), democratisation pursues state- and macro-level reforms as complex as democratic control of the armed forces, including oversight and accountability as well as the overall SSR. Sometimes, processes of transitional justice are included within a democratisation process (such as the 'trials of the Junta' in Argentina) or even within a leading mature democracy (such as the Saville Report in the United Kingdom). From the previous chapters and other cases, the impact of democratisation on the transformation from bullets to ballots is generally positive in terms of both initiation and sustainability. Specific processes necessary for successful democratisation – namely SSR and DDR – were either a condition for transformation, as in the cases of South Africa, El Salvador and Colombia, or supported the sustainability of the process as in other cases. There are exceptions, however.

Generally, democratic systems serve as non-violent conflict resolution mechanisms by which the contestation for power is done by non-violent, (liberal) constitutional means. Given the non-violent, inclusive nature of the system(s), Keefer and Getmansky consistently found that democracies are less than half as likely to experience armed insurgency onsets compared to non-democracies.[30] The regime-type – democratic or non-democratic – impacts the incumbents' and the insurgents' initial decision to become involved in combat as well as whether to escalate or de-escalate the levels of political violence, including state repression and nonstate terrorism.[31] As we have seen in the previous chapters, the relationship however can be more complicated.

Democracy has other impacts. The 'combat costs' do transcend the organisational and state leadership and do have implications for the electorate.

In Colombia, 6.43 million citizens rejected a peace agreement between the incumbent government and the FARC insurgents in October 2016, against 6.38 million citizens who supported it (most of whom were residents of regions affected by the conflict).[32] The referendum was supposed to inaugurate the transformation of the FARC towards non-violent politics. When the FARC did transform in March 2018, it was 'punished' at the ballot box. It only secured 0.38 per cent of the overall votes; any myths about rural or periphery popular support were shattered. Support for the peace agreement and the transformation of the FARC did not mean support for the FARC itself.[33] Still, the transformed organisation was granted five seats in the senate and 5 seats in the house of representatives, as per the peace agreement. In Uruguay, the Filtro violent episode and the alleged support of ETA's suspects might have cost the Frente Amplio and its candidate Tabaré Vázquez the 1994 presidential elections. During Libya's first ever free and fair elections in July 2012, the LIFG had to split supporting votes between two factions: the Homeland Party, led by the LIFG's former commander Abd al-Hakim Belhaj and the Centrist Nation Party, led by the LIFG's former ideologue Sami al-Saadi. The first party did not secure any seats and the second secured only one seat in the General National Congress. The 'stain' of direct involvement in nonstate violence – even though Qaddafi's state violence and international terrorism was of a different scale and intensity – coupled with the fear that 'Taliban-like' laws would be implemented in the country – have pushed the overall voting behaviour against former jihadists.[34]

In a way, democratisation in these cases has served as both a structural inducement and a punishment. Its inducement stems from state-level structural changes, which allow political inclusion, promote the legitimacy of non-violent activism and the transformations towards it, support security sector reform (successfully, partially or unsuccessfully), *may* address past violations and allow for the holding of periodic free and fair elections. The punishment for using violence or for allegedly supporting it occurs during the latter, at the ballot box.[35]

On International and Regional Support

International and regional support (or lack thereof) for the transformations towards non-violence is the other critical macro-level variable. As demonstrated throughout this book, both initiation and sustainability for collective de-radicalisation and transformation processes have either directly benefited from, or were undermined by, international and regional varying interventions. In Western Europe and (mainly post-Cold War) Latin America, regional and international powers were more likely to directly support the transformations, and less likely to undermine or spoil it. This has been demonstrated by the critical role of the European Union in supporting the Provisional IRA's transformation to non-violence, in softening the borders between the UK and Ireland and in investing to sustain the transformation and financing other peacebuilding activities. Although its role was significantly diminished in the case of ETA, the European Union was still relatively supportive of the peace process in the Basque country.[36] The United States, especially under the Clinton administration, also had a strong supportive role and took significant risks in the case of Northern Ireland.[37]

In post-Cold War Latin America, and for different reasons, both the United States and Cuba were either directly supportive of the transformations or did not invest in spoiling them (depending on a case-by-case policy). The United States congress threatened to freeze funds when El Salvador's right-wing incumbents attempted to impede voter registration in areas supportive of the leftist FMLN insurgents and therefore both undermine their transformation to a political party and threaten a peace agreement and a fragile democratic transition process.[38] Similar US policies were pursued in Guatemala. Cuba was the host and a mediator between the Colombian government, the FARC and the ELN rebels and ultimately supported the transformation of the former M-19 guerrillas.[39] The Organisation of American States (OAS) was also supportive of multiple cases of transformations and peace processes, including the 2016 Colombian peace agreement and the transformation of the FARC into a legitimate political party.[40] This can be starkly contrasted with the cases of the Middle East and South Asia, where both international powers and regional states have almost always conflicting policies and regional interstate organisations such as the Arab League have either a negligible or a negative role. Overall, it is not an uncommon policy in either of the two regions – from Algeria to Afghanistan – to invest in spoiling collective transformation processes towards non-violence. Whereas there is significant research available on nonstate spoilers of peace agreements and transformations to non-violence, there is relatively limited scholarly research (as opposed to partisan and opinion pieces) on states acting as spoilers.

Concluding Observations and Strategic Implications

The 'Arab Spring' has provided scholars and practitioners with several important lessons about how changes within socio-political environments can affect transformations towards unarmed activism. The success of mainly unarmed civil resistance tactics in bringing down two authoritarian regimes in Tunisia (2010, 2011) and Egypt (2011) has briefly undermined the rationale that violence is the most effective (and, according to some ideologies, the most legitimate) means of bringing about social and political change. However, the transformation of the uprisings in Libya and Syria in 2011 and onward, and the regional developments in Iraq (during and after April 2013) and Egypt (during and after July 2013) have led to different conclusions: soft power and civil resistance tactics have their limits and, to pursue real change, hard power is necessary. In such an environment, radicalisation, recruitment and ideological frames supportive of political violence are more likely to grow, survive and expand. Still, a few policy implications can be offered to stakeholders and end-users.

Firstly, in the Arab world, almost all of the once-armed large groups upheld their transformation from armed to unarmed activism during the brief period of the 'Arab Spring'. This should not be taken for granted and should certainly be treated as a strategic gain that could have implications at both national and regional levels. [41] Like the Colombian cases (from the M-19 to the FARC) and other Latin American ones, lessons learned through research and practice should be upheld to promote sustainability and continuity, and to avoid reverting back to political violence. The lessons can be organised within interdisciplinary, scholar–practitioner–activist forums with the aim of garnering both practical lessons and state-of-the-art scholarship about transformations to non-violent activism and collective de-radicalisation on a regional and global scale. Many of these forums and events have already been conducted, bringing together academics, officials, practitioners and leaders of the transformations to share experiences form different standpoints. It is important, however, that they continue to be organised on a regular basis in order to act as a brainstorming hub on future scenarios, trajectories, initiations and the sustainability of transformation processes to unarmed activism, with regular forecasts and policy implications and recommendations based on a global, comparative and critical perspectives.

Secondly, a key lesson learned is how popular support for national reconciliation, compromise, inclusion and general de-escalation is crucial to collective de-radicalisation and transformations to unarmed activism. Popular support for national reconciliations is a variable and should not be taken for granted. It can be diminished by populist politicians, demagogues, warlords, state and nonstate violent extremists, hysteric media and regressive education. But it can certainly be enhanced partly by a responsible elite, progressive education, professional free media and a strategy to deal with spoilers.[42]

Thirdly, media campaigns that promote reconciliation, compromise, inclusion and general de-escalation are essential to support transitions to unarmed activism, as opposed to propaganda and narratives that promote social decohesion and sectarian polarisation. The same applies to education where there is a need – in many Arab states specifically – to promote the importance of national compromises between diverse components of the societies, civic peace and the supremacy of reconciliation via elementary, secondary and higher education. Essential elements of reformist curricula should include the understanding of the risks, implications – and even the de-glorification – of various forms of political violence (including military coups, state repression, civil wars and both state and nonstate terrorism) and the importance of non-violent conflict resolution mechanisms. Reformist curricula should also foster respect and celebrate diversity and difference of opinion with an emphasis on human security and its importance to state, regional and international security.[43]

Fourthly, SSR remains a critical factor. It comes out clearly from the chapters in this book that transitions from armed to unarmed activism are less likely to be sustained unless there is a thorough process of reforming the security sector, usually within a democratisation framework.[44] The reform process must entail changing standard operating procedures (SOPs), training and education curricula, leadership and promotion criteria, as well as oversight and accountability by elected and judicial institutions, and partly by civil society organisations. The violations of the security sector, and the lack of accountability to address such violations, have been a major contributor to sparking and sustaining nonstate political violence. Also, reconfiguring and rebalancing civil-military relations in such a way that armed state institutions become more accountable to elected and judicial authorities.[45] The supremacy of the armed over the elected and the judicial/constitutional has created a political context in which bullets are more significant than ballots and laws as methods for attaining and remaining in political power. Compared to arms and coups, votes, constitutions, good governance and socio-economic achievements are by far secondary means for attaining or remaining in power in several Arab countries.

Finally, though demobilisation, disarmament and reintegration processes are costly and difficult, they are certainly worth the investment. The politicisation of such a process and its failure in Libya and Yemen in the aftermath of the Libyan and Yemeni armed revolutions have led to the rise of multiple armed state and nonstate actors, unbound by any constitutional or legal frameworks. This DDR failure facilitated the necessary resources and logistics to warlords, violent extremists, ethnic, regional and sectarian armed entrepreneurs and their likes. DDR is an integral part of any transformation to unarmed activism and it is inherently connected to SSR, CMR and the organisational dimension of collective de-radicalisation. Most armed nonstate actors in post-conflict environments will refuse to disband and demobilise if there is no mutual trust or guarantees with the official armed institutions and armed state actors. This is especially the case when the latter has traditionally been above oversight, accountability and law. Hence, the sustainability of the transformation from bullets to ballots is also tied to DDR, on which the ultimate success or failure of the process depends.

All around the world, the problems of transformations from bullets to ballots have remained as complicated as ever and, in many cases, have faced more challenges. This book has proffered a focus on the determinants of initiation and sustainability of collective transformation and de-radicalisation processes. We have shown how these determinants have worked within multiple organisations and states. Hopefully, such understandings and lessons learned from the testimonies and the analytical chapters will help to curb or end political violence and to sustain a better peace.

Notes

1. However, Nelson Mandela remained on a US terrorism watchlist until 2008. See for example: Olivia B. Waxman, 'The U.S. Government Had Nelson Mandela on Terrorist Watch Lists Until 2008: Here's Why', *Time*, 18/7/2018, accessed on 10/12/2020, at: https://bit.ly/2JK78lc

2. At the time of writing of this book, the IG is still designated. See: 'Country Reports on Terrorism 2017', *United States Department of State* (2018), p. 292.

3. Omar Ashour, 'Will Egypt's Muslim Brotherhood Return to Political Violence?', *BBC*, 30/7/2014, accessed on 10/12/2020, at: https://bbc.in/3qJoDT9

4. Heraldo Munoz, *The Dictator's Shadow: Life Under Augusto Pinochet* (New York: Basic Books, 2008), pp. 15–17, 97.

5. Ibid.

6. Maria Jimena Duzan, 'Political Reintegration of Demobilised Combatants in Colombia', paper presented at the first annual conference of the Strategic Studies Unit entitled 'From Bullets to Ballots: Transformations from Armed to Unarmed Political Activism', Arab Centre for Research and Policy Studies, Doha, 3–4/11/2020.

7. Ibid.

8. Frank Pearl, conversation with the author, Doha, 4 November 2018.

9. 'Colombia: Killing of Rights Defenders, Social Leaders, Ex-fighters, Most Serious Threat to Peace', *UN News*, 14/7/2020, accessed on 10/12/2020, at: https://bit.ly/3qI4KvK

10. Nicholas Casey and Lara Jakes, 'Colombia's Former FARC Guerrilla Leader Calls for Return to War', *The New York Times*, 29/8/2019, accessed on 10/12/2020, at: https://nyti.ms/2K83C3K

11. Edith M. Lederer, 'UN Envoy Says Many Ex-Combatants in Colombia Being Killed', *U. S. News*, 14/10/2020, accessed on 10/12/2020, at: https://bit.ly/3m1XFT5

12. Juan Franco, 'Colombian President's Veto Threat Challenges Peace Process', *Just Security*, 7/3/2019, accessed on 10/12/2020, at: https://bit.ly/2VWEu2J; Juan Arredondo, 'The Slow Death of Colombia's Peace Movement', *The Atlantic*, 30/12/2019, accessed on 10/12/2020, at: https://bit.ly/3n3X2K5

13. See for example: Steven Stedman, 'The Spoiler Problems in Peace Processes', *International Security*, vol. 22 no. 22 (1997), pp. 5–53.

14. Known as the Umm al-Thalathin massacre; it occurred in July 1997.

15. 'A Meeting with Madani Mezraq: The National Emir of the Islamic Salvation Army', [in Arabic] *Mashahid wa Ara'*, Al-'Arabiya, 18/10/2004.

16. Ibid.

17. David Snow and Scott Byrd, 'Ideology, Framing Processes, and Islamic Terrorist Movements', *Mobilisation*, vol. 12, no. 2 (2007), pp. 119–36.

18. For an overview see: Omar Ashour, 'Sinai's Insurgency: Implications of Enhanced Guerilla Warfare', *Studies in Conflict and Terrorism*, vol. 42, no. 6 (2019), pp. 541–58.

19. Interview by author, Cairo. May 2012. See also: Omar Ashour, 'Jihadists and Post-Jihadists in the Sinai', *Foreign Policy*, 5/9/2012, accessed on 10/12/2020, at: https://bit.ly/3qGSgV7

20. See for example: James Reynolds, 'Abdullah Ocalan: A Bridge between Kurds and Turks?', *BBC*, 4/2/2013, accessed on 10/12/2020, at: https://bbc.in/2W1hzmQ; Jake Hess, 'Turkey's PKK Talks', *Foreign Policy*, 8/1/2013, accessed on 10/12/2020, at: https://bit.ly/37NO6lT; Murat Yesiltas, 'When Politics is not Enough: Explaining the Failure of the Peace Process and the PKK's Urban Insurgency in Turkey (2015–2016)', paper presented at the first annual conference of the Strategic Studies Unit entitled 'From Bullets to Ballots: Transformations from Armed to Unarmed Political Activism', Arab Centre for Research and Policy Studies, Doha, 3–4/11/2018.

21. Edward Luttwak, 'Give War a Chance', *Foreign Affairs* (1999), pp. 36–44.

22. See: Ch. 6, this volume, where Gordon Clubb argues that 'framing the conflict as being stuck in a stalemate was important for the Provisional IRA's transition because it saved face, but it also fed into a developing narrative of 'changing conditions' which justified the abandonment of violence.'

23. Roberto Cajina, 'The Changing Ethos of the Nicaraguan Military: Three Stages and Three Different Identities', paper presented at the first annual conference of the Strategic Studies Unit entitled 'From Bullets to Ballots: Transformations from Armed to Unarmed Political Activism', Arab Centre for Research and Policy Studies, Doha, 3–4/11/2018.

24. Ibid.

25. See for example: Omar Ashour, 'De-Radicalisation of Jihad? The Impact of Egyptian Islamist Revisionist on al-Qaeda', *Perspective on Terrorism*, vol. 2, no. 5 (2008), pp. 11–12. See also: Lisa Blaydes and Lawrence Rubin, 'Ideological Reorientation and Counterterrorism: Confronting Militant Islam in Egypt', *Terrorism and Political Violence*, vol. 20, no. 4 (2008), pp. 461–79.

26. Mamduh Ali Yusuf, Commander of the Armed Wing of the Egyptian Islamic

Group (1988–90), Interview by Salwa al-'Awwa, *al-Jama'a al-Islamiyya al-Musallaha fi Misr: 1974–2004 [The Islamic Armed Group in Egypt: 1974–2004]* (Cairo: Al-Shuruq, 2006) qtd in Omar Ashour, *The Deradicalisation of Jihadists: Transforming Armed Islamist Movements* (London and New York: Routledge, 2009), p. 98.

27. Combat effectiveness and conflict outcomes are two different variables that should not be conflated. The former affects but does not determine the latter. See for example: Omar Ashour, *How ISIS Fights: Military Tactics in Iraq, Syria, Libya and Egypt* (Edinburgh: Edinburgh University Press, 2021); Kenneth Pollack, *Arabs at War* (New York: Bison Books, 2004).

28. Examples including the case of Ali Ben Hajar, the emir of the demobilised Islamic League for the Call and the Jihad (LIDD), who refused a request from the regime to call on other armed organisations to put down their arms as a result of the regime reneging on their promises. President Bouteflika had realised the importance of acknowledging the state's failure to fulfill its promises, and as a result, he 'apologised' publicly to the former militants. See for example Ali Ben Hajar, 'The Commander of an Armed Group Refuses the Demand from the Authorities to Call on Armed Militias to Cease Violence', Interview by Bou Allam Ghimrasa, *Al-Sharq Al-Awsat*, 27/9/2005. In Tajikistan, Following the regime's failure to fulfil a power-sharing formula that granted the United Tajikistani Opposition, led by the Islamic Renaissance Party (IRP), a 30 per cent of the ministerial positions, several IRP militia commanders started rearming and taking positions in the mountains surrounding the capital of Dushanbe in 1999 and 2000. See for example: Muzzafar Olimov and Soadat Olimova, 'Region Early Warning Report: Political Islam in Tajikistan', *Forum on Early Warnings*, 31/7/2001, pp. 10–26.

29. Joe Parkin, 'Former Farc Commanders Say They Are Returning to War Despite 2016 Peace Deal', *The Guardian*, 29/8/2019, accessed on 10/12/2020, at: https://bit.ly/3n6DZ1I

30. Anna Getmansky, 'You Can't Win If You Don't Fight', *Journal of Conflict Resolution*, vol. 7, no. 4 (2012), p. 710; Philip Keefer, 'Insurgency and Credible Commitment in Autocracies and Democracies', *The World Bank Economic Review*, vol. 22, no. 1 (2008), pp. 33–61.

31. Alexander B. Downes, *Targeting Civilians in War* (Ithaca: Cornell University Press, 2008), p. 711.

32. Annette Idler, 'Colombia Just Voted No on its Plebiscite for Peace. Here's Why and What it Means', *The Washington Post*, 3/10/2016, accessed on 10/12/2020, at: https://wapo.st/375HUqi

33. Similar patterns were shown elsewhere. In Algeria, the 2005 national reconciliation referendum have shown an overwhelming support for the reconciliation (over 97 per cent of the voters voted 'yes' for the Charter for Peace and National Reconciliation project that Bouteflika's government has proposed). This did not mean in any way support for the GIA, the AIS or other armed nonstate actors.

34. For more details see: Omar Ashour, 'Between ISIS and a Failed State: The Saga of Libyan Islamists', in: Shadi Hamid and William McCants (eds), *Rethinking Political Islam* (Oxford: Oxford University Press, 2017).

35. There were also violent retaliations against de-radicalised former insurgents (at the town or village level), including hundreds of recorded cases in Colombia, Algeria, Egypt, Tajikistan, Afghanistan and elsewhere. In Algeria, for example, the state's security services had to distribute personal weapons on former insurgents for self-defence.

36. See for example: Alexander Ramsbotham and I. William Zartman (eds), *Paix sans frontières: Building peace across borders*, Accord, no. 22 (London: Conciliation Resources, 2011).

37. See for example: Jonathan Powell, *Talking to Terrorists: How to End Armed Conflicts* (London: The Bodley Head, 2015), pp. 103, 130, 224, 232, 455.

38. I am grateful to Frank Pearl and Maria Jimena Duzan for these observations. Frank Pearl, former official negotiator with the FARC and the ELN, conversation with the author, Doha, 4 November 2018. Maria Jimena Duzan, author of *Santos: Paradojas de la Paz y del Poder*, conversation with the author, Doha, 4 November 2018. For more details see: Human Rights Developments, 'El Salvador', *Human Rights Watch*, accessed on 10/12/2020, at: https://bit.ly/3m3DwMF

39. Eumelio Rodriguez, Cuban Ambassador to Qatar, conversation with the author, Doha, June 2018. See also: John Otis, 'Cuba's Dictator Was Colombia's Peacemaker: How Fidel Castro Helped End Conflict with FARC', *CBC*, 2/12/2016, accessed on 10/12/2020, at: https://bit.ly/2VXPwo7

40. Kimberly Inksater and Paola Jiménez, *The Organisation of American States Mission to Support the Peace Process in Colombia* (Stockholm: International Institute for Democracy and Electoral Assistance, 2016).

41. That is, one successfully transformed organisation could influence or act as a model for armed organisations and interact with and incentivise them to abandon political violence. On the 'domino effects', see: Omar Ashour, 'De-Radicalisation of Jihad? The Impact of Egyptian Islamist Revisionists on Al-Qaeda', *Perspectives on Terrorism*, vol. 2, no. 5 (2008), pp. 11–14; Mathew

Charles, 'Farc Deal Opens Path for Colombia's Other Rebels: "The Future has to be about War"', *The Guardian*, 7/1/2018, accessed on 12/12/2018, at: https://bit.ly/2CFCGzD; Gordon Clubb and Marina Tapley, 'Conceptualising De-radicalisation and Former Combatant Re-integration in Nigeria', *Third World Quarterly*, vol. 39, no. 11 (2018), pp. 2053–68.

42. On spoilers and ways to deal with them see Stephen John Stedman, 'Spoiler Problems in Peace Processes', *International Security*, vol. 22, no. 2 (1997), pp. 5–53.

43. 'Threats to Human Security Impede Development in the Arab Countries', *United Nations Development Programme*, 21/7/2009, accessed on 12/12/2018, at: https://bit.ly/2ro1Z5h; Simone Young, 'Order From Chaos: Why Human Security Is National Security for Small Island Developing States', *Brookings*, 12/6/2017, accessed on 12/12/2018, at: https://brook.gs/2UhrVNe

44. Youssef Chaitani, Omar Ashour and Vito Intini, 'An Overview of the Arab Security Sector amidst Political Transitions: Reflections on Legacies, Functions and Perceptions', *United Nations Economic and Social Commission for West Africa* (New York: 2013); Omar Ashour, 'Security Sector Reform and the Arab Spring', *SETA Perspective*, no. 16 (2014), pp. 1–4; Yazīd Ṣāyigh, 'Missed Opportunity: The Politics of Police Reform in Egypt and Tunisia', *Carnegie Paper* (2015).

45. See for example: Azmi Bishara, 'The Army and Political Power in the Arab Context: Theoretical Problems', *Studies*, Arab Centre for Research and Policy Studies (2017); Omar Ashour, 'Collusion to Collision: Islamist-Military Relations in Egypt', *Brookings Doha Center Analysis Paper*, no. 14, Brookings (2015), pp. 1–50; Zoltan Barany, *How Armies Respond to Revolutions and Why* (Princeton: Princeton University Press, 2016).

BIBLIOGRAPHY

Abbas, Hassan, *The Taliban Revival: Violence and Extremism on the Pakistan-Afghanistan Frontier*, London: Yale University Press, 2014.

Abrahms, Max, 'Why Terrorism Does Not Work', *International Security*, vol. 31, no. 2 (2006), pp. 42–78.

Africa in 50 Years' Time: The Road Towards Inclusive Growth, Tunis: African Development Bank, 2011

Aguiló, Hernan, 'Inicio de un balance autocrítico de mi militancia revolucionaria', 2005. Accessed on 29/8/2020, at: https://bit.ly/32H5t5o

al-'Awwa, Salwa, *al-Jama'a al-Islamiyya al-Musallaha fi Misr: 1974–2004 [The Islamic Armed Group in Egypt: 1974–2004]*, Cairo: Al-Shuruq, 2006.

Al-Arian, Abdullah, *Answering the Call: Popular Islamic Activism in Sadat's Egypt*, New York: Oxford University Press, 2014.

Aldrighi, Clara, *La Izquierda Armada: ideología, ética e identidad en el MLN-Tupamaros*, Montevideo: Ediciones Trilce, 2001.

al-Hudaibi, Hassan, *Du'at la Qudat [Preachers Not Judges]*, Cairo: Dar al-Tawzi' wa'l-Nashr al-Islamiyyah, 1973.

Aliverti, Eduardo, 'Un comando de maniaticos', *El Porteño*, February 1989.

All According to Plan: The Rab'a Massacre and Mass Killing of Protesters in Egypt. New York: Human Rights Watch, 2014.

Almeida, Paul D, *Waves of Protest: Popular Struggle in El Salvador, 1925–2005*, Minneapolis: University of Minnesota Press, 2008.

Almustafa, Hamzah, *al-Majal al-'Amm al-Iftiradi fi'l-Thawra as-Suriyya: al-Khasa'is, al-Ittijahat, Aliyyat San' ar-Ra'y al-'Amm [The Virtual Public Sphere in the Syrian Revolution]*, Doha and Beirut: The Arab Centre for Research and Policy Studies, 2012.

Almustafa, Hamzah, 'The al-Nusra Front: From Formation to Dissension', *Policy Analysis*, Arab Center for Research and Policy Studies (2014).

Alonso, Rogelio, 'The Madrid Bombings and Negotiations with ETA: A Case Study of the Impact of Terrorism on Spanish Politics', *Terrorism and Political Violence*, vol. 25, no. 1 (2013), pp. 113–36.

Alterman, Jon B. et al, 'How Terrorism Ends', United States Institute of Peace, *Policy Brief* (1999).

Arrarás, Astrid, 'Armed Struggle, Political Learning and Participation in Democracy: The Case of the Tupamaros', PhD Dissertation, Princeton University: New Jersey, 1998.

Ashour, Omar, 'Lions Tamed? An Inquiry into the Causes of De-Radicalization of Armed Islamist Movements', *Middle East Journal*, vol. 61, no. 3 (2007).

Ashour, Omar, 'Islamist De-Radicalization in Algeria: Successes and Failures', *Middle East Institute*, 1/11/2008. Accessed on 11/12/2018. at: https://bit.ly/2rlZVLd

Ashour, Omar, 'De-Radicalization of Jihad? The Impact of Egyptian Islamist Revisionists on Al-Qaeda', *Perspectives on Terrorism*, vol. 2, no. 5 (2008), pp. 277–91.

Ashour, Omar, *The De-Radicalization of Jihadists: Transforming Armed Islamist Movements*, London and New York: Routledge, 2009.

Ashour, Omar, 'Post-Jihadism: Libya and the Global Transformations of Armed Islamist Movements', *Terrorism and Political Violence*, vol. 23, no. 3 (2011), pp. 377–97.

Ashour, Omar, 'Security Sector Reform and the Arab Spring', *SETA Perspective*, no. 16 (2014).

Ashour, Omar, 'Collusion to Collision: Islamist-Military Relations in Egypt', *Brookings Doha Center Analysis Paper*, no. 14 (2015).

Ashour, Omar, 'Sinai's Insurgency: Implications of Enhanced Guerrilla Warfare', *Studies in Conflict and Terrorism*, vol. 42, no. 6 (2019), pp. 541–58.

Ashour, Omar, 'From Bullets to Ballots: Transformations from Armed to Unarmed Political Activism', *Strategic Papers*, no. 1, The Arab Centre for Research and Policy Studies (2020).

Ashour, Omar, 'From Militias to Political Parties: How and Why Do Armed Organizations Take up non- violent Activism?' [in Arabic] *Siyasat Arabiya*, vol. 8, no. 44 (2020).

Ashour, Omar, *How ISIS Fights: Military Tactics in Iraq, Syria, Libya and Egypt*, Edinburgh: Edinburgh University Press, 2021.

Avendaño, Daniel and Mauricio Palma, *El Rebelde de la Burguesía: La Historia De Miguel Enríquez*, Santiago, Chile: Ediciones CESOC, 2001.

Barany, Zoltan, *How Armies Respond to Revolutions and Why*, Princeton: Princeton University press, 2016.

Barfield, Thomas, *Afghanistan: A Cultural and Political History*, Princeton: Princeton University Press, 2010.

Barnard, Niel, *Secret Revolution: Memoirs of a Spy Boss*, Cape Town: Tafelberg, 2015.

Barrell, Howard, 'Conscripts to Their Age: African National Congress Operational Strategy, 1976–1986', PhD Dissertation, Oxford University, Oxford, 1993.

Belhaj, Abdul Hakim, 'From the "Fighting Group" to the "Homeland Party": Observations on the Transformations in Libya', paper presented at the first annual conference of the Strategic Studies Unit entitled 'From Bullets to Ballots: Transformations from Armed to Unarmed Political Activism', Arab Centre for Research and Policy Studies, Doha, 3–4/11/2018.

Berhe, Mulugeta Gebrehiwot, *Laying the Past to Rest: The EPRDF and the Challenges of Ethiopian State Building*, London: Hurst & Company, 2019.

Berman, Eli, *Radical, Religious, and Violent: The New Economics of Terrorism*, Cambridge, MA: The MIT Press, 2009.

Biney, Ama, *The Political and Social Thought of Kwame Nkrumah*, 1st edn, New York: Palgrave Macmillan, 2011.

Bishara, Azmi, *Suriya: Darb al-Alam Nahw al-Hurriyya: Muhawala fi'l-Tarikh al-Rahin [Syria: A Way of Suffering to Freedom]*, Doha and Beirut: The Arab Centre for Research and Policy Studies, 2013.

Bishara, Azmi, 'The Army and Political Power in the Arab Context: Theoretical Problems', *Studies*, Arab Centre for Research and Policy Studies (2017).

Bishara, Azmi, 'Opening Remarks', paper presented at the first annual conference of the Strategic Studies Unit entitled 'From Bullets to Ballots: Transformations from Armed to Unarmed Political Activism', Arab Centre for Research and Policy Studies, Doha, 3–4/11/2018.

Bjørgo, Toro and John Horgan (eds), *Leaving Terrorism Behind: Individual and Collective Disengagement*, Abington: Routledge, 2009.

Blaustein, Eduardo, 'Un alfiler menos', *El Porteño*, February 1989.

Blaydes, Lisa and Lawrence Rubin, 'Ideological Reorientation and Counterterrorism: Confronting Militant Islam in Egypt', *Terrorism and Political Violence*, vol. 20, no. 4 (2008), pp. 461–79.

Blixen, Samuel, *Conversaciones con Gorriarán Merl: treinta años de lucha popular*, Buenos Aires: Editorial Contrapunto, 1988.

Brockett, Charles D., *Political Movements and Violence in Central America*, Cambridge: Cambridge University Press, 2005.

Buchanan, Cate and Joaquín Chávez, 'Guns and Violence in El Salvador Peace Negotiations', *Negotiating Disarmament*, Country Study 3, Geneva: Centre for Humanitarian Dialogue, 2008.

Cajina, Roberto, 'The Changing Ethos of the Nicaraguan Military: Three Stages and Three Different Identities', Paper presented at the first annual conference of the Strategic Studies Unit entitled 'From Bullets to Ballots: Transformations from Armed to Unarmed Political Activism', Arab Centre for Research and Policy Studies, Doha, 3–4/11/2018.

Callinicos, Luli, *Oliver Tambo: Beyond the Engeli Mountains*, Cape Town: David Philip Publishers, 2004.

Cardenal, Ana Sofía, *La democracia y la tierra: Cambio político en El Salvador*, Madrid: CIS, 2002.

Carnovale, Vera, *Los Combatientes: Historia Del PRT-ERP*, Buenos Aires: Siglo Veintiuno Editores, 2011.

Castañeda, Jorge G., *La utopía desarmada. Intrigas, dilemas y promesa de la izquierda en América Latina*, Barcelona: Ariel, 1995.

Cavatorta, Francesco and Fabio Merone, 'Moderation through Exclusion? The Journey of the Tunisian Ennahda from Fundamentalist to Conservative Party', *Democratization*, vol. 20, no. 5 (2013), pp. 857–75.

Celesia, Felipe and Pablo Waisberg, *La Tablada: A vencer o morir: La última batalla de la guerrilla Argentina*, Buenos Aires: Aguilar, 2013.

Chaitani, Youssef, Omar Ashour and Vito Intini, 'An Overview of the Arab Security Sector Amidst Political Transitions: Reflections on Legacies, Functions and Perceptions', *United Nations Economic and Social Commission for West Africa*, New York: 2013.

Chávez, Joaquín Mauricio, *Poets and Prophets of the Resistance: Intellectuals and the Origins of El Salvador's Civil War*, New York: Oxford University Press, 2017.

Chaya, Nada, 'Poor Access to Health Services: Ways Ethiopia is Overcoming It', *Research Comment*, vol. 2, no. 2 (2007).

Clark, Robert P, *The Basques: The Franco Years and Beyond*, Reno: University of Nevada Press, 1979.

Clubb, Gordon and Marina Tapley, 'Conceptualising De-radicalisation and Former Combatant Re-integration in Nigeria', *Third World Quarterly*, vol. 39, no. 11 (2018), pp. 1–16.

Clubb, Gordon, *Social Movement De-Radicalisation and the Decline of Terrorism: The Morphogenesis of the Irish Republican Movement*, London: Routledge, 2016.

Cochrane, Marisa, *The Fragmentation of the Sadrist Movement*, Iraq Report 12, Washington, DC: Institute for the Study of War, 2009.

CODEPU, *Informe de Derechos Humanos: 1990–2000*, Santiago: LOM, 2001.

Colburn, Forrest D., 'The Tragedy of Ethiopia's Intellectuals', *The Antioch Review*, vol. 47, no. 2 (1989), pp. 133–45.

Collier, Paul and Anke Hoeffler, 'Greed and Grievance in Civil War', *Oxford Economic Papers*, vol. 56, no. 4 (2004), pp. 563–95.

'Contra la dictadura y por la liberación popular', *Comunicado del IV Congreso del MIR (Politico)* (1988). Accessed on 29/8/2020, at: https://bit.ly/3b8RVTH

Cordesman, Anthony (with assistance from Emma R. Davies), *Iraq's Insurgency and the Road to Civil Conflict*, Washington, DC and London: Center for Strategic Studies (CSIS)/ Praeger Security International, 2008.

'Country Reports on Terrorism 2017', *United States Department of State* (2018).

Crenzel, Emilio, *La Historia Política del Nunca más: La Memoria de las Desapariciones en la Argentina*, Buenos Aires, Argentina: Siglo Veintiuno Editores, 2008.

Crews, Robert D., and Amin Tarzi (eds), *The Taliban and the Crisis of Afghanistan*, Cambridge, MA: Harvard University Press, 2008.

Cronin, Audrey Kurth, 'How Al-Qaida Ends: The Decline and Demise of Terrorist Groups', *International Security*, vol. 31, no. 1 (2006), pp. 7–48.

Cronin, Audrey Kurth, *How Terrorism Ends: Understanding the Decline and Demise of Terrorist Campaigns*, Princeton: Princeton University Press, 2009.

Danza, Andrés and Ernesto Tulbovitz, *Una oveja negra al poder: Pepe Mujica, la política de la gente*, Barcelona: Debate, 2016.

Davenport, Christian, Hank Johnston and Carol Mueller (eds), *Repression and Mobilization*, Minneapolis: University of Minnesota Press, 2005.

Davenport, T. R. H., *The Transfer of Power in South Africa*, Cape Town: David Philip, 1998.

De Zárate, Verónica Valdivia Ortiz, Rolando Alvarez Vallejos and Julio Pinto Vallejos, *Su Revolución Contra Nuestra Revolución: Izquierdas y derechas en el Chile de Pinochet (1973–1981)*, vol. 1, 2. Santiago: LOM, 2006 / 2008.

Decision Regarding Delimitation of the Border Between Eritrea and Ethiopia: 13 April 2002, vol. XXV, New York: United Nations, 2006.

Deonandan, Kalowatie, David Close and Gary Prevost (eds), *From Revolutionary Movements to Political Parties: Cases from Latin America and Africa*, New York: Palgrave Macmillan, 2007.

Diamond, Larry and Richard Gunther (eds), *Political Parties and Democracy*, Baltimore and London: The Johns Hopkins University Press, 2001.

Dominguez, Florencio, *La agonia de ETA: una investigacion inedita sobre los ultimos dias de la banda*, Madrid: La esfera de los libros, 2012.

Donoso, Igor Goicovic, 'Transición y Violencia Política: En Chile (1988–1994)', *Ayer Revista de Historia Contemporánea* (2010).

Downes, Alexander B., *Targeting Civilians in War*, Ithaca: Cornell University Press, 2008.

Dubow, Saul, *The African National Congress*, Stroud: Sutton, 2000.

Dudouet, Veronique (ed.), *Civil Resistance and Conflict Transformation: Transitions from Armed to Nonviolent Struggle*, London: Routledge, 2015.

Dunkerley, James, *The Pacification of Central America. Political Change in the Isthmus 1987–1993*, London: Verso, 1994.

Dupuy, Kendra and Siri Aas Rustand, 'Trends in Armed Conflict, 1946–2017', Peace Research Institute Oslo (PRIO), *Conflict Trends*, vol. 5 (2016).

Duzan, Maria Jimena, 'Political Reintegration of Demobilized Combatants in Colombia', paper presented at the first annual conference of the Strategic Studies Unit entitled 'From Bullets to Ballots: Transformations from Armed to Unarmed Political Activism', Arab Centre for Research and Policy Studies. Doha, 3–4/11/2018.

Edwards, Aaron and Cillian McGrattan, 'Terroristic Narratives: On the (Re) invention of Peace in Northern Ireland', *Terrorism and Political Violence*, vol. 23, no. 3 (2011), pp. 357–76.

'El 'fenómeno Mujica': La seducción de un intruso', *Brecha*, 8/10/1999.

Elorza, Antonio et al., *La Historia de ETA*, Madrid: Temas de Hoy, 2000.

Engel, Jakob and Pauline Rose, 'Ethiopia's Progress in Education, a Rapid and Equitable Expansion of Access', *Research Reports and Studies*, London: Overseas Development Institute, 2011.

Ethiopia: Demographic and Health Survey, Addis Ababa: Central Statistical Agency; Calverton, MD: ORC Macro, 2006.

Eugenia, María Allier, *Batallas por la memoria*, Montevideo: Trilce, 2010.

Feld, Claudia and Marina Franco, *Democracia, hora cero: Actores, políticas y debates en los inicios de la posdictadura*, Buenos Aires: Fondo de Cultura Económico, 2015.

Federal Democratic Republic of Ethiopia, 'The Foreign Affairs and National Security Policy and Strategy', *Ministry of Information Press and Audiovisual Department*, no. 7 (2002).

Feroz, Emran, 'Death by Drone: America's Vicious Legacy in Afghanistan', *Foreign Policy*, 27/3/2020. Accessed on 17/9/2020 at: https://bit.ly/2Ftk6BH

Fitzgerald, Mary and Emad Badi, 'The Limits of Reconciliation: Assessing the Revisions of the Libyan Islamic Fighting Group (LIFG)', *Institute for Integrated Transitions* (2020).

Fombad, Madeleine, 'An Overview of Accountability Mechanisms in PPP In South Africa', *Ufahamu: A Journal of African Studies*, vol. 37, no. 1 (2013). Accessed on 07/02/2021 at: https://escholarship.org/uc/item/18j0h3ng

Freeman, Michael (ed.), *Financing Terrorism: Case Studies*, London and New York: Routledge, 2012.

Gaili, Ahmed, 'Federalism and the Tyranny of Religious Majorities: Challenges to Islamic Federalism in Sudan', *Harvard International Law Journal*, vol. 45, no. 2 (2004), pp. 503–47.

Garaño, Santiago and Werner Pertot, *Detenidos-Aparecidos: Presas y Presos Políticos desde Trelew a la Dictadura*, Buenos Aires: Editorial Biblos, 2007.

Garcé, Adolfo, *Donde Hubo Fuego: el proceso de adaptación del MLN-Tupamaros a la legalidad y a la competencia electoral (1985–2004)*, Montevideo: Editorial Fin de Siglo, 2006.

Garcés, Mario and Sebastián Leiva, *El golpe en La Legua: Los Caminos de la Historia y la Memoria*, Santiago: LOM Ediciones, 2005.

Gardner, Tom, 'Will Abiy Ahmed's Bet on Ethiopia's Political Future Pay Off?', *Foreign Policy*, 21/1/2020. Accessed on 7/9/2020 at: https://bit.ly/3lXeq3b

Gates, Scott et al., 'Trends in Armed Conflict, 1946–2014', Peace Research Institute Oslo (PRIO), *Conflict Trends*, vol.1 (2016).

Gatto, Hebert, *El Cielo Por Asalto: el Movimiento de Liberación Nacional (Tupamaros) y la Izquierda Uruguaya (1963–1972)*, Montevideo: Taurus, 2004.

Gerhart, Gail M., and Clive L. Glaszer, *From Protest to Challenge: A Documentary History of African Politics in South Africa, 1882–1990*, vol. 6: Challenge and Victory, Bloomington: Indiana University Press, 2010.

Getmansky, Anna, 'You Can't Win If You Don't Fight', *Journal of Conflict Resolution*, vol. 7, no. 4 (2012), pp. 709–34.

Gillespie, Richard, *Soldiers of Perón: Argentina's Montoneros*, Oxford and New York: Clarendon Press / Oxford University Press, 1982.

Giustozzi, Antonio, *Afghanistan's Endless War: State Failure, Regional Politics, and the Rise of the Taliban*, Seattle: University of Washington Press, 2001.

Giustozzi, Antonio, *Koran, Kalashnikov, and Laptop*, Oxford: Oxford University Press, 2009.

Giustozzi, Antonio, *Decoding the New Taliban: Insights from the Afghan Field*, New York: Columbia University Press, 2012.

Giustozzi, Antonio, *The Army of Afghanistan: The Political History of Fragile Institution*, New York: Oxford University Press, 2015.

Giustozzi, Antonio, *The Taliban at War: 2001–2018*, New York: Oxford University Press, 2019.

Gleijeses, Piero, *Visions of Freedom*, Cuito Cuanavale: Wits University Press, 2013.

Green, James, *We Cannot Remain Silent: Opposition to the Brazilian Military Dictatorship in the United States*, Durham, NC: Duke University Press, 2010.

Gregor, Thomas (ed.), *A Natural History of Peace*, Nashville: Vanderbilt University Press, 1996.

Grenier, Yvon, *The Emergence of Insurgency in El Salvador: Ideology and Political Will*, Pittsburgh: University of Pittsburgh Press, 1999.

Hafez, Mohammed M., *Why Muslims Rebel: Repression and Resistance in the Islamic World*, Boulder: Lynne Rienner, 2004.

Hamid, Shadi and William McCants (eds), *Rethinking Political Islam*, Oxford: Oxford University Press, 2017.

Hamid, Shadi, *Temptations of Power: Islamists and Illiberal Democracy in a New Middle East*, New York: Oxford University Press, 2014.

Harvey, Robert, *The Fall of Apartheid: The Inside Story from Smuts to Mbeki*, Basingstoke: Palgrave Macmillan, 2003.

Hegghammer, Thomas, 'The De-Radicalization of Jihadists: Transforming Armed Islamist Movements', *Perspective on Politics*, vol. 9, no. 2 (2011), pp. 472–4.

Hilb, Claudia, 'La Tablada: el último acto de la guerrilla setentista', *Lucha armada en la Argentina*, vol. 9, no. 3 (2007). Accessed on 29/8/2020 at: https://bit.ly/3hGOTbT

Hinnebusch, Raymond, 'Syria: From "Authoritarian Upgrading" to Revolution?', *International Affairs*, vol. 88, no. 1 (2012), pp. 95–113.

Horgan, John, *Walking Away from Terrorism: Accounts of Disengagements from Radical and Extremist Movements*, London–New York: Routledge, 2009.

Horgan, John, 'De-radicalization or Disengagement?', *Perspectives on Terrorism*, vol. 2, no. 4 (2008), pp. 3–8.

Huges, Michelle A., and Michael Miklaucic (eds), *Impunity: Countering Illicit Power in War and Transition*, Washington, DC: National Defense University/ Center for Technology and National Security Policy/ Center for Complex Operations and Peacekeeping and Stability Operations Institute, 2016.

Huidobro, Eleuterio Fernandez, *Historia de los Tupamaros*, three volumes, Montevideo: TAE, Tupac Amaru Editores, 1986–1988.

Huntington, Samuel, 'Political Development in Ethiopia: A Peasant-Based Dominate-Party Democracy', Report to USAID/Ethiopia (1993).

Hutcheon, Nick, *Intra-State Immigrants as Sub-State Nationalists: Lived Experiences in the Basque Country*, London: Routledge, 2020.

Inksater, Kimberly and Paola Jiménez, *The Organization of American States Mission to Support the Peace Process in Colombia*, Stockholm: International Institute for Democracy and Electoral Assistance, 2016.

International Monetary Fund, 'The Federal Democratic Republic of Ethiopia: Joint Staff Advisory Note on the Growth and Transformation Plan 2010/11–2014/15', *IMF Country Report*, no. 11/303 (October 2011).

Jabar, Faleh A., *The Shi'ite Movement in Iraq*, London: Saqi Books, 2003.

Johnson, David E., M. Wade Markel and Brian Shannon, *The 2008 Battle of Sadr City: Reimagining Urban Combat*, Santa Monica: RAND Corporation, 2013.

Johnson, Thomas H. and Ludwig Adamic, *The Historical Dictionary of Afghanistan*, Lanham: Rowman & Littlefield, forthcoming, May 2021.

Johnson, Thomas H. and M. Chris Mason, 'Understanding the Taliban and Insurgency in Afghanistan', *Orbis*, vol. 51, no. 1 (2007), pp. 71–89.

Johnson, Thomas H. and M. Chris Mason, 'Obama's Indecent Interval', *Foreign Policy*, 10/12/2009. Accessed on 17/9/2020. at: https://bit.ly/33ANbmB

Johnson, Thomas H. and M. Chris Mason, 'Refighting the Last War: Afghanistan and the Vietnam Template', *Military Review* (2009).

Johnson, Thomas H., 'Taliban Adaptations and Innovations', *Small Wars and Insurgencies*, vol. 24, no. 1 (2013).

Johnson, Thomas H., *Taliban Narratives: The Use and Power of Stories in the Afghanistan Conflict*, Oxford: Oxford University Press, 2018.

Johnson, Thomas H., *The 2019 Presidential Election: A Continuation of Problematic Processes and Results*, Constitutional and Political System Reform Studies, Series VI, Kabul: The Afghanistan Institute for Strategic Studies, 2020.

Jones, Cara and Katrin Witting, 'The 2015 Legislative and Presidential Elections in Burundi: An Unfinished Post-Conflict Transition', *Electoral Studies*, vol. 43 (September 2016), pp. 206–8.

Jones, Seth G., and Martin C. Libicki, *How Terrorist Groups End: Lessons for Countering al Qa'ida*, Santa Monica: RAND Publications, 2008.

Kasrils, Ronnie, *A Simple Man: Kasrils and the Zuma Enigma*, Johannesburg: Jacana Media, 2017.

Katz, Richard S., and William Crotty (eds), *Handbook of Party Politics*, New York: SAGE Publications, 2006.

Keefer, Philip, 'Insurgency and Credible commitment in Autocracies and Democracies', *The World Bank Economic Review*, vol. 22, no. 1 (2008).

Kelemen, Barbara, 'China's Economic Stabilization Efforts in Afghanistan: A New Party to the Table?', *Middle East Institute*, 21/1/2020. Accessed on 17/9/2020, at: https://bit.ly/3c4RkTM

Keys, Barbara J., *Reclaiming American Virtue: The Human Rights Revolution of the 1970s*, Cambridge, MA: Harvard University Press, 2014.

Klapador, Dominik, 'From Rebels to Politicians: The Case of Nepal', *London School of Economics Paper Series*, February 2009.

Khalfiyyat al-Thawra: Dirasat Suriya [Backgrounds of Revolution: Syrian Studies], Doha and Beirut: The Arab Centre for Research and Policy Studies, 2013.

Koehler, Daniel, *Understanding Deradicalization: Methods, Tools and Programs for Countering Violent Extremism*, London: Routledge, 2016.

Krause, Peter, 'The Political Effectiveness of Non-State Violence: A Two-Level Framework to Transform a Deceptive Debate', *Security Studies*, vol. 22, no. 2 (2013), pp. 259–94.

Lafeber, Walter F, *Inevitable Revolutions: The United States in Central America*, New York: W. W. Norton & Co., 1993.

Lastra, Soledad, 'Los retornos del exilio en Argentina y Uruguay. Una historia comparada de las políticas y tensiones en la recepción y asistencia en las posdictaduras (1983–1989)', PhD Dissertation, Facultad de Humanidades y Ciencias de la Educación (UNLP), La Plata, 2014.

Leicht, Federico, *Cero a la izquierda: una biografía de Jorge Zabalza*, Montevideo, Uruguay: Letraeñe Ediciones, 2009.

Leogrande, William M., *Our Own Backyard: The United States in Central America, 1977–1992*, Chapel Hill: The University of North Carolina Press, 1998.

Lessa, Alfonso, *La Revolución Imposible: Los Tupamaros y el Fracaso de la vía Armada en el Uruguay del siglo XX*, Montevideo: Editorial Fin de Siglo, 2002.

Lia, Brynjar, *The Society of the Muslim Brotherhood in Egypt: The Rise of an Islamic Mass Movement 1928–1942*, Reading: Ithaca Press, 1998.

Lister, Charles R., *The Syrian Jihad: Al-Qaeda, the Islamic State and the Evolution of an Insurgency*, Oxford: Oxford University Press, 2015.

Loveman, Brian and Elizabeth Lira, *Las Ardientes Cenizas del Olvido: Vía Chilena de Reconciliación Política 1932–1994*, Santiago: LOM Ediciones / DIBAM, 2000.

Lund, Aron, 'Struggling to Adapt: The Muslim Brotherhood in a New Syria', *Carnegie Middle East Center*, 7/5/2013. Accessed on 13/4/2017, at: https://bit.ly/303GOr3

Luttwak, Edward, 'Give War a Chance', *Foreign Affairs* (1999).

Lyons, Terrence, 'Closing the Transition: The May 1995 Elections in Ethiopia', *The Journal of Modern African Studies*, vol. 34, no. 1 (1996), pp. 121–42.

Maley, William (ed.), *Afghanistan and the Taliban*, New York: New York University Press, 1998.

Maley, William (ed.), *Fundamentalism Reborn? Afghanistan and the Taliban*, New York: New York University Press, 1998.

Mandela, Nelson, *Long Walk to Freedom: The Autobiography of Nelson Mandela*, London: Abacus, 1997.

Manning the Barricades: Who's at Risk as Deepening Economic Distress Foments Social Unrest, Special Report, London: Economist Intelligence Unit, 2009.

Manning, Carrie and Ian Smith, 'Political Party Formation by Former Armed Opposition Groups after Civil War', *Democratization*, vol. 23, no. 6 (2016), pp. 972–89.

Marais, Hein, *South Africa: Limits to Change: The Political Economy of Transition*, London: Zed Books, 2001.

Marchesi, Aldo, *Latin America's Radical Left Rebellion and Cold War in the Global 1960s*, Cambridge: Cambridge University Press, 2018.

Markarian, Vania, *Left in Transformation: Uruguayan Exiles and the Latin American Human Rights Networks, 1967–1984*, New York: Routledge, 2005.

Mar-Molinero, Clare and Angel Smith, *Nationalism and the Nation in the Iberian Peninsula: Competing and Conflicting Identities*, Oxford: Berg, 1996.

Marsden, Peter, *The Taliban: War and Religion in Afghanistan*, New York: Zed Books, 2002.

Martín Álvarez, Alberto and Eudald Cortina Orero, 'The Genesis and Internal Dynamics of El Salvador's People's Revolutionary Army (ERP): 1970–1976', *Journal of Latin American Studies*, vol. 46, no. 4 (2014), pp. 663–89.

Martín Álvarez, Alberto, 'De guerrilla a partido político: El Frente Farabundo Martí para la Liberación Nacional (FMLN)', *Historia y Política: Ideas, Procesos y Movimientos Sociales*, no. 25 (2011).

Maru, Mehari Taddele, 'A Basic Introduction to Ethiopian Electoral System', paper presented to the EU Delegation to Ethiopia, Addis Ababa, January 2014.

Maru, Mehari Taddele, 'Migration, Ethnic Diversity and Federalism in Ethiopia', Unpublished PhD Dissertation, University of Oxford, Refugee Studies Centre, Queen Elizabeth House, Oxford, 2004.

Maru, Mehari Taddele, 'Federalism in Ethiopia: After Fifteen Years', *Journal of the Horn of Africa*, vol. 37, no. 134 (2006), pp. 29–52.

Maru, Mehari Taddele, 'Report of a Baseline Study of Violent Conflicts in Ethiopia', *NCA & FES*, 2009.

Maru, Mehari Taddele, 'Federalism and Conflicts in Ethopia', *Conflict Trends (African Centre for the Constructive Resolution of Disputes (ACCORD)*, no. 1 (2010), pp. 36–46.

Maru, Mehari Taddele, 'Federalism and Conflicts in Ethiopia', *African Journals Online (Africa Insight)*, vol. 39, no. 4 (2010). Accessed on 07/02/2020, DOI: 10.4314/ai.v39i4.54669

Maru, Mehari Taddele, 'Ethiopia's Regional Diplomacies: A Dominant Interpretation of the Horn of Africa', South African Institute of International Affairs (SAIIA), *SAIIA Policy Briefing*, no. 112. 27/10/2014. Accessed on 7/9/2020. at: https://bit.ly/334wOyj

Maru, Mehari Taddele, *The Kampala Convention and Its Contributions to International Law: Legal Analyses and Interpretations of the African Union Convention on the Protection and Assistance of Internally Displaced Persons*, Hague: Eleven Publishers, 2014.

Matthies-Boon, Vivienne, 'Shattered Worlds: Political Trauma amongst Young Activists in Post-revolutionary Egypt', *The Journal of North African Studies*, vol. 22, no. 4 (2017), pp. 620–44.

McAdam, Doug, 'Tactical Innovation and the Pace of Insurgency', *American Sociological Review*, vol. 48, no. 6 (1983), pp. 735–54.

Merlo, Enrique Gorriaran and Darío Díaz, *Memorias de Enrique Gorriarán Merlo: de los Setenta a La Tablada*, Buenos Aires: Planeta, 2003.

Mitchell, Richard P., *The Society of the Muslim Brothers*, New York: Oxford University Press, 1993.

Mohammad Khan, Riaz, *Afghanistan and Pakistan: Conflict, Extremism, and Resistance to Modernity*, Baltimore: The Johns Hopkins University Press, 2011.

Moloney, Ed, *A Secret History of the IRA*, New York: W. W. Norton & Co., 2003.

Montaña, Benjamín Tejerina, 'Nationalism, Violence and Social Mobilization in the Basque Country: Factors and Mechanisms of ETA's Rise and Fall', *Papeles del CEIC*, vol. 3, no. 136 (2015).

Moss, Dana, 'Repression, Response, and Contained Escalation Under 'Liberalized' Authoritarianism in Jordan', *Mobilization*, vol. 19, no. 3 (2014), pp. 261–86.

Moyano, María José, *Argentina's Lost Patrol: Armed Struggle, 1969–1979*, New Haven: Yale University Press, 1995.

Moyn, Samuel, *The Last Utopia: Human Rights in History*, Cambridge, MA: Harvard University Press, 2010.

Mueller, McClurg, Hank Johnston and Christian Davenport (eds), *Repression and Mobilization*, Minneapolis: University of Minnesota Press, 2005.

Munoz, Heraldo, *The Dictator's Shadow: Life Under Augusto Pinochet*, New York: Basic Books, 2008.

Muro, Diego, 'Nationalism and Nostalgia: The Case of Radical Basque Nationalism', *Nations and Nationalism*, vol. 11, no. 4 (2005), pp. 571–89.

Muro, Diego, 'The Politics of War Memory in Radical Basque Nationalism', *Ethnic and Racial Studies*, vol. 32, no. 4 (2009), pp. 659–78.

Murua, Imanol and Txema Ramírez de la Piscina, 'Ceasefire as Bad News: The Coverage of the End of ETA in the Basque and Spanish Press', *Revista Latina de Comunicación Social*, vol. 72 (2017), pp. 1453–67.

Murua, Imanol, 'No More Bullets for ETA: The Loss of Internal Support as a Key Factor in the End of the Basque Group's Campaign', *Critical Studies on Terrorism*, vol. 10, no. 1 (2017), pp. 93–114.

Naranjo, Francisco García, *Historias Derrotadas: Opción y Obstinación de la Guerrilla Chilena (1965–1988)*, Morelia: Universidad Michoacana de San Nicolás de Hidalgo, 1996.

Naranjo, Pedro et al., *Miguel Enríquez y el proyecto revolucionario en Chile: Discursos y Documentos del Movimiento de Izquierda Revolucionaria*, Santiago, Chile: LOM Ediciones, 2004.

National Research Council, *International Conflict Resolution After the Cold War*, Washington, DC: The National Academies Press, 2000.

Nega, Sebhat, 'Corruption Could Undermine Ethiopia's Development Goals', *Addis Fortune*, vol. 12, no. 617 (February 2012).

Neltume, Comité Memoria, *Guerrilla en Neltume: Una historia de lucha y resistencia en el sur* chileno, Santiago de Chile: LOM Ediciones, 2003.

Novaro, Marcos and Vicente Palermo, *La Dictadura Militar, 1976–1983: Del Golpe de Estado a la Restauración* Democrática, Buenos Aires: Paidós, 2003.

O'Donnell, Lynne, 'Factional Struggles Emerge in Virus-Afflicted Taliban Top Ranks', *Foreign Policy*, 9/6/2020. Accessed on 17/9/2020, at: https://bit. ly/32DlFFN

O'Mailey, Padraig, *Shades of Difference: Mac Maharaj and the Struggle for South Africa*, New York: Viking Press, 2007.

O'Kane, Eamonn, 'Decommissioning and the Peace Process: Where Did It Come from and Why Did It Stay So Long?', *Irish Political Studies*, vol. 22, no. 1 (2007), pp. 81–101.

Opp, Karl-Dieter and Wolfgang Roeh, 'Repression, Micromobilization, and Political Protest', *Social Forces*, vol. 69, no. 2 (1990), pp. 521–47.

Orellana, Patricio and Elizabeth Quay Hutchison, *El movimiento de derechos humanos en Chile: 1973–1990*, Santiago de Chile: Centro de Estudios Políticos Latinoamericanos Simón Bolívar, 1991.

Pape, Robert A., 'The Strategic Logic of Suicide Terrorism', *American Political Science Review*, vol. 97, no. 3 (2003), pp. 343–61.

Paszyn, Danuta, *The Soviet Attitude to Political and Social Change in Central America, 1979–90: Case-Studies on Nicaragua, El Salvador and Guatemala*, London: Palgrave Macmillan, 2000.

Pearl, Frank, 'Talking to Guerrillas: Reflections on the FARC and the Colombian Peace Accords', paper presented at the first annual conference of the Strategic Studies Unit entitled 'From Bullets to Ballots: Transformations from Armed to Unarmed Political Activism', Arab Centre for Research and Policy Studies, Doha, 3–4/11/2018.

Pfetsch, Frank and Christoph Rohloff, *National and International Conflicts, 1945–1995: New Empirical and Theoretical Approaches*, London: Routledge, 2000.

Pirker, Kristina, *La Redefinición de lo Posible: Militancia Política y Movilización Social en El Salvador (1970 a 2012)*, México: Instituto Mora, 2017.

Pirnie, Bruce R. and Edward O'Connell, *Counterinsurgency in Iraq (2003–2006)*, Santa Monica: National Defense Research Institute (RAND), 2008.

Polakow-Suransky, Sasha, *The Unspoken Alliance: Israel's Secret Relationship with Apartheid South Africa*, Johannesburg: Jacana Media, 2010.

Policy Analysis Unit, 'Jaysh al-Islam: al-Bahth 'an Dawr fi Mustaqbal Suriya', *Case Analysis*, Arab Center for Research and Policy Studies, 2015.

Policy Analysis Unit, 'Tatawwur al-Mawqif al-Amriki min al-Nizam al-Suri: Min Da'wat al-Islah ila'l-Tafawud', *Policy Analysis*, Arab Center for Research and Policy Studies (2015).

Policy Analysis Unit, 'Syria's Armed Uprising: The Status Quo', *Case Analysis*, Arab Centre for Research and Policy Studies (2016).

Pollack, Kenneth, *Arabs at War*, New York: Bison Books, 2004.

Powell, Jonathan, *Talking to Terrorists: How to End Armed Conflicts*, London: The Bodley Head, 2014.

Pozzi, Pablo A., *Por las Sendas Argentinas: El PRT-ERP, La Guerrilla* Marxista, Buenos Aires: Eudeba, 2001.

Pruitt, Dean G., 'Readiness Theory and the Northern Ireland Conflict', *American Behavioral Scientist*, vol. 50, no. 11 (2007), pp. 1520–41.

Qutb, Sayyid, *Ma'alim fi'l-Tariq [Milestones]*, Cairo: Dar al-Shorouq, 1973.

Rabasa, Angel et al., *Deradicalizing Islamist Extremists*, Santa Monica: RAND, 2010.

Ramsbotham, Alexander and I. William Zartman (eds), *Paix sans frontières: Building peace across borders*, Accord, no. 22, London: Conciliation Resources, 2011.

Rashid, Ahmed, *Taliban: Militant Islam, Oil, and Fundamentalism in Central Asia*, London: Yale University Press, 2000.

Rashwan, Diaa, *Transformations of Islamic Groups in Egypt*, Strategic Pamphlets. no. 92. Cairo: Al-Ahram Center for Political and Strategic Studies, 2000.

'Resoluciones de la V Convención Nacional', *MLN-T*, Junio-Julio 1990.

Reynolds, Andrew (ed.), *Election '94 South Africa: The Campaigns, Results and Future Prospects*, London: James Currey, 1994.

Robinson, William I., *Transnational Conflicts: Central America, Social Change and Globalization*, London: Verso, 2003.

Rosas, Pedro, *Rebeldía: Subversión y Prisión Política*, Santiago: LOM, 2004.

Rosencof, Mauricio and Eleuterio Fernández Huidobro, *Memorias del Calabozo*, Montevideo: Tae, 1988.

Ross, Jeffrey Ian and Ted Robert Gurr, 'Why Terrorism Subsides: A Comparative Study of Canada and the United States', *Comparative Politics*, vol. 21, no. 4 (1989), pp. 405–26.

Ross, Robert, Anne Kelk Mager and Bill Nasson (eds), *The Cambridge History of South Africa: volume 2, 1885–1994*, Cambridge: Cambridge University Press, 2012.

Rouquié, Alain, *Guerras y paz en América Central*, México: Fondo de Cultura Económica, 1994.

Rufyikiri, Gervais, 'The Post-Wartime Trajectory of CNDD-FDD Party in Burundi: A Facade Transformation of Rebel Movement to Political Party', *Civil Wars*, vol. 19, no. 2 (2017), pp. 220–48.

Sampson, Anthony, *Nelson Mandela: The Authorised Biography*, Johannesburg: Harper Collins and Jonathan Ball Publishers, 1999.

Sandoval, Carlos, *M.I.R, (una historia)*, Santiago: Sociedad Editorial Trabajadores, 1990.

Ṣāyigh, Yazīd, 'Missed Opportunity: The Politics of Police Reform in Egypt and Tunisia', *Carnegie Paper* (2015).

Schmid, Alex, 'Radicalisation, De-Radicalization, and Counter-Radicalisation: A Conceptual Discussion and Literature Review', *ICCT Research Papers* (2013).

Schwedler, Jillian, 'Can Islamists Become Moderates? Rethinking the Inclusion-Moderation Hypothesis', *World Politics*, vol. 63, no. 2 (2011), pp. 347–76.

Schwedler, Jillian, *Faith in Moderation: Islamist Parties in Jordan and Yemen*, Cambridge: Cambridge University Press, 2006.

Sha'bo, Ratib, 'Harakat Ahrar al-Sham al-Islamiyya: Bayn al-Jihadiyya wa'l-Ikhwani-yya', Democratic Republic Studies Center, 2016.

Shadid, Anthony, *Night Draws Near*, New York: Henry Holt and Company, 2005.

Shirlow, Peter et al., *Abandoning Historical Conflict? Former Political Prisoners and Reconciliation in Northern Ireland*, Manchester: Manchester University Press, 2010.

Sikkink, Kathryin, *The Justice Cascade: How Human Rights Prosecutions Are Changing World Politics*, New York: W. W. Norton & Co., 2011.

Simpson, Thula, *Umkhonto we Sizwe: The ANC's Armed Struggle*, Cape Town: Penguin, 2016.

Siraj Centre for Composition (Fulfilment and Translation), *League of the Righteous: Information Booklet*, D. M. Iraq: Dar al-Kafeel.

Smidt, Wolbert & Kinfe Abraham, 'Discussing Conflict in Ethiopia: Conflict Management and Resolution', *LIT Verlag* (2007).

Smith, Michael Lawrence Rowan, *Fighting for Ireland? The Military Strategy of the Irish Republican Movement*, London: Routledge, 2002.

Snow, David and Scott Byrd, 'Ideology, Framing Processes, and Islamic Terrorist Movements', *Mobilization*, vol. 12, no. 2 (2007), pp. 119–36.

Soliman, Yumna, 'al-Bunya al-Mu'assasiyya li'l-Ikhwan al-Muslimin: Iqtirab Tahlili', *Institute Articles*, Egyptian Institute for Political and Strategic Studies (2017).

South Sudan: A Study on Competitiveness and Cross Border Trade with Neighbouring Countries, Tunis: African Development Bank, 2013.

Sparks, Allister, *Tomorrow is Another Country: The Inside Story of South Africa's Negotiated Revolution*, Sandton: Struik, 1994.

Stedman, Steven, 'The Spoiler Problems in Peace Processes', *International Security*, vol. 22, no. 22 (1997), pp. 5–53.

Steinberg, Guido, 'Ahrar al-Sham: The "Syrian Taliban"', German Institute for International and Security Affairs, *SWP Comment*, no. 27 (2016).

Stern, Steve J., *Reckoning with Pinochet: The Memory Question in Democratic Chile 1989–2006*, Durham, NC: Duke University Press, 2010.

Steward, Frances, 'Inequality in Political Power: A Fundamental (and Overlooked) Dimension of Inequality', *The European Journal of Development Research*, vol. 23, no. 4 (2011), pp. 541–5.

Shugart, Matthew, 'Guerrillas and Elections: An Institutionalist Perspective on the Costs of Conflict and Competition', *International Studies Quarterly*, vol. 36, no. 2 (June 1992), pp. 121–51.

Tammam, Husam, *Abdul Moniem Abulfotouh: Shahid 'ala tarkikh al- haraka alislam-iyya [Abdul Moniem Abulfotouh: A Witness of the Islamist Movement's History]*, Cairo: Dar al-Shorouq, 2010.

Tekle, Amare, 'The Determinants of the Foreign Policy of Revolutionary Ethiopia', *The Journal of Modern African Studies*, vol. 27, no. 3 (1989), pp. 479–502.

Tellidis, Ioannis, 'Peacebuilding Beyond Terrorism? Revisiting the Narratives of the Basque Conflict', *Studies in Conflict and Terrorism*, vol. 43, no. 6 (2020), pp. 529–47.

Thomas, Clayton, 'Al Qaeda and Islamic State Affiliates in Afghanistan', *Congressional Research Service*, 24/6/2020. Accessed on 17/9/2020, at: https://bit.ly/3krLdvO

Thomas, Clayton, 'Afghanistan: Background and U.S. Policy: In Brief', *Congressional Research Service* (2020).

Tlemçani, Rachid, 'Algeria Under Bouteflika: Civil Strife and National Reconciliation', *Carnegie Papers*, no. 7 (2008).

Todman, Will, 'Gulf States' Policies on Syria', *Middle East Program*, Center for Strategic and International Studies (2016).

Tomsen, Peter, *The Wars of Afghanistan*, New York: PublicAffairs, 2013.

Tonge, Jonathan, Peter Shirlow and James McAuley, 'So Why Did the Guns Fall Silent? How Interplay, Not Stalemate, Explains the Northern Ireland Peace Process', *Irish Political Studies*, vol. 26, no. 1 (2011), pp. 1–18.

Tonge, Shirlow and McAuley; Eamonn O'Kane, 'When Can Conflicts Be Resolved? A Critique of Ripeness', *Civil Wars*, vol. 8, no. 3–4 (2006), pp. 268–84.

Tse Tung, Mao, *Mao Tse Tung on Guerrilla Warfare*, Hawthorne: BN Publishing, 2007.

Tucker, Robert, 'Deradicalization of Marxist Movements', *American Political Science Review*, vol. 61, no. 2 (1967), pp. 343–58.

'Una nueva propuesta política. Todos por la Patria', *Entre Todos*, no. 17 (1986).

'Única vía a la democracia,' *El Combatiente. Periódico oficial de la Comisión Militar*, no. 1 (1988).

United Nations, 'Plan of Action for Preventing Violent Extremism', *Report of the Secretary-General* (2015).

van Zyl Slabbert, Frederik, *Duskant die Geskiedenis: 'n persoonlike terugblik op die politieke oorgang in Suid-Africa*, Cape Town: Tafelberg, 2006.

Vaughan, Sarah, 'Ethnicity and Power in Ethiopia', PhD Dissertation, University of Edinburgh, Edinburgh, 2003.

Villalobos, Joaquín, *Perspectivas de Victoria y Modelo Revolucionario*, El Salvador: Sistema Radio Venceremos, 1988.

Viterna, Jocelyn, *Women in War. The Micro – Processes of Mobilization in El Salvador*, Oxford: Oxford University Press, 2013.

Waldmeir, Patti, *Anatomy of a Miracle: The End of Apartheid and the Birth of a New South Africa*, London: Penguin, 1998.

Walter, Barbara, 'Why Bad Governance Leads to Repeated Civil War', *Journal of Conflict Resolution*, vol. 59, no. 7 (2015), pp. 1242–72.

Walter, Knut, 'Estados Unidos y El Salvador: la década de 1980', *Estudios Centroamericanos*, nos. 713–714 (2008), pp. 197–208.

Watson, Cameron, *Modern Basque History: Eighteenth Century to the Present*, Reno: Center for Basque Studies, 2003.

Wedeen, Lisa, *Ambiguities of Domination: Politics, Rhetoric, and Symbols in Contemporary Syria*, Chicago: The University of Chicago Press, 1999.

Weinstein, Jeremy M., *Inside Rebellion: The Politics of Insurgent Violence*, Cambridge: Cambridge University Press, 2007.

Welsh, David, *The Rise and Fall of Apartheid*, Jeppestown: Jonathan Ball, 2009.

Whitfield, Teresa, *Endgame for ETA: Elusive Peace in the Basque Country*, Oxford: Oxford University Press, 2014.

Wickham, Carrie R., *Mobilizing Islam: Religion, Activism, and Political Change in Egypt*, New York: Columbia University Press, 2002.

Wood, Ellen J., *Insurgent Collective Action and Civil War in El Salvador*, Cambridge: Cambridge University Press, 2003.

Woodworth, Paddy, *Dirty War, Clean Hands: ETA, the GAL and Spanish Democracy*, London and New Haven: Yale University Press, 2002.

Worsnop, Alec, 'Who Can Keep the Peace? Insurgent Organizational Control of Collective Violence', *Security Studies*, vol. 26, no. 3 (2017), pp. 482–516.

Yesiltas, Murat, 'When Politics is not Enough: Explaining the Failure of the Peace Process and the PKK's Urban Insurgency in Turkey (2015–2016)', Paper presented at the first annual conference of the Strategic Studies Unit entitled 'From Bullets to Ballots: Transformations from Armed to Unarmed Political Activism', Arab Centre for Research and Policy Studies, Doha, 3–4/11/2018.

Zabalao, Julen and Mikel Saratxo, 'ETA Ceasefire: Armed Struggle vs. Political Practice in Basque Nationalism', *Ethnicities*, vol. 15, no. 3 (2015), pp. 362–84.

Zahid, Mohammed, *The Muslim Brotherhood and Egypt's Succession Crisis: The Politics of Liberalisation and Reform in the Middle East*, London: I. B. Tauris, 2012.

Zartman, William, *Ripe for Resolution: Conflict and Intervention in Africa*, Oxford: Oxford University Press, 1989.

Zollner, Barbara, *The Muslim Brotherhood: Hasan al-Hudaybi and Ideology*, London: Routledge, 2011.

Zulaika, Joseba and Imanol Murua, 'How Terrorism Ends–and Does not End: The Basque Case', *Critical Studies on Terrorism*, vol. 10, no. 2 (2017), pp. 338–56.

INDEX

Note: page numbers in *italic* refer to tables; page numbers in **bold** refer to figures

Abboud, Hassan, 71, 83
Abdel Ghaffar, Ibrahim, 49
Abdel-Ghani, Safwat, 63
Abdel-Rahman, Omar, 52
al-Abnoudi, Abd al-Rahman, 47
Abrahms, Max, 118
Abu al-Nasr, Alaa, 63
Abu Jaber (Hashim al-Sheikh), 73–4, 75
Adams, Gerry, 137
Afghanistan *see* Taliban
African National Congress (ANC), 3, 12,
    17, 23, 24–6, 120, 129–30
  ban lifted, 33–4, 239–40
  compared with IG, 282–3
  election manifesto 1994, 254–5
  four pillars of struggle strategy, 41
  Groote Schuur Minute, 240–1
  Harare Declaration, 34, 240
  involvement in Convention for a
    Democratic South Africa (CODESA),
    244–8
  involvement in talks, 242–4
  isolation of apartheid, 31
  national elections 1994, 36
  'Negotiations: A Strategic Perspective',
    249–50
  negotiations with South African
    government, 34–6, 41–2, 256
  Operation Vula, 241
  outlawed, 30
  political activism, 37
  power sharing agreement, 250
  relations with other liberation
    movements, 25–6
  terrorism, rejection of, 28–9
  unity kept intact, 34
Ahern, Bertie, 137
al-Albani, Nasiruddin, 76
Alfonsín, Paul, 189–90, 191–2
Algeria, 10, 25, 27, 58, 139, 286–7, 288,
    292, 295
Alloush, Abdullah Mohammed, 76
Alloush, Mohammad, 89
Alloush, Zahran, 77, 78, 83
Almustafa, Hamzah, 15, 68–94
al-Qaida, 1, 12, 27, 53, 58, 60, 65, 71, 97,
    160, 177
Al Shabab, 27
Álvarez, Alberto Martin, 16, 213–37
Amin, Muhammad, 51
Angola, 26
Annan, Kofi, 137

Arab Socialist Union (ASU), 45
Arab Spring, 65, 296
Arafat, Yasser, 123
Argentina, 11, 187, 204, 205, 206–7, 208, 284, 292
  Cuartel de la Tablada assault, 1989, 193
  de-radicalisation processes, 189–94
  Entre Todos (magazine), 190–1
  exiled militants, 188–9
  militants' press projects, 190–1
  political prisoners, 190, 207
  political processes and individual trajectories, 188–9
Armed Islamic Group (GIA), 58
Army of Conquest (AoC, Syria), 81–2
Army of Islam (*Jaysh al-Islam*), 3, 10, 76–7, 83
  external determinants of the transformation process, 85–7
  factional conflicts and dynamics, 84–5, 87–8
  ideological changes, 88–9
  organisational transformation, 89–90
  transformation process determinants and mechanisms, 82–4
Arraras, Astrid, 195, 206
Ashour, Omar, 1–22, 119, 129, 131, 282–303
al-Assad, Bashar, 69
al-Assad, Hafiz, 68

Badr Corps, 96, 98
Badr, Zaki, 48–9, 50
al-Banna, Ali, 49
Baradar, Mullah Abdul Ghani, 171–2, 177
Basque Homeland and Liberty/Country and Freedom (ETA), 3, 10, 16, 134–52, 197–8, 283–4, 295
  Aske gunea (Free Place) mobilisations, 144
  Basque national identity and language, 138, 142
  casualties of violence, 142
  ceasefire, 137, 143
  changes in attitude towards, 140–1
  civil disobedience, 144
  disengagement of former militants, 147–8
  dissolution, 134, 140, 147, 148, 149

elections, 143–4
  end of ETA, 144–7
  Euskal Herria Bildu (EH Bildu), 143–4
  factions, 139–40
  history of, 1959–2018, 137–40
  ideology, 139
  Izquierda Abertzal (IA) (Basque Nationalist Left), 134–5, 141, 142, 143, 144, 145, 146, 147–8, 149
  political advantages of unarmed activism, 143–4
  political objectives, 135–6
  post-conflict, 147–9
  relationship with the Spanish state as a disputed conflict, 135–7
  social conditions in the Basque Country, 148–9
  Spanish constitution and secession, 136
  Spanish government's counter-terrorism measures, 135, 144, 146
  state repression, 141, 144–5
  state view that ETA was defeated, 146, 149
  unarmed activism, appeal of, 140–4
  and unilateralism, 145–6
Belhaj, Abdul Hakim, 1
Bin Laden, Osama, 53, 58, 65, 160
Boko Haram, 27
Bolivia, 187, 207–8, 284
Bonafini, Hebe de, 193–4
Botha, Pik, 239, 243–4, 246, 248, 257
Boutros-Ghali, Boutros, 246, 247, 249
Brazil, 11, 187, 204, 205, 207–8, 284
Brigade of Islam (*Liwa' al-Islam*), 77
Building and Development Party (BDP, Egypt), 61–3
Bush, George W., 53–4, 97, 160, 228

Camp David Accords, 47
Carpio, Salvador Cayetano, 230–1
Carter, Jimmy, 203, 225, 226
Castro, Fidel, 228
Chile, 11, 187, 204, 205, 206–7, 208, 284, 292
  counterinsurgency strategy, 201–2
  de-radicalisation processes, 199–202
  political prisoners, 201, 202

political processes and individual trajectories, 188–9
Public Security Coordinating Council, 202, 287
Civilian Protection Commission (CPC, Syria), 80–1, 84
Clark, Robert P., 138
Clinton, Bill, 120
Clubb, Gordon, 15, 116–33
Colombia, 3, 11, 12, 27, 145, 284–5, 293, 294, 295, 296
combat pressure, 8–9, 288–9
Committee for Liberation of the Levant, 75–6
Congressional Research Service, 167
constitutional liberalism, 5, 6, 7, 9–10
Coptic Church of Asyut, 9
Cosatu, 37
counter-terrorism strategy, 16, 135, 144, 146
Covid-19 pandemic, 164
Cristiani, Alfredo, 224, 225
Cuba, 204, 228–9, 295
Cuito Cuanavale, Battle of, 32

de Klerk, F. W., 33–4, 36, 39, 238, 239–40, 242, 248, 256, 257–8
de-radicalisation/transformation processes
and abandonment of ideology, 120–1, 131
armed groups, numbers transformed, 4
behavioural de-radicalisation, 6–7, 70
collective de-radicalisation cases, 9–12
collective de-radicalisation, causes of, 7–9, 50–1
collective de-radicalisation, conceptual framework, 5–9
collective de-radicalisation, reflections on the study of, 285–96
comprehensive de-radicalisation, 8
de-radicalisation analysed as draw or defeat, 117–19
demobilisation, disarmament and reintegration processes (DDR), 298
and democratic transitions, 203–7
failure of, 1–2, 12–13
framing disengagement, 121–4

ideological de-radicalisation, 53–7, 70, 120–1
international and regional support, 294–6
jihadism and ideological de-radicalisation, 57–60
literature on collective transformations, limitations of, 13–14
macro-level factors, 10–11
meso-level variables, 8–9, 10–11
organisational de-radicalisation, 70
political costs and policy implications, 7
pragmatic de-radicalisation/disengagement, 8, 120–1
radical collective entities, features of, 6
substantive (or factional) de-radicalisation, 8
terminology, 5–7
theorising structure, interplay and de-radicalisation framing, 119–21
transformation during combative phases, 10
variables that facilitate a transition from violence, 119–20
Declaration of Aiete (2011), 137
democratisation/democracy, 9, 194, 282–3, 293–4
de-radicalisation processes under democratic transitions, 203–7
democratic centralism, 273–4, 275
Derbala, Essam, 54, 60, 63
disengagement, 5, 120–1
framing disengagement, 121–4, 127–30
reframing objectives to justify disengagement, 126–7
Doha peace agreement, 16
Duarte, Napoleón, 226

education, 297
Egypt, 45–67, 296
Building and Development Party (BDP), 61–3
conflict between Islamic Group (IG) and the state, 47–50
democratisation, 282–3
elections, 61
ideological de-radicalisation and IG, 53–7
IG's initiative for ceasing violence, 50–3

Egypt (*cont.*)
  Luxor massacre 1997, 51–2
  military coup July 2013, 62–3
  release of IG detainees, 60
  revolution of 25 January, 60–1, 62
  Sinai insurgency, 287–8
  'Thieves Uprising' 1977, 45
Egyptian Arab Socialist Organisation
    (EASP), 46
Egyptian Jihad Organisation (EJO), 57–8,
    59
Ejército Revolucionario del Pueblo (ERP),
    217
El Salvador, 16–17, 213–37, 293
  ARENA party, 222, 224, 225, 232
  Catholic action groups, 218
  ceasefire, 233
  changes in the position of the FMLN's
    allies, 228–30
  Chapultepec Peace Accords 1992, 215,
    221, 222, 235
  civil war, 213–15
  civilian-military junta, 219
  civilian victims, 222
  economic changes, 223–5
  elections, 222–3, 233
  Farabundo Martí National Liberation
    Front (FMLN), 3, 16–17, 220, 221,
    222, 225, 227
  FMLN internal dynamics and political
    development, 230–3
  Government of Broad Participation
    (GAP) proposal 1984, 231
  internal conflicts in the armed left, 214
  liberalisation of the political regime,
    221–3
  Political-Military Coordination Body
    (CPM), 220
  protest waves and emergence of the armed
    left, 215–18
  Revolutionary Coordinating Committee
    of the Masses (CRM), 220
  road to war, 215–21
  transition to peace, 221–33
  urban guerrillas to political-military
    movements, 218–21
  US policy changes, 225–8, 295

El-Sisi, Abdel Fattah, 62
elections, 9, 36, 61, 110, 143–4, 180, 197,
    198, 222–3, 233, 254–5, 256, 275–6,
    294
Eritrean People's Liberation Front (EPLF),
    269, 271
ETA *see* Basque Homeland and Liberty/
    Country and Freedom (ETA)
Ethiopia, 11–12, 17, 265–81
  armed groups in political transition,
    276–8
  armed groups under imperial rule, 268
  coalition politics, 277
  common elements of armed groups,
    269–70
  corruption, 274–5
  democratic reform, lack of, 273–4
  elections 2020, 275–6
  future policy needs, 279–80
  influential armed groups, 266–8, *267–8*
  military junta 1974–91, 268–70
  re-emergence of armed groups, 278
  security sector reform, 272–3
Ethiopian People's Revolutionary
    Democratic Front (EPRDF), 3, 265–6
  aversion to change, 273–4
  democratic centralism, 273–4, 275
  ideology, 272–3, 276
  nation and state-building attempts, 272
  transformation post-2018, 276
  transition to a ruling party, 270–2
Ethiopian People's Revolutionary Party
    (EPRP), 266, 268, 269
European Commission, 64–5
European Union, 64–5, 120, 295

Farabundo Martí National Liberation Front
    (FMLN), 3, 16–17, 220, 221, 222
  changes in the position of the FMLN's
    allies, 228–30
  internal dynamics and political
    development, 230–3
Farabundo Martí Popular Liberation Forces
    (FPL), 217–18, 230–1
fatwas, 50, 58, 59
Fernández Huidobro, Eleuterio, 194, 196
Finnie, John, 136

framing/frame dynamics, 120–1
  framing disengagement, 121–4, 127–30
  framing the end of armed struggle, 124–7
  reframing objectives to justify
    disengagement, 126–7
Franco, Francisco, 137–8, 141
Free Syrian Army (FSA), 71, 80
Freemen of the Levant (*Ahrar al-Sham*), 3,
  10
  Abboud's assassination, effects of, 83
  emancipation from Salafi jihadism, 70–6
  external determinants of the
    transformation process, 85–7
  factional conflicts and dynamics, 84–5,
    87–8
  ideological changes, 89
  massacre of leaders 2014, 73
  organisational transformation, 89
  Shura Council, 73
  transformation process determinants and
    mechanisms, 82–4
Frente Amplio (FA, Broad Front), 186, 196,
  197, 198
Frente Patriótico Manuel Rodríguez
  (FPMR), 199–200, 201, 205

Garcé, Adolfo, 197
Geneva Convention, 28–9
Ginbot 7, 266, 277
Good Friday Agreement, 10, 16, 116, 118,
  119–20
Goodwill Zwelithini (Zulu King), 253–4
Gorriarán Merlo, Enrique, 190, 191, 192,
  207
guerrilla warfare, 24, 25, 156–7
  universal context, 26–7
Guevara, Che, 187

al-Hakim, Nasir, 79, 84
Harare Declaration, 34, 240
Hezbollah, 77, 97–8, 110
human rights, 52, 55–6, 63, 65, 73,
  189–91, 192, 202, 203, 204, 206
Hutcheon, Nick, 16, 134–52

Ibn Taymiyya, 50
inducements, 12–13, 292–3

Inkatha Freedom Party (IFP), 241, 242,
  243, 246, 248, 253, 254
interactions and interplay, 120, 121–4, 130,
  131, 289–92
Iran, 48, 78, 82, 98, 109, 112, 178,
  179
Iraq, 10, 12, 15, 95–115, 283, 296
  challenges and conflicts for Shiite political
    society, 101–2
  conflict within the Sadrist Movement,
    104–10
  elections, 110
  Mahdi Army as an embodiment of the
    Sadrist Movement, 100–4
  Operation Charge of the Knights, 96,
    104, 109, 111
  rehabilitation/deradicalisation
    programme, 2
  Shiite clerical establishment and the
    Mahdi Army, 98–100
  studies of the Mahdi Army, 96–8
Iraqi Governing Council (IGC), 98
Irish Republican Army *see* Provisional Irish
  Republican Army (IRA)
al-Islam Gaddafi, Saif, 1
Islambouli, Khaled, 47
Islamic Front (IF), 73
Islamic Group of Egypt (IG), 3, 9–10, 15,
  45–67, 292
  arrests and ill-treatment of members,
    48–9, 50, 51
  Building and Development Party,
    establishment of, 61–3
  compared with ANC, 282–3
  Conceptual Corrections, 54
  conflict with the state, 47–50
  ideological de-radicalisation, 53–7
  initiative for ceasing violence, 50–3
  interactions and interplay, 290
  international position on, 64–5
  leadership, 286, 287–8
  Luxor massacre 1997, 51–2
  publications, 55
  release of detainees, 60
  revolution of 25 January, 60–1,
    62
  Shura Council, 55, 62

Islamic Salvation Army (AIS), 3, 10, 286–7, 292
Islamic State of Iraq and Sham (ISIS), 2, 12, 27, 60, 97
  in Syria, 72, 78, 87–8

jihadism
  and ideological revisions, 57–60
  intra-jihadists conflict and rivalry in Syria, 87–8
  Salafi jihadism, 70–6
Johnson, Thomas H., 16, 153–85
Juntade Coodrinación Revolucionaria (JCR, Revolutionary Coordination Board), 187
just war, 25, 41

Kasrils, Ronnie, 14–15, 23–44, 241, 245–6
Kennedy, John Fitzgerald, 24, 42n
Khalilzad, Zalmay, 153, 161, 162, 163, 169
Kharijites, 78, 87, 92n
Khazali, Qais, 107, 108, 109

Laufer, Rafael, 79–80
leadership, 8–9, 10, 12, 24, 83–4, 128, 129–30, 286–8
League of the Righteous, 107–8, 109, 110, 111
Lenin, V. I., 27
Levant Corps (*Faylaq al-Sham*), 3, 10
Libya, 1–2, 294, 296, 298
Libyan Islamic Fighting Group (LIFG), 1, 3, 9, 294
Lund, Aron, 80
Luttwak, Edward, 288

Mahdi Army (*Jaysh al-Mahdi*), 3, 10, 15, 95, 283, 292
  compared with the Badr Corps, 96
  conflict within the Sadrist Movement, 104–10
  as an embodiment of the Sadrist Movement, 100–4
  fragmentation and splinter groups, 109–10, 111–12
  and the Shiite clerical establishment, 98–100

studies of, 96–8
suspension of operations, 104–5, 106–7, 111
al-Maliki, Nouri, 104, 111
Mandela, Nelson, 12, 24, 26, 28, 32–3, 39, 40, 239, 241, 244, 246, 253, 286
  becomes president, 36, 255
  meeting with de Klerk, 248
  release of, 33–4, 240
Manuel Rodríguez Patriotic Front (FPMR), 3
Mao Tse Tung, 27
  On Guerrilla Warfare, 156, 157
Marchesi, Aldo, 16, 186–212
Markarian, Vanya, 206
Maru, Mehari Taddele, 17, 265–81
al-Masri, Mohannad, 75
media campaigns, 297
moderation, 7, 19n, 72, 74, 226
Moloney, Ed, 120
Montoneros, 3, 190
Morsi, Mohamed, 62
Movimento de Izquierda Revolucionaria (MIR, Left Revolutionary Movement, Chile), 187, 189, 192, 199–201, 202, 205
Movimento Todos por la Patria (MTP, Argentina), 191, 192–3
Mubarak, Mohamed Hosni, 46, 47, 48, 50, 53–4
Mujahid, Mullah Mohammed Omar (Mullah Omar), 155, 156, 158–9
Mujica, José, 186, 198–9, 287
Munoz, Heraldo, 284
Muslim Brothers/Brotherhood (MB), 3, 47, 58, 68–9, 283
  Syrian MB, 79–80, 84

al-Nahhas, Labib, 74
National Coalition for the Syrian Revolution (NCSR), 79
Najaf Hawza (seminary), 100–1
National Action Group (NAG), 79
National Democratic Party (NDP, Egypt), 46
National Party (South Africa), 35, 36, 37
Negm, Ahmed Fouad, 47

9/11 terror attacks, 53, 160
Nicaragua, 11, 206, 229, 289
Northern Ireland
    compared with the Basque Country,
        148–9
    see also Provisional Irish Republican Army
        (IRA)
Nusra Front (*Jabhat al-Nusra*, JN), 75, 76,
    81
Nzo, Alfred, 238, 241

Obama, Barack, 161
al-Omar, Ali, 75
Ogaden National Liberation Front (ONLF),
    269, 270, 271, 272, 277
Organisation of African Unity (OAU), 25,
    34, 37, 239
    Resolution 765, 246–7
Organisation of American States (OAS),
    295
Organización Político Militar (OPM), 197–8
Oromo Liberation Front (OLF), 266, 269,
    270, 271, 272, 276, 277, 278
Al-Otaifi, Majid, 49
Otegi, Arnaldo, 145–6

Palestinian Liberation Organisation (PLO),
    26, 123
Partido Demócrata Cristiano (PDC, El
    Salvador), 216, 219, 220, 221, 222
Partido dos Trabalhadores (PT, Workers'
    Party), 186
Partido Nacionalista Vasco (PNV), 139, 142
Partido Revolucionario de los Trabajadores-
    Ejército Revolucionario de Pueblo
    (PRT-ERT, Argentina), 187, 189,
    190–2, 205
People's War, 25, 27
PKK, 11
Popular Party (PP Spain), 135–6
popular support, 27, 134, 141, 189, 221,
    227, 230, 294, 297
Powell, Jonathan, 137
prisons and prisoners, 2, 12
    political prisoners, 190, 207
    role in disengagement, 128–30
protest, social protest, 186–7

Provisional Irish Republican Army (IRA), 3,
    10–11, 15, 116–33, 144, 145, 283–4,
    295
    ceasefire, 116
    de-radicalisation analysed as draw or
        defeat, 117–19
    disbandment, 124
    framing disengagement, 121–4, 124,
        127–30
    framing the end of the armed struggle,
        124–7
    generational hegemony, 126, 128, 130
    Good Friday Agreement, 10, 16, 116,
        118, 119–20
    interaction and interplay, role of, 120,
        121–4, 130, 131, 290
    leadership, 128, 129–30, 287
    legitimacy, 124, 127
    pragmatic de-radicalisation/
        disengagement, 120–1
    prisons, role in disengagement, 128–30
    reframing objectives to justify
        disengagement, 126–7
    socio-economic factors and transition,
        120
    stalemate narrative, 122, 123–5, 127, 131
    theorising ideology and an end to
        violence, 131–2
    theorising structure, interplay and de-
        radicalisation framing, 119–21

Qassem, Talaat Fouad, 64

Rahma, Haitham, 79, 80, 84
Rahmani, Mohammed Arif, 178
Reagan, Ronald, 28, 226–7
religion, 12, 27, 47, 61, 72, 76, 81, 96, 99,
    102, 105, 154, 290, 291
Revolutionary Armed Forces of Colombia
    (FARC), 3, 11, 12, 145, 284–5, 292,
    293, 294, 295
Revolutionary Democratic Front (FDR, El
    Savador), 220, 222
Rifaat, Mustafa, 54
ripeness theory, 124–5, 131
Romero, Carlos Humberto, 219, 225
Rousseff, Dilma, 186, 207

Rushdi, Osama, 15, 45–67
Russia/Soviet Union, 88–9, 229–30, 239

Sadat, Anwar, 45, 46
    assassination, 47–8
al-Sadiq, Abu Muhammad, 74
al-Sadr, Muhammad, 101
    The Jurisprudence of Tribes, 102
al-Sadr, Muqtada, 96, 98, 99, 100, 102,
    103, 106, 109, 111
Sadrist Movement (*al-Tayyar al-Sadri*), 95,
    96, 97, 100
    compared with Hezbollah, 110
    conflict within the Movement, 104–10
    and identity issues, 107–8, 111
    Mahdi Army as an embodiment of,
        100–4
    and religious authority, 105
    social networks, 105
Saeed, Haider, 15, 95–115
Salafis, 70–6
    Scholarly Salafism, 76–7
Sandinista National Liberation Front of
    Nicaragua, 3, 11, 229, 289
Saudi Arabia, 12, 58, 82, 159
Saudi Wahhabism, 10, 38n
security sector, 11, 272–3, 293–4, 297–8
Sham Legion (*Faylaq al-Sham*), 70, 79–82
    external determinants of the
        transformation process, 85–7
    factional conflicts and dynamics, 84–5,
        88
    leadership, 83–4
    transformation process determinants and
        mechanisms, 82–4
Sharia law, 72, 73, 78
al-Sharif, Sayyed Imam, 57–60
Simpson, Thula, 16, 238–64
Sinn Fein, 119, 120
Sisulu, Walter, 24
Slabbert, Frederik van Zyl, 258
Slovo, Joe, 241, 249
Soufan, Hassan, 83
South Africa, 12, 14–15, 17, 23–44,
    238–64, 293
    Afrikaner Weerstandsbeweging (AWB),
        251, 252–3

aftermath of negotiations and elections,
    255–8
ANC political activism, 37
apartheid system, 23–4, 29–30, 31
armed force, use of, 24–6
background to negotiations, 239–41
civilian victims, 254, 255
climate of violence, 242–4, 246, 248
Convention for a Democratic South
    Africa (CODESA), 244–8, 290
democratisation, 282–3
elections 1994, 254–5, 256
emergency rule in Natal, 241
guerrilla warfare, universal context,
    26–7
historic compromises, 248–50
historical background, 29–32
international involvement in the peace
    process, 246–7, 253–4
and majority rule, 257–8
Mandela's release and ANC ban lifted,
    33–4
military's involvement in negotiations,
    38–40
national elections 1994, 36
National Peace Accord 1991, 244
negotiations, 32–3, 34–6, 41–2
Operation Exit, 245–6
police, 238, 240, 243
power sharing agreement, 250
reasons for dismantling apartheid, 31–2
Record of Understanding, 35, 248, 249
Sharpeville massacre, 25, 30
terrorism, 28–9
transition period, 252–4
war years 1960–90, 30–1
South African Communist Party (SACP),
    30, 240, 249
South African National Defence Force
    (SANDF), 38, 39–40
Soviet Union *see* Russia/Soviet Union
Spain *see* Basque Homeland and Liberty/
    Country and Freedom (ETA)
Spanish Socialist Workers Party (PSOE),
    135–6
Spear of the Nation *see* Umkhonto we Sizwe
    (MK)

spoilers, 38–9, 286–7
stalemate, 122, 123–5, 127, 131
standard operating procedures (SOPs), 2, 297
Steinhoff, Patricia, 208
Syria, 10, 15, 68–94, 283, 289, 296
    Astana negotiations, 85
    charismatic leadership in Islamist factions, 83–4
    Civilian Protection Commission (CPC), 80–1
    determinants and mechanisms of the transformation process, 82–4
    dimensions of collective transformations, 88–90
    external determinants of the transformation process, 85–7
    factional conflicts and dynamics, 84–5
    intra-jihadists conflict and rivalry, 87–8
    Islamist groups, emergence of, 69
    revolution, 70–1
    Revolutionary Code of Conduct, 85
    Salafi jihadism, 70–6
    Umma project, 73, 85, 87
Syrian Islamic Front (SIF), 71–2, 87
Syrian Islamic Liberation Front (SILF), 71

Taha, Rifai, 52, 53, 55
Tahan, Abu Saleh, 74
Taliban, 3, 10, 16, 71, 153–85, 284, 289, 292
    Afghan civilian casualties of ANSDF, US and NATO forces, 166–7
    attacking enemy arms depots, 157–8
    attacks carried out by Taliban forces, 168, 178–9
    ceasefires, 162
    cohesion, 164
    domestic policies under Taliban rule, 157–61
    foreign policies, 159
    ideology, 155, 157–61
    and an Islamic Emirate, 159, 164, 168, 178, 181
    key issues for negotiations, 178
    leadership changes, 176–7
    military/government employee's defection to, 167–8, **168**, 171, **171**, 175, **175**
    negotiations with the US, analysis of, 162–5, 171–2
    non-involvement of Kabul in peace negotiations, 162–3
    offensive and defensive operations, 169, **170**, 173–4, **173**
    organisation of, 156–7
    origins and background, 154–6
    peace agreement with US, 153–4, 161
    prisoner exchange/release, 162–3, 177
    propaganda videos, 169
    pure Islamic state policy, 158
    research implications, 176–80
    role of external actors in negotiations, 179
    Twitter statements analysis 2018–20, 165–76, **170**, **173**, **174**, **175**
    war crimes claimed, 165–6, **166**, 169, 170–1, **170**, 174–5, **174**
Tambo, Oliver, 31, 32–3, 34, 239, 241
Task Force 134, 2
Tendencia Proletaria (Proletarian Tendency), 195
terminology, 5–7, 23
TerreBlanche, Eugene, 251, 252
terrorism, 28–9, 117–18
Thatcher, Margaret, 28, 239
Tigray People's Democratic Movement (TPDM), 266, 277
Tigray People's Liberation Front (TPLF), 269
torture, 48, 49, 50
transformation processes *see* de-radicalisation/transformation processes
Trump, Donald, 161, 180
Tupamaros National Liberation Movement (MLNT), 3, 11, 187, 189, 194–5, 287
    Fifth Convention, 1991, 196–7
    The Seventeen Group, 196
    social actions and communications, 195–6
Turkey, 11
Twitter, analysis of Taliban's use of, 165–76, **166**, **168**, **170**, **171**, **173**, **174**, **175**

Umkhonto we Sizwe (MK), 3, 12, 15, 17, 28, 31, 34–5, 38–9, 239, 240, 244, 248
  manifesto, 30
United Democratic Front (UDF), 37
United Kingdom, 10, 64, 160, 293
United Nations, 34, 37, 64
  Security Council, 246–7
United States, 2, 16, 64, 78, 97, 98, 138, 154
  Afghan coalition, 160–1
  and El Salvador, 223–4, 225–8, 295
  invasion of Afghanistan, 156–7
  negotiations with the Taliban, analysis of, 162–5
  peace agreement with the Taliban, 153–4, 161
Uruguay, 11, 187, 204, 205, 206, 208, 284, 292
  de-radicalisation processes, 194–9
  democracy, 194
  elections, 197, 198
  Fifth Convention of MLN-T, 1991, 196–7
  Filtro massacre, 197–8, 294
  MLN-T group, 3, 11, 187, 189, 194–6
  political prisoners, 194, 195, 197–8, 207
  political processes and individual trajectories, 188–9

The Seventeen Group, 196
Tupamaros' social actions and communications, 195–6

Viljoen, Constand, 252, 255–6, 256–7
Villalobos, Joaquín, 233
violence, 118
  glorification of, 291, 297
  political violence, 1, 5, 6–7, 12, 13, 136, 186, 241, 247, 254, 258, 283, 296, 297–8
  variables that facilitate a transition from violence, 119–20

Waldmeir, Patti, 255
War on Terror, 53, 160, 270
Wedeen, Lisa, 68

al-Yaqoubi, Muhammad, 103
Yemen, 12, 82, 298

Zabalza, Jorge, 196
al-Zarqawi, Abu Musab, 58
al-Zawahiri, Ayman, 53, 58, 59
Al-Zomor, Tariq, 64–5
Zuhdi, Karam, 56–7
Zulu Nationalist Inkatha movement, 12, 17, 36
Zwerman, Gilda, 208